Living on the Black

Living on the Black

TWO PITCHERS, TWO TEAMS, ONE SEASON TO REMEMBER

John Feinstein

LITTLE, BROWN AND COMPANY

New York   Boston   London

Little, Brown and Company
Hachette Book Group USA
237 Park Avenue, New York, NY 10017
Visit our Web site at www.HachetteBookGroupUSA.com

First Edition: May 2008

Little, Brown and Company is a division of Hachette Book Group USA, Inc.
The Little, Brown logo is a trademark of Hachette Book Group USA, Inc.

Library of Congress Cataloging-in-Publication Data

Feinstein, John.
    Living on the black : two pitchers, two teams, one season to remember /
John Feinstein. — 1st ed.
        p. cm.
    ISBN-13: 978-0-316-11391-5
    ISBN-10: 0-316-11391-3
    1. Glavine, Tom.   2. Mussina, Mike.   3. Pitchers (Baseball) —
United States — Biography.   4. Pitching (Baseball)   5. New York Mets
(Baseball team)   6. New York Yankees (Baseball team)   I. Title.
    GV865.G53F45 2008
    796.357092'2 — dc22   2007050618
    [B]

10   9   8   7   6   5   4   3   2   1

RRD-IN

Printed in the United States of America

This is for Chris Bauch, who deserves
far more than this

CONTENTS

INTRODUCTION

THE IDEA TO WRITE A BOOK about pitching first crossed my mind while driving down the New Jersey Turnpike in the middle of a monsoon on a February morning in 1999. The rain was coming down in sheets, the visibility was about six feet, and the radio was tuned to New York's WFAN, which had debuted as the very first all-sports radio station back in 1987.

The host that morning was Suzyn Waldman, then the station's New York Yankees beat reporter and a sometimes weekend host. She was leaving for Tampa the next morning for the start of spring training, and most of her callers wanted to talk about the Yankees' prospects for the coming season. New York and Boston are probably the last two cities on earth where the fortunes of the baseball teams are more important than those of the local NFL teams.

A caller wanted to know what kind of a year Waldman expected from David Cone. "Well," she said, "I'm not sure. There isn't a person who knows David Cone who doesn't want to see him do well because we all love the guy . . ."

I really didn't hear the rest of her answer. I was thinking about Cone, as likable and bright as any athlete I'd ever met. I'd gotten to know him during the 1992 season, when I was working on my first baseball book, and had kept in occasional touch with him since then. It was always fun to talk to him about almost anything, from the art of pitching to union issues to good restaurants.

An idea came into my mind: why not do a book on a year in the life of a major league pitcher? Pitching is one of those sports skills few of us really understand. We know how hard someone is throwing; we know their pitch count; and we think we know what pitches they are throwing. But so much about pitching is, for lack of a better term, truly "inside baseball." What do pitchers really do during the off-season — especially as they get older — to prepare for spring training? What do they do while "throwing a bullpen," which is what pitchers call the time they spend throwing in the bullpen on the day or days that they pitch to a catcher between starts. In fact, they will often refer to "having a good bullpen," which is a lot different than a team having a good bullpen.

There's more: How do pitchers and catchers relate to one another; what in the world do pitching coaches *really* say when they jog to the mound; and what does a pitcher, especially one who can't just rear back and throw 95-mile-an-hour fastballs, do to get out of a slump? How do they interact with umpires? Opposing hitters? The manager? Their wives?

Cone, I thought, would be perfect for such a book. He was a very good pitcher who was getting near the end — he would be thirty-seven in 2000, which was when I was contemplating doing the book. He was smart, personable, and articulate. I already had a good relationship with him. I knew Joe Torre, his manager, well. More than anything, it would be fun to spend a year watching baseball and talking about pitching — and, no doubt, a lot of other things — with someone I genuinely liked.

And, perhaps most important at that particular moment, it meant I would spend most of February in Florida and *not* on the New Jersey Turnpike.

THREE WEEKS LATER, I made the trip down I-4 from Orlando to Tampa on a Saturday morning. There were no monsoons in sight. It was a glistening March day, and exhibition baseball had just begun. I knew that Cone would be finished with his workout by 10 a.m. That's the way spring training is — if you aren't playing in a game, most days your work is over long before noon.

I hadn't called Cone in advance, because there's never been a more approachable athlete than Cone, and I've always liked to spring ideas on people in person. I was actually talking to Roger Clemens, newly arrived as a Yankee, when Cone walked into the clubhouse, sweat-soaked from his workout. As usual, he was warm and friendly.

"What brings you to spring training in the middle of the [NCAA] basketball tournament?" he asked, shaking my hand.

"To be honest," I said, "I came to see you. Have you got a few minutes?"

"Let me take a shower," he said. "We'll go get breakfast."

Which we did, at a diner down the road that Cone said George Steinbrenner frequented. "Never been here myself," he said as we walked in. "But I hear it's pretty good."

Inside it was apparent that Steinbrenner hung out in the place because there were pictures of him all over. There was also one of Cone. "Thanks for the great soup!" it said.

"I thought you'd never been in here."

"I didn't think I had been," Cone said, laughing.

We sat down, and, over eggs and coffee, I laid out the idea.

"Boy, I think that would be a lot of fun," Cone said. "There's only one potential problem."

He explained to me that he had been friends almost since the beginning of his career with Roger Angell, the nonpareil baseball writer of *The New Yorker*. "I always promised Roger that if I ever did a book, I'd give him first crack," he said. "I really think I have to talk to him before I commit to you. I'd feel funny if I didn't."

Part of me couldn't help thinking, *Great, I get the one baseball player in America not only literate enough to read Angell but with a conscience too.* Another part of me thought I'd be okay: Angell had never actually written a baseball book, only collections of his *New Yorker* pieces. He was seventy-nine at the time. I figured the chances that he'd want to take on such a project weren't all that great.

"I understand completely," I said. "But I think there's a good chance he'll pass."

"In which case, I'm in," Cone said. "I'll call you sometime in the next week."

When I didn't hear anything for ten days, I began to get nervous. "Don't worry about it," my friend Dave Kindred counseled. "Even really good guys like David Cone don't always call back when they say they're going to call back."

I waited until after the Final Four before I finally got impatient enough to call Cone myself. As soon as I heard his voice, I knew the news wasn't good.

"Roger wants to do the book," he said. "I'm really sorry. I should have called you."

The lack of a phone call didn't bother me at that moment. The lack of a book did.

ANGELL WROTE THE BOOK (as I had planned) during the 2000 season. As it turned out, that was Cone's last year with the Yankees. I enjoyed reading the book because if Angell wrote a book about paint drying it would be enjoyable to read. But the fact that Cone pitched hurt for most of the season made Angell's task monumentally difficult, and the book, even though it got good reviews, sold only about twenty-two thousand copies in hardcover and far less than that—about six thousand copies—in paperback. Cone's lost season clearly didn't help sales.

I still thought my initial idea had a lot of merit. But it needed the right subject or, I was now convinced, subjects. You can't chronicle an entire season in a pitcher's career if he only pitches half the season or less. I decided I needed two pitchers, so that if one got hurt, I could compare and contrast what a pitcher on the disabled list went through with one who was healthy and pitching.

I came up with a short list of potential subjects: Tom Glavine, Greg Maddux, Mike Mussina, John Smoltz, Al Leiter, and Curt Schilling. Maddux and Glavine were, I believed, lock Hall of Famers. Smoltz was borderline, and Mussina and Schilling had a shot if they finished their careers on a high note. Only Leiter, I thought, was definitely not a Hall of Famer, merely a very good pitcher. All six were smart, the kind who would understand a project like this and not chafe (or at least not chafe that often) at the sort of detail and time I would need, and I knew Glavine, Mussina, and Smoltz well from past contact with them.

I decided to ask Glavine and Mussina because I liked the contrasts they brought to the table: Glavine was a lefty who hadn't gone to college and had been (like Cone) a very vocal and visible part of the players union during the player-owner battles of the 1990s. He had pitched in the National League his entire career. Mussina was a righty who had gone to Stanford and graduated in three and a half years. He had also been a union rep but never an especially visible one. He had pitched in the American League, Eastern Division, his whole career.

One started in Atlanta, the other in Baltimore. Both landed in New York—one a Met, one a Yankee. The notion of comparing and contrasting the culture of the Mets with that of the Yankees as part of the story also appealed to me.

What's more, I knew that both would be able to explain to me exactly what it is they do to be successful pitchers. Neither has ever won on pure power. Glavine never threw in the 90s. Mussina did, but what made him an All-Star was his ability to keep hitters off balance with a variety of off-speed pitches. Both pitchers have always relied on their ability to throw the ball almost exactly where they want to most of the time.

"They're like scientists out there," Detroit Tigers manager Jim Leyland said. "They don't beat you with their arms so much as they beat you with their minds."

Both understand the importance of not giving the batter a good pitch to hit. "What you don't want," Glavine explained once, "is white on white. You have to be around the black."

"The black" is a reference to the outside edges of home plate. The plate is seventeen inches wide. The outside edges are framed in black, and a pitcher with great control is someone who can "hit the black." In other words, he can throw pitches that just nick the corners of the plate, making it difficult for batters to hit but forcing umpires to call strikes if batters don't swing. If you get the white baseball over the white part of the plate — Glavine's "white on white" — you're in trouble, especially if you're not a power pitcher.

Thus, Glavine and Mussina, neither a power pitcher, have had to hit the black to be successful, and now, near the end of their careers, their margin for error would be tiny. I looked forward to watching them face that challenge over a season.

The two of them are also extremely different personalities. If there's a baseball player as friendly and as approachable as David Cone, it is Tom Glavine. He has a knack for taking an unbelievably stupid question and making the questioner think he's giving the answer great thought. He's unfailingly polite, whether you've talked to him a hundred times or never talked to him at all. He has never ducked a postgame meeting with the media, no matter how poorly he may have pitched. If you can't get along with Tom Glavine, something is wrong with you.

Here, in total, are the discussions we had about doing the book:

JF: I'd like to do a book on a year in the life of two aging, smart, and very good pitchers. I think you'd be ideal.

TG: Okay. When do you think you'd want to do it?

Mussina is completely different. In fact, when he first signed with the Yankees prior to the 2001 season, he was given the locker in the Yankee clubhouse that had belonged to Cone.

"Part of my problem that first year was that I had David Cone's locker," he said six years later. "The guys in the media wanted me to be David. I am *not* David Cone."

Not by any stretch of the imagination. The New York writers—most of whom very much like and respect Mussina now—talk about "paying the Mussina toll."

Rarely does a conversation with him begin with "Have you got a minute?" And rarely is the answer "Sure."

More likely the answer is "What do you want to talk about? And I don't believe for one minute that this will only take one minute."

Our discussions about doing this book took almost as much time as our discussions for the book did. Mussina worried about how much time I would need and when I would need the time. What if he pitched lousy—would that ruin the book? He also asked a question he later forgot he had asked: "What if I get so frustrated at some point in the season that I just don't feel like talking for a while?"

My answer was honest: "That's the luxury of a book. If you need a break, we can take a break, as long as I keep tracking what you're doing and talking to the people around you." That would turn out to be very important late in the season.

After about four different discussions and a number of e-mail exchanges, Mussina also said yes. And he was more than true to his word about giving me the time I needed once he pledged it.

And, true to his reputation, he *did* point out stupid questions.

On a cold, wet, rainy afternoon at Shea Stadium in May, with the Yankees well under .500 and Mussina's record 2–3, we sat in the visitors' dugout talking. Rumors were swirling that Joe Torre was about to get fired. Mussina's answers, normally thoughtful and lengthy, were short and biting. Finally I said, "You're not in a good mood today, are you?"

He gave me a look I had by then become familiar with.

"No, I'm in a great mood," he said. "I've already been on the DL once this season, and I'm pitching right now like a solid, Triple-A pitcher. My team sucks, and there's no sign it is going to stop sucking anytime soon. Everyone wants my manager fired, the temperature is about forty degrees, it's raining, and there are about five hundred people in the clubhouse right now wanting to ask me questions like, 'So, what do you think is wrong with you guys?' Why the hell *shouldn't* I be in a bad mood?"

THE SEASON I CHRONICLED was filled with twists and turns. Glavine began the year ten wins shy of three hundred, and Mussina started eleven away from 250. Both reached their milestones but took routes to them none of us would have imagined when spring training began.

The Mets, who looked like a lock for the playoffs all season, ended up blowing a seven-game lead in the last seventeen games, their collapse climaxed on the season's last day by what was arguably the worst performance of Glavine's storied career.

The Yankees, 22–29 in May and 42–43 at the All-Star break, made the playoffs for a thirteenth consecutive season. In August, for the first time in seventeen years, Mussina found himself yanked from the rotation. And yet, most Yankee fans headed into winter wishing he had had been the starter in Game Four of the American League Division Series against the Cleveland Indians rather than Chien-Ming Wang.

What I got to see and hear and learn up close had little to do with wins and losses, even though they were obviously very important to both pitchers.

The results produced by Tom Glavine (13–8 record, ERA 4.45) and Mike Mussina (11–10 record, ERA 5.15) in 2007 are there in black-and-white for all to see. What I set out to do was give people a sense of what went into those numbers, what the process is for a pitcher who isn't ready to walk off into the sunset just yet.

"The physical part of doing this is pretty easy," Mussina said at one point last summer. "You know what you have to do to prepare, to try to stay healthy or get healthy, to take care of your arm so you can take the ball every fifth day.

"The hard part is mental—especially when you aren't pitching well. You can't escape it. The physical part you can leave at the ballpark—you do your work and you're done. Not the mental part. You can be playing with your kids, reading a book, talking to your wife, eating a meal, and it's there. What can I do to get better? What am I doing wrong? What am I missing? Is this the end or just a slump? It never goes away."

He smiled. "I guess the day it does go away is the day you're done. So, I guess I'm not done just yet."

Neither man felt done during 2007, even when doing his job was really, really hard. This is the story of that season.

Living on the Black

1

The Gifted Lefty

IF YOU HAVE ATTENDED A BASEBALL GAME at Yankee Stadium at any time during the past fifty-five years, you have heard the voice of Bob Sheppard, who has been the public address announcer there since 1951. No one introduces a starting lineup quite like Sheppard, who for years taught diction at St. John's University.

In deep, sonorous tones, Sheppard, who turned ninety-seven during the 2007 season, introduces each player in a booming, deliberate voice: "And pitching for the Yankees...Number thirty-five...Mike Mussina...Number thirty-five."

There are none of the theatrics that many of today's PA announcers make a part of their act. Sheppard isn't acting. He's just informing, in remarkably clear, perfectly pronounced English.

It is different at Shea Stadium, where the Mets PA announcer Alex Anthony has only been on the job for a few years. Sheppard had been on the job in the Bronx for eleven years by the time the Mets played their first game as a team, and Anthony doesn't even introduce the players. He simply says, "Batting ninth, the pitcher..." and at that point the player in question will appear on the Diamond Vision screen behind the left-field fence, smile, and tell the fans his name and his hometown.

When Tom Glavine is introduced, he smiles for the camera and says, "Tom Glavine, Billerica, Massachusetts."

What he actually says is "Bill-uh-rica," which is different from the way most people say it. They say "Bill-rica," leaving out the *uh*. "That's the short way," Glavine says with a laugh. "If you're a true Billerican, you say it with the *uh*."

Glavine is a true Billerican. The town is located about twenty-five miles northwest of Boston, a classic New England community of about thirty-seven thousand people. Glavine likes to point out that when it snows, which is often, Billerica looks like something straight out of a Norman Rockwell painting.

Tom's parents, Fred and Mildred Glavine, met there while in high school. Fred was a star athlete, playing football, basketball, and baseball. A superb football player, he would later tell his sons to stay away from the game because of the injuries that continued to plague him as he got older.

After he got out of the military, Fred Glavine started a construction business with one of his brothers, building pools and laying foundations for homes. Tom worked for him for several summers and came away from the experience with great respect for what his father did and no desire to follow in his footsteps.

From a very early age it was apparent that Tom was a gifted athlete. All the Glavine kids were good athletes, but Tom always ended up competing with older kids because of his talent.

"I remember when I was ten, I was playing on Little League teams with twelve-year-olds," he said. "I wasn't all that big, but I could throw hard when I pitched, and I never felt out of place competing with older guys."

All three Glavine boys played baseball and hockey. As passionate as most New Englanders are about the Red Sox, hockey is the sport almost every kid plays growing up. "You usually start out skating on an outdoor pond somewhere when you're very young, and by the time you're four or five you're comfortable on skates," Glavine remembered. "When I was young, hockey was definitely my number one sport and my first love. Baseball came later."

Glavine's interests were like those of most boys growing up in Billerica: he rooted fanatically for the Red Sox and the Bruins and liked the Patriots and the Celtics. "It was more the Red Sox and the Bruins," he said. "I never really got into basketball, and my dad wouldn't let me play football. Plus, the Patriots weren't very good back then. Now, it's different."

Several times a year, Fred and Millie Glavine would take the family to see the Red Sox or the Bruins. Glavine remembers sitting in the right-field seats at Fenway Park watching Dwight Evans, one of the better right fielders of the 1970s. "When I played the outfield, I always imitated the way he caught the ball and got into position to make a throw," he said. "I was old enough [nine] to remember the '75 World Series. I remember [Carlton] Fisk's home run, but I also remember feeling crushed when they lost the seventh game."

Glavine was a pitcher and a center fielder in baseball and a center in hockey. By the time he was in high school, he was a local star and he was starting to draw attention from college coaches and scouts in both sports. "More hockey though," he said. "I would say ninety percent of the letters I got from coaches my junior year were for hockey. I was a more polished hockey player than I was a pitcher, which isn't surprising because most pitchers aren't very polished when they're sixteen. My thinking at the time was that I wanted a college scholarship, and my best bet was hockey. If I could go someplace and play both sports, that would be ideal. Turning pro after high school wasn't really on my mind at all."

College made sense for a number of reasons. For one thing, Glavine was an excellent student. His grade point average floated between about 3.8 and 3.9, and, in a high school with about 550 students in each grade, he usually ranked in the top sixty in the class, eventually graduating fifty-eighth in a class of 558.

It was during his junior year that Glavine decided exactly what he wanted to do after high school: go to Harvard. A friend of his had a brother who was playing hockey at Harvard, and one day he took Tom to a game. Glavine loved the campus, loved the atmosphere at the game, and loved the idea that this was *Harvard* and decided that playing hockey at Harvard was what he wanted to do—even though it meant he would have to apply for financial aid, and his parents would have to pay at least part of his tuition.

"My parents were all for it," he said. "I mean, come on, it was Harvard."

Bill Cleary, the longtime Harvard hockey coach, loved Glavine's game. He was a slick center with great quickness and passing skills. And he was a good student. There was just one catch: the SATs.

"I simply could not do well on them," Glavine said. "I can't even tell you why. I was just a complete disaster."

Disaster is a relative word. The first time Glavine took the boards as a high school junior, he scored 1100. Almost any college in America would kill to have a star athlete with a 3.8 GPA and 1100 on the boards. Harvard is, needless to say, not most schools. Cleary was allowed to recruit one player each year with under 1200 on the boards. (One more than longtime Harvard basketball coach Frank Sullivan was ever allowed.) Glavine spent the summer between his junior and senior years being tutored on how to take the SATs. He took the test twice more. "Best I could do was eleven fifty," he said. "To this day, I can't tell you why I couldn't do better."

After Glavine had taken the SATs for the last time, Cleary called him. "I'd love to have you," he said. "But I've only got one exception, and I'm desperate for a defenseman, so I'm going to give it to Don Sweeney."

As it turned out, Cleary knew what he was doing: Sweeney played in the National Hockey League for fifteen years. Glavine, the Harvard dream gone, had to go to plan B. The problem was he didn't really have a plan B.

"I was still thinking more about hockey than baseball," he said. "But by then I was starting to get a lot of attention for baseball too."

Glavine had started to notice the scouts behind home plate

during his junior year. They were easy to spot because they all came equipped with radar guns that they pointed at him each time he went into his windup. When Tom was older, Fred Glavine told his son that he had first started seeing scouts at his games as early as the eighth grade but never said anything because he didn't want Tom to get a swelled head or to think he was better than he was. When he first spotted the radar guns, Glavine reacted like any teenager might be expected to react: "I tried to throw harder," he said. "I wanted to impress them. After a while I just got used to the fact that they were there."

Glavine also benefited from the fact that he had a coach who recognized his potential and protected his arm. Jon Sidorovich never pitched his star on short rest, never let him pitch more than nine innings, and resisted risking his arm regardless of what was at stake.

The best example of that came in the state championships during Glavine's senior year. Glavine had pitched in the quarterfinals — going head-to-head with Pete Smith, who would later be a teammate in Atlanta. "We won the game seven-six," Glavine said. "Two future major leaguers, and that was the score. Real pitcher's duel."

The next day Glavine played center field in the semifinals, and, with two pitchers on the mound who would never sniff the big leagues, the score was tied 1–1 after nine innings. Coming in from the outfield after the ninth, Glavine went to Sidorovich and told him he was ready, willing, and able to pitch the tenth. Sidorovich put his hands on Glavine's shoulders and looked him in the eye: "You're not pitching today, Tom," he said. "I know how much you want to win, and so do I. But I'm not risking your future to win one game."

Glavine stayed in the outfield. Billerica lost 2–1 in the tenth. "As disappointing as it was to lose, I understand now what Jon was doing," Glavine said. "A lot of coaches wouldn't have worried about risking my future; they'd have wanted to win the game and the championship."

By that time Glavine was being pursued by college coaches from all over. At first it was exciting, but after a while it became a burden. In those days there were no limits on how often coaches could call a recruit. Glavine can remember lying in bed on Saturday mornings and hearing the phone ring again and again.

"The coaches all figured I'd be home on a Saturday morning, so they'd call," he said. "I'd hear the phone, and I'd just yell, 'Mom, tell them all I'm not home.' My parents protected me from a lot of it."

Since he couldn't go to Harvard, Glavine decided to sign a letter of intent with the University of Lowell, which was close to home, very good academically, and, even though a small school, played very good Division 1 hockey. Plus, the baseball team wasn't bad either. It seemed ideal. The plan was to go to Lowell, play both sports, and see what might be waiting for him as an athlete after college. Even so, Glavine was intrigued by both the hockey and baseball drafts, wondering if all those scouts who had shown up to see him would still be interested.

They were—although his announcement that he was planning to go to college clearly affected him in the hockey draft. The Los Angeles Kings took him in the fourth round and made no attempt to sign him. "I remember on the day of the draft [Kings general manager], Rogie Vachon called me and told me they would be keeping an eye on me at Lowell," Glavine said. "In hockey, they retained your rights for five years. So, in theory, I could have played at Lowell for four years, graduated, and then signed with the Kings, who would still have my rights."

Baseball's rules were different. If a team drafted him and he didn't sign and went to college, he wasn't eligible to be drafted again for at least three years—and then he went back into the draft. Thus, it was a far bigger gamble for a baseball team to risk a pick on a high school player, especially one who had already signed a letter of intent to attend college.

Even so, as Glavine's senior season moved along, he noticed more and more scouts. The Toronto Blue Jays and the Cleveland

Indians both showed a lot of interest, and other teams also had scouts keeping an eye on him. Although Glavine considered himself far more polished as a hockey player than as a pitcher, he was considered quite advanced for a left-handed pitcher by most of the scouts following his progress.

He was not overpowering in big league terms. His fastball topped out most of the time at 88 or 89 miles an hour, perhaps inching to 90 on occasion. He had a good curveball, and his control had improved steadily throughout high school. "When I was young, I threw very hard for a high school kid, but I was also wild," he said. "I might strike out twelve and walk ten in a game. By the time I was a senior, I wasn't doing that anymore."

The scouts also liked his demeanor on the mound: he never seemed to lose his cool, unusual in one so young. He was also a good athlete—if his hockey prowess wasn't proof of that, the fact that he played center field and hit third on the days he didn't pitch did. All of that added up to what scouts call "good makeup." Not only was he advanced for someone who had turned eighteen during March of his senior season, he was also someone who clearly had the potential to get to the big leagues fairly quickly. If his fastball had topped at 95, he would have been a top-five pick in the draft.

Because he wasn't overpowering and because he appeared likely to go to college, no one took him in the first round. Risking a first-round pick on someone who says he's going to college is something teams do only if they are willing to overspend greatly to sign someone. Historically, those players who have been talked out of college by big money have ended up not panning out.

Surprisingly, it wasn't the Blue Jays or the Indians who picked Glavine; it was the Atlanta Braves. Although the Braves had scouted Glavine, they had never contacted him to try to get a gauge on how serious he was about college.

On the day of the 1984 draft, Glavine was at baseball practice, when he saw his mother pull up to the field—not exactly a normal thing for her to do. He remembered the draft was that day—nowadays a player projected to go high in the draft would be at least glued to a cell phone, waiting for a call—and wondered what was up. Millie Glavine stopped to talk to Sidorovich, who waved Glavine over.

"The Braves took you in the second round," Millie Glavine reported.

"Okay, cool," Tom replied and went back to finish practice.

Glavine had expected to be taken somewhere in the first three rounds by either the Indians or the Blue Jays, although he had secretly hoped to be taken by the Red Sox. "If it had been the Red Sox, I probably would have gotten excited," he said. "If it had been the first round, I'd have been a little surprised but excited. Going in the second round was okay, and going to the Braves was okay, even though I knew just about nothing about them. That's why I didn't have that much of a reaction.

"It's funny looking back because at the time that was my thought, 'Okay, cool; let me get back to practice,'" Glavine says now, laughing at the memory. "It really was no big deal. I remember thinking, 'Second round, that's nice; they must think I'm pretty decent.' But in my mind I was going to finish the state championships, graduate, and go to Lowell. The only thing that could change that was if the Braves offered big money."

At that moment, Glavine didn't have an agent, and when the Braves called and asked for a meeting to discuss a possible contract, it was Fred Glavine who acted on Tom's behalf. Father and son sat down to discuss strategy. They decided that if the Braves offered a bonus that was big enough to ensure that he would have enough money to pay for college if baseball didn't work out, he would sign. Otherwise, he'd say thanks but no thanks and head to college.

A week after the draft, the Braves came to the house to negotiate with Fred Glavine. Paul Snyder, the team's scouting director, and Tony DeMacio, the scout who had recommended drafting

Glavine, represented the Braves. The offer was a $60,000 bonus to sign. That was a fair offer for a second-round pick, but it wasn't enough for Fred Glavine.

"If that's the offer, I guess Tommy will go to school," he said.

Snyder and DeMacio asked him to think about it. Fred Glavine told them there was nothing to think about. A few days later they called and asked if they could talk again — they had another offer to make. Father and son consulted again: the standard bonus for a first-round pick in those days was between $75,000 and $90,000. If the Braves offered first-round money, it would mean they were very serious about Tom as a prospect. It would also mean he could almost certainly pay his way to college if he decided after a few years that he wasn't good enough to make it as a baseball player.

"Okay," Tom finally said. "If they offer first-round money, let's take it."

He hadn't really thought about what it would mean if he signed: no summer vacation hanging out with his pals or Chrissy Sullivan, his girlfriend; no fraternity parties; no more hockey. If the Braves were willing to guarantee his future — one way or the other — he was ready to jump. He got in his car and drove to a friend's house for a pre-graduation party, leaving his father to deal with Snyder and DeMacio.

He was in the backyard a few hours later when his friend's mother came out to tell Tom his dad was on the phone. "They offered $80,000," Fred Glavine said. "I took it."

Glavine raced to the backyard to tell his pals the news: he was an Atlanta Brave. "Everyone thought it was really cool," he said. "I did too. Of course I had absolutely no idea what I was getting into."

TWO WEEKS LATER, graduation over, Glavine was on a plane to Bradenton, Florida. He had made a quick trip to Atlanta to be introduced to the media with the Braves' other draft picks and to work out briefly at Atlanta-Fulton County Stadium. Now, though, he was leaving home for the first time.

He was met at the airport by Pedro Gonzales, the manager of the Braves' rookie team. Glavine liked Gonzales right away — he was high energy, enthusiastic, and clearly happy to be managing very young, inexperienced players. The rest wasn't quite as easy or comfortable. The Braves were headquartered at the Pittsburgh Pirates' training facility, and the players stayed in dorms in what was called "Pirate City."

Glavine's roommate was Mark Lemke, who would end up traveling through the minor league system to become a starting second baseman with the Braves. Most of the other players were Hispanic. They spoke little English; Glavine spoke no Spanish. "I felt a little bit out of it," he said. "I really wasn't used to being a minority. It was a very different experience."

He went through all the normal homesickness an eighteen-year-old experiences and spent a lot of time waiting in line for the one pay phone in the basement of the dorm. "The worst part was that it was July in Florida, and it wasn't air-conditioned down there," he said. "You'd get eaten alive by all the bugs while you waited."

He figured he could deal with all that as long as he was playing baseball. During his second start, he began to feel pain in his shoulder. He pitched through it and hoped it would go away before his next start. It didn't. Frightened, he went to Gonzales's room and told him he was hurt.

"I think I need to see a doctor," he said. "Something is wrong."

Gonzales told him not to throw the next day while he contacted the front office. Glavine figured he would be told to fly to Atlanta to see a doctor. Instead he was told to stay in Bradenton. Johnny Sain would be coming down to see him.

In those days, Sain was a roving pitching instructor for the Braves. He was a legendary baseball figure, having been half of the famous "Spahn and Sain and pray for rain" duo that had pitched the Boston Braves to the World Series in 1948. He had been a pitching coach for several teams, including the New York Yankees, and had been immortalized in Jim Bouton's ground-breaking book, *Ball Four.*

Bouton had, for all intents and purposes, written that Sain was by far the best pitching coach he had ever had. Sain was unconventional. Most pitchers run in the outfield almost every day of their lives. Sain didn't believe in running. "You can't run the ball across the plate," he liked to say.

Glavine was vaguely aware of who Sain was and ready to do whatever he was told to do. Sain arrived and asked him what his symptoms were. "My arm hurts," Glavine answered. Sain said, "Okay, fine; you're going to throw the next ten days in a row."

At that moment Glavine was fairly convinced that Sain was *in*sane.

But he was eighteen and this was what the great Johnny Sain was telling him to do. For the next ten days he played long toss in the outfield every day. Long toss is just what it sounds like. It is how most pitchers begin their off-season workouts, and something they continue throughout the season.

A long-toss session usually begins with the pitcher and whomever he is throwing to—frequently in spring training, two pitchers will throw to one another—standing no more than twenty feet apart, softly throwing the ball back and forth. Gradually, they will move back as their arms start to loosen up, usually about ten feet at a time, until they are standing anywhere from 100 to 120 feet apart. (The pitching rubber is sixty feet, six inches from home plate.) A major league pitcher can throw a ball on a straight line from 120 feet if he wants to, but most pitchers don't throw at much more than 60 percent of their velocity when long tossing.

An early-winter session can last for as little as ten minutes, with no more than ten or twelve throws from the maximum distance. When a pitcher is well into spring training or the regular season, he might throw as many as forty or fifty times from the full distance. There's no windup involved, no throwing from the stretch. It is, essentially, a game of catch played at a very high level.

Glavine long tossed with Sain for ten days. He still felt some soreness the first few days, but after about six or seven days he noticed that he was pain free. By the time the ten days were up, he was throwing free and easy from 120 feet for fifty tosses.

Sain asked how his arm felt. "Great," Glavine said. "Pain free."

"Okay; tomorrow you'll throw off a mound out of the bullpen," Sain said. "If that goes well, we'll get you back in a game in a few days."

At that juncture if Sain had suggested to Glavine that he pitch standing on his head, Glavine would no doubt have done as he was told. The bullpen session—another fifty pitches at about 80 percent of full velocity with some breaking pitches mixed in—went fine. Two days later, Glavine was back on the mound.

"Never felt another twinge again," he said. "Johnny's theory was simple: my arm just wasn't stretched out because in high school you don't pitch that much. Plus, even though I probably didn't know it, I was trying to throw harder than I had in high school. The rest of the season went fine."

Baseball's minor leagues, except at the Rookie League level, are filled with players of all ages and varying experiences: Triple-A is one step from the majors, and teams there are often full of play-ers who have been in the majors and will be back there shortly. Double-A has a handful of players who might be ready to jump straight to the majors but know, for the most part, they're still probably a year away from being ready to go there. The Single-A level is divided into "high-A" and "low-A," which are exactly as described. Once upon a time, the minor leagues went as low as "Class D" ball, but someone somewhere decided that classifying anyone below A-level was somehow insulting. Thus, there is high-A and low-A and, below that, rookie ball and short-season rookie ball, which is where Glavine had been sent initially. Short-season is almost exclusively for players who have just finished high school in June, although there are occasional exceptions.

When short-season was over, Glavine went home for a week and then flew back to Florida to play for the Braves Instructional League team.

Instructional leagues, which are held in the fall, are just that: a place where younger players are sent to learn their craft. There are no Crash Davises in instructional leagues, only younger players deemed by their teams to have the potential to make the majors. I-league games aren't really games in the traditional sense.

"You might start the first inning like a regular game, then go out in the second, and they say, 'Okay; man on first. Let's work on your pickoff move this inning,'" Glavine remembered. "They might keep you out there for five outs if you have an inning where you don't throw a lot of pitches, or get you out of there after one or two if you're struggling."

Glavine had a good fall but was happy to return home for the holidays. He had been gone for most of six months. Because his bonus money was being banked in case it was needed down the road and his minor league pay was about $650 a month, he went to work during the winter on his father's construction crews.

"Dad steered me clear of the real heavy lifting," he said. "But I can remember carrying cement on a few occasions and thinking, 'Whoo boy; be careful with that left shoulder.'"

The shoulder survived the winter, and Glavine found himself promoted to low-A ball the following spring in Sumter, South Carolina. He was a little disappointed not to be sent to Durham, home of the higher A team (not to mention "Bull Durham") but felt better when it was explained to him that the Durham team was, generally speaking, for older players—guys who had gone to college or had slipped back from higher levels of the minors.

It turned out Sumter was a team filled with genuine prospects: Lemke was there, as were Jeff Blauser and Ron Gant, all of whom would end up with the Braves and have lengthy major league careers. Friendships were cemented that summer. The players even found time to tour Fort Sumter, the spot where the first shots of the Civil War had been fired. "Not a whole lot else to do in that town," Glavine remembered. He pitched well at Sumter, but the thing he remembers most is the heat.

"Just absolutely smoking; every day, every night," he said. "Hottest summer of my life, bar none."

Even in the stifling heat, Glavine pitched well, leading the league in ERA (2.35) while striking out 174 batters in 168 innings. "I guess at that level I was still a flamethrower," he joked. "I had learned a lot in the Instructional League. I was starting to become a pitcher."

He returned to the Instructional League that fall and was promoted to Class-AA Greenville at the start of the 1986 season. He was on the All-Star team in July and pitching so well that he began to hear rumors that he might get called up to the big leagues in September. The Braves were an awful team—they would go on to finish the season 72–89 after going 66–96 a year earlier—and the thought was that calling up some of the team's bright young prospects in September, when the roster limit was expanded from twenty-five players to forty, might give Braves fans (those that were left) some hope for the future.

Early in August, Bill Slack, Glavine's pitching coach in Greenville, sat him down to tell him not to listen to the rumors. "You're staying right here until the end of the season," he said. "Don't listen to any rumors about moving up."

A week later Slack called Glavine in again. "You're going to Richmond," he said, simply.

Richmond was the Braves' Triple-A farm team—one step away from the majors. Glavine was excited and disappointed.

"We had a group of really good guys," he said. "I felt very comfortable where I was, and, mentally, I was thinking I'd finish the season there and, with luck, make it to Richmond the following spring. On the other hand, I was being promoted; I felt ready to make the move, and I was one step from the major leagues."

The jump to Richmond wasn't an easy one. "It was the first time I felt a little bit intimidated," Glavine said. "You could go out there to pitch, and half the lineup might be guys who were in the majors a month earlier. I was twenty years old, and most nights I was facing a lot of guys who had ten or twelve years of professional experience. I had two."

He struggled during the last month of the season, going 1–5 with an ERA of more than 5 runs a game. During the playoffs, he pitched out of the bullpen and did better. He even got a save one night. "I didn't know it because coming out of the bullpen was so confusing for me; I didn't know what the score was," he said. "I thought we were up four, and we were only up three. I'd have probably been more nervous if I'd have known."

The Braves ended up winning the International League championship, giving Glavine a small taste of what that success felt like. Shortly after the season had ended, Glavine was at home preparing for a nonbaseball off-season. As a Triple-A player he was too advanced for the Instructional League, and he was looking forward to some extended time at home. One afternoon the phone rang, and Glavine heard a voice say, "Tom, hi; it's Hank."

That would be Hank as in Hank Aaron, then (and still in the minds of many) baseball's all-time home-run king. Aaron was director of player personnel for the Braves. The team wanted him to play winter ball in Central America. Glavine's gut told him that would be a mistake.

"I'd been playing ball almost nonstop since graduating from high school," he said. "I thought I needed a rest, a winter to take it easy and be fresh for spring training. Being twenty years old and telling Hank Aaron no wasn't easy, but I was convinced I was doing the right thing."

Aaron pushed a little bit, telling Glavine that playing winter ball would probably enhance his chances of making the team the following spring. "Maybe," Glavine said. "But if I'm good enough to make the team next year, I'll make it. If I'm not, some more time at Triple-A probably wouldn't be bad for me." He hung up, convinced he was right but still feeling a little bit strange about saying no to Hank Aaron.

"The funny thing is, these days, that call never happens," Glavine said. "A young pitcher like me — the last thing they would want to do is have me pitch all winter. In fact, occasionally, they tell guys who want to pitch in the winter not to pitch. They're far more careful about babying young pitchers now than they were then."

As he expected, Glavine began the season at Richmond. A year older, a little more experienced, he pitched much better, even though his record (6–12) didn't reflect it. His ERA was 3.35 — more than two runs lower than it had been the previous summer. "I lost a lot of games two-one and three-two," he said. "It was frustrating, but I knew I was pitching well, and I was starting to hear again that I might get called up."

The Braves weren't any better than they had been a year earlier (they would win three fewer games), but they were starting to make over their roster under the leadership of Stan Kasten, the team president, and Bobby Cox, who had been hired after the 1985 season as general manager. Kasten and Cox had a simple plan: build around young pitching. Glavine was one of those young pitchers they were counting on to make their future brighter. There were others, including Pete Smith, whom Glavine had competed against in high school. In fact, during the first four years Kasten and Cox were in charge, they had six first-round draft picks; five of those picks were pitchers.

They also made a decision in the winter of 1987 to re-sign Doyle Alexander, a thirty-seven-year-old journeyman pitcher who clearly would not be around when the team became a contender again. "We signed him for one reason," Kasten said. "We thought he was still good enough that a contending team might trade us a young pitcher for him during the summer."

They were right. On August 13, the Braves traded Alexander to the Detroit Tigers, who were fighting for the American League East pennant. In return, they got a twenty-year-old prospect named John Smoltz. Alexander went 9–0 for the Tigers and did help them win their division. But the trade certainly worked out for the Braves.

Glavine was in Toledo when the Braves made the trade. On the night of the trade, he pitched what had become a typical game for him: seven innings, one run; then he was lifted for a pinch hitter in the eighth, trailing 1–0. He took the loss. He was back in his hotel room when the phone rang. It was Triple-A manager Roy Majtyka: "The Braves traded Doyle Alexander to Detroit," he said. "You're going up. You'll meet the team in Houston."

The next few days are still a blur in Glavine's mind. He had to call his parents, his friends, his sister, and his two brothers. He had to find a way to get from Toledo to Houston, and he had to figure out how to get enough tickets to get his family and friends into the Astrodome four nights later when he was scheduled to make his major league debut.

He had no idea who John Smoltz was. All he knew was that his presence in the Braves organization had gotten him promoted to the majors. He had no idea that Smoltz would become a key part of the Braves staff and his best friend in the game. "If I had known that Smoltzy would spend the rest of our lives telling me *he* was the reason I got to the majors, I might not have gone," he said, laughing. "But I guess, in the end, it was worth it."

He reported to Houston on August 14 and began preparing for

his first start as a big leaguer. His opponent would be Mike Scott, who had won the National League Cy Young Award the previous season.

Glavine was twenty-one years old, and any thoughts about giving up baseball to go to college were in the past. He was nervous but excited. *Bring on Mike Scott,* he thought.

2

The Lawyer's Son

WHILE IT MAY BE EASY to describe the whereabouts of Billerica to someone—twenty-five miles northwest of Boston—it is not nearly as simple to tell someone exactly where Montoursville, Pennsylvania, can be found.

"It's the next town over from Williamsport" lets people know that it is on the doorstep of the place where the Little League World Series is held every year but still doesn't help that much unless you have *been* to the Little League World Series.

If you check a map, you will find that Montoursville is 180 miles northwest of Philadelphia and 215 miles northeast of Pittsburgh.

In short, Montoursville is near almost nothing. According to the 2000 census, it has a population of 4,777. And, depending on your point of view, the second most famous person to have grown up in Montoursville was either Tom O'Malley, who spent several years playing in the major leagues; Blaise Alexander, a semisuccessful NASCAR driver; or Kelly Mazzante, who plays in the WNBA.

There is no doubt, however, about who Montoursville's most famous native son is: Michael Cole Mussina.

Montoursville is where Mike Mussina grew up, where he still lives today, and where he plans to live when he is finished playing baseball.

"It's home," he says with a shrug. "I'm comfortable here."

These days his home sits on a two hundred–acre tract of land that he purchased in 1994 for $510,000 during his third full season with the Baltimore Orioles. There are three main buildings on the property: a large, comfortable house, where Mussina, his wife, Jana, and their three children live; a gym that is larger than some college gyms; and "the barn," which houses not animals, but several dozen old cars Mussina has collected through the years.

Mussina has come a long way—though moving only a short distance—since his days growing up as the best athlete ever to come out of Montoursville. Malcolm, his dad, was, and is, a local lawyer; Eleanor, his mom, is a retired nurse. Mike is the older of their two sons—his brother, Mark, also still lives in town—and quickly established himself as a star in every sport he tried. While Glavine's first love was hockey, Mussina's was basketball.

He can still tell you off the top of his head that he scored 1,421 points as a three-year starter at Montoursville High School (then again he can recite almost any of his lifetime stats in an instant), and even now he and Mark often begin their winter workouts in the family gym by playing basketball—anything from a shooting contest to full-court one-on-one, depending on the day.

Mussina also played football growing up and was a good enough placekicker and punter—he also played wide receiver—to get some scholarship interest from various colleges during his junior and senior years of high school. "If I had thought I was good enough to play Division 1 basketball, that probably would have been my first choice," he said. "But I wasn't that good. I was a reasonably good high school player; I probably could have gone to a D-3 school and played, but not D-1. I knew my best shot was going to be baseball."

Like Glavine, Mussina was a star pitcher from an early age. He wasn't all that big, but he threw hard—very hard for a kid—and he had good control. He enjoyed trying to throw different pitches, in addition to his fastball, and was always fooling around with different grips.

"One thing people don't understand sometimes is how much we [big league pitchers] study pitching and study baseball," he said. "I enjoy pitching and I enjoy competing, but I also enjoy the game itself. I like to watch other guys pitch, especially guys who are good at what they do. After all these years, I know a lot about pitching. I can watch a young pitcher throw three pitches and probably have a good idea about his potential. It isn't just how hard he throws, but *how* he throws: his delivery, the look on his face, and, after a few pitches, how he responds to any suggestions I might make.

"Pitching isn't just physical. Sure, you need certain tools and ability. But if you're going to do it well for a long time, you need more than that. You need an understanding of what goes into it."

To some, Mussina might sound immodest when he talks about how much he knows about pitching—and about a lot of things. He can come off at times as one of those people who believes he's always the smartest guy in the room. One reason for that is that he frequently *is* the smartest guy in the room.

In 2006 Mussina appeared in the documentary *Wordplay*, which is about people who are fascinated by crossword puzzles. He was one of a handful of famous people the filmmakers found who did crosswords regularly. The others were former President Bill Clinton, *Daily show* host Jon Stewart, and former *New York Times* ombudsman Daniel Okrent. Not the kind of company most baseball players keep on a regular basis.

"They were different than me," Mussina explained. "They all do the *Times* puzzle on a regular basis. I prefer *USA Today*. I've done the *Times*, but it's really hard. I enjoy *USA Today* because it's easier and I can get through it faster."

That's sort of typical Mussina. He knows he's smart, but he doesn't feel any need to prove he's any smarter than he really is. The main reason people frequently get upset with him is that he doesn't feel a need to massage people's egos. He is completely honest when he answers questions and never gives a knee-jerk answer. Often, he will pause a while before answering the question because he is thinking it through. Sometimes he will challenge the premise of the question before answering it.

By Mussina's junior year he was being scouted by major league teams and could throw in the 90-mile-per-hour range, with good control. But the thought of signing a contract straight out of high school never crossed his mind.

"It was just sort of a given in my family that you went to college," he said. "Plus, for me, there was a lifestyle question. Did I want to spend three or four years riding buses around in the minor leagues, staying in little towns in lousy hotels, or did I want to have the chance to experience college while playing baseball at the same time. To me, it was a no-brainer."

His choice of college was also pretty much a no-brainer once he saw Stanford. It was a long way from home, but that didn't bother him. It was a great school with a great baseball team — a perennial national contender. In fact, the Cardinals won the college World Series during Mussina's senior year of high school.

"One thing I wanted to do was go someplace where they played a lot of games," Mussina said. "If I had stayed in the East, I would have been at a school where they played a forty- or forty-five-game schedule. In the South or in California, it was more like seventy games."

At the end of his senior year, even though he and his family had put out the word very clearly that he was going to Stanford and had no interest in signing with a major league team, he was drafted anyway — by the Baltimore Orioles, in the eleventh round. Frequently teams will take a flyer on a player they think has potential in the later rounds of the draft on the off-chance that a big bonus might change his mind.

Doug Melvin, who is now the general manager of the Milwaukee Brewers, was the chief scout for the Orioles back then, and, even though he had been told Mussina had no interest in signing, he took a drive into central Pennsylvania to see him pitch that spring.

"I can still remember watching Mike and thinking this was a kid who would be a big leaguer and probably get there faster than most kids coming out of high school," Melvin said. "He had a very mature way about him on the mound. He threw hard, which you expect, but he also threw a lot of different pitches. He looked more like twenty-eight out there than eighteen because of his demeanor."

Melvin stuck all that in the back of his mind, knowing it would be at least three years before the Orioles would have another chance to draft Mussina. The Orioles did make a phone call to see if Mussina had any interest in signing but were quickly told no, so they backed off and never made a formal offer.

Unlike most kids leaving home, especially small-town kids, Mussina felt no sense of dread or any real homesickness when he arrived at Stanford. "When I got there, we had a team that was coming off a national championship and had a number of experienced pitchers coming back," he said. "I don't think I've ever lacked for self-confidence, but I do remember wondering if I would be good enough to pitch on a team that experienced and that deep. I can still remember riding my bicycle across campus one day and thinking to myself, 'Okay, here you are; are you going to be good enough?'"

He was good enough, fitting into the rotation right from the beginning. The only setback—and it was a major one—came early in his sophomore year. He was pitching against Stanford's archrival, California, when he felt pain in his shoulder while throwing a pitch.

"It was certainly scary," he said. "I had never been injured before, and I had no idea if I'd pitch again or be the same pitcher I had been before. I guess there were a few moments when I wondered if I might be through, but not many, to tell the truth. My focus was really on getting healthy and getting back on the mound and pitching again. I think I always thought I would be okay. I was young enough to be an optimist, I suppose.

"But the other thing I realized was that this was one of the reasons I'd come to college. People do get hurt; you hear about it all the time. If by some chance I couldn't pitch again, well, a Stanford degree wasn't a bad alternative. I didn't want my baseball career to be over at the age of nineteen, but I knew if for some reason things turned out that way, I still had plenty of alternatives. My life wasn't going to be over."

In a sense, Mussina was lucky to be injured when he was so young. The damage wasn't serious enough to require surgery, and by the fall of his junior year he was pitching pain free. And not only was he pain free, he was emerging as a star. Under baseball's draft rules, he was eligible for the June 1990 draft because he had been in college for three years. Mussina had filled out while at Stanford, and, as Doug Melvin had expected, had become a much better pitcher — even with the time lost to injury — than he had been in high school. The scouts were back in droves that spring, and this time Mussina was happy to see them.

"By then I felt I was ready," he said. "I had taken some extra courses with the idea that if I got drafted high enough at the end of my junior year, I would only need one semester to graduate in the fall after I finished playing baseball that summer. I had a good junior season, and I was fairly certain I'd be a first-round pick, although you can never be sure. I'd heard everything from the top ten to somewhere in the second round."

It wasn't the top ten and it wasn't the second round. The Orioles were once again very interested but weren't sure Mussina would still be there when they picked twentieth in the first round. "At one point we heard Texas was going to take him," Melvin said. "They were a couple of spots in front of us. It was going to be Mike or Daniel Smith. When they picked Smith we were very happy because we were pretty certain at that point [Mike would] be there when we picked."

He was there, but it was a closer call than Melvin imagined. The Oakland Athletics, picking before Texas and Baltimore, also liked Mussina a lot. But they were fascinated by the potential of high school phenom Todd Van Poppel. The A's were torn: take a chance that they could sign Van Poppel, who everyone was convinced was going to be a superstar, or go with Mussina, who most thought would be a very good major league pitcher.

"I think the decision in the end was to roll the dice," said Tony LaRussa, the A's manager at the time. "I know everyone really liked Mike Mussina a lot. But the thought was we might be passing on the next great pitcher if we didn't go after Van Poppel. Obviously, Mussina has turned out to be a great pitcher."

Mussina was extremely happy to be drafted by the Orioles, which appeared to be a team on the rise. They had bottomed out in 1988, losing twenty-one straight games to start the season, but had bounced back to go 87–75 in 1989. What's more, Baltimore was less than two hundred miles from Montoursville.

"I had grown up a Yankees fan, even though I was right between the Phillies and Pirates," he said. "It was only a couple of hours to go into New York to see a game every once in a while, and I could watch their games on TV and listen to them on radio most of the time. But if I wasn't going to the Yankees, I was perfectly happy to be taken by the Orioles."

Since he was twenty-one years old and had three years of college-pitching experience, Mussina was sent straight to Hagerstown, the Orioles Double-A affiliate, meaning he was only two steps from the major leagues. It isn't unusual at all for college players to start out in Double-A, especially since the top level of college baseball is usually considered to be about the equivalent of Double-A ball.

"Except," Mussina said, "when you get to the minors, guys

aren't using metal bats anymore. That makes the adjustment to the pro game considerably easier for a pitcher."

Mussina reported to Hagerstown on July 4, meeting the team just as it was returning from a long road trip. "They had played poorly on the road trip," he remembered. "I walked into the club-house the first day, and the first thing that happened was we had a team meeting. Jerry Narron was the manager, and he was really angry. He just aired the whole team out. I sat there thinking, 'Welcome to pro ball, kid.'"

The rest of his welcome that first season went about as well as he might have hoped. Not wanting to rush a first-round draft pick, the team gave Mussina what amounted to two weeks of spring training to get ready to pitch in his first game. When he made his debut, on July 19, he was lifted after four innings, even though he hadn't given up a run.

"It became apparent pretty quickly that Mike was ready for just about anything we threw at him," Melvin said. "I remember talking to one of our minor league pitching scouts a little while after he got to Hagerstown. I asked him how Mike was adapting, and he said to me, 'Adapting? Doug, he's going to be adapting to the majors very soon. This kid isn't going to spend much time in the minors.'"

Mussina was already throwing a variety of pitches, including a knee-buckling knuckle-curveball that he had starting throwing in high school and had developed further at Stanford. "He was twenty-one but pitched like he was thirty-one," Melvin said. "He had a presence on the mound; he had command of his pitches; and he had great control."

By mid-August, Mussina had started seven games and had a sporty 1.49 ERA. He had struck out forty batters in forty-two innings and had walked only seven, a mind-bending number for someone so young and inexperienced. "I really didn't feel that inexperienced, though," Mussina said. "I had faced a lot of good hitters in college."

The Orioles decided there was no sense keeping Mussina at Double-A and moved him to Triple-A Rochester to finish the season. He was even better there, pitching to an ERA of 1.35 and then pitching well in two playoff games. He was so good, there was talk during the off-season that he might be ready to make the big league team the next spring, even though he had only pitched half a season of minor league ball.

Before spring training, though, there was the matter of returning to Stanford to complete his degree requirements. He did that in the fall, helped by the fact that Stanford didn't start classes until mid-September, which dovetailed perfectly with the end of the minor league season. He graduated in December, with a degree in economics. To this day when people talk about all of Mussina's accomplishments, one of the first things that comes up is the fact that he graduated from Stanford in three and a half years while playing baseball.

"Graduating from college doesn't mean you're smart," Mussina likes to say. "But it does mean you were smart enough to know that having a degree is a good thing."

A college grad, Mussina reported to spring training in 1991, figuring he would be headed for Triple-A Rochester in April. He was given number 42—a low number for a nonroster player—but he harbored no illusions about where he fit in at that moment.

"I knew I'd start the season in Rochester, and if I pitched well, depending on how the big league team was doing, there was a chance I'd get called up. I figured at worst, unless I really screwed up, I'd get called up in September.

"I didn't give up a hit the first nine innings I pitched that spring. All of a sudden, I looked up and we were only about a week away from breaking camp, and I was still with the team. But I also knew there were still nine starting pitchers in camp, and I was a nonroster player. So, when they told me I was going down, I wasn't that surprised."

The Orioles were playing their final season in Memorial

Stadium and were hoping to contend for the American League East title. They never came close, playing so poorly that team legend Frank Robinson was replaced as manager by Johnny Oates midway through the season. With the team out of contention, there was no reason not to start bringing up prospects from the minor leagues. By midsummer, there was no brighter prospect in the system than Mussina.

Mussina had been more than okay at Triple-A in 1991, winning ten games with a league-leading ERA of 2.87. He also led the league in strikeouts. On July 30, he pitched in Columbus against the Clippers, the Yankees farm club, and threw a shutout.

"I was pitching as well as anyone in the league and better than anyone on the team. The Orioles were going nowhere. I knew there were business considerations involved: if they called me up during the first half of the season, I would be arbitration-eligible a year earlier, and teams think about things like that. But now it was late July, and all of that was past. I kept wondering, when was the call going to come?

On July 31, Mussina was in his hotel room in Columbus when the call came. Only it wasn't for him. It was for his roommate, Jim Poole. "Someone from the Orioles called; I don't even remember who it was," Mussina said. "They asked for Pooley, who was out. They said, 'Please have him call us right away; we're bringing him up.' I went and found him and told him. Then I went to the weight room to work out because I was *so* frustrated. I mean, I was happy for Pooley, but I was thinking, 'What about me? What do I have to do to get called up? I was angry.'"

He went back to his room after about an hour and found Poole packing. The Orioles were in Seattle, and Poole had been told to fly there to meet the team. "Where've you been?" Poole asked. (Very few people had cell phones in 1991.) "The team called a little while ago. You're going up too."

Mussina was baffled. "I just talked to them an hour ago when they called for you; why wouldn't they have told me then?" he asked.

Poole laughed. "They didn't know it was you. They just asked for my room. They didn't realize we were roommates. They called back asking for you right after I hung up with them."

Mussina called Baltimore and was told that yes, he was being called up. He was not to fly to Seattle, though, because his first start would be in Chicago in four days. That gave him time to throw his bullpen session that day in Columbus, fly to Rochester, pack up his car, and drive to Baltimore. Then he flew to Chicago to meet the team.

"The funny thing was there was some kind of Orioles fan-club trip to Chicago for the weekend," he said. "They were all on my flight. So was Chuck Thompson [the Orioles Hall of Fame radio announcer]. He was traveling with the fan-club group for some reason. He recognized me from spring training and said, 'Hey, come on and ride the bus with us to the hotel.' So, I threw my stuff underneath the bus and rode to the Hyatt with the fan club and Chuck."

The Orioles had been convinced for a while that Mussina was ready for the call-up. But they were a team that had traditionally treated young pitchers with care, and this was no different.

"One thing you don't do with young pitchers is rush them," Oates said after Mussina was pitching for him. "Mike walked into the clubhouse and looked like he had been there for years. He probably needed less input from me and Boz than almost anyone on our staff."

"Boz" was Orioles pitching coach Dick Bosman, who had been Rochester's pitching coach when Mussina first arrived there. There wasn't all that much Bosman had wanted to change in the young pitcher, except for helping him do a better job of holding runners on first. Because a right-handed pitcher has his back to a runner on first, he often has trouble knowing just how big the runner's lead might be. Bosman suggested to Mussina that he bend way down, almost to his knees, while getting into the stretch position, so he could sneak a look at the runner through his legs before standing up to his set position. Years later, even after he had become adept at holding runners, Mussina still used the Bosman dip on his way to getting set.

"It worked, and it became habit," he said. "There's really been no reason to change."

Mussina's big league debut on August 4 was mostly an auspicious one. He pitched seven and two-thirds innings and made one mistake—giving up a home run to Frank Thomas—that cost him the game. Charlie Hough, the White Sox veteran knuckleballer, pitched a shutout, and Mussina, in spite of giving up just four hits and the one run, lost the game 1–0. Ten days later, in his third start, he got his first win, beating the Texas Rangers 10–2 in Memorial Stadium. At that point he was only a little more than a year removed from the campus at Stanford.

He had clearly arrived in the Major Leagues. And almost everyone expected him to stay for quite a while.

3

Cy Young ... Cy Almost

By THE TIME MIKE MUSSINA made his major league debut, Tom Glavine was in his fourth full season with the Braves.

He remembered his debut on August 17, 1987, more for his first major league at bat than for anything he did on the mound. As would become part of a pattern throughout his career, he had struggled in the first inning, giving up two runs before getting Dale Berra—son of Yogi—to fly out to center with the bases loaded. In the top of the second, he had come up against Mike Scott, who had won the Cy Young Award the year before, amid constant complaints that his sudden emergence as a star had as much to do with his ability to scuff balls as to throw them.

"What he threw at me didn't need to be scuffed," Glavine said, laughing. "First pitch came out of his hand and was by me before I could start to move the bat. I remember it made this *whooshing* sound that I had never heard before in my life. I thought to myself, 'Oh, so this is what the big leagues is like.' My lasting impression of that night was trying to hit against Scott as much as anything else."

Glavine lasted less than four innings, giving up five runs, and took the loss. It hardly mattered. He would have liked to have pitched better, but the thrill of making it to the majors, of having all his family and friends there, took a lot of the sting out of the loss. That and the fact that he had lost to Mike Scott, who he could now testify firsthand was unhittable.

Five nights later, he made his first start in Atlanta, with half of Billerica again in attendance. Mike Scott was nowhere in sight. The Pirates' starting pitcher was Bob Walk, and Glavine, feeling much more relaxed both on the mound and at the plate, pitched seven and a third innings, gave up three runs, and left with a 10–3 lead. The bullpen held the Pirates right there, and Glavine was 1–1 as a big leaguer.

"I honestly can't remember the last couple innings of that game," he said. "I remember that I stayed in the dugout, and I remember I was a wreck in the ninth inning and thought the game would never end."

He and the family celebrated at length following the victory, taking pictures on the field, making sure all the appropriate souvenirs were collected. In addition to his first win, Glavine had his first brush with big league practical jokes.

When the game was over, Willie Stargell, the Pittsburgh Pirates Hall of Famer who was then a Braves coach, walked over to Glavine in the clubhouse and handed him the game ball, giving him a heartfelt handshake. "You should give this to your mom," he said.

Glavine thought that was a cool idea until he looked at the inscription Stargell had written on the ball. "Hey, Mom," it said. "This is the ball from my first fucking major league win."

Glavine almost gagged.

Stargell reached into his pocket and produced the actual game ball, a huge smile on his face. Glavine could see a number of his teammates standing behind Stargell, cracking up.

"They got me," he said. "It was the first time I saw what big league humor was like."

The rest of the season was predictably up and down for a rookie on a bad team. Glavine was 2–4 with a 5.54 ERA. He wasn't going to overpower hitters throwing a fastball that topped out at maybe 90 miles per hour. He was still looking for an effective changeup and hadn't found it. Like most young pitchers, he had tried different grips and arm motions, but nothing had really worked.

"No matter how hard you throw, you have to have at least one good breaking pitch to go with your fastball," Glavine said. "It sounds simplistic, but pitching is really about two things: changing speeds and location. The location part is obvious: if you throw the ball over the plate to major league hitters, they're going to crush it unless they're fooled by the speed of the pitch. If you can throw every pitch on the black or just off the black, then fooling a guy with pitch speed becomes a little less important. Most of us can't do that all the time so we have to be able to change speeds."

In *Ball Four,* Jim Bouton describes Sal Maglie, the pitching coach for the Seattle Pilots, going through a lineup in a pitcher's meeting and saying of every hitter, "Keep the ball low and on the outside corner, and he won't hit it."

That was accurate, as Bouton pointed out, because no hitter can hit a pitch low and outside. The trouble is that no pitcher can throw every pitch—or even a majority of his pitches—in that spot.

So, assuming a pitcher can't place every pitch exactly where he wants it—in today's baseball vernacular it's called *locating*—he has to keep hitters off balance by changing speeds. At twenty-one, Glavine was pretty good at locating, especially for a young lefty, but he was still working on changing speeds.

Even so, he was part of the Braves' starting rotation when the 1988 season began. The Braves were even worse in 1988 than they had been the previous three years. Manager Chuck Tanner was replaced thirty-nine games into the season by Russ Nixon, but it didn't make much difference. By season's end, the Braves were 54–106 (two games were mercifully rained out) and had drawn only 848,000 fans at home. Glavine's season fit right in with all that: he was 7–17 and his ERA was 4.56. Not only was he going through on-the-job training, he was doing it with a very bad team behind him.

"Part of me understood that this was the deal," he said. "I was still learning, and we were bad. Some days I was just bad; other days I was pretty good, and the team was bad. Either way, it made for a long year."

One positive during that season was the arrival in Atlanta of another young pitcher: John Smoltz. Glavine and Smoltz became fast friends. They shared a love of golf, a love of giving people a hard time, and, most of all, a love of competing.

Both young pitchers—Glavine was a little more than a year older than Smoltz—were learning on the job and sharing the suffering that went with it. A year later, the Braves weren't much better, 63–97, but Glavine believed he had turned a corner. His 14–8 record and ERA of 3.68 were a big part of that feeling. But believing he had finally found the changeup he needed to be a successful pitcher was even more significant.

Early in his minor league career, Glavine threw three pitches most of the time: fastball, curveball, forkball. The forkball is a pitch that starts out looking like a fastball but drops hard and fast as it gets near the plate, causing batters to swing over it. It isn't all that different from the split-fingered fastball, or splitter, that many pitchers throw nowadays. The grip is different, and the split-finger tends to be thrown harder, but the principle—fooling the batter into thinking a fastball is on the way—is the same.

Glavine loved his forkball while he was in A-ball and Double-A ball. "I could throw it fifty-five feet, and guys would still swing at it," he said. "I thought it was a great pitch."

Two things changed his thinking while he was pitching in Greenville in 1986. The first was the arrival of Ned Yost as a minor league pitching instructor. One night after Glavine had struck out a number of hitters with his forkball, Yost walked over to him and asked how he felt about his forkball.

"I love it," Glavine said. "Look at what it did for me tonight."

"Yeah, well, the pitch sucks," Yost said. "You can get Double-A hitters out with it, but major league hitters will laugh at it. They'll just wait until you leave one up and hit it a million miles."

Glavine was skeptical. After all, he was twenty years old and knew everything there was to know about baseball. Yost was just a washed-up old catcher. What could he possibly know about pitching?

A few weeks later, Glavine found himself pitching to Bo Jackson, the famous two-sport athlete who was trying to make his way to the big leagues and had recently started his minor league career.

"I had faced him about a month earlier, and he was completely clueless about how to hit a breaking ball," Glavine said. "I think I struck him out three times with the forkball. So, first time up, I threw him one and waited for him to flail at it. He just waited on it; it was up just a little, and he hit it, honestly, about six hundred feet. The ball may still be going."

Glavine was impressed by how much Jackson had improved in a month and by the fact that someone not yet in the big leagues had hit the pitch so hard. He remembered what Yost had said. "From that moment on, I was searching for a way to throw a good straight changeup."

Fast-forward to March of 1989. Glavine was shagging balls in the outfield during spring training when a ball rolled up to him. He picked it up, and, as he went to throw it back toward the infield, it slipped in his hand, causing him to grip it between his middle finger and his ring finger rather than the more natural way between the middle finger and the index finger. When he released the ball, he noticed that it dropped more rapidly than his other breaking pitches did and, at least it appeared to him, darted to his left as opposed to his right, the way most breaking pitches do when thrown by a lefty.

Intrigued, Glavine attempted to throw some pitches like that from the mound when he next threw a bullpen, and, sure enough, the pitch dropped quickly and to his left, meaning he was throwing a breaking pitch that broke away from a right-handed batter. He asked Bruce Dal Canton, the pitching coach, and Bruce Benedict, the catcher, what they thought.

"If it feels good, give it a shot" was the response from both of them.

"Until then I had two problems with my changeup," Glavine said. "If I tried to throw it with enough sink and enough change of speed from my fastball, I was slowing my arm motion down. The batters at the big league level are good enough to read that, and they would know I was throwing a change as a result. When I didn't slow my arm motion down, the pitch might go seventy-eight [Glavine's fastball was in the 86- to 88-mile-per-hour range at that point], or it might go eighty-two or eighty-three—which isn't nearly enough change of speed—and batters would rip it. I just never knew what was coming out of my hand. With the new grip, I had both break and change of speed without slowing my arm motion down. I couldn't throw it faster than seventy-eight even if I wanted to."

Glavine began using the new grip and pitch in exhibition games and carried it over to the regular season. Bobby Cox, who was still the general manager, was impressed. "It's one thing for a young pitcher to mess around with a new pitch," he said. "Tommy was throwing it in tough spots right from the beginning. He was never afraid of it."

By the end of 1989, Glavine was convinced he was now ready to be a big-time major league pitcher. He had won fourteen games with a bad Braves team, and he had found the changeup he needed. Then, in 1990, he went backward again. He started the season feeling pain in his shoulder—it turned out to be tendinitis—and the confidence he had gained the previous year rapidly disappeared. It hurt to pitch, and it hurt just as much to watch his fielders kick the ball around.

Sixty-five games into another lost season, with the Braves 25–40 and sitting in their usual spot—last place—Cox fired

Nixon and came down to the dugout to become the manager. Cox brought an entirely new coaching staff with him. Dal Canton was fired and replaced by Leo Mazzone.

Glavine knew Mazzone a little bit from Instructional League baseball. He knew Mazzone was a disciple of Johnny Sain. Even so, he was shocked when Mazzone told the pitchers that they were going to throw almost every day and would always throw not one but two bullpens between starts.

"It was a little bit like that first year in Bradenton," Glavine said. "My arm is killing me, and here's a guy saying I should throw more. It had worked with Johnny, but I was very skeptical because I wasn't working my way back starting with long tossing and then eventually getting on a mound. I was pitching in the majors every fifth day. It was kind of scary."

Glavine didn't complain though — partly because it's not his way, partly because he was still a little nervous he might be yanked from the rotation because he wasn't pitching well. He went along with the program, and, sure enough, his arm started to feel better. For most of the second half of the season, he pitched without pain and pitched much better. Even so, life with Leo was an adjustment.

Dal Canton had been an upbeat, friendly guy, someone who soothed when things weren't going well and always tried to find something good to say. That wasn't Mazzone's style.

"If you were throwing a bullpen and not hitting your spots, he'd let you have it," Glavine said, smiling at the memory. "Sometimes he'd come to the mound to calm you down; other times he'd just blast you.

"I remember one night in San Diego, I was really struggling in the first inning — not unusual for me. Leo comes to the mound and he says, 'Tommy, are you okay? Are you hurt?' I said no, I felt fine. He says, 'Well, then, do me a favor and get some people out! Otherwise, I'm gonna yank you and get someone in here who *will* get some people out!' I pitched out of it, settled down, and we won the game."

Glavine finished 10–12 that year but pitched much better down the stretch. In fact, the entire team played better down the stretch, even though their record (65–97) wasn't much better than it had been in the past.

"You just got the sense that we had some guys by then," Glavine said. "Smoltzy was clearly going to be a star; we'd picked up Charlie Leibrandt the previous winter and he could really pitch. We had gotten Terry Pendleton and Sid Bream; [Jeff] Blauser was up too. You looked around and said, 'You know what? There's a chance to get better.' I'm not saying we knew it was going to happen as fast as it did, but by the end of '90, we were starting to see some light at the end of the tunnel."

In 1991 the Braves pulled one of the all-time turnarounds in baseball history. With Glavine, Smoltz, Leibrandt, and a young lefty named Steve Avery leading the way, they emerged as one of the best starting-pitching staffs in baseball. Glavine was the star, his arm healthy. The Mazzone method was working for him, and with the changeup now a true weapon, he dominated throughout most of the season, finishing 20–11 with a 2.55 ERA.

The Braves became a worst-to-first story, beating the Los Angeles Dodgers down the stretch for the National League West title. Atlanta suddenly became a baseball city, with attendance jumping from 980,000 in 1990 to more than 2.1 million in 1991. Fulton County Stadium was full and frenzied every night as the Braves made their run.

The Braves upset the Pittsburgh Pirates in seven games in the National League Championship Series, with Smoltz pitching a shutout in the seventh game. They led the Minnesota Twins (who had also gone from worst-to-first that year) 3–2 in the World Series, before losing two remarkable games in Minnesota: the first on an eleventh inning home run by Kirby Puckett off Leibrandt; the second 1–0 in ten innings. Smoltz was brilliant that night; Jack Morris was a little more brilliant.

Glavine lost Game Two of that series, pitching a complete

game but losing 3–2 before coming back to win Game Five. As disappointing as the loss in the World Series was, the exhilaration of the remarkable season lingered in Atlanta all winter. Glavine was named the Cy Young Award winner, which vaulted him into stardom at the age of twenty-five.

WHILE GLAVINE WAS BECOMING A STAR, Mussina was trying to become a major leaguer. Like Glavine, he believed that wearing a major league uniform alone didn't cut it.

"It isn't really something you can define," Mussina said. "There's no set time when you look in the mirror and say, 'Okay, now I'm a *real* big leaguer.' I can tell you for sure that when I first came up in '91, I in no way felt as if I was a big leaguer. I was happy to have the uniform and the chance to pitch, but when I looked across the clubhouse and saw Cal Ripken, I knew there was a substantial difference between what he was and what I was."

Ripken was one of the game's true superstars. Even then, four years before he would break Lou Gehrig's record, his consecutive-games streak was the stuff of lore. He was having a great season on a bad team in 1991, en route to winning the MVP Award for the second time in his career. Smart and savvy as he was, Mussina was in awe of Ripken and a little bit overwhelmed by the other veterans on the team.

"Mostly I just sat at my locker very quietly and watched the other guys," he said. "I didn't say much to them; they didn't say much to me." He smiled. "I'm pretty sure the first time Ripken spoke to me was when he came over to the mound to ask me something during a game."

The first veteran to speak to him was Dwight "Dewey" Evans — Glavine's boyhood hero. The Orioles had flown home from Chicago after Mussina's debut, and Mussina arrived at the ballpark early to get out and stretch and go through his day-after-pitching routine.

"In Memorial Stadium, the player's parking lot was outside the left-field fence," he said. "You'd park, then walk in from there to our clubhouse on the third-base side. I was out stretching when Dewey came walking in. He looked at me and said, "You were good yesterday, kid. I'm glad you aren't taking it for granted, though, and you're out here working."

Mussina wasn't likely to take anything for granted. That just wasn't his way. He pitched solidly the rest of that season, going 4–5 but with a 2.87 ERA — exactly the same as his ERA in Rochester. He pitched two complete games and had the thrill of matching up against Nolan Ryan on a steamy night in Texas. "I pitched well but lost," he said. "But, heck, how badly can you feel losing to Nolan Ryan when you're twenty-two-years old and fifteen months out of college?"

The Orioles finished that season 67–95, not all that different from the Braves team that Glavine was called up to in 1987. Mussina was fairly certain he had won a spot in the starting rotation for the next season. The Orioles moved into their sparkling new ballpark in April of 1992 and became the surprise of the American League, contending right from the start and chasing the Toronto Blue Jays deep into September.

No one played a bigger role in their renaissance than Mussina. He began the season as the number four starter in the rotation, but by the All-Star break it was apparent that he was the team's best pitcher. He opened the season 5–0 and was selected for the All-Star team, a rare honor for a pitcher in his first full year. In July, he pitched a one-hitter against the Rangers in Texas, giving up a single to Kevin Reimer in the fifth inning. He didn't beat Ryan, but he did beat Kevin Brown, a twenty-game winner. The Orioles ended up 89–73 that season, and Mussina was 18–5 with an ERA of 2.54. He finished fourth in the Cy Young voting.

Then did he think of himself as a major leaguer?

"Maybe," he said with a smile. "Seriously, I did have a great year in '92. But if you look back through history, there have been a lot of one-year wonders in this game. Mark Fidrych? Joe Charboneau? They were Rookies of the Year, weren't they? There are lots of other examples. I was very happy to pitch that well, believe me, but I felt as if I had to come back and do it again to really prove myself."

In many ways 1992 became symbolic of Mussina's career. By any definition, he was outstanding. But it was a season of almosts: The Orioles almost won the American League East (they ended up seven games behind the Blue Jays). Mussina almost won twenty games. He almost pitched a no-hitter, and he was almost a serious contender for the Cy Young Award.

At that moment though, neither he nor anyone else in the organization was thinking in those terms. Ripken was still the number one star in Baltimore and would always be that, until the day he retired in 2001. But Mussina was clearly established as the number one pitcher, as an All-Star, as someone the team would count on to lead its pitching staff for years to come.

He was solid again in 1993, but the year did not go as well for him or for the team as 1992 had. The league had now seen Mussina and his array of pitches and had settled in against him a little bit. What's more, Mussina missed six weeks of the season and was on the disabled list shortly after the All-Star break, with a strain in his right shoulder brought on by neck and back pain. He still won fourteen games that season—proving that he wasn't a one-year wonder—but his ERA (4.46) was considerably higher than it had been the year before.

"There were factors involved," Mussina said. "My shoulder, the team not being as good, the fact that I was still learning about life in the big leagues—but it was still a learning experience for me. I was only twenty-four, but after going to the All-Star game the year before I was kind of surprised when I *wasn't* an All-Star. When you're young and things are going well, there's a tendency to figure they'll keep going well as long as you keep working at getting better."

He did work during that off-season, wanting to prove that Mussina '92 — not Mussina '93 — was the real Mussina. Sure enough, the work paid off. Right from the start, Mussina was the dominant pitcher he had been in 1992. He was 13–4 at the All-Star break and was cruising along with sixteen wins and an ERA of 3.06 on August 7, clearly on his way to a twenty-win season, when baseball came to a screeching halt.

The players and the owners had been parrying with one another for most of two years, headed in the direction of another work stoppage. The owners had sent a clear message in 1992 when they had fired commissioner Fay Vincent, who had counseled against going to war with the players, both publicly and privately, and installed one of their own, Milwaukee Brewers owner Bud Selig, as his replacement. They had also hired Richard Ravitch, who had established a reputation as a union buster, as their new negotiator.

Ravitch's negotiating stance was simple and direct: nothing that had been negotiated in the past mattered. The owners wanted a new financial system. Don Fehr, the head of the union, wasn't about to allow that, and it became apparent by midsummer in 1994 that the two sides were headed for a collision.

It came on August 12 when the players carried out their threat to go on strike. Mussina was 16–5 when the strike hit. Only one pitcher in baseball, the Yankees Jimmy Key, had more wins (17) than Mussina did at that moment.

The strike would be the ugliest in the history of baseball. There was no postseason in 1994; Major League Baseball shut down for good with one-third of the regular season unplayed. Congress held hearings, and President Bill Clinton called both sides to the White House, all without a resolution. The owners, with the exception of Orioles owner Peter Angelos, decided to start spring training in 1995 with "replacement players" — scabs — and threatened to begin the season with scab teams, mimicking the tactics used by the football owners in 1987, when three regular-season games were played with scab teams.

That decision had worked out for the football owners. Many players crossed their union's picket line to play, and to this day the NFL is the only major professional sport in which the players' contracts are not guaranteed. This was not the football union, though. This was a powerful union with smart leadership. It was not about to back down, and the players weren't going to cross any picket lines.

Major League Baseball decided to hand out awards at the end of 1994, even though the season had been shut down. David Cone of the Kansas City Royals, who had a 16–5 record, identical to Mussina's, won the Cy Young Award. Key was second, Randy Johnson was third, and Mussina was fourth.

Glavine was 13–9 when the strike ended the season, not having a banner year. But he had a fairly good excuse for not pitching quite as well as he had the previous three seasons: No one was more involved in the player-owner battle than he was. In fact, to fans in Atlanta, he would become the symbol of the strike. It would make 1995 the most difficult season of his career.

4

Crossroads

GLAVINE WAS FIRST ELECTED as the Braves' player rep in 1990, replacing Dale Murphy, when he was only twenty-four. Mussina was twenty-five when he became the Orioles' rep. Each was in his third full season in the big leagues when elected.

The job is not exactly coveted in major league clubhouses. It is a no-fun, no-win job. It can be time consuming, which is why pitchers, especially starting pitchers, are frequently elected to the job; they have more free time than most players. A lot of the work is just plain dull: conference calls to discuss insurance plans, setting up meetings for players to listen to union lawyers, negotiating whether a team will give up a required off-day in order to make up a rainout.

And when it isn't boring, it's because the players and the owners are doing battle — again. Baseball's recent history is littered with work stoppages, dating back to 1972, when the start of the season was delayed by a player strike. During the next thirty years players and owners negotiated eight collective-bargaining agreements. Each and every time, there was some kind of work stoppage. But nothing like the strike of 1994–1995.

Mussina was probably fortunate because he was a new player rep in 1994. His job was to report back to his teammates on the work being done by the negotiating committee and, when the time came, to take the strike vote.

It wasn't nearly as simple for Glavine. He was on the negotiating committee. What's more, the union's leadership—Don Fehr and Gene Orza—decided early on that the two players they wanted to put out front were Glavine and David Cone. Both were smart and articulate and didn't get nervous in front of microphones. Both also had absolutely no chance of being viewed by the public as anything but villains.

Anytime there is a strike or a lockout, most people assume it is all about the players, already rich and famous, demanding more money. That was certainly not the case in 1994. The crux of the issue was the owners' demand for some form of a salary cap and the players' insistence that a salary cap was not necessary. The owners claimed many franchises were in financial trouble. The players asked to see their books. The owners said no.

The owners never really intended to negotiate with the players. Their plan was to wait until the contract expired, declare an impasse with the union, and then simply announce that, in the absence of a contract, they were going to change the rules—which would include a salary cap, although they were euphemistically calling it a "luxury tax."

The players believed their only chance to get the owners to negotiate was to strike. "Our thinking was if we went out early enough, there would be owners who wouldn't want to give up the postseason TV money, and they might seriously negotiate with us," Glavine said. "We were wrong."

Ravitch had convinced the owners that if they stuck it out and imposed new rules, they would get what they wanted, and that a long-term victory was more important than the short-term losses they would suffer by wiping out a postseason.

Even before the strike began, Glavine was being pilloried in Atlanta for his role as a union negotiator and spokesman. To a large degree, he had no chance. He was seen as the spokesman for a group of young, greedy athletes who were making millions of dollars—Glavine's salary that year was $5 million—and were still about to go on strike. He also made a mistake that haunted him for a long time. He said that fans didn't understand that players loved the game and didn't play just for the money: "I would gladly play for $1 million a year," he announced at one point, not realizing how that would sound to people who weren't making 10 percent of that.

"It certainly didn't come out the way I meant it to," he said, years later. "The problem is, when you're asked so many questions on so many different occasions, sometimes you say something you don't really mean. I was trying to make a point about the fact that we weren't all about money, that we did love the game, and it just came out wrong."

Even if Glavine hadn't made that mistake, the public was going to be against the players. The notion of young men — many of whom flaunted their money — being wealthy or, so it seemed, wanting more wealth didn't sit well. Most polls taken during the strike ran two to one in the owners' favor.

The owners began spring training in 1995 with scab teams in place and prepared to play the season with the "replacement teams" if necessary.

Fortunately for everyone, the courts stepped in. On March 31, a federal court judge in New York granted an injunction requested by the National Labor Relations Board, finding that the owners' attempt to unilaterally invoke a contract was against federal labor laws. Even though they were without a new contract, the owners had no choice but to open spring-training camps.

And even though both the NLRB and a federal court had found that the owners were the bad guys in the dispute, it was still the players — and Glavine — who had to deal with angry fans.

"I actually had people throw money at me warming up in the bullpen," Glavine said. "Pitching in Atlanta was actually worse than pitching on the road for most of the '95 season. It really hurt because I thought I had done the right thing and that what we had fought for was right. Certainly the NLRB and the courts thought we were right."

Glavine also got in trouble because he said on a number of occasions that he understood that it was "tough for fans to understand all the issues." He was trying to give those who were critical of the players a pass; instead it came off as if he were saying that fans weren't smart enough to understand the issues.

GLAVINE HAD MOVED to Atlanta five years earlier, following the 1990 season. It was during that year that he had met Carri Dobbins, who worked for a friend of his at a tanning salon. He had liked the fact that she wasn't a big baseball fan and didn't seem all that impressed with the notion that he had just won the Cy Young Award. In fact, she really didn't know what the Cy Young Award was or who Cy Young had been. She just liked Glavine.

For Glavine, meeting Carri could not have come at a better time. He was young and single and wealthy and obviously well known around Atlanta. "It isn't as if my lifestyle was wild or crazy or I got into any serious trouble," he said. "But I did go out, and at times I stayed out late. When I started dating Carri and settled down, it was a good thing. If nothing else, it was good for my pitching because I was better rested."

Glavine asked Carri to marry him on Christmas Day in 1991, and they planned their wedding for the following November — right after the World Series. The scheduling had worked out fine — the Braves made the World Series for a second straight season — although the result was the same as 1991, except that this time the Braves lost in six games instead of seven.

Glavine pitched very poorly in Game Six of the National League Championship Series against the Pirates, giving up eight runs in one inning-plus, but he pitched superbly in the first game of the World Series, beating the Toronto Blue Jays and Jack Morris 3–1.

The victory was gratifying for several reasons. To begin with, Glavine had outpitched Morris, who had been the Braves' nemesis in Game Seven the previous year when he had still been with the Twins. Beyond that, Cox had been pilloried for deciding to bring Glavine back to pitch Game One after his awful performance in Game Six against the Pirates.

Glavine heard it all, and it angered him, which was good. "It kind of focused me," he said. "I might have been a little bit nervous pitching Game One of the World Series [he had pitched Game Two the previous year], but hearing what people were saying really got me into just the right mood to pitch."

Glavine pitched so well that Cox opted to bring him back on three days' rest in Game Four, with the Braves down two games to one. He pitched well again, but Jimmy Key was a little bit better. Two nights later, the Blue Jays won Game Six in eleven innings to win their first World Championship.

That off-season Glavine and his agent Gregg Clifton negotiated his first big-money, long-term contract. The Braves had guaranteed him $18 million for four years — pretty good money for a newlywed. That 1992 contract had made Glavine an easy target for fans during and after the strike. In 1994, he was young, rich, and walking off the job. It was all about perception. Intellectually, Glavine understood that, but the boos still hurt.

Even so, Glavine pitched well in 1995. The season was shortened to 144 games because of the strike, and Glavine went 16–7 with a 3.08 ERA. The Braves made it into a fourth consecutive postseason, and, for the first time, under the new wild-card system that would have started in 1994 if not for the strike, the team had to get through two rounds of playoffs to reach the World Series. Glavine pitched well, and the Braves easily beat both the Colorado Rockies and the Cincinnati Reds to reach their third World Series in four seasons.

He then won Game Two of the Series and watched his team take a 3–1 lead over the Cleveland Indians. This was as close as the Braves had been to finally winning a World Series. But the Indians came back to beat Greg Maddux in Game Five, sending the Series back to Atlanta for Game Six. Glavine was scheduled to pitch against Dennis Martinez, and he knew—and everyone in Atlanta knew—that the last thing the Braves wanted was to face a Game Seven after blowing a 3–1 lead.

There was one problem: two hours before game time, no one was sure if Glavine would be able to pitch. He had somehow gotten an infection in his thumb—he thought because of the way the thumb rubbed against his ring finger when he released his changeup. It had never become serious enough to create a problem in the past, but now it was creating a very serious problem.

While his teammates got ready to play, Glavine was in the training room with doctors looking at his thumb to see if he would be able to pitch. He couldn't tape it because a pitcher can't have anything on his hands while on the mound since it might be used to scuff the baseball. While Glavine was being worked on, the training staff put towels on the windows so no one could see what was going on.

"It was scary," said Milwaukee Brewers manager Ned Yost, who was a Braves coach at the time. "Everything was so secretive with the towels and all. We all knew something was wrong, but we had no idea what was wrong. Finally, Glav came out and said he was ready to go as if nothing was wrong."

Glavine's injury was so secret that when he wrote his autobiography that winter, he never mentioned it. It wasn't until 2007 that Stan Kasten, who was the team president in 1995, heard about the thumb issue. "Typical Tommy," he said. "My God, if he had been healthy that night, imagine what he might have done."

Kasten insists that Glavine's performance that night, thumb or no thumb, was the greatest game he has ever seen pitched in a World Series. Against a loaded lineup—Albert Belle, Jim Thome, Kenny Lofton, Carlos Baerga, among others—Glavine was almost flawless. Over eight innings, he allowed one hit—a bloop single in the sixth inning to Tony Pena. In the bottom of the sixth, David Justice homered off relief pitcher Jim Poole, Mussina's old minor league roommate, to give the Braves a 1–0 lead.

Mazzone was absolutely convinced at that moment that the Braves had just won the World Series. "Tom came in after the fifth, sat down, and said, 'I hope we score a run soon because I *know* they're not scoring.' That was so unlike him. I was completely convinced there was no way he would give up a run."

He didn't. After he had retired the Indians in the eighth, he surprised Mazzone and Bobby Cox by telling them he'd had enough. That wasn't like him either, but he was tired, his thumb was feeling sore, and he had not felt as if his pitches had much snap left in them in the eighth. Cox and Mazzone brought Mark Wohlers in to pitch the ninth, and he closed out the Indians one-two-three.

Most Atlanta fans forgave Glavine for his union sins after his Series-clinching masterpiece. It was the first championship in any sport for the city of Atlanta, and the town went nuts. Glavine's first child, Amber, had been born during the strike, in January, so he was now a husband, a father, and a hero.

All was right with the world. As is almost always the case in real life, it would not stay that way.

THE STRIKE OF 1994 could not have come at a worse time for Mike Mussina. He completely supported the decision to strike, not just because he was a player rep but because he didn't think the players should give things up they had won at the negotiating table simply because the owners were crying poverty.

The Orioles were different from any other team in baseball during the strike for two reasons: Peter Angelos, their owner, was the only team owner in baseball who refused to field a replacement team. Angelos had made millions of dollars as a lawyer representing unions, and he wasn't going to damage his relationship with the leaders of other unions by hiring scabs, even if the union in question was made up of, for the most part, millionaires.

There was also the Cal Ripken question. When the strike hit in 1994, Ripken was 118 games away from breaking one of baseball's most cherished records: Lou Gehrig's 2,130 consecutive games played. Had the season not been canceled, he would have broken the record prior to the 1995 All-Star break. If the Orioles didn't field a team, would Major League Baseball declare their games forfeits and claim that Ripken's streak had been broken? What if the other owners forced Angelos to field a team. What then? Some players said publicly that they would understand if Ripken crossed the picket line to keep the streak alive. Mussina, the Orioles' player rep, was caught squarely in the middle of the issue.

Ripken himself stayed quiet, hoping it would all go away. Fortunately for him and for everyone else, replacement baseball never made it beyond spring training, and the record wasn't jeopardized.

Ripken broke the record on September 6, 1995, in Baltimore. President Bill Clinton not only attended the game but was sitting in the Orioles radio booth with play-by-play man Jon Miller when Ripken homered in the third inning. As the ball came off Ripken's bat, Clinton's voice could clearly be heard: "Go baby, get out!" The ball listened to the leader of the free world.

Two innings later, after the Angels had been retired in the fifth inning, and the game became official, Ripken had the record. The pitcher who got the last out of the fifth and who went on to be the winning pitcher was Mike Mussina, who still has a copy of the lineup card from that night.

"Obviously I was happy to have a small part in that night," he said. "But it was a *small* part. We weren't in contention. If not for Cal, it would have been a meaningless early-September game with a lot of no-shows. Because of Cal, it was a celebration, not just for the Orioles, but for the game of baseball. I felt proud that night to be his teammate. I think we all did."

Perhaps the most touching sight during the twenty-two minutes that the game stopped so Ripken could circle the park and shake almost every hand in the place was the Angels on the top step of their dugout, clapping and cheering and reaching for Ripken's hand, just like everyone else who was there.

The Orioles finished that strike-shortened season 71–73, their first losing season since 1991.

On a mediocre team, Mussina went 19–9, tying for the league lead in wins in a season that was eighteen games short of the normal 162. If the season hadn't been shortened, he would have gotten at least three more starts, perhaps four, to try to win twenty games.

The case can easily be made that the strike cost Mussina two twenty-win seasons. In 1994, the Orioles played 112 games—a little more than two-thirds of a normal season. Mussina was 16–5 when the strike hit, and the Orioles still had fifty games to play. If the season had been completed, Mussina would have started at least ten more games. Healthy—his ERA when the season ended was 3.06—it is difficult to believe that he would not have won at least four more times. It is just as difficult to believe that with three or four more starts the next year that he would not have won at least once more.

"Some things are out of your control," he said. "I know people talk about the fact that I've never won twenty games in a season. I certainly can't prove that I would have done it in '94 or '95, but the evidence is there that I had a pretty good chance. At the very least, you can say I pitched well enough to look like I would have gotten it done if the seasons hadn't been cut short."

Mussina is matter-of-fact when he talks about the almosts in his career, but there is no doubt that they sting. He's also completely honest about 1996 when he came within one inning of winning twenty games and didn't.

"That may have been the worst year of my career," he said. "I just wasn't very good. We had a good team and a very good hitting team, and I won a lot of games when I didn't pitch well. That doesn't mean it wasn't disappointing when I didn't get the twentieth; it just means I know there were a lot of years where I pitched better than I did in '96."

The Orioles finally made it back to the playoffs in 1996 after a thirteen-year drought. Mussina's ERA that season was 4.81, which was almost two runs higher than his ERA had been during the two strike-shortened seasons. Not until 2007 — his sixteenth full season in the big leagues — would his ERA be higher. But the Orioles scored a lot of runs for him in '96. As a result, he went into his last start of the season on a Saturday afternoon in Toronto with a chance to win twenty games.

The Orioles were a hot team; they had rallied in the second half of the season and needed one victory in the final two games to become the American League's wild-card team. Mussina pitched one of his best games of the year that afternoon and left after eight innings with a 2–1 lead. Armando Benitez, who would go on to earn a reputation as one of the worst in-the-clutch closers in baseball history, came in to pitch the ninth.

"Two batters," Mussina said. "There wasn't much suspense."

The second batter Benitez faced was Ed Sprague. He hit a long home run to tie the game at 2–2. The Orioles went on to win the game in extra innings to clinch the playoff spot, but Mussina's chance to win twenty disappeared the minute Sprague's home run cleared the fence. "I probably didn't deserve to win twenty games that year," he said. "And there have definitely been other years where I deserved it far more than that year. But I would be lying if I said it wasn't disappointing when it happened. It was mitigated when we won the game and made the playoffs, because that was my first chance to pitch in postseason."

He didn't pitch especially well in the postseason, although he wasn't terrible by any means. In Game Three of the Division Series against the Cleveland Indians, he pitched six innings and gave up three earned runs in an outing the Orioles bullpen ended up losing after he left. In the American League Championship Series, the Yankees hit him hard. He gave up five runs in seven and two-thirds innings and was the losing pitcher in the third game of the series, which the Yankees went on to win four games to one.

"Actually the way I pitched in postseason that year was about the way I pitched in the regular season," he said. "I wasn't awful, but I certainly wasn't very good."

A year later, he was more like his old self. His ERA was 3.20, and his 15–8 record was a reflection of the fact that, even though this was the best Orioles team he would ever pitch for, the team just didn't score many runs when he pitched. In May, Mussina retired the first twenty-five Cleveland Indians he faced on a Friday night in Baltimore before catcher Sandy Alomar Jr. lined a single to center field to break up his bid for a perfect game.

Another almost.

The playoffs were more of the same. Mussina probably never pitched better in his life than he did that October. The Orioles had won the American League East with a wire-to-wire performance, going 98–64. In the Division Series they faced the Seattle Mariners, and Mussina matched up twice with Randy Johnson — and beat him twice. Mussina pitched seven innings in each game and gave up a total of three runs, pitching the fourth game on three days' rest. He struck out sixteen and walked only three. In short, he was dominant.

The Orioles won the series 3–1 and moved on to face the Indians in the ALCS. Cleveland had beaten the Yankees in five games in the other Division Series, thanks to a late home run in the deciding game by Mussina's old pal Sandy Alomar Jr. With the Yankees out of the way, everyone in Baltimore fully expected the Orioles to move on to the World Series.

That it didn't happen certainly couldn't be blamed on Mussina. He was better against the Indians than he had been against the Mariners. In Game Three, he pitched six shutout innings only to see the Orioles lose the game in twelve innings. He again came back on three days' rest to pitch the sixth game with the Orioles down 3–2. In what may have been the most dominant performance of his career, Mussina pitched eight shutout innings, striking out fifteen batters. Unfortunately, Indians starter Charles Nagy also pitched shutout ball, and the game went into extra innings, with both starters long gone. It ended in the eleventh inning when Tony Fernandez hit a home run off, surprise, Armando Benitez, and the Indians won 1–0 and advanced to the World Series.

If nothing else, Mussina's performance that October proves that it is unfair to criticize a pitcher for not having been on a World Championship team. In four starts, Mussina pitched twenty-nine innings and gave up four runs—an ERA of 1.24. He struck out forty-one and walked seven. Those are astounding numbers. But his team failed to win the ALCS games in which he pitched shutout ball and didn't reach the World Series.

"That's the way baseball is," Mussina said. "There's only so much you can control. Sometimes, when you aren't good, your team bails you out. Other times, when you're good, it isn't good enough. I've always taken the approach that if I go out and pitch six or seven innings and we lose three-two, I'm not going to say, 'Hey, I pitched well enough to win.' No, I didn't. If I had pitched well enough to win, I would have given up one run instead of three, and we'd have won two-one. But if you go out and give up no runs, then you've done everything you can possibly do, and the rest is out of your hands. In '97, I felt like I did everything I could possibly do. That hasn't always been the case in my career, but that year I did honestly feel that way during those playoffs."

Mussina had signed a three-year contract extension with the Orioles earlier in the season, passing up the chance to try the free-agent market at the end of that year. Glavine had also re-signed before reaching free agency during 1997. His contract was guaranteed for $34 million—four years at $8 million a year, with a $2 million buyout if the Braves did not pick up the $10 million option for a fifth year. The two-year difference would be the subject of considerable discussion for the two men—even though they would never speak directly to one another about it.

5

Rich and Richer

Tom Glavine's life had changed considerably in the two years that had passed since his one-hit, Series-clinching gem in 1995. He had coauthored a book that winter, *None but the Braves,* with the *Boston Globe*'s Nick Cafardo, that, as athlete autobiographies go, was extremely honest — especially when discussing the issues surrounding the strike of 1994–95.

He also talked about how he had met Carri, how he had proposed to her, and how thrilled they had both been when Amber was born in January 1995, but he said little else in the book about his personal life. There was a reason for that: his marriage was falling apart.

In June 1996, the story broke: Tom and Carri Glavine were filing for divorce. At that point, no one in Atlanta was a bigger star than Glavine. Going through the divorce was difficult for him for all the reasons that divorce is difficult, especially with an eighteen-month-old child involved. To have to go through it in public made it that much more painful.

"I guess the only good thing was that Amber was too young to read the papers," Glavine said, forcing a laugh. "I don't think any of us ever gets married thinking we're going to end up divorced. So, when it happens, it's a shock to your system. When you see it in the papers, and you know people are talking about you and gossiping about you, it's that much harder.

"I was probably lucky, looking back, that it happened during the season. It meant I had an escape at the ballpark and on the field. I think if it had happened during the off-season it would have been that much tougher."

Glavine pitched well in 1996, and the Braves made it back to the World Series, only to blow a 2–0 lead and lose to the New York Yankees in six games. Glavine pitched well in Game Three, but was outpitched by his union buddy David Cone. He would have been the Game Seven pitcher but there was no Game Seven.

His divorce was still pending the next spring when a friend of his told him that Christine St. Onge was in town. He wondered if Glavine wanted to get together with her.

Glavine already knew St. Onge. They had first met in spring training in 1988. She had been living in Palm Beach and working for Home Depot in their computer division, and the two of them had been introduced at a party.

"I had no idea who he was," Chris said years later. "But I thought he was cute."

Glavine thought the same thing about Chris. They dated off and on for the next couple of years, even though she lived in Florida and he lived in Atlanta. The relationship tailed off when Glavine started dating Carri, and Chris began dating someone she worked with in Florida. Each got married in 1992. They became parents within three months of one another—Chris's son Jonathan being born in October 1994.

And then, in 1996, they both went through divorces. Each was on the rebound, but when they met again in the spring of 1997 they remembered liking one another, and a relationship began to bloom.

"At first it was just good fun," Chris said. "We were both still finalizing divorces, and it was comfortable. But after a while it started to get a little bit serious, and I kind of wanted to know where we stood—or at least how Tom thought we stood. I had not yet introduced him to Jonathan [who was not quite three], and I said to Tom one night in August, 'You know, if we're going to keep going forward with this, I think you should meet my son. But if all we're doing is having a good time and there's nothing more to it, I don't want you to meet him. I don't want you in his life one day, out of it the next. If I'm just the girl you call on Tuesdays and Fridays and that's it, fine, just tell me. But if it's more than that, you should meet Jonathan.'"

Glavine said he understood. He said she was absolutely right to feel the way she did. And then he didn't call for three months. "I guess I kind of freaked out a little," he said. "The wound of the divorce was still kind of fresh; in fact I wasn't legally divorced yet. I knew where Chris was coming from and that she wasn't trying to pin me down. I guess I just wasn't ready to deal with anything that involved moving forward in any kind of serious manner right at that moment."

Chris was still working for Home Depot—out of Atlanta rather than Florida at that point. Not hearing from Glavine was disappointing, but she figured the message was that the relationship had just been a lark for him. "It made me sad," she said. "Because I really liked him a lot."

She was at work one morning just prior to Thanksgiving when someone told her that Tom Glavine was on the phone for her. The Braves' season had ended in disappointment that October: after winning a sixth straight Division title they had been beaten in the National League Championship Series by the wild-card Florida Marlins. Chris waited a moment or two and then picked up the phone.

"Hi, Chris. It's Tom."

"Tom who?" she said coolly. "Do I know you?"

Glavine wasn't stunned but still caught a little bit off guard. "I guess I deserve that," he said.

"You bet you do," she answered.

Glavine wanted to see her again. He was sorry about the

lengthy gap between phone calls. That wasn't good enough. "If you want to go out with me again, you have to make a list of the ten reasons I should say yes," she told him.

That night when Chris got home, there was a message on her answering machine. "I've come up with six so far," Glavine said on the message.

The list included things like "really good tickets to Braves games" but did not include the one reason Chris really wanted to hear. "There was," she said smiling, "nothing romantic. I don't think he could quite bring himself to do it."

Chris was torn. She knew she wanted to see Tom again, but a part of her was worried that she was just another jock date, the flavor of the month or week. Finally she decided to really put him to the test. "Why don't you go with me to my office Christmas party," she said. Tom agreed.

"For someone like Tom, there can't be anything worse than a party like that," she said. "There was no way he was going to get thirty seconds of peace. Everyone in Atlanta knew Tom Glavine. It was going to be autographs and pictures and 'What happened in the playoffs?' all night long. I figured if he was willing to go through that, then maybe he really did like me."

Glavine went through it and never complained. He knew the drill. Having paid his penance, he began dating Chris seriously again. He met Jonathan. She met Amber. They were married the next fall.

At the start of the 1997 season, Glavine began negotiating a new contract with the Braves. They had picked up his option for that year at $5 million, which was fine with him, even though he was probably underpaid given his status and the market for pitchers at the time. Braves president Stan Kasten told Glavine and Gregg Clifton, Glavine's agent, that he wanted to sign Glavine to a long-term contract before the end of the season so he would not file for free agency.

"They actually made me a very good offer," Glavine said. "It was four years at $32 million with a club option for a fifth year at $10 million. I really thought I deserved a fifth year. Which led, of course, to one of my sessions with Stan."

Kasten and Glavine have what can only be described as a unique employer-employee relationship. Kasten, who is now president of the Washington Nationals, was something of a boy wonder among sports executives. He had been named general manager of the Atlanta Hawks in 1979, making him, at twenty-seven, the youngest general manager in NBA history. Five years later, Ted Turner—who owned both the Hawks and the Braves—asked him to take over the Braves too, and Kasten's first important move was to hire Bobby Cox as general manager. By the time Glavine arrived in Atlanta, Kasten was president of both the Braves and the Hawks.

Kasten quickly understood that Glavine wasn't just a promising young pitcher; he was also bright and a clubhouse leader, albeit in a quiet way most of the time. Glavine liked the fact that Kasten was anything but buttoned-down, spent time with the players, and had a sharp sense of humor.

But they also clashed. They sat across from one another during many tempestuous negotiation sessions during the 1994–95 strike, and they frequently argued with one another about union issues and other political issues. Kasten, the management hawk, the antiunion man, was a Democrat. Glavine, the union man, was a Republican.

"Ask Tom to explain how *that* works," Kasten liked to say. "One minute he's Mr. Union Guy, the next he's voting for whomever is going to lower taxes for the rich."

"He makes a good point," Glavine would reply.

When Kasten and Glavine met in the spring of 1997 to discuss a possible fifth year in Glavine's contract, Kasten was adamant. "Look, Tom, I'm going to get a lot of heat from other owners for giving you this contract," Kasten said. "You're going to be the highest paid pitcher in baseball. We just aren't going to give anyone a guaranteed fifth year."

It was, as Glavine often says, "typical Stan."

"First, he lectures me on why I should be grateful when I think the money he's paying me is good but not in any way out of line based on my performance," he said. "Second, he knows I will never pitch a game as the highest paid pitcher in baseball. For one thing Greg [Maddux] is up at the end of that year, and he's going to get more than me. Kevin Brown is up too, and, as a free agent, he's going to get more too."

Glavine signed the contract. It was, he knew, good money. What rankled was when the Braves signed Maddux a month later—to a five-year guaranteed contract. "He deserved it," Glavine said. "But I sat and listened to Stan say, 'No way will we give anyone five years guaranteed.' A month later he gave Greg five years guaranteed."

Even so, Glavine was happy with the deal. It meant he would be in Atlanta until he was at least thirty-five, perhaps thirty-six if the fifth year kicked in. He felt he had held up his obligation to the union to get as much money as possible—he was the highest paid pitcher in the game, at least in theory, when it was announced—and he didn't have to leave Atlanta or even shop himself on the free-agent market. Having been one of the leaders of the strike in 1994 and 1995, Glavine did not want to take a "hometown discount" to stay in Atlanta. Kasten understood that and made him an offer he felt comfortable taking.

"I had no desire to leave Atlanta, then or ever," he said. "By then I had a daughter who was living there with her mother, and I liked where I was. It had become home, and I certainly didn't want to leave the Braves or Bobby [Cox] or Leo [Mazzone] or Doggy [Greg Maddux] or Smoltzie."

Maddux had come to the Braves as a free agent in the winter of 1992, after beating Glavine for the Cy Young Award while pitching for the Cubs. He had promptly won the next three Cy Young Awards and was the game's dominant pitcher. Glavine and Smoltz, both likely Hall of Famers at the rate they were going, were the number two and number three pitchers in what was clearly one of the great rotations in baseball history.

If their personalities had been different, the three might not have gotten along. They were extremely competitive: as pitchers, as hitters, as golfers—but they enjoyed one another's company and recognized that each made the others better.

"When I first signed, I was really a little bit nervous about how it would all work," Maddux said. "These guys were already very established. They had won back-to-back pennants, and now I come along. Plus, for all intents and purposes, I took Charlie Leibrandt's place, and Tom and John were both very close to him."

There was nothing subtle about the way the Braves made the switch from Leibrandt to Maddux. On the same day that Maddux signed—December 9, 1992—Leibrandt was traded to Texas. Signing Maddux was an upgrade—if he wasn't the best pitcher in baseball, he was one of the three or four best—but Leibrandt's departure was difficult for both Glavine and Smoltz.

Leibrandt had been the big brother in the trio, a few years older, someone who had pitched in the World Series (with Kansas City in 1985) in key situations before the Braves became contenders. He had come over from Kansas City prior to the 1990 season and had taken Glavine and Smoltz under his wing. The three were virtually inseparable, playing golf together almost every day, especially on the road.

"If we had a weeklong road trip, the only day we didn't play was on the day we pitched," Glavine said. "We'd usually pick up a fourth somewhere or just the three of us would go out, but it was a ritual."

Fortunately, Maddux was also a golfer. He wasn't quite as good as Glavine, who isn't quite as good as Smoltz. Glavine's handicap is usually in the five to eight range; Maddux's is a little bit higher. Most days Glavine and Maddux would play against Smoltz, and the competition was fierce. "You just didn't want to lose to John at anything because you weren't likely to hear the end of it anytime soon — or ever," Glavine said. "It just wasn't any fun."

Maddux was quickly accepted into the circle but says he was never quite as competitive with Smoltz and Glavine as they were with each other. "Maybe it was because they'd been together so long," he said. "Or maybe it was just personalities. I always wanted to win, always wanted to do well, but Tom and John would do just about anything to beat one another at everything. If John got two hits in a game, Tom had to get two hits the next game by hook or by crook. The golf thing never stopped. Sometimes I just sat back and watched the show."

In 1997, Tiger Woods moved to Orlando's Isleworth, an exclusive megabucks golf community not far from where the Braves had just relocated their spring-training camp. Isleworth was one of many places where the Braves trio went to play golf during the spring, and they struck up a friendship with Woods. On occasion, the three of them would play with Woods — their best ball against his one ball.

"One time he beat us pretty soundly, and I gave him five hundred-dollar bills that I stuck in an envelope to pay him off," Smoltz said. "As it turned out, that was the last time that spring we got to play with him. Almost a year later, we played again, and this time we whipped him — for five hundred bucks. When we're done, he reaches inside his golf bag and pulls out the envelope I'd given him a year earlier and just hands it to me. It had never made it out of the bag. He just shrugged and said, 'I figured you guys would get me back someday.'"

Smoltz was always the golf organizer. Whenever the Braves arrived in town somewhere, he would get on the phone and set up a game, usually at the best-known golf course in the area. There weren't many places — if any — where the three famous pitchers couldn't get on.

"The thing I miss most about those days is the golf," Maddux, now with the San Diego Padres, said. "The best thing was that

Tom and I never had to do anything except show up. Smoltzie made all the arrangements."

One of the culture shocks for Glavine years later, when he left Atlanta for New York, was not only finding new golf partners but often having to make arrangements himself. In 2007 he was the only Mets starter who played much golf, so he often played with relief pitchers like Aaron Heilman, Scott Schoeneweis, and Aaron Sele. "It's different because those guys may have to pitch on any given day; they aren't on a schedule the way a starter is, so they can't play as regularly," he said. "Plus, some of the time I have to make the phone call myself to get us in certain places."

In fact, when the Mets were in Pittsburgh in the summer of 2007, Schoeneweis called Oakmont Country Club where the U.S. Open had been held in June to try to get the pitchers a tee time. No room at the inn—or on the golf course—he was told. Glavine made the same call a day later. "What time do you guys want to come out?" was the answer he got.

The rules of Oakmont are clear: relief pitchers can play as long as they are accompanied by at least one future Hall of Famer.

During the glory years in Atlanta, no one would go to greater lengths for a laugh than Smoltz. Once, when Glavine had gotten in the habit of hanging out in the clubhouse during games—starting pitchers will often do that when they aren't pitching, especially if the weather isn't good—Smoltz took masking tape and spent a good hour on his hands and knees putting it on the floor to create a trail from Glavine's locker in the clubhouse to the dugout. When Glavine walked in that day, Smoltz presented him with a map and said if he ever *did* get lost to just follow the tape.

"It was a good laugh," Glavine said. "Only Smoltzie could put in an hour on his hands and knees to get a good thirty-second laugh."

Smoltz admits now that there were times when he felt like the third brother and that it constantly drove him to try to prove himself. "My sense is that I was the guy riding in the backseat most of the time," he said. "As good as Greg was, Tom was definitely riding up there with him. He was the first of us to establish himself as a star. He was the World Series hero. The two of them shared turns at the steering wheel through the years. I was in the backseat kind of waiting my turn."

Unlike Maddux and Glavine, who have been on the disabled list just once (Maddux for fifteen days), combined, in their careers, Smoltz has had his share of injuries. He has been on the disabled list nine times in his career, has had elbow surgery three times, and missed the entire 2000 season after having "Tommy John surgery" on his elbow. While Maddux was the winningest pitcher in baseball in the 1990s with 176 wins and Glavine was second with 164, Smoltz was fifth with 143.

The one area where Smoltz has clearly outshone the two guys in the front seat has been in the postseason. Glavine is 14–16 in postseason play; Maddux is 11–14. Smoltz is 15–4 and would probably have even more wins if he had not spent four seasons as the Braves closer after the Tommy John surgery.

Regardless of who was sitting where in the car, Glavine had no desire to pitch for anyone else after the '97 season. The Braves certainly didn't want to break up the staff or see Glavine leave, which is why they made sure to get him signed before free agency became a factor.

MUSSINA DIDN'T FILE for free agency either. Like Glavine, he was in a situation where he did not want to leave the team he was pitching for. He had been eligible for arbitration after the 1996 season. Arbitration is the first step a player takes before he reaches free agency, which comes after he has been in the major leagues for six years.

How much an arbitration-eligible player makes depends on how much other players with similar statistics are making at the time. The team will submit a proposed figure, and the player and his agent will submit a proposed figure. The arbitrator, after a hearing in which both sides present their case, chooses one figure or the other. There is no compromise.

Because of this, most teams and players try to make a deal before actually going to arbitration. If a player is asking for $7 million for one year and the team offering $5 million, they will frequently agree to compromise at $6 million. Another reason teams don't want to go to arbitration is that arbitration hearings can get ugly. The team will point out—with the player sitting in the room—every flaw a player has. Players don't like hearing all the weaknesses they allegedly have from their employer.

In the winter of 1996–97, Mussina and the Orioles agreed on a one-year contract worth $6.85 million. They continued to negotiate on a contract extension during spring training since Mussina would be a free agent at the end of that season. When they couldn't make a deal, Mussina assumed he would simply file for free agency in the fall.

It never happened. Orioles owner Peter Angelos asked Mussina to have breakfast with him. He told him how much he wanted Mussina to stay in Baltimore. He said he didn't want to give him a five-year contract because contracts that long were risky for pitchers, no matter how good and how healthy they were at the time. He told him he would pay him top dollar for a three-year contract.

By early May, the deal had been made. Mussina signed for three years and almost $21 million, making him the fourth-highest-paid pitcher in baseball in terms of annual salary. As good as the money was, the case could certainly be made that Mussina would have gotten more money and more years on the contract had he elected to put himself on the open market at the end of the season. In that sense he had given the Orioles a hometown discount. Clearly, Mussina would not have signed with any other team in baseball for only three years and probably would have commanded more money had he gone someplace else. But he didn't.

Mussina had gotten engaged that spring to Jana McKissick, someone he had known since boyhood, and he very much wanted to stay in Baltimore since it was less than 200 miles from Montoursville. Jana had been married once before and had an eight-year-old daughter. That meant Mussina had an instant family. What's more, both he and Jana wanted to have more children, so they were thinking about how far away Mussina might have to travel as a free agent.

"Even though my agent told me I could probably get more on the open market, what if the best offer was in Los Angeles or Texas or someplace far from home?" Mussina said. "I was about to get married, I had an eight-year-old daughter, and I didn't want to be that far away for six or seven months of the year. I was comfortable in Baltimore, and we had a good team. It also crossed my mind that if I continued to pitch well, a three-year deal might work to my advantage because I would have the chance to be a free agent again in 2000."

So, Mussina accepted the Orioles' offer. It was a coup for the team because they had gotten a premier pitcher at the peak of his powers for a relatively cheap price. And it was the kind of contract that made all owners happy because they could point to Mussina's contract when negotiating with other pitchers and say, "If Mike Mussina took a three-year deal, why shouldn't you?" Which, naturally, didn't make the union very happy, particularly since Mussina was not only visible for his pitching prowess but was the Orioles' player representative.

"If a guy wants to give a team a hometown discount, I can understand that, if he thinks it is the best thing for him," Glavine was quoted as saying after Mussina signed. "But it doesn't help the rest of the guys for him to sign a contract like that."

As is always the case in these situations, Glavine and Mussina never actually spoke. Glavine insists now that he wasn't trying to put Mussina down, and he wasn't angry with Mussina for signing the deal that he signed. He was simply trying to make a point.

"I did probably have my union hat on when I said it," Glavine said. "But it really wasn't personal at all. Would I have preferred that Mike hold out for four or five years or, if necessary, go on the open market? Yes. But did I understand him not wanting to move? Yes. I didn't want to move either."

But Glavine's choice had been relatively easy. He had gotten four years plus an option and top money. If the Braves had offered only three years, he probably would have gone to free agency.

"I think I would have felt obligated to do it given my involvement with the union," he said. "That doesn't mean I would have wanted to do it. I can certainly see Mike's side of it."

That wasn't exactly how the quote came across when Mussina read it. He wasn't angry about it, but he remembered it. Years later when the subject came up, he referred to Glavine having "ripped me" for giving the Orioles a hometown discount.

"Actually it turned out very well for me," Mussina said. "Three years later, I was a free agent again when the market was about as flush as it's ever been. Tom had to wait five years, and by then the market wasn't as good. I probably ended up making more than Tom by taking the three years, although, to be fair, I wasn't that smart. That wasn't why I signed when I did. I just didn't see any reason to leave Baltimore."

Three years later, that would no longer be the case.

6

From Camden Yards to Yankee Stadium

ALTHOUGH HE PROBABLY DIDN'T KNOW IT at the time, the beginning of the end of Mike Mussina's career in Baltimore came on November 5, 1997. That was the day that Davey Johnson "resigned" as the Orioles' manager.

Johnson had managed the team for two years and taken it to the playoffs both times. Prior to that he had managed the New York Mets to a World Championship and the Cincinnati Reds to the playoffs. Johnson was good at what he did, knew he was good at what he did, and didn't mind telling people that.

In the end, the given reason for Johnson's departure was a dispute with Orioles owner Peter Angelos over a fine that Johnson made second baseman Roberto Alomar pay to a charity that Johnson's wife, Susan, worked for. In truth, Angelos just wanted Johnson out and used "charity-gate" as an excuse to force him out. During that same off-season, Angelos also forced the departure of longtime radio play-by-play man Jon Miller, generally regarded as one of the best in the business. Miller, it seemed, wasn't enough of an Orioles' homer during the broadcasts.

With Johnson gone, the 1998 season was a disaster for the Orioles. They never contended and finished 79–83, an amazing thirty-five games behind the Yankees, who won a near-record 114

72

games. As bad as the season was for the Orioles, it was worse for Mussina. He went on the disabled list two weeks into the season with an infection on his right index finger. Twelve days after he returned, he was pitching against the Cleveland Indians in Baltimore when his old friend Sandy Alomar Jr., who had broken up his perfect game almost exactly a year earlier, came to the plate.

From the time they are very young, pitchers are taught to get themselves into a defensive position if a ball comes up the middle. Mussina is one of the best fielding pitchers in the history of baseball, having won six Gold Gloves (given to the best defensive player at each position each year) during his career. His follow-through almost always puts him in position to field a ball because he doesn't fall off the mound in one direction or other but ends up square to the plate, balanced, and ready to throw up his glove if a line drive comes his way.

This one he never saw. "I'm not sure if it was the angle the ball came off the bat or the time of night [it wasn't completely dark yet], but I never saw the ball. The next thing I knew, I was on my back, and it looked like there was blood all over the place."

It was one of those scary baseball moments. The good news was that neither his nose nor his eye socket was completely smashed because the ball landed in between the two. He doesn't remember much about what happened next, other than being in the hospital and being told his nose was broken and his eye was damaged but not so seriously that his vision would be compromised.

"Looking back, I was lucky," he said. "The ball could have hit me anywhere, and the damage could have been a lot worse."

Remarkably, Mussina was back on the mound twenty-four days after the incident. "It was one of those get-back-on-the-horse things," he said. "I thought it was important that I get back out there and pitch as soon as I possibly could. But it was a mistake. For one thing, it wasn't one of those injuries where I could throw while I was recovering—I couldn't. Plus, there's no doubt that even though I tried not to think about it or worry about it, I was gun-shy. I was probably flinching on almost every pitch I threw for the rest of the season."

He wasn't awful by any means, finishing 13–10 with a 3.49 ERA, but he knew he wasn't himself. Plus, the team was clearly headed in the wrong direction. Pat Gillick resigned as general manager at the end of the season, tired of being told by Angelos that the owner knew more about baseball than he did. The new manager in 1998 was Ray Miller, who had been the team's longtime pitching coach. A year later, Mussina was healthy and confident again and went 18–7 on another mediocre (78–84) team. Cal Ripken's streak had ended at the end of the 1998 season, and he was beginning to fade.

Prior to the 2000 season, Mussina and his agent, Arn Tellem, began negotiating a possible contract extension with the Orioles. This time, Mussina wasn't willing to settle for three years. He was in the prime years of his career and was convinced, having just turned thirty-one, that this would be his last big contract. He thought he deserved five years. Tellem asked Angelos for five years at $60 million—$12 million a year—which wasn't at all out of line in the pitchers' market at the time.

Angelos said no. Mussina decided it was time to test the free-agent market. There would be no hometown discounts this time around.

If Mussina had any doubts at all about going through with free agency, they were washed away during the 2000 season. If 1996 was the year when his record was better than he was, 2000 was the year when he was much better than his record. Mussina pitched well all year—"In some ways, as well as I've ever pitched," he said—and finished the season with the first and only losing record of his career: 11–15.

The Orioles were a bad team on their way to getting worse. They were still clinging to Ripken like a lifeboat on the *Titanic*, even though Ripken was turning forty and was a shell of himself. For the year, he hit .256 and was able to play in only eighty-three games.

"That was, without doubt, the longest season of my life," Mussina said. "We were bad. I lost a lot of games I should have won, and the atmosphere was just awful. People in Baltimore were upset because they thought I was leaving, and they let me have it, which hurt because I didn't think they understood what was going on. What we asked for in spring training was not at all unreasonable in the market we were in. By the end of the year, I knew it was time to go someplace else."

Brycen, Mussina's first son, had been born a year earlier, and Mussina wanted to be near his family. Teams like the Yankees, Mets, Red Sox, Phillies, and Pirates fit the geographic profile best. The Yankees were coming off their fourth World Series victory in five years, but everyone knew that David Cone wasn't going to be back. He had been plagued by injuries all year, and the Yankees no longer believed they could count on him for thirty-plus starts. They were looking for a reliable starter on the free-agent market.

Shortly after the Yankees had beaten the Mets in a five-game World Series, Mussina was relaxing at home when he heard the phone ring. Jana answered, then walked into the room and pointed at the phone. "It's Joe Torre," she said.

Needless to say, Mussina was a little bit surprised that the manager of the Yankees was calling him out of the blue less than a week after winning the World Series.

"I'm leaving on vacation tomorrow," Torre told Mussina. "But before I go, I wanted to talk to you because I've been hearing some things, and whenever I hear things I wonder if they're true."

"What have you heard?" Mussina asked.

"That you've got concerns about living in New York during the season," Torre answered. "I think you need to come in here and see where you and your family could live. New York isn't just

Manhattan. You can live in the suburbs, have a fairly easy commute, and be quite comfortable. I live in Westchester. Just take a look."

Mussina was touched and flattered that Torre had taken the time to call. He *did* have some concerns about living in New York, but beyond that, Torre's reaching out to him told him that the Yankees — or at least the manager — really wanted him to pitch for them. Having grown up as a Yankee fan, knowing what kind of team and organization they had at the time, he was extremely intrigued by the idea of going to New York.

"The fact that Joe took the time to call me was a big deal," he said. "I certainly didn't know him well at the time, although my sense had always been that he was someone who would be good to play for. What the phone call said was that I was a priority for him. That made me feel very good, especially since I didn't really feel that the Orioles felt that way about me at that stage."

It took less than a month to nail down the deal. On November 30, the Yankees and Mussina agreed to a six-year deal worth $88.5 million — an average of $14.7 million a year. In the blink of an eye, Mussina went from being a very good pitcher on what had become a mediocre team (the Orioles had just finished their third straight losing season) to a key member of baseball's best team and rotation.

He joined a Yankee staff that included Roger Clemens, Andy Pettitte, and Orlando Hernandez, each very much a star in his own right.

"I think that was a good thing for Moose," Torre said. "In Baltimore he was *the* guy, and they felt they had to win every time he pitched because they didn't have anybody nearly as good. A lot of times when we faced him, our strategy was just to wait him out, try to run deep counts on him and stay close, because we knew they would leave him out there for the extra inning, and that was going to be our chance to get him when he was a little tired and should probably be out of the game.

"On our staff, he was one of the guys we counted on, but that was it: *one* of the guys, not *the* guy."

Mussina was fine with that aspect of his new team. And, as Torre had predicted, he was able to find a comfortable house in Westchester that was about a twenty-minute drive from Yankee Stadium on most days. Like many players who sign for big money in New York, especially with the Yankees, Mussina thought he knew what to expect when he arrived: increased media scrutiny, the pressure to perform up to the numbers on his contract, the expectations that the team would win every year.

He was mistaken.

"You can read about it; you can talk to other players who have been through it; you can tell yourself a thousand times that you can handle it. There's just no way to walk into that atmosphere on a daily basis and be prepared for it. You have to learn it, adapt to it, adjust to it, and, most important, accept it. You can't fight it. Every guy who has tried to fight it has ended up failing."

Mussina had gotten along with most of the media in Baltimore, especially once he became comfortable and established. "There were times when I felt like he enjoyed talking to us more than the other players," said Mark Maske, who covered the Orioles for the *Washington Post* in the '90s. "He would talk to us about things that had nothing to do with baseball, knowing, I guess, that we were more likely to be interested in that stuff."

But the Yankees clubhouse is a far cry from the Orioles clubhouse. It is packed every day with a minimum of fifty media members—frequently more. The clubhouse is open to the media three and a half hours before the first pitch and closes one hour before the game starts. Because of that, there are plenty of areas that are off-limits to the media: the hallway that leads to the manager and coaches' offices, the players' dining area, and the training area. Many players spend a good deal of time in the off-limits areas so they don't have to deal with the media. Those who venture to their lockers are frequently pounced on.

"The toughest part was that there was never a day off," Mussina said. "Every day there were guys who wanted to talk to you. Sometimes they wanted to talk about you, but just as often they wanted to talk about whatever was going on with the team or something else. Some of the guys I knew; a lot of the guys I didn't know. I really didn't deal with it very well the first year."

There were days when Mussina just didn't feel like talking because he had talked the previous four days. Sometimes he didn't think the subject was worth his time, or, on occasion, he got snappish. As a result, his early relationship with the New York media was rocky.

What saved him was the way he pitched. Unlike many players who allow adapting to New York to affect their performance, Mussina had a very good first season as a Yankee in 2001. He was 17–11 with an ERA of 3.15 and pitched, arguably, the two best games of his career.

The first came in early September in Boston, a place where Mussina had never pitched especially well. On this night he was perfect for twenty-six hitters, coming within one out and one strike of a perfect game. It was broken up by pinch hitter Carl Everett, who punched a 1–2 pitch to left field, the only hit and only base runner of the game for the Red Sox.

Yet another almost. Actually, Mussina set a record of sorts that night. It was the fourth time in his career that he had taken a no-hitter into at least the eighth inning, en route to pitching a one-hitter. That was the most times anyone had ever gone into the eighth with a no-hitter without recording one.

A month later, Mussina found himself back in postseason for the first time since 1997. The Yankees quickly found themselves down 2–0 to the Oakland Athletics and flew to the West Coast facing elimination in Game Three of the Division Series. Mussina pitched seven superb shutout innings, and the Yankees won the game 1–0. What most people remember about that game is not how well Mussina pitched but the extraordinary play that

Derek Jeter made in the seventh inning to preserve the Yankee lead.

With Jeremy Giambi steaming toward home plate with the tying run, Jeter somehow got from his shortstop position to the first-base line to grab a wayward throw to the plate, and, in one motion, backhanded the ball to catcher Jorge Posada, who managed to pick the ball out of midair and tag Giambi, who was so certain he was going to score that he failed to slide. That play ranks with Willie Mays's catch on Vic Wertz in Game One of the 1954 World Series and Ron Swoboda's diving catch on Brooks Robinson in the 1969 World Series as among the most spectacular in postseason history.

Mussina had a great view of the play since he was backing up home plate. "The funny part of it is, Derek was exactly where he was supposed to be when he made the play, which people don't understand," he said. "His job on the play is to be in the middle of the infield and read the throw from the outfield—in this case from the right-field corner. The throw (from rightfielder Shane Spencer) missed two cut-off men. Derek saw that, got over to the line, and made the play.

"What was unbelievable was that he was able to backhand and, in one motion, get it to Posada and that Posada was able to grab it and make the tag in one motion."

That play allowed Mussina to hand the ball to Mariano Rivera in the eighth inning with a 1–0 lead, and that was the final score. The Yankees ended up winning the series in five games and then beat the 116-win Seattle Mariners in five games. Mussina pitched Game Two of that series as well and gave up two runs in six innings as the winning pitcher. That set up what turned out to be a classic seven-game World Series that the Yankees lost when Rivera couldn't hold a 2–1 lead in the ninth inning of the seventh game.

Mussina pitched twice in his first World Series. He pitched poorly in Game One but pitched very well in Game Five, leaving in the eighth inning, trailing 2–0. The Yankees rallied to win that game in twelve innings. In Game Seven, the Yankees had a 2–1 lead in the eighth, only to lose 3–2 after two Arizona runs in the bottom of the ninth.

"I think of all the almosts in my career, that one was the toughest to take," he said. "We were three outs away from winning a championship, and we had Mo [Rivera] out there. You can talk about blowing the Boston series [in 2004], but even if we win that series, we still have to win the World Series. In Arizona, it was right there."

The Yankees have not been that close to winning a World Series since that night. In fact, they have only reached one World Series in the last six seasons, and, if you were to ask Joe Torre, the person most responsible for that one appearance was Mussina.

It was the seventh game of the 2003 American League Championship Series: Yankees-Red Sox in Yankee Stadium. Mussina had started and lost two games in the series, not pitching horribly but not pitching especially well. The seventh-game pitchers that night were Roger Clemens and Pedro Martinez.

"You would have thought it would be a low-scoring game," Mussina said. "But you never know. Since it was Game Seven, it was all hands on deck. Joe and [pitching coach] Mel [Stottlemyre] told me to be ready to come out of the bullpen just in case."

Mussina had never pitched a game in relief in thirteen seasons in the major leagues. In fact, he had never pitched in relief at any level of pro ball or at Stanford or in high school. "I don't think I'd ever relieved in my life," he said. "There had been times when I'd been in the bullpen in a 'just in case' situation, but it had never happened."

By the time Mussina made his way out to the bullpen in the third inning, the Yankees were down 3–0.

"You better be ready to pitch," Mike Borzello, the bullpen coach and his best friend on the team, told him when he arrived.

"You really think so?" Mussina answered.

Borzello nodded. "Roger's struggling. How far can you go?"

Mussina shrugged. "Probably not more than an inning."

"An inning?" Borzello said. "What are you doing here, then? You go in, you better be ready to go longer than that."

The call came in the top of the fourth inning. The score by then was 4–0, and the Red Sox had men on first and third, with no one out. Torre and Stottlemyre had told Mussina they wouldn't bring him in except to start an inning. This wasn't exactly starting an inning.

"It was four-nothing," Mussina said, "and I'm thinking that, best-case scenario, maybe I get us out of it with only one run scoring. That means we're down five-nothing, and Pedro Martinez is pitching for them. I really didn't think we stood much chance."

Mussina gave the Yankees a chance. He got a strikeout and a double-play ground ball and kept the Yankees within four runs. When he got to the dugout, he said to Torre and Stottlemyre, "I thought you were only going to bring me in to start an inning."

"We lied," Torre answered.

Two Jason Giambi home runs cut the lead to 4–2, and Mussina pitched two more shutout innings. Still, when David Wells gave up a home run to David Ortiz in the eighth to make it 5–2, it looked as if Mussina's effort had been for naught.

But Martinez ran out of gas in the eighth inning. Manager Grady Little famously left him in the game too long (and was fired as a result), and the Yankees tied the score 5–5. Mariano Rivera pitched three shutout innings, and then Aaron Boone led off the eleventh inning by hitting a Tim Wakefield knuckleball into the left-field seats to win the game and the pennant for the Yankees. Not surprisingly, Boone still has vivid memories of that night — one of them being Mussina after the game.

"I'd been around for half the season and I certainly respected him," Boone said. "He's kind of the consummate pro — all business, always prepared. He had a dry sense of humor, but you didn't see him get excited. We all know that I never get the chance to hit that home run if not for him.

"My memories of what happened right after the game ended are a little hazy. I remember being mobbed and how great it felt. I came back out of the clubhouse, and I was doing a TV interview on the field when someone poured champagne on my head. I looked behind me, and it was Moose. He had this look of absolute, pure joy on his face. I don't think I'll ever forget that. It was just neat to see."

Borzello remembers the same thing. "That's the happiest I've ever seen him," he said. "I've seen him satisfied after pitching well or after a milestone victory. But never quite like that. He was just absolutely happy, thrilled. I don't think Mike gets thrilled a lot. That night, he was thrilled. He knew he had done something special, and it meant a lot to him. Everyone in the clubhouse knew that Boone's home run was going to be replayed a million times, but Mike's fourth inning and the two after that saved the game."

Mussina doesn't argue. "Maybe it was because I did something I'd never done before. When I start a game, I know I have a job to do. If I do my job, that's great, but I go out there expecting to do it. If I don't do my job, I'm angry with myself. That night I had no expectations, especially when I walked to the mound. To have it turn out the way it did was just an amazing thing and an amazing feeling."

The last two people out of the clubhouse that night were Mussina and Borzello. They sat in the corner of the room, next to Borzello's locker, until close to 2 a.m., going over the events of the evening.

"I just couldn't believe we had actually won," Mussina said. "I don't think I've ever had a feeling like that in all the years I've played the game."

It looked as if Mussina was finally going to get his World Series ring when the Yankees went up 2–1 on the Florida Marlins after Mussina won Game Three in Florida, giving up one run over seven innings, striking out nine. But the Yankees lost Game Four in extra innings, then David Wells could only pitch one inning in Game Five and they lost that one too, to trail 3–2. Josh Beckett shut them out in Game Six to wrap up the Series. Thus, Mussina is currently the answer to a trivia question he wishes didn't exist: name the last Yankee pitcher to win a World Series game.

7

A Bitter Divorce

Tom Glavine watched Game Seven of the 2003 American League Championship Series on television. He had nothing better to do that night or that month because for the first time since 1990 (other than the strike year) he was not playing postseason baseball.

The Braves were in postseason, playing the Chicago Cubs in the National League Division Series. But Glavine, the man who had coauthored a book titled *None but the Braves,* was no longer a Brave. He was a New York Met.

The story of how Glavine came to be a Met is a convoluted one that still sparks controversy and anger in Atlanta to this day. The general assumption as the 2002 season wore down was that Glavine would sign a contract with the Braves that would allow him to finish his career in Atlanta. Glavine thought that's what would happen. Everyone in Braves management thought that was what would happen. Everyone in an Atlanta uniform thought the same thing.

"I don't think it ever seriously occurred to anyone that Tom would leave Atlanta," said John Smoltz. "I mean Tom, not a Brave? There was no way. Or at least that's what we all thought."

Glavine had continued to be one of the best pitchers in baseball after signing the contract that kicked in beginning in 1998. During that season, he was 20–6 with a 2.47 ERA and won his

84

second Cy Young Award. Over the four guaranteed seasons of the contract, he was 71–33 and never missed a start as the Braves continued to win Division titles every year — although they never could win a second World Series. The Braves were more than happy to exercise the $10 million fifth year in the contract at the start of 2002. It was then that the trouble began.

Once again, the collective-bargaining agreement was up at the end of the season. Once again, the owners were demanding changes. Specifically, they were insisting that they *must* have some kind of luxury tax, which the players again saw correctly as being a euphemism for a salary cap.

"Stan [Kasten] told me that the team didn't want to negotiate any new deals until we knew if there was going to be another work stoppage," Glavine said. "I understood that."

But when the negotiations began, they were rancorous. Once again, Glavine and Kasten found themselves on opposite sides, and the two of them argued almost constantly with each other.

"It got to the point," Kasten remembered, "where most of our conversations would end with one of us saying to the other, 'You must be the single stupidest person on the face of the earth!' And the other one saying, 'Right back at ya, pal.'"

In July, the players set a strike date — August 30. Another blown-up postseason loomed. The players had actually agreed to some form of a luxury tax, meaning that any team that went over a certain figure in payroll would have to pay a "tax" to Major League Baseball. It was a "soft" salary cap — that is, an owner would have the option of going over it if he was willing to pay the tax — as opposed to a "hard" cap, which would have prohibited anyone from going over that number under any circumstances.

The question was how high the tax threshold should be. The owners wanted it lower, naturally. And just as naturally, the players wanted it higher.

As the deadline neared, tempers got short. Jim Bowden, then

the general manager of the Cincinnati Reds, went on a radio show and accused the players of "steering Major League Baseball right into the World Trade Center," as if a threatened strike could somehow be akin to the events of September 11, 2001.

Kasten's phone rang that day. "*Who* is the stupidest person on the face of the earth?" he heard Glavine's voice say.

Kasten had to laugh. "Okay, Tommy, you win," he said. "Today, you are no better than number two when it comes to stupidity."

Just prior to the strike date, Glavine flew to Pittsburgh to meet with other members of the players' negotiating committee and union leaders Don Fehr and Gene Orza. The players and owners were now $10 million apart on the luxury tax threshold, but neither side seemed ready to budge another inch. The players had already lowered the number they had initially demanded by a considerable margin.

Glavine knew that if the negotiating committee went back to the players and said the strike was on, it would be on. The votes had already been taken in all thirty clubhouses. He also remembered 1994 and how long it had taken baseball to recover from that strike. The owners had lost millions of dollars; the players had lost millions in salary, and their image had taken a pounding.

"Fellas, I just don't think we can do this," he finally said late on the eve of the strike date. "I don't think we can go back to our guys and say we're walking because of a $10 million difference in a luxury tax level that probably isn't going to affect very many teams, regardless of where it's set. I think, even if it means we have to give in to the owners a little bit, we can't afford to stop playing again."

The others in the room listened. They knew Glavine was as loyal to the union as anyone, that he had been one of the out-front guys the last time there had been a strike. Fehr and Orza never wanted to give in to the owners because history showed that the players were always proven right in the end, especially when arbitrators or the courts got involved. But Tom Glavine saying that a strike would be a bad thing—especially when they were so close to an agreement—was a voice worth listening to. Early the next morning, with several teams sitting in their clubhouses waiting for word on whether to leave on a team bus to the airport to a game that night or in a cab to the airport to go home, the players and owners reached an agreement. There would be no strike.

"From what I've been told by others—not by Tom—no one played a more important role in averting a strike than he did," Kasten said. "He deserves a lot of credit for standing up and saying what he said. I don't think he's really gotten it." He smiled. "Of course I would never tell him that to his face."

The strike averted, teams began negotiating with their free agents to be. The Braves made an initial offer to Glavine: one year, $9 million.

"Which was a joke," Glavine said. "They weren't offering me a raise of any kind, and if I wanted to sign for one year I could go to arbitration and get a good deal more than that based on my past performance."

Glavine had pitched well again in 2002, going 18–11, and he was still as durable as any pitcher in baseball. Since he didn't rely on throwing hard, there was no reason to think he didn't have several more good years left in his arm.

But the Braves didn't want to commit to three years for a thirty-seven-year-old pitcher. Period. They had just signed Smoltz to a three-year, $30 million contract and didn't want to make a similar commitment to a pitcher who was a year older—even if his medical history was far superior. That was where the parting of the ways began: To Glavine, asking for the same contract Smoltz had gotten was fair. To Kasten, it was fair but it wasn't practical.

Just before the free-agency period began, the Braves offered Glavine $18 million for two years.

"By then I was going to file anyway," Glavine said. "I had told Stan I wanted three years and $30 million. I thought that was reasonable. He told me he didn't think I could get that from any-one. I thought he was wrong."

Glavine and Kasten ran into each other at a hockey game in early November. By then, Kasten was also running Atlanta's hockey team, the Thrashers. As part of Glavine's previous con-tract, Kasten had sold the old hockey player a suite to use at Thrashers games.

"You go do your 'Tommy over America Tour' and call when you get back," Kasten said.

Glavine said fine. Except in the crowded room they were in, he thought Kasten had said, "We'll call you when you get back."

Glavine was still convinced he was going to end up with the Braves, even after he filed for free agency. Smoltz, who had signed his new contract a year earlier, told him this was all part of the game, that he had to go "on tour" to other cities to find out what people would pay him, and then sit down with the Braves and hammer out a deal.

Within days of filing for free agency, Glavine had visited with the Mets and the Phillies. There had also been a phone call from the Yankees. The Mets' first offer was three years for $28 million. The Phillies' offer was almost identical, three years and $29 million. "Which meant I could now go back to Stan and say, 'You see, there are teams who will give me three years, and you know they'll go to at least $30 million if I pursue a deal. So now can we please get serious and talk?'"

Glavine came home and waited for the Braves to call. The Braves were waiting for him to call. Finally, a reporter called Glavine. Frustrated, Glavine said, "The Braves were supposed to call me and didn't. I think it's unprofessional."

The next day Kasten called. There was some shouting about who was supposed to call whom, but a meeting was set up. The phone conversation was not filled with pleasantries. "It was," Glavine said, "typical Stan."

"I guess it was," Kasten said. "I called him and said, 'Congratulations! I read in the papers that you have now officially discovered that New York and Philadelphia both have nice restaurants. Who would have thought it? Now, are you ready to talk?'"

Glavine was ready. He figured this was playing out just as Smoltz had told him it would. He and Gregg Clifton went to Kasten's office and met with Kasten and general manager John Schuerholz. The meeting lasted well into the night.

"Their first offer was exactly the same as before," he said. "Two years, $18 million. I think I said something like, 'Are you guys fucking kidding me?'"

Round and round they went. Kasten screamed. Glavine screamed. This wasn't a philosophical union argument; this was genuine anger, on both sides. Kasten's description of the meeting is simple and direct: "Gregg and John didn't say very much. Tom and I just sat there and motherfucked each other for most of six hours."

After those six hours, with the building completely empty except for the four men in Kasten's office, Kasten and Schuerholz made their best offer: three years at $30 million, with $9 million from the last year deferred.

"You guys already owe me $4 million in deferred money from the last contract," Glavine said. "I don't want you to owe me $13 million interest free."

"That's the last, best offer," Kasten said. "It's the best we can do."

It wasn't good enough. Stunned and saddened, Glavine went home. He told Clifton to tell the Mets and Phillies that the Braves were out of the picture. The Mets immediately responded by upping their offer and raising the possibility of adding a fourth year to the contract.

The fourth year was important to Glavine for reasons that had nothing to do with money. He had finished 2002 with 242 career victories. He had won a total of sixty-nine games over the previous four seasons and believed if he stayed healthy—he had never been on the disabled list—there was a good chance he could win fifty-eight during the next four and get to three hundred wins.

"I hadn't really thought about it until that point," he said. "When I was younger, I never thought I'd pitch past thirty-five, just because guys didn't do that. But the game had changed a lot in the time that I had gone from a twenty-one-year-old rookie to a thirty-six-year-old veteran. I was thirty-six, and I felt great, and I was still pitching well. There was no reason for me to think I couldn't pitch another four years and get to three hundred."

Even as he got older, Glavine had never given any thought to steroids. For one thing, his style of pitching wasn't built on strength. Like any pitcher, his legs were an important part of his delivery, but he wasn't a power pitcher by any stretch of the imagination. "Soft-tossing lefty" he likes to call himself.

Several years before Major League Baseball finally got around to drug testing (2003), Glavine did take creatine, a vitamin supplement that allows people to recover more quickly after a rigorous workout. "It really worked," he said. "I felt great. It made my work between starts a lot easier for me."

Creatine is not a banned substance, but as soon as MLB started drug testing, Glavine stopped using it. "It just wasn't worth the risk," he said. "What if, somehow, there was something in what I took that was banned, even a tiny bit. I just didn't think it was worth the risk. I know anytime someone tests positive and says 'I was using a legal supplement; there must have been something wrong with it,' no one believes him. I didn't want to somehow be the guy who *was* using a legal supplement and tested positive for some crazy reason."

Glavine was still a very good pitcher at the end of 2002, and the Mets certainly thought he could help them. They were coming off an awful season, and adding someone like Glavine to their pitching rotation would give the team an immediate credibility boost.

The deal was finalized on the first Thursday in December:

four years, $42.5 million. If nothing else, Glavine had proven Kasten wrong. But from the moment Clifton told Glavine the deal had been made, Glavine began to have buyer's remorse.

"It had nothing to do with the Mets or with New York, and certainly it had nothing to do with the deal," he said. "My family lived in Atlanta. I had a daughter I shared custody on whose mother lived in Atlanta, and Chris had a son in the same situation. We had two boys who, at that point, were four and two. It just hit me that they were going to be on airplanes all the time between New York and Atlanta during the season. I wasn't sure I could go through with everything that was going to be involved for *them*. Chris was the one who would be doing most of the work, and she said she was fine with it. I wasn't so sure if I was fine with it."

After the announcement that he was coming to New York, Glavine spoke to the New York media. He said he was disappointed with the way the Braves had handled the negotiations. They had failed to call when they said they were going to call. He didn't think they had negotiated in good faith. He didn't really believe they had wanted him back.

Kasten picked up the Friday papers and went ballistic. He called a press conference of his own and blasted Glavine. It was Glavine, he said, who had failed to call (both men now agree they had an honest misunderstanding about who was to call whom). The Braves had negotiated in good faith; they had wanted Glavine back, but he wanted every last dollar he could make.

Glavine woke up on Saturday morning, read Kasten's comments, and went into a state of anger and semipanic. Since his contract would not be formally filed with the union until Monday morning (at 12:01 a.m.), he was not yet officially a Met. He called Bobby Cox. He wasn't sure he could leave the Braves. Was the door still open? Cox called Kasten and Schuerholz. They agreed that Schuerholz should be Glavine's contact at that point.

Schuerholz called Glavine. Did he still want to talk? Yes.

Schuerholz drove to the house, and Chris went down to the wine cellar and opened a good bottle of wine.

"Right now the best we can do for you is two years, $10 million," Schuerholz said.

"Is that per year or total?" Glavine asked, in such a daze he honestly wasn't sure what Schuerholz was offering.

"Per year," Schuerholz said.

"I think I want to do it," Glavine said. "I don't want to leave Atlanta."

Schuerholz told Glavine he needed to call Clifton and Jeff Wilpon immediately. He left to call Kasten and Cox. They decided to call a 1:30 p.m. press conference for the next day.

"If Tommy had ended up staying, he would have been the fair-haired boy in Atlanta all over again," Kasten said. "But I wasn't convinced the deal would hold once he talked to Clifton."

It didn't. Clifton told Glavine he understood why he felt the way he did, but he had given his word to the Mets. Even if the contract wasn't signed, it would be wrong for him to back out for numerous reasons. Glavine knew Clifton was right. He also knew he wanted to stay in Atlanta. He spent the next day in a complete fog, talking to no one.

"Even when his parents called, I told them he just couldn't talk," Chris Glavine said. "He was really tormented."

So tormented that at one point he sat down and wrote a letter announcing that he was retiring. At that moment, it seemed like the only way out. "I was a mess," he said. "I didn't want to renege on the Mets deal, and I didn't want to leave Atlanta. For a few hours, I thought if I just retired that would be the best thing to do."

That was when Chris made the decision to call Jeff Wilpon. "You've got to get us out of here," she said. "If Tom sits around and thinks and rethinks, I don't know how it will come out."

Jeff Wilpon sent a plane to pick up Tom and Chris. They went through all the details of the deal the next day: where the family would live; the private airport Chris and the kids would fly into; Tom being able to fly home to Atlanta while the kids were in school when the team had an off-day. Glavine calmed down. He decided he could go through with it. The next day—finally—he was formally introduced as a Met.

"Hardest four or five days of my life," he said, looking back. "I felt guilty about my family, guilty about the Mets, guilty about the fans in Atlanta—just guilty. I remember going downstairs in an elevator at Shea Stadium to meet the media, and it hit me, 'I'm not a Brave anymore; I'm a Met. We're really doing this.' Chris said to me on the way home, 'You just went through a divorce after eighteen years of being married to the Braves. Don't feel bad about feeling bad.' She was right. I felt hurt and confused about it all. In the end, though, I felt like I'd made the right decision."

There would be times over the next two years—many times—when he wouldn't be so sure.

GLAVINE MADE HIS DEBUT as a Met on Opening Day 2003, March 31—a cold, blustery day in New York—pitching against the Chicago Cubs.

He wasn't out in the cold for long. He lasted only three and two-thirds innings and was pummeled for eight runs en route to a 15–2 loss. Less than an hour into his Mets career, he heard boos from the hometown fans. That game turned out to be a harbinger. For the first time, he had to deal with injuries: he left a game in Milwaukee in early June with inflammation in his elbow and missed his next start. It was the first time in his big league career that he had missed a start. Later in the month, a Derek Jeter line drive smacked him in the chest, and he was forced to leave the game.

Even healthy, he didn't pitch terribly well—especially against the Braves, who looked like they were taking batting practice whenever they faced him. "We just told our guys to look for the ball outside and take it to the opposite field," Bobby Cox said. "We had an advantage because we knew how he had been pitching for sixteen years. If there was one guy in baseball who could think along with Tommy it was Leo [Mazzone]."

Glavine missed Mazzone. The Mets' pitching coach, Vern Ruhle, let him continue his regimen of throwing twice between starts (most pitchers throw only once), but it wasn't the same for Glavine without Mazzone. The team was bad again. The Mets had hired Art Howe as their manager. Howe had been very successful in Oakland, but his quiet see-no-evil approach just wasn't going to work in New York. Mike Piazza was aging and balking at moving from catcher to first base. The team was a wreck, finishing 66–95.

Glavine was no better. He went 9–14 — the first time since his rookie year he hadn't won at least ten games. His ERA was 4.52, and he was 0–4 against the Braves, which really stung.

That was also the year that Major League Baseball first began using Questech, a videotaping system that judged umpires on balls and strikes in ten major league parks. As luck would have it, Shea Stadium was a Questech park. Glavine, who had spent most of his career getting pitches on or just off the outside corner called in his favor, found that he wasn't getting those pitches anymore. Umpires didn't want Questech showing that a Glavine pitch just outside was a strike while someone else's pitch in the same spot was a ball.

"Whether that was actually happening or not doesn't matter," Glavine said. "I *believed* it was happening, and it affected my confidence and the way I pitched. I think I could go back and show you pitches that had been strikes that weren't strikes anymore. But even if I couldn't, I thought that was what was happening."

The only good news was off the field — his family loved New York. The Glavines had found a house in Greenwich, Connecticut, that was a relatively easy commute to the ballpark. The kids loved the area and so did Chris, especially the fact that they were away from Atlanta's brutal summer heat for almost three months.

Still, it was a long year. Glavine wondered if perhaps his decision to leave Atlanta might end up costing him his chance to win three hundred games. He was now forty-nine wins away, meaning he would have to average a little more than sixteen victories per year if he was to reach that milestone by the end of his contract.

The 2004 season started far better than that of 2003. The Mets had hired a new pitching coach, Rick Peterson, who had worked wonders with a young Oakland staff when Howe had been the manager there, helping make Tim Hudson, Mark Mulder, and Barry Zito into twenty-game winners. Peterson was the polar opposite of Mazzone in just about every way possible. He was a college-educated, literature-quoting, vegetable-eating, Zen master. Or, at the very least, a Zen pitching coach.

"To say that Leo and Rick are different is one of the great understatements of all time," Glavine said, laughing. "If you put the two of them in a room and they talked to each other for an hour, I'm not sure either one would understand a word the other was saying."

Peterson grew up in a baseball family—his dad was the general manager of the Pittsburgh Pirates when he was a kid—and was a pitcher with some promise until he blew out his arm in college when his coach left him in a game to throw 164 pitches. "I was never the same after that," he says now, without rancor. "I'm not saying I would have been a big leaguer if that hadn't happened, but after that there wasn't any doubt."

He graduated from Jacksonville University in 1976 with a degree in psychology and was drafted in the twenty-first round by the Pirates. He spent the next four years pitching at the A-ball level in the Pirates' system before deciding it was time—at age twenty-five—to move on. He had already decided what he was going to do when he was finished playing, so moving from playing to coaching seemed like a natural step at the time.

"I always loved the game; I grew up with it," he said. "After I got hurt in college, I was pretty sure I wasn't going to make it very far in pro ball, but I wanted to take the shot and see how far I got. I was into a lot of other things by then—art, reading. I loved to paint—still do.

"Not long after I graduated, I was in San Diego visiting some friends, and I went on a seven-day fast. I've been a vegetarian since I was a kid, and I just felt like this was something good to do—cleanse my body entirely for a little while.

"I was walking on the beach during the fast—and I'm not really sure how to describe this—but I was looking up at the sky, and the sun came slanting down in a certain way, and something inside me said, 'You're supposed to teach.' I know how that sounds, but that's how it happened. The thing I knew best was baseball; the thing I know best in baseball is pitching. So, here I am."

Peterson almost never raises his voice to a pitcher. He is constantly looking for analogies they can relate to and always talks about the process of pitching—constantly telling his pitchers not to worry too much about results. If they focus on the process, the results will be there.

After all those years with Mazzone, Glavine went through a little bit of culture shock working with Peterson. Even four years into their relationship, he would still occasionally roll his eyes when Peterson would point out a butterfly in the bullpen.

"Do you realize what a miracle that is?" Peterson was likely to say. "Not that long ago that beautiful creature was a caterpillar. Think about that, Tom—a caterpillar! Now look at it. Seeing it *has* to be a good omen."

"That's great, Rick," Glavine would likely reply. "Now would you mind taking a look at my changeup?"

Glavine and the other pitchers may occasionally mock what Glavine calls "all the Zen stuff," but they respect Peterson.

"He may go on for a while, but he's smart, and he understands people as well as he understands baseball," Glavine said. "When we first talked, he asked me a lot of questions about golf, which I wondered about. But after a while, he began using golf analogies that really made sense to me, especially when I was struggling."

Glavine was superb for the first half of the 2004 season. He was 3–1 with a 1.64 ERA in April, and he pitched a one-hitter against Colorado—taking a no-hitter into the eighth inning—in May. The Mets were bad again (71–91), but Glavine made his ninth All-Star team in July.

Then disaster struck—again. The Mets had wrapped up an early-August road trip in St. Louis, and Glavine had flown home on Sunday night to spend an off-day with his family. Chris and the kids had just returned to Atlanta to get ready for the start of school. He caught a late-morning flight to New York on Tuesday, landed at LaGuardia Airport, and got into a cab to make the one-mile trip to Shea Stadium. The cab pulled out into traffic while Glavine called Chris to let her know he had landed safely.

"I was getting ready to hang up with her, and I remember thinking, 'Short trip, but I probably should put my seat belt on,'" he said. "Just as I thought that, I heard the cabbie say something loudly—I think I was looking down at that moment for my seat belt—and the next thing I knew, I got slammed headfirst into the partition between the front seat and the backseat."

The cab had been cut off by a car trying to weave through traffic on the ramp leading onto the Grand Central Parkway. Glavine's face went directly into the partition and shattered it.

"I remember kind of going down and wondering if I was going to pass out," he said. "I didn't, and I thought, 'Okay, that's good,' and then I felt this pain in my mouth. I looked down, and I saw blood all over my hands. Then I saw a tooth in my hands too."

Glavine actually managed to call Chris back while he was spitting up blood and teeth (two were knocked out) to tell her he'd been in an accident but he was okay. Then he called Mets public relations director Jay Horwitz to tell him what had happened and that he suspected he wouldn't make it to the ballpark as planned.

Horwitz immediately called Jeff Wilpon, who made arrangements to have Glavine taken to the Manhattan hospital where the Mets send their players.

When the police arrived, they put Glavine in a squad car and waited for the ambulance.

"How do I look?" Glavine asked the first cop on the scene.

"I've seen worse," the cop said. "But not a lot worse."

Once he got to the hospital, they began giving him one novocaine shot after another because of all the work they needed to do on his gums and his teeth. "After about the tenth one, I said, 'Enough; do what you have to do. I'll deal with the pain.'"

Before they dug in to do the major work, Glavine asked if he could go to the bathroom. "When I finished, I made the mistake of looking at myself in the mirror," he said. "That was it. I went down."

He was in the hospital until late that night and ended up having to go through several rounds of dental surgery—the final one done in January of 2007. He missed a total of thirteen days—just two starts—and came back on August 21 to pitch against the Giants.

"It was probably a mistake," he said. "I couldn't throw at all while I was out because they were afraid I might rip open the stitches in my mouth on my follow-through. I came back too quickly, and I was probably a little bit afraid of hurting myself when I went back. I was pretty bad the rest of the season."

He finished 11–14 with a respectable 3.60 ERA, but nine of the wins came before the accident. He could easily have had a dozen wins before the All-Star break if the Mets had been better, but he didn't. He was now at 262 victories, and it was clear that he wasn't getting to three hundred by the end of 2006 when his contract was up. People in New York were calling his signing yet another Mets mistake in a parade of them during that period.

The 2005 season began much the way the 2004 season had ended. Glavine was still struggling. He had almost grown accus-

tomed to not getting the outside pitches called in his favor anymore, but he hadn't come up with a way to consistently get hitters
out without his bread-and-butter pitch — the one just off the outside corner — working for him.

He opened the season by getting bombed in Cincinnati — five
runs in three and two-thirds innings, and it just kept getting worse.
The bottom came in June when the Mets made an interleague
road trip to Oakland and Seattle. Glavine was merely mediocre in
Oakland — four runs and ten hits in six innings. But then he was
awful in Seattle, giving up six runs while getting just seven outs
before new manager Willie Randolph mercifully came to get him.

Glavine was just about at the end of his rope. He was 4–7 for
the season, and his ERA was 5.06. The notion that he might stick
around long enough to win thirty-four more games was laughable.
He was, as you might expect, getting hammered in New York.
One radio talk show host wondered on the air if the driver who
had slammed into Glavine's cab the previous August could be
found for a reprise.

On the long flight home from Seattle, Rick Peterson sat in the
front of the plane trying to decide what to do next. He had tried
just about everything he could think of to get Glavine out of his
funk. Because Peterson had so much respect for Glavine as a
pitcher and liked him so much as a person, Glavine's pitching was
tearing him up almost as much as it was tearing up Glavine.
Finally, he made a decision. Peterson got out of his seat, walked
back to where Glavine was, and slid into the empty spot next to
him. He knew Glavine wasn't in the mood for any Zen soothing,
and he had none to give. He asked the flight attendant if they
could have a couple of beers.

"I was really nervous going back there," he said. "I'm very aware
of who Tom Glavine is and how much he's accomplished in baseball. I never got close to the major leagues as a pitcher. But I had
decided I had to tell him that he had to blow up the way he had
pitched for eighteen years and try something completely new."

Once the beers arrived, Peterson started out with a golf question.

"How many clubs are you allowed to have in your bag?" he asked Glavine.

Glavine wasn't really in the mood for a golf analogy at that moment, but he isn't the kind of guy to tell someone to leave him alone, and he liked Peterson enough to play along.

"Fourteen," he answered.

"Well, as a pitcher right now, you're using about seven clubs. Does it make any sense to use only half the clubs you're allowed to use?"

Glavine looked at him quizzically.

"You have to start pitching inside," Peterson said. "Not once in a while to get a guy off the plate — all the time."

Glavine had never pitched inside because his game had always been to get batters to chase pitches outside. When his changeup is working and his location is good, he likes to say he has batters "playing the chase game." Pitching inside for a nonpower pitcher was high risk because if a batter is ready for an inside pitch and it isn't located perfectly, he is apt to crush it.

"Pitch inside?" Glavine said. "Me?"

Peterson nodded. "Every team in the league has the same scouting report on you: lay off on the pitch off the plate; wait for him to come over the plate, and then take the ball to the opposite field or up the middle. They're sitting on your pitches, Tom. Your game is keeping guys off balance. No one is off balance right now."

Glavine couldn't argue with that. It had been a while since he had felt as if he had hitters off balance. They talked for a while longer about when to throw inside and what pitches to throw inside and when to go back outside. Glavine's thinking was simple: I can't pitch any worse. Why not try it?

He unveiled his new self in Yankee Stadium a few nights later. He was inside, and he was outside. The Yankee hitters were surprised. "He was a different guy completely," Joe Torre remembered. "A couple of times, I was tempted to check his uniform number to make sure it was Tom."

He pitched six innings that night and gave up two earned runs and got the win. Each time out, he got a little more confident with his new style, and even after word got around the league that he was pitching differently it didn't seem to matter.

"They knew I was willing to come inside," he said. "But they didn't know *when* I was going to come inside. It was like the old days; I had them chasing again."

The turnaround was remarkable. In his first 15 starts through Seattle, Glavine had given up 48 earned runs in 85 innings. In his last 19 starts of the season, he gave up 35 earned runs in 126 innings, pitching to an ERA of 2.50. He finished with a flourish, winning his last three starts, including a masterful two-hit, eleven-strikeout shutout of the Colorado Rockies in his final start of the season. He was 9–6 after the late-night talk on the plane with Peterson and could have been considerably better if the bullpen hadn't blown several leads for him.

"I felt like a new man, a new pitcher," he said. "Rick deserves a lot of credit because he convinced me I had to change the way I was pitching. It isn't easy to get someone who has been pitching as long as I have to start all over again, but he did it."

The new Glavine was just about as good in 2006 as he had been late in 2005. He went 15–7, and except for a stretch in July where he struggled with his control, he was outstanding all year. The Mets had finally turned around after Randolph had been hired as the manager, Omar Minaya had taken over as general manager, and Pedro Martinez had joined Glavine in the rotation, with Billy Wagner as the closer. After going 83–79 in 2005, the Mets dominated the National League East throughout 2006, taking complete control of the pennant race by the All-Star break. They cruised home with a 97–65 record and won the division by twelve games, finally ending the Braves' run of fourteen consecutive division titles.

There were really only two down moments for Glavine all season, although one of them was potentially serious.

The first came in July, when he was struggling. On June 23, he had raised his record for the season to 11–2 with a victory over Toronto. Over his next six starts, nothing went right. He gave up twenty-one runs in thirty-four innings and was fortunate to lose only twice, getting off the hook with no decisions in the other four games.

"Every year you go through a period where you just can't get anyone out," he said. "This lasted a little longer and was a little more worrisome, if only because I was forty years old. I mean, I wasn't panicking or anything, but I was definitely frustrated."

On a hot Sunday in Atlanta, Glavine went out for his sixth start of July. The Mets promptly staked him to a 3–0 lead. Still struggling against his old team, Glavine let the Braves close to 7–3 by the end of the second, but then the Mets scored again to make it 8–3 in the third.

"At that point, given the heat and my pitch count, I'm just thinking about getting through five so I can get the bullpen to finish it off for me and get a win," he said.

He almost didn't make it through the fourth. The Braves scored three runs, with two out, the score now 8–6. Glavine steadied and got the final hitter out to maintain the lead. He walked into the dugout, put a towel on his neck, and saw Randolph approaching.

"You're done, Tommy," Randolph said. "The bullpen will take it from here."

Glavine was stunned. He knew he wasn't pitching well, but he thought at worst either Randolph or Peterson would ask him if he thought he had another inning in him. "I've never been a guy who always says I'm okay no matter what," he said. "After the eighth inning in Game Six [of the '95 World Series], I told Bobby [Cox] and Leo [Mazzone] that I thought I was done, and I was pitching a one-hitter.

"If Willie had come and gotten me during the fourth, I would have understood. But I got out of the inning. At the very least, especially given how I was scuffling and needing a win to get some confidence back, I thought he'd let me start the fifth. If I put someone on, fine, come get me. But at least give me a shot."

If Randolph had it to do all over again, he probably would do just that. But he was thinking he had an older pitcher who was struggling in the heat. Peterson was worried about Glavine's pitch count. The Mets had a comfortable lead in the pennant race — eleven games — but it was still Atlanta and it was still the Braves. So, Randolph made the move.

"When Tommy and I sat down and talked about it, I understood why he was upset," Randolph said later. "I respected his point of view, and I think he respected mine. I think it's fair to say that was a learning experience for me as a manager."

Once he knew he was out of the game, Glavine went back to the clubhouse and, by his own description, proceeded to go ballistic. "I was hot," he said. "About as angry as I can ever remember being. I don't throw things around very much, but that day I did."

When Randolph heard what had happened in the clubhouse, he asked Glavine to come to his office the next day to talk. Both men explained their thinking. There was an agreement to disagree. "And then it was over," Glavine said. "I was still a little upset, but you get over it. I think Willie knew where I was coming from and that was all I could ask."

It helped that Glavine ended his seven-game no-victory skein with seven solid innings against the Phillies six days later. Eleven days later, Glavine pitched against the Phillies, this time in Philadelphia. He pitched seven innings and left for a pinch hitter in the eighth, with the Mets trailing 3–0.

Sitting in the dugout in the top of the eighth — Glavine always waits until the end of an inning to go to the clubhouse after he comes out of a game — he felt some coldness in the ring finger on his pitching hand. It was a comfortable night, so the coldness wasn't caused by the weather. After he had gone back to the club-house and gone through his twenty-minute postgame routine with an ice pack on his shoulder, the finger still felt cold.

"Very early in my career [1990], I'd had a problem with my index finger and my middle finger where they got cold that way," he said. "I had it checked out, and the doctors decided it was something called Raynaud's disease, which means, basically, that when your hand gets cold, the blood doesn't flow properly through your fingers sometimes. They put me on some Procardia — a pill I took once a day — and I never had a real problem with it again.

"This was a little different because it was my ring finger, but my first thought was that maybe the Raynaud's was flaring up a little. I decided I probably shouldn't take any chances and should tell someone about it."

The first person he found was assistant trainer Mike Herbst, who agreed the finger was abnormally cold and suggested he pack it in heat that night and see how it felt the next day. When the finger was still cold and the knuckle on it was sore (something that hadn't happened with the Raynaud's in the past), the Mets decided to send Glavine to see a hand specialist in New York.

He showed up at the hospital on the east side of Manhattan the next day, thinking he would be at the ballpark at four o'clock, just a little later than he normally arrived for a seven o'clock home game. He left the hospital nine hours later.

First, the specialist looked at his hand and performed an MRI. Nothing unusual showed up. Then he asked Glavine to stick his hand into a bucket of ice and hold it there for two minutes. "I remembered doing that in '90 and how much it hurt," he said. "It hurt just as much this time."

And the results were similar: his thumb and pinky returned to normal circulation in less than five minutes. The three middle fingers were still cold. "They said, 'Probably the Raynaud's, but, since you're here, let's do an ultrasound.' I was sitting there while they were doing the ultrasound when I heard the doctor say, 'Uh-oh.' When a doctor says 'uh-oh,' that gets your attention."

The doctor showed him what he had seen. On the screen there was clearly something that was darker in his blood flow in one area than in the others. "Not sure what it is," the doctor said. "But I think we better get a full MRI"—An MRI from Glavine's shoulder down to the hand would show what was causing the darker color on the screen, what might be cutting off the circulation to his hand. Since an MRI can only be done for small portions of a person's body, Glavine had to spend four hours going in and out of the MRI machine. "They would set it on my shoulder, leave me in there for forty-five minutes, and then move it down my arm a little," he said. "A couple of places they couldn't get the camera positioned exactly right, so I had to go in and out like four times. It was absolutely brutal."

When the MRI was finally over, the doctors told him they still couldn't be sure what was wrong with him. "Could be something minor," they said. "We want to do an angiogram on you on Monday."

Great, Glavine thought. *I have to wait until Monday, and the closest thing I have to a diagnosis is a doctor saying "uh-oh."* He drove home exhausted and a little bit frightened.

"I went from thinking it was no big deal and I probably wouldn't miss a turn to thinking maybe my season was over. I didn't even want to *think* my career was over. But the thought sneaked into my head briefly."

As luck would have it, his parents and his sister and brother-in-law were in for the weekend, so it was a full house. Glavine told them and Chris what was going on. "No one panicked or anything," he said. "But the uncertainty was kind of tough."

He went to the ballpark briefly the next day, avoiding the media only because there was nothing he could tell them. When his teammates asked what was going on, his answer was honest: "I don't know. Could be nothing. Or my season could be over."

Not surprisingly, when he arrived at the ballpark on Sunday, several writers were waiting for him. They had heard his season might be over. True? Glavine talked to everyone that day, saying he would know more after the angiogram, and, yes, he was nervous about what was going on.

The next day he and Chris drove back to the hospital. The angiogram took close to two hours. When he came out of the fog from the light anesthesia he'd been given, he found Dr. Anne Winchester, who had performed the angiogram, looking at him, concern on her face. The angiogram showed a small blood clot, not one that was life-threatening, but one that might make it risky to pitch again.

"I was sort of freaking out at that point," Glavine said. "Then Dr. [David] Altchek and the other doctors who work with the Mets came in. I was still a little groggy, but at one point I heard someone say something about when I started pitching again. I kind of sat up and said, 'Pitching again? You guys think I can pitch?' Dr. Altchek kind of nodded and said, 'Sure, in a little while; why not?'"

Glavine was less groggy but more confused. Chris was concerned. Why, she wanted to know, did the baseball doctors think it was okay to pitch but the nonbaseball doctor didn't? Glavine was wondering the same thing when, as if on cue, Dr. Winchester came into the room.

She told him that she had been discussing the angiogram results with Altchek and the other doctors. She was in agreement that there was no reason why he shouldn't pitch. The clot had probably been developing for years and years — in fact, it might have been the cause of his problems in 1990, not Raynaud's — as a result of the way he twisted his body when he released the ball. It had probably started in his chest, traveled to his hand, and was creating a circulation blockage there.

"The only way you would really be at risk by pitching is if you have a bunch of symptoms that you choose to ignore," she said. "If the finger feels cold again, you tell someone right away."

Glavine was relieved. He and Chris both asked if there was any chance he could have a heart attack or a stroke. Dr. Winchester said almost none, unless he ignored symptoms. And over the next several days, his finger began to feel normal again.

Eleven days later, he was back on the mound in Houston, feeling nervous, wondering what would happen. "It was almost like the first game in spring training," he said. "I'd done my work, gotten back on the mound, but I had no idea where the ball would go when I got out there. Would the finger get cold again? I didn't know."

He pitched three good innings, a bad fourth inning, and left after five. He was almost as happy as he would have been if he had pitched a shutout. "The finger was fine; I felt fine," he said. "The problems I had in the fourth were normal pitching problems—I put a couple guys on and tried to make perfect pitches instead of good ones. That had nothing to do with the finger. I was fine."

He pitched well throughout September and October and had no further issues with the finger. His only complaint during the last nine weeks of the season was that the Mets came up one victory short of reaching the World Series.

"After it was over, I realized how lucky I was," he said. "If I had needed surgery, the rehab would have been six to eight months. At my age, that could have been the end. To get back on the mound so quickly and to do it pain free and be pretty effective was a blessing. I felt very lucky."

And, when he beat the Washington Nationals 13–0 in his final regular season start, he had won his 290th game.

8

One More Contract

TOM GLAVINE AND MIKE MUSSINA both became free agents not long after the 2006 season ended.

Mussina's six-year, $88.5 million contract with the Yankees had a $17 million team option for 2007, but he knew they were not going to execute it. "Given the market, there was no way they were going to pay me that kind of money," he said. "But I knew they wanted me back."

Yankees general manager Brian Cashman had made that clear to Mussina before the season ended. In 2006 Mussina had had his best year since 2002. He had been completely healthy — making thirty-two starts — and had pitched to a 15–7 record with a 3.51 ERA, his lowest since the 3.15 he'd put up his first year in New York.

There were other reasons why the Yankees would want Mussina back. For one thing, their starting pitching was as shaky as it had been in years. Although Chien-Ming Wang had emerged as a star, winning nineteen games, the rest of the staff — behind Mussina — was full of question marks.

On the orders of owner George Steinbrenner, the Yankees had traded for forty-two-year-old Randy Johnson and given him a two-year, $32 million contract prior to the 2005 season. Johnson's stay in New York had been disastrous. It had taken him about fifteen minutes to get into a scuffle with a local cameraman when he first arrived in town, and his pitching had been consistently mediocre. Even though he had won seventeen games in '06, he had pitched to a horrific 5.00 ERA, and then, for the second year in a row, had pitched poorly in the critical third game of a Division Series.

The fourth starter had been Jaret Wright, who had won eleven games and managed to stay healthy for the first time in years but was a free agent, a question mark for '07, and a six-inning pitcher at best.

And then there was the fifth starter. Cashman had signed Carl Pavano as a free agent prior to the 2005 season, giving him a four-year contract worth just under $40 million. Pavano was about to turn twenty-nine and was coming off a superb season in which he had gone 18–8 with a 3.00 ERA pitching for the Florida Marlins. He had been a part of the staff that had beaten the Yankees in the 2003 World Series and had given up just one run in eight innings in the game he started against the Yankees.

Given Pavano's age and his 2004 season, signing him seemed to make sense. But he had really had only one outstanding season in the major leagues, and, as Mussina often says, a lot of guys have had one good year. By the end of 2006, Pavano still had just one good year.

He pitched poorly during the first half of 2005 — 4–6 record, 4.77 ERA — and had gone on the disabled list at the end of June with tendinitis in his right shoulder. He hadn't pitched in a major league game since then because of various injuries. Three times Pavano had begun rehab stints in the minor leagues, and each time he had returned to the DL without making it back to New York.

The last time had been most galling to the Yankees. Pavano had started the season on the DL because of tendinitis, had undergone arthroscopic surgery to remove a bone chip from his elbow, and had started to pitch rehab games in Tampa in August. On August 25, he had come out of a game complaining about soreness under his right armpit. Only then did Pavano tell the trainers that he had been in a car accident ten days earlier and had experienced pain since then. For Mussina and other Yankees, that was about the last straw.

"You're being paid a lot of money, and you haven't pitched for more than a year, and you don't tell people about an accident for ten days?" he asked rhetorically, incredulous at the thought. "That's just irresponsible. I think a lot of us decided after that happened that, for whatever reason, he really didn't want to pitch. I mean, every time he'd start back and it would look like he might get back to New York, something would happen. The car accident was the topper."

Mussina had been skeptical about Pavano even prior to the accident. Shortly before going to Tampa to begin rehab, Pavano had come to New York to throw a bullpen session with pitching coach Ron Guidry and bullpen coach Joe Kerrigan (an ex-pitcher and pitching coach). Mussina was standing by his locker when Kerrigan walked by on the afternoon Pavano was going to throw.

"Pav's going to throw," Kerrigan said to Mussina. "You want to come watch?"

"Not really," Mussina said.

When Kerrigan walked away, Mussina shook his head and said, "Why watch? There's no way the guy is pitching for us this season."

He had been proven correct.

All of which meant the Yankees had exactly one starter — Wang — under contract for 2007 they felt they could absolutely count on. Wright was going to be allowed to sign elswhere; the team was hoping to trade Johnson; and Pavano was, at best, a major question mark.

"We wanted Mike back; we needed Mike back," Cashman said. "He had earned every single dollar we had paid him for six years. He was a great investment, and, given the way he pitched in '06, there wasn't any reason not to want him back. Plus, he'd become an important guy in our clubhouse."

That last point was a development few people would have foreseen. As well as he had pitched in 2001, Mussina had, by his own admission, gone through a rocky time adapting to the Yankeee clubhouse. Unlike a lot of players who struggle early in New York and throw their arms up and say "This is impossible," Mussina had taken the opposite tack. "I had to learn how to deal with it," he said. "I had a six-year contract. I wasn't going anywhere, and neither was the New York media."

He learned to accept the fact that a day off from pitching was not necessarily a day off from talking to the media. He began to make a point of not keeping people waiting after he had pitched poorly, although he still might make them wait a few extra minutes after he had pitched well. Writers figured out that Mussina would give smart, thoughtful answers as long as he was approached correctly.

What's more, Mussina had become the leader of the pitching staff. When Roger Clemens, Andy Pettitte, and David Wells had all departed after the 2003 season, Mussina had been the one remaining veteran with New York experience. He began to go out of his way to talk to younger pitchers and to newcomers. In fact, Torre had called him in early in the 2006 season to ask him to counsel the struggling Johnson.

"Moose had been through the New York wringer when he first got here," Torre said. "He had figured out how to deal with it all. Not everyone does that. Randy was really struggling with it. I thought maybe he could help."

Mussina tried. He sat Johnson down and talked to him about his early struggles in 2001.

"Does it ever stop?" Johnson asked.

Mussina shook his head. "No, it doesn't," he said. "You have to accept the fact that it isn't going to stop. A lot of it is your attitude when you talk. If you pitch six innings, give up three runs, and we lose 4–3, they don't want to hear you say, 'Well, I pitched pretty well; I gave the team a chance to win.' Because we *didn't* win. What you should say is, 'Hey, my job was to hold the other guys to one or two if we're only scoring three today, and I didn't get it done. That's on me.' No one in this town wants to hear excuses because in the end, that's what they are, excuses."

Johnson listened, and Mussina sensed at times that he was trying. But Johnson just couldn't do it. Often, Mussina would look at Johnson, who lockered a few yards away from him, and see him just staring into space, looking completely alone in a packed room.

"I felt for him," Mussina said. "He was just never happy here."

Mussina was happy in New York and was pleased that the Yankees wanted him back. He would be thirty-eight when the 2007 season began, and, in the back of his mind, he thought it possible, though not likely, that he could get to three hundred wins.

"The odds are against it at this point," he said. "I've won two hundred thirty-nine games, which means I would have to average fifteen wins a year [plus one] for four years to get to three hundred. I pitched well this year [2006], and I was healthy all year, and I won fifteen games. The chances are I won't do that for the next four years, the last year coming when I'll be forty-one. But we'll just have to see. Two years from now, I'll see where I am and reevaluate."

He could wait two years because Cashman offered him a new two-year deal shortly after the team had formally let Mussina and his agent, Arn Tellem, know they wouldn't exercise the 2007 option. Although Tellem closes Mussina's deals, Mussina will often talk to Cashman during the negotiations.

Not long after the season had ended — the Yankees had been eliminated by the Detroit Tigers in the Division Series, with Mussina pitching a mediocre Game Two in a 4–3 loss — Cashman called Mussina to talk about a new contract. His first offer was for two years at $18 million. Mussina's response was swift and to the point: "Brian, you're *not* paying me less than you're paying Carl Pavano," he said. "Don't insult me."

Point taken. Months later, Cashman laughed when that conversation came up. "I don't remember a lot of details," he said. "But I do remember *that*."

It didn't take long for Cashman to come up to a respectable above-Pavano level. On November 27, the Yankees announced that Mussina had signed a two-year contract worth $23 million.

With Mussina and Wang under contract, the team then went on to bring Andy Pettitte back as a free agent, and, after losing out to the Boston Red Sox in the Daisuke Matsuzaka sweepstakes, they signed their own Japanese free agent, Kei Igawa, for a lot more money (five years at a cost of $46 million) than most baseball people thought he was worth.

In January, Johnson was traded to Arizona for four prospects. Wright signed with Baltimore. And so, the Yankees headed into spring training with a starting rotation of Wang, Mussina, Pettitte, Igawa, and . . . Carl Pavano.

LIKE MUSSINA, Glavine had been outstanding in 2006, also finishing 15–7, and then pitching superbly in the postseason, allowing just three runs in seventeen innings over three starts against the Dodgers and Cardinals. His strong season had put him at 290 career wins, and, given the way he had pitched, there was no reason to think he would not be able to get the ten wins he needed to reach three hundred the following season.

The question was, where would he be pitching?

Both Glavine and the Mets had options for 2007 that each knew would not be exercised: the Mets could have signed Glavine for $16 million. Once the Mets did not exercise that option, Glavine could have exercised his own for $7.5 million. Team and player were in agreement: Glavine should be paid more than $7.5 million and less than $16 million.

"Money was never really an issue with the Mets," Glavine said. "I knew that Jeff [Wilpon] and Omar [Minaya] would make me a fair offer if and when the time came."

The if, as in 2002, was the Braves.

Things had changed in Atlanta since Glavine's rancorous departure four years earlier. Stan Kasten was now CEO of the Washington Nationals. The two had long since made up, having sat down over lunch during the 2003 season. They were now back to their friendly bickering.

During the 2006 season, when the Mets had come to play in Washington, Kasten wanted to introduce Mark Lerner, one of the Nationals' new owners, to Glavine. He spotted him signing autographs down the left-field line and walked up behind him.

"You know, Mark," he said as they approached, "the last time I tried to get this guy to sign an autograph, he wanted me to give him $40 million for it."

"Thirty million," Glavine answered, not even pausing as he signed.

Glavine was also still close with Braves manager Bobby Cox, whom he had never had an issue with. This was not the case, however, with general manager John Schuerholz.

"Some of it is just personality," Glavine said. "My relationship with Stan was that we could curse each other out for hours, and when it was over, it was over. John's not like that. Things tended to linger — on both sides — with him."

There was also the issue of Schuerholz's autobiography. It had been published early in the 2006 season, and, among other things, it detailed the Glavine negotiations of 2002, including the Saturday when Glavine had thought he wanted to back out of the New York deal and return to Atlanta. That had never been publicized before, and Glavine was upset that Schuerholz went public about his last-minute doubts.

"There were two issues to me," he said. "The first was I considered what happened that day private, which may be naive because, ultimately, in sports nothing is private. Beyond that was the timing. I had just gotten to the point where people had accepted me in New York, and now John comes along saying I didn't want to go there. This was three years later; my doubts about New York were long gone."

Fortunately, Glavine pitched so well through most of 2006 that few people in New York were concerned about any doubts he'd had in 2002. He and Schuerholz sat down together in August during a Mets-Braves series to hash out their differences and did . . . sort of.

"He explained what he was trying to do, and I told him how I felt," Glavine said. "It cleared the air — at least to some extent."

Was the air clear enough for Glavine to return to Atlanta? The Mets had told Glavine they wanted him back, and Glavine knew he would probably be paid about $11 million for 2007 if he went back to the Mets. Still, he couldn't help thinking about going back to the Braves.

"In some ways it would have been perfect," he said. "Obviously, for the family it would be much easier — no more airplanes, no more packing and unpacking all the time. It would have been nice in a lot of ways to come back and try to get my three hundredth with the Braves. Full circle. It was certainly something worth checking into."

The Braves appeared to have some interest when the free-agent signing period began in November. They could certainly use some help on their pitching staff. John Smoltz was back in the starting rotation, and Tim Hudson was certainly solid, but there were lots of question marks after that. Cox made it clear he would love to have Glavine back.

While Glavine waited to see what the Braves would offer, the Mets were asking for an answer — one way or the other. If Glavine wasn't coming back, they needed to make a move to fill his spot in the rotation. Baseball's annual winter meetings, where a lot of trading is done, were in early December. Glavine finally told Jeff

Wilpon he would give him an answer in time for the winter meetings.

And then he waited. And waited. The Braves never made an offer.

Schuerholz had a problem: new owners were about to take over the team, and he didn't know exactly what kind of budget he was going to have for player payroll. He needed to make some moves—several at the winter meetings—to gain some payroll flexibility. If Glavine could have waited a little longer, Schuerholz might have been able to make an offer.

Glavine understood, but he couldn't wait. He had given Wilpon his word. On December 9, several days after telling the Mets he was coming back, he re-signed with the Mets: one year, $11 million. More money than Carl Pavano was making, and more than Glavine would have been willing to take to play for the Braves.

"I'm honestly not sure what went on with the Braves," Glavine said when it was over. "I know they had payroll issues; I get that. I wasn't one hundred percent sure they wanted me back. Maybe they weren't either. I understood that.

"Going back to the Mets is absolutely fine with me," he said. "We had a good team last year; we should have a good team this year. We've done the travel thing for four years; no reason we can't do it for five. I'm ready to go."

HOW ATHLETES PREPARE FOR THE NEXT SEASON changes as they get older, especially for pitchers. As pitchers age, their off-seasons get shorter. After the season ends, neither Glavine nor Mussina will go more than a week or two without at least working out.

"I might put on a little bit of weight through Thanksgiving," Glavine said. "But the cookies and the desserts start to go away in December, and once New Year's comes around, I'm done with them."

In today's world, most professional athletes never really get out of shape. The days when baseball players reported to spring training twenty-five pounds overweight and spent February and March getting into playing shape are long gone.

Both Glavine and Mussina have workout facilities in their homes. Glavine has lived at the Country Club of the South, a posh, gated community, since the early 1990s. He and Chris spent the 2007 season building a new home a few doors down from their old one. The new house, at fifteen thousand square feet, will be slightly smaller than the old one. In the basement of his old house, Glavine had all the workout equipment he needed. He begins a daily workout regimen within a week of the season ending and starts to throw shortly after New Year's.

"When I was younger I would take a longer break after the season ended," he said. "But as I got older, I found that even taking a few weeks off made it hard to start working out again. I was just so sore and it hurt so much I figured I'd be better off not taking that break and not being as sore."

Four mornings a week, after taking the kids to school, Glavine works out with Frank Fultz, the Braves' longtime strength coach. They work for about an hour each day, doing different exercises to work on different parts of the body. The first two months of the off-season are devoted mostly to exercises that build strength—heavier weights, fewer reps. After New Year's, the weights are lighter, and the exercises are designed to stretch out muscles and get them loose and ready for pitching. The one part of Glavine's workout routine that has changed radically in the past few years is the amount of work he does on his rotator cuff. Once, he did exercises to strengthen that part of his shoulder on a daily basis, even during the season. Now, he does it just two days a week.

"Basically, it was something [Mets assistant trainer] Mike Herbst suggested," Glavine said. "He said there's a point where you do so much in that area—especially when you're a little older—that you're tearing down muscle rather than building it up. I tried cutting back to a couple days a week, and I've felt much stronger ever since."

Glavine's winter preparation is almost scientific and goes according to the calendar. Just as he gives up eating sweets and fast foods after Christmas, he begins throwing a baseball.

"Obviously you start out throwing very lightly," he said. "You're just playing catch, and the first few days you don't throw for very long; you don't throw for much distance; and you certainly don't throw hard. How quickly you build up really depends on how the arm and the shoulder feel."

A pitcher protects his throwing arm and shoulder the way the Secret Service protects the president. "If I pull open a refrigerator that's stuck a little during the off-season, I'm apt to feel something in my shoulder," Glavine said. "I understand that's from not using it for a while. But if I feel any pain at all, I'll ice it."

One of the more remarkable aspects of Glavine's career is how resilient his arm has always been. He has never been on the disabled list and has only missed one start in his career because of anything arm related: he had a bone spur in his elbow that forced him to miss a start in June 2003.

"One reason I didn't get panicked about getting to three hundred when I struggled my first couple of years with the Mets was that people have always told me, 'Hey, you can pitch until you're forty-five,' because of the way I pitch—not throwing that hard and not putting that much pressure on my arm with my motion," he said. "Sometimes, early in the season, I actually feel too strong. When I'm a little tired, like a lot of pitchers, I tend to pitch better because there's more natural sink on the ball when I throw."

As healthy as he had been throughout his career, Glavine was amazed by how good he felt during the 2006–07 off-season. Even the normal misery of building up his early workouts wasn't as pronounced as it usually was. When he began to throw, there was little of the soreness he had come to expect.

"I can't really explain it," he said, sitting in his kitchen one morning sipping coffee after a workout. "It's always a little different every winter, but this year has just been easier than the past few years. Maybe my arm is a little looser because I pitched into October. I'm certainly not going to complain, but I'm also going to be careful not to push too hard too soon just because I feel good."

Glavine spends most of January working his way backward in his game of long toss. He starts out at thirty or forty feet the first few days and works back to no more than eighty feet, tossing the ball rather than throwing it. Before he actually steps onto a mound, he and Fultz stand about 120 feet apart when they throw. "I like to get to a point where I'm throwing at maybe sixty or seventy percent before I get on a mound," he said. "I'm not trying to hum the ball from a hundred twenty feet by any means or put it on a string, but I'm not just lobbing it either."

By the end of January, Glavine is on a mound. There is an indoor baseball training facility with both batting cages and mounds, run by Mussina's old minor league roommate Jim Poole, a few miles from Glavine's house, and he and Fultz drive there and Glavine gets on the mound at least five times before he heads to Florida in mid-February. Those sessions are very much like the bullpen sessions he throws between starts during the season: about forty pitches at first—one day from the windup, the next from the stretch. He starts out building up his fastball but throws all his pitches and might get up to 90 percent the last few times on the mound. The final session or two can go as long as sixty pitches, depending on how his arm feels.

"It's funny, though; no matter how well your throwing sessions go at home, it all changes when you get to Florida," he said. "I'm not sure if it's being in the heat and the humidity or throwing with other guys around, but you still feel kind of sore the first couple of times you throw in Florida. I've had years where I feel great throwing in January and terrible in March. As scientific as you might try to make it, as much as you try to regiment it and point toward being ready to really pitch seriously that first week in April, there's no way of knowing for sure that what you're doing is going to work."

Glavine would turn forty-one a week before Opening Day, but he felt great physically. In his mind he was probably preparing for his last spring training.

Probably.

"If Chris had her way, I'd be retired already," he said before heading to Florida. "But she knows what I'm trying to do, and she's been great about it. I think in her mind the plan is for me to get this done and then be home next year. That's the way I'm thinking too. But if I have a great year and I can still pitch and someone wants to pay me well to keep pitching, I think I have to at least consider it."

He wasn't going to close the door on pitching for another year if he didn't have to. "One thing I don't want is some kind of farewell tour," he said. "If I say I'm definitely quitting, then I'll be getting rocking chairs everywhere I pitch on the road. That's really not for me. Plus, I don't want to be one of those guys [does the name Roger Clemens ring a bell?] who says he's retiring and then turns around and says, 'Never mind.'"

Still, he went through all his preseason rituals as if it might have been the last time.

MUSSINA, WHO TURNED THIRTY-EIGHT ON DECEMBER 8, had no such musings, although retirement was something he thought about more and more often. "I really don't want to be one of those dads who is gone until his kids are already teenagers. My kids are still young now [Brycen had turned eight in September and Peyton was five in January], but if I pitched four more years, Brycen would be just about a teenager by the time I got home. From everything I've heard, kids are done with you by twelve or thirteen until they're twenty. Right now, they both want to be with me. I don't want to miss out on that."

Mussina was sitting on a comfortable couch on a Saturday morning in January in the workout room of his gym as he spoke. Outside, snow was falling steadily, the norm in Montoursville on most winter days. "You can pretty much expect to have snow on the ground from Thanksgiving on around here," he said. "If it's what you're used to, it's no big deal."

Mussina starts his off-season throwing sooner than Glavine does. After Thanksgiving, he begins throwing lightly in his gym — which has a moose head at the center-court jump circle and room to seat at least a couple thousand people if needed — with his younger brother, Mark, who lives a few miles away. Like Glavine, Mussina starts throwing easily without very much on the ball and gradually builds up to the point where he is throwing at something approaching 100 percent before he heads south.

"It really is amazing how it comes and goes," he said. "It's actually like pitching itself. You'll have nights during the season where you warm up and have nothing and go to the mound and you're lights out. Then on other nights, it will be just the opposite. When I start throwing at this time of year, I really have no idea how good my arm will feel. I expect it to get stronger as I throw more, but it isn't necessarily a steady improvement."

The brothers usually begin their workouts by playing basketball, not because it helps Mussina's pitching but because they enjoy it. More often than not, they play shooting games — horse, pig — rather than all-out ball. Mussina loves basketball enough that he spent several winters coaching the junior varsity team at Montoursville High School. He is always keenly aware of how good Stanford's basketball team is each winter. Once the shooting contests are over, Mussina will loosen up, gradually moving backward and picking up the pace of his throwing.

Until you have stood very close to a major league pitcher

throwing a baseball, it is difficult to comprehend exactly how hard they throw. When a scoreboard shows that a fastball has been thrown to a hitter at 90 miles per hour and you are watching from the stands, it hardly seems like a big deal. But when you stand a few feet away from someone who is throwing at 80 miles per hour—and not trying all that hard to do it—and hear the *whoosh* of the ball as it goes past, you have a clearer understanding of why the very best hitters are fortunate to get a hit three times out of ten.

On this winter morning, Mussina stood at one end of the basketball court while Mark crouched at the other end. They were about eighty feet apart, and Mussina was uncoiling from his tight, compact windup and effortlessly throwing the ball, as if on a string, to his brother time after time.

"This is about as good as I've felt all winter," he said at one point. "I could pitch in a game today."

He threw about forty-five pitches to Mark, then sat down to relax, breathing only a little bit harder than usual. A few minutes later his father arrived, bringing with him a friend whose son was a high school senior—and a pitcher. Mussina had agreed to spend some time with the father and son.

He spent several minutes throwing with the young pitcher— acting as his catcher. "Is your arm okay to throw a breaking pitch?" he asked. Eagerly, the youngster threw several breaking pitches. Then, Mussina spent forty-five minutes talking pitching—what to do, what not to do, how to protect his arm. He asked the young pitcher what his plans were for the next fall.

Mussina was completely unhurried, answering questions, showing father and son the kind of weight work he did. When they had left he said, "The kid is doing the right thing" going to a Division 2 college.

He could tell that from fifteen pitches?

"I could tell from five. He's got a decent arm; I like his attitude."

He smiled. "I'm a month away from my seventeenth major league training camp. I *should* know something about pitching by now."

Outside, the snow fell harder. Mussina was in no rush to get to that seventeenth training camp. Clearly, though, he was ready for it.

9

The Rites of Spring

"PITCHERS AND CATCHERS REPORT." It is one of those sports phrases that true baseball fans understand has magical qualities. That is the day each year that baseball fans look forward to because it is so full of symbolic meaning. It signals the return of baseball and the approaching end of winter. Exhibition games will soon be played in Florida and in Arizona, and later real games will begin. There will be standings to peruse, box scores to examine, and that day's probable pitchers to speculate about.

But why exactly do pitchers and catchers report before the rest of the team?

"It's simple," Mike Mussina explains. "Spring training is forty-five days long because of five guys—the starting pitchers on every team. We need the full forty-five days to get our arms to the point where we can pitch five, six, seven innings once the season starts. Everyone else needs three weeks, four weeks max. But we need that extra time."

The pitchers need someone to throw to when they arrive. That's why the catchers are also asked to show up early.

The first few days of spring training before—as the pitchers call them—"the players" arrive is little more than a bunch of guys playing catch. Fans will turn up to watch, partly because it is spring training, but also because, traditionally, they can get closer to the players during spring than during the regular season.

Sadly, this isn't nearly as true as it once was. Players are more likely to stop and sign autographs during spring because they have more time, but the days when fans could surround players walking in and out of their training facilities are long gone. All the new spring-training ballparks were built with added security in mind. Players park inside a fence and have the option of not getting anywhere near the waiting fans if they don't want to do so.

These days pitchers are expected to be ready to throw off a mound when they arrive in training camp. Mussina and Glavine are typical of most pitchers, especially veterans, in that they have spent anywhere from six to ten weeks getting their arms ready to throw regularly off a mound. What's different in spring training is that every pitch thrown is monitored and recorded; time on the mound is noted; and there is a very specific schedule to be followed. There's no pushing back the start of the day to take kids to school or to play a game of horse.

"In a lot of ways, the last few days before we go to Florida are bittersweet for me," Glavine said a few days prior to his February 14 departure for the Mets camp in Port St. Lucie, Florida. "Part of me is excited about getting down there, seeing the guys, getting ready to start another season. But there's another part of me that's going to miss taking the kids to school, being there when they come home, and having free time to pretty much do whatever I want.

"The worst day of the year for me, without fail, every year is the first Monday of spring training: Chris and the kids always fly down with me, spend a long weekend, and then leave first thing Monday morning so the kids can get back to school. That morning really sucks because it hits me that I'm only going to see them on weekends for most of the next six weeks."

Mussina's feelings are similar. His boys are younger — Peyton was not yet in school in 2007, and Brycen, because he's a smart kid, had flexibility to miss some school time — but they were still in and out during the spring. "The good news is they have a really good time when they're here," he said. "The bad news is I miss them when they have to go back north."

There is no doubt about the best part of spring training: seeing the guys. Any retired athlete you talk to will instantly tell you that what he misses most about his playing days are the guys. It isn't just the camaraderie of a clubhouse—baseball locker rooms are never called locker rooms, they are called clubhouses, which is instructive if you think about the meaning of the word *club*—it is the notion of having a place, of being a part of a very exclusive club that most boys grow up dreaming of being in at some stage of their lives.

"I'm pretty sure the thing I'll miss most is having a locker," Mussina said. "That's *your* place, no one else's, and having it isn't just a practical thing—a place to put your stuff—it's a symbolic thing. It means you belong inside that clubhouse. My boys love being able to walk in and hang out around my locker after a game. When I'm retired, I know I'll be welcome to come in; I know there will be times I can bring the kids. But it won't be the same. It can't be. I'll be an outsider; I won't have a place anymore."

Glavine feels the same way. "It's very tough to explain to someone who has never been on the inside what that feels like," he said. "The clubhouse is open to outsiders a lot. You've got media in there and other people who come through for different reasons. But there are times when it's just the guys, when you say and do things that you wouldn't say or do anyplace else. It's nothing terrible or bad; it's just being able to revert to being a kid, playing practical jokes, giving each other a hard time." He smiled. "It's a way to feel young, even when you aren't young anymore."

Of course that place in the clubhouse has to be earned. On the first day that an entire team reports to spring training—usually about five days after pitchers and catchers—the clubhouse feels overrun. Most teams invite between sixty and seventy players to spring training. Usually, no more than thirty—sometimes fewer—have a realistic chance to make the big league roster.

"You walk in there on the first day, and you see faces you absolutely don't recognize, people you don't know, and, in many cases, people you'll never know," Mussina said. "If someone walks up and introduces himself, that's certainly fine with me, but I'm not going to go around introducing myself to people I'm pretty sure I'll never play with except maybe in a spring-training game."

On the first day that the entire team is in camp, the manager will hold a meeting before the first workout. Many of the players in the room are new: youngsters in their first big league camp; players acquired by trade or free agency; older players who have signed a minor league contract hoping to make a team. As a result, the manager will introduce the entire staff: coaches, minor league instructors working in camp, doctors, training staff, public relations staff. There will be warnings about staying out of trouble, and a curfew—usually 1 a.m.—will be announced though it is never enforced.

"It's there more in case someone gets in trouble," Glavine said. "If a guy gets stopped by a cop at three o'clock in the morning, well, he's violated curfew, so the manager can suspend him or fine him regardless of what happens with the police. It's just a way of reminding guys that they're public figures, and they should try to stay out of trouble."

One thing that takes up some time is the introduction of the public relations staff. Playing baseball in New York isn't like playing baseball anyplace else. There is more media in New York than in any other city in the country, and the pressure on players to perform and to make themselves available to the media there is higher than elsewhere.

Jay Horwitz has been the Mets' public relations director for twenty-eight years. He has outlasted eight managers and seven general managers and has survived dealing with charmers like Vince Coleman, Jeff Kent, and Eddie Murray, among others. When he talks to the players, his warnings to be careful about what they say are infused with humor, but at the same time he reminds them that part of their job is dealing with the media.

If there's a tougher job in baseball than Horwitz's, it is that of the Yankees' public relations director. In 2007, that job fell to Jason Zillo, who succeeded Rick Cerrone during the winter. Zillo had been with the team for eleven years, but this was his first year in charge. As much coverage as the Mets get, the Yankees get more. In addition to all those who cover the team for local and national media outlets, the Yankees have a regular coterie of Japanese media who follow Hideki Matsui. The signing of Kei Igawa only increased the Japanese media presence.

Zillo's job is challenging because of the number of people he deals with, but also because the Yankees are a powder keg. Any four-game losing streak can lead to speculation about the immediate future of the manager, the general manager, and the high-priced stars. In addition to giving the usual talk about dealing with the media, Zillo shows the players a film that is best described as "how to deal with the media, and, more important, how *not* to deal with the media." It shows a number of instances when athletes have made themselves look foolish by blowing up on camera. Example one in 2007 was Randy Johnson's first encounter with the New York media in 2005.

Once the first meeting is over, the rituals begin. Players are expected on the field at a specific time to begin their stretching, and then at appointed times they move on to drills. Pitchers report to specified locations to play catch (usually with another pitcher during spring) or to throw off a mound or to work on pitcher's fielding practice, or PFP.

On the morning that Yankee pitchers and catchers first reported, Mussina went through his drills, threw off a mound for eight minutes, iced his arm, and got something to eat. It then took him about another ten minutes to become embroiled in the Yankees' first controversy of the spring.

Mussina was not, by any stretch of the imagination, the only

Yankee who had become extremely skeptical about Carl Pavano. In fact, manager Joe Torre, who rarely said anything even a little bit negative about a player in public, had made the comment during the winter that Pavano was going to have to "earn back the confidence of the clubhouse." In other words, Pavano hadn't performed for two years; there had been serious questions raised about how he had handled his injury problems; and until he got himself healthy and performed, the other players would continue to have doubts about him.

Asking Pavano how he felt about having to prove himself to his teammates seemed a logical first-day-of-camp story to a lot of media members. When Pavano finished his drills and came inside to his locker, a number of people asked him how he felt about it all.

"That's just the media saying those things," Pavano answered, taking the age-old, "it's the media's fault" route. "I'm not worried about it. I don't think I have to prove anything to my teammates."

Actually, the media hadn't said those things; his manager had. Among others.

Pavano's locker inside the clubhouse at Legends Field in Tampa is no more than ten feet from Mussina's, which is in a corner — giving him a little extra room in a crowded place — to the left of the front door. As soon as Pavano was finished blaming the media for his troubles, several writers made a beeline for Mussina.

This made sense for several reasons: Mussina is now considered a go-to guy by the Yankees media. He's smart and honest and isn't likely to duck a question. What's more, many of the reporters knew how Mussina felt about Pavano. When they repeated Pavano's comments, Mussina was genuinely stunned.

"He said that? Really? He really said that?" was his opening response. He then went on to say in blunt terms that Pavano was in for a big surprise if he thought he did not have a problem with his teammates. "What Joe said is completely true," he said. "The guy has a lot to prove. This has nothing to do with you guys."

It is worth remembering that this was mid-February. The Super Bowl was over; college basketball had not yet reached March Madness, and this was day one of spring training. Mike Mussina blasting a fellow Yankee pitcher would be news any time of year, but in mid-February it was *big* news.

"I really didn't think it would make the back pages," he said later with a wry smile. "Guess I was wrong."

He found out he was wrong when he walked into the club-house the next day and was shown several newspaper headlines. He hadn't just made the tabloid back pages, he had been the lead story in the sports section of the *New York Times*. Mussina wasn't happy about it, but he wasn't upset either. He'd known he was going to be quoted, and he knew Pavano would see what he said and that was fine with him.

Shortly after he returned to the clubhouse from his morning drills, Mussina was approached by Jason Zillo. "Pav wants to know if you're willing to talk to him about this," Zillo said.

"Sure, why not?" Mussina said, looking over at Pavano's locker, which was empty at the moment. "Why doesn't he just ask me himself."

"He's nervous about it," Zillo said. "He's afraid you won't talk to him."

"Of course I'll talk to him," Mussina said. "Where is he right now?"

"He's waiting for you in Rob Cucuzza's office," Zillo said. Cucuzza is the Yankees' equipment manager.

Mussina walked out of the locker area of the clubhouse, down a short hallway, and found Pavano waiting for him.

"Were you quoted accurately in the papers today?" Pavano asked.

"Absolutely," Mussina said.

Pavano was upset, not so much with Mussina, but with the situation. He told Mussina how much he respected him and how much it bothered him that Mussina felt the way he did. Mussina said he appreciated that and that he would try to help Pavano in any way possible.

"Do you think I need to address the team about this?" he asked Mussina.

Mussina shook his head. "No. There's nothing for you to say to anyone. You just have to get on the mound and pitch. Talking isn't the answer now; going out and pitching is."

Pavano nodded, and the two men shook hands. They then told the media, who had first seen Pavano and then Mussina walk down the hallway and were awaiting their return, that all was well.

"We had a good talk," Mussina said.

What he didn't say was what he had said to Pavano: talking at this point was meaningless.

THE FIRST REAL TEST for a pitcher in spring training comes when he throws batting practice. Starting pitchers will throw off a mound every other day when they first get to camp. In Port St. Lucie, Glavine threw thirty pitches his first day on the mound, forty-five his second day, and forty-five his third. That got him to Thursday, February 21, when he would throw batting practice for the first time. The Yankees' sessions are done strictly on time: Mussina threw for eight minutes the first day, ten the second, and twelve the third. His new catch partner for the spring was Andy Pettitte, the veteran lefty who had come back to the team after three years in Houston.

"Until the games start, we're pretty much on the same schedule, so it makes sense for us to be catch partners," Mussina said. "Once the games start, I'll probably have to find someone else since we'll be on different schedules."

Pitchers hate throwing batting practice. Years ago pitchers actually threw batting practice on their off-days during the season. Now, teams have batting-practice pitchers—frequently they are coaches—and pitchers never throw BP during the season.

"I remember guys did it on their throw days," Joe Torre said. "It was a way of getting in your bullpen session while also having someone who could throw BP for you. But no one really liked it. The hitters didn't like it if pitchers wanted to throw breaking pitches, and the pitchers always hated the screen."

The "screen" is, quite simply, a screen set up in front of the mound during BP so whomever is pitching doesn't have to worry about getting hit by a screaming line drive hit back through the box off an 80-mile-an-hour batting-practice fastball. Pitchers despise throwing from behind the screen.

"Part of it is just vision," Glavine said. "You really can't see the corners of the plate from behind it, particularly for me the outside corner against a right-handed hitter. You have to remind yourself that it's okay to follow through, that the screen isn't going to impede you because it looks like it will. It's just one of those spring-training things you have to get through."

The biggest difference for a pitcher throwing BP — other than the screen — as opposed to a bullpen session is obvious: there's a hitter in the batter's box. Hitters aren't crazy about taking BP from pitchers trying to find their spring form. It isn't like in-season batting practice when the pitcher is lobbing the ball up there to be hit.

"The hitter is trying to do his job; you're trying to do yours — so it's different," Mussina said. "But that's not a bad thing. It gives both of you an idea of how well you're doing."

Before their batting-practice sessions, the pitchers will warm up in the bullpen, almost the way they would before a game. "You don't go as long," Glavine said. "Probably no more than five or six minutes. As soon as you feel loose, you stop. You have to remember that it's still early, and there's no need to push yourself."

When a pitcher steps onto the mound to throw his first spring BP session, it is the first time he has faced a hitter since October. There is always an adrenaline rush, even though there is no umpire, no count, no scoreboard, and no reason to be concerned if the hitter takes a ball deep.

"It's interesting because, on the one hand, especially after doing it for so many years, it really doesn't mean a thing," Glavine said. "In truth, you don't *want* to throw all that well because it's February, and there isn't much point in wasting any nasty pitches in February. But there are people watching, and whenever that's the case, you don't want to embarrass yourself by throwing the ball all over the place or getting the ball hit five hundred feet by someone."

The top Yankee pitchers — all those on the forty-man major league roster — throw their batting-practice sessions from the mound inside Legends Stadium. There are always several hundred fans watching, and the media gawks as if the Yankees and Red Sox are playing in September.

The Mets' camp is more casual. The Mets do all of their pre–exhibition season work on the back fields around the facility at Port St. Lucie, allowing fans to wander from one field to another to watch different players do different drills. Still, there is a little bit of a buzz when one of the big names trots out to begin a BP session.

Most veteran pitchers will throw BP twice — no more than three times — before their first exhibition-game start. Mussina isn't as bothered by throwing BP as Glavine, and, since he wasn't pitching until the Yankees' third exhibition game, he and pitching coach Ron Guidry decided he would throw BP three times. Glavine, who was starting the second exhibition game for the Mets, two days earlier than Mussina's start, would only throw BP twice.

"Thank God," he said. "When I retire, I want to take one of those BP screens home with me and do a ritual burning."

Glavine was scheduled to throw thirty pitches in his first session, forty-five in his second. He wasn't all that pleased with either of his BP sessions, but that was par for the course. During his second session, when he was trying to throw his breaking pitches, he kept stopping to ask the hitter and the catcher where the pitch had been.

"Was that okay?" he kept repeating. "Where was that?"

"I just couldn't see," he said later. "That's the screen. At this point in my career, I have a pretty good feel for whether or not I've thrown a strike when I release the ball. This time of year, though, you aren't so sure, so if you can't see you ask."

Glavine threw forty-eight pitches in his second session, wanting to throw a few extra pitches from the stretch. He worked first with a runner on first base, then with a runner on second, working on his pickoff move—not actually throwing over but spinning as if to do so—between pitches. After he left the mound, his spot was taken by Philip Humber, a twenty-four-year-old right-hander who had been the third overall pick in the 2004 draft. Humber was six-foot-four and 225 pounds, and, even though he'd undergone elbow surgery in 2005, his fastball was at least ten miles an hour faster than Glavine's.

"You don't need a radar gun to see he's throwing a little harder than I did," Glavine said, laughing. "Fortunately for me, there's more to this game than throwing hard."

He was clearly relieved to have both his BP sessions behind him. He would throw in the bullpen once, perhaps twice, before starting against the St. Louis Cardinals in five days.

As he went through the spring rituals, it occurred to Glavine every so often that he might be doing things he had been doing all his adult life for the last time.

"I thought about it this morning, getting dressed," he said. "If that *was* my last BP session, all I can say is good riddance."

He went off to do his running. Chris and the boys were down for the weekend, and the rest of the day was his. It was 10:30 in the morning.

"THAT'S THE IRONY OF SPRING TRAINING," Mike Mussina said, sitting in his house shortly after noon on the day he threw his second BP session. "It's forty-five days long, basically to accommodate five guys—maybe six or seven if you aren't certain about your rotation—and we spend less time at the ballpark than anyone."

Pitchers do three things on a typical spring-training day: stretch, throw—either catch, in the bullpen, or BP—and run. Then they're done for the day. Occasionally on a day when they aren't scheduled to throw, they will take PFP, something that Glavine and Mussina take very seriously. They are both good athletes and two of the best fielding pitchers in the game. Mussina has won six Gold Glove Awards as the best fielding pitcher in the American League during his career. Glavine has won none, but that's only because he's pitched in the National League at the same time as Greg Maddux, who many consider the best fielding pitcher of all time. In 2007, Maddux would win his seventeenth Gold Glove.

"To be honest, I think I deserved to win it at least once," Glavine says, when the subject of Gold Gloves comes up. "Don't get me wrong, Greg's a great fielder, and he always has more assists than I do because he's more of a ground-ball pitcher than I am. But I think what happens with that award is that once a guy wins it more than once, it's almost automatic that he keeps winning it. It's a little bit frustrating to me that I never did win one."

Glavine *has* won the Silver Slugger Award as the best hitting pitcher in the National League four times, something he is almost as proud of as his two Cy Young's. He has never been an automatic out at the plate and works hard on both his hitting and his bunting. When he was in Atlanta he, Smoltz, and Maddux were always extremely competitive about their hitting.

"Especially Smoltzie," he remembered. "That was always the nature of the relationship. That's not to say Doggy [Maddux] wasn't competitive. Among the three of us, he was the one most likely to take a bat up the tunnel and bash it all over the place if he thought he'd screwed up on the mound."

Glavine believes that being proficient at the plate can be worth a minimum of two wins a year to a National League pitcher.

What's more, he enjoys hitting. He always hit third when he was in high school and has hit as high as .274 for an entire season in the majors. Four times in his career he has been used as a pinch hitter. In 1995 he hit his first and only career home run off of Pittsburgh's John Smiley, who at the time was one of the better pitchers in baseball.

"I remember that I hit to the opposite field, which is pretty amazing in itself," he said. "And I remember running around the bases pretty fast. The last thing I wanted to do was show Smiley up by cruising because I know just how I would have felt if I had been him in that situation."

Beyond that, Glavine has more sacrifice bunts — 216 — than any other pitcher in major league history. In an era when bunting has become a lost art, when some pitchers look as if they don't know which end of the bat to hold when asked to bunt, he almost never fails to get a bunt down when asked.

"It amazes me during spring to watch young guys in bunting drills clearly not trying and not paying attention," he said. "Every once in a while I'll say something to one of them because it's pretty clear to me they don't understand how helpful it can be to you to be a good bunter.

"If we're late in a game and I have to come out for a pinch hitter, fine, I can live with that. But if we were ever in a situation where I'm coming up and a bunt was called for and they didn't think I could get it down, I would be furious with myself. I still get angry with myself if I don't get one down. Through my career, being able to bunt has probably been worth at least one extra win a year to me."

That's why, unlike a lot of young pitchers, he takes PFP and pitchers' BP seriously. When the subject of young pitchers and hitting comes up, Glavine sighs and shakes his head before saying anything.

"My guess is if you go back a hundred years in baseball and ask any veteran then about younger players, he'll shake his head and say, 'These young guys just don't get it.' That's the nature of the game; it's the nature of life. But the game *has* changed a lot since I first came up, and a lot of it has not been for the good.

"Some of it is money—that's always changing things. When I first got called up to the Braves in 1987, I got a huge raise because I was making a [prorated] salary of $62,000. Back then, that was a lot of money, especially for a twenty-one-year-old. The next year, my first full year, I got bumped to $65,000. Still good money. But now, even if you put aside the huge bonuses kids sign for—well into the millions—the minimum salary they make in the big leagues is $320,000. I'm all for that; I fought for it all those years with the union. But having that kind of money does change your attitude, especially when you're young, and, in a lot of cases, immature.

"Sometimes when pitchers take BP, there's a lot of joking around and giving each other a hard time. I'm all for that; I enjoy it as much as anyone. But it's like with anything else—there comes a time when you have to go to work. When I get in the cage, that's work time. It isn't as if you're being asked to carry cement around; you're being asked to swing a bat or put down a few bunts for five or ten minutes. That's not exactly heavy lifting. But there are guys who just won't concentrate. They think their job is to just throw the ball. It's not, especially in our league."

It is different in the American League. Because of the designated-hitter rule, American League pitchers hit only during interleague play—fifteen games—and during the World Series. In spring training, those games are so far away that there is no pitchers' BP, even though a pitcher might get up once or twice when playing in a National League park.

Early in spring training 2007, the Yankees made the trip down I-4 to play the Braves in Orlando. Mussina, making his second start of the spring, came up in the third inning against the Braves' Tim Hudson and hit a fly ball fairly deep to right field. As he trotted off the field, he went past Hudson and said thanks. Hudson had thrown him an 85-mile-an-hour fastball right down the middle to make sure he didn't make Mussina look bad. An inning later, Mussina returned the favor.

"We'll take some BP a week or so before we play interleague," Mussina said. "Tom's right. A lot of guys don't take it seriously. Obviously, it isn't nearly as big a deal for us. I mean for me, I might get to hit ten or twelve times during a season, maximum. But if two of those times are crucial—if I need to get a bunt down or if I come up with two outs and the bases loaded—I like to feel I have a chance to be competitive at the plate."

Mussina bats lefty and was a decent hitter in high school, though not as good as Glavine. He learned to hit lefty at the age of eleven because he thought it gave him an edge since most pitchers are right-handed. "Just gives me a better shot to hit someone's breaking ball," he said. "In a real game, a guy isn't likely to just throw you a batting-practice fastball. They need to get you out."

Both men take spring training seriously. "One of the things you don't want to fall into during spring is the idea that you're down here on vacation," Mussina continued. "It can happen. It isn't like football where guys are pounding on each other in practice every day during preseason. It is more relaxed than that. But you are here to work. There are certain things you need to get done every day so that when April comes, you're ready to go. It isn't like we have to be at the ballpark all that long every day. You're up early, and you're done early."

Before exhibition games begin, spring training is very much a rite of morning. Mussina is usually out of his house by no later than 7:45, and on weekdays he will take back roads to get from his house to Legends Field. "If I go straight down Dale Mabry [the main road near his house] with lights and traffic on a weekday, it will take me at least forty-five minutes and some days more than that. So I go back roads, and it's twenty-five minutes. On a weekend, I can go straight down Dale Mabry, and it's about twenty minutes."

Both the Yankees and the Mets have chefs who will prepare just about anything the players want to eat. Mussina is a Froot Loops and juice guy most mornings—he's not a coffee drinker—and then will spend some time in the weight room before going into the clubhouse to deal with any media types who want to talk to him before workouts begin.

Glavine is a coffee drinker. He will usually have a cup at home and may make a Starbucks stop en route to Tradition Field, the new name of the Mets' ballpark in Port St. Lucie. His commute from the house he rents is a little shorter than Mussina's, although he is just as apt to hit traffic on weekdays. He also eats when he arrives, sometimes cereal, sometimes—"when I'm in a mood to try to be healthy"—egg whites.

Until the games start, a pitcher's day is always over before noon, even with a leisurely shower, getting another bite to eat, and dealing with postworkout media. Glavine, the avid golfer, will often have a tee time to get to when his day is done at the ballpark. Mussina rarely plays golf, and when his family isn't down he is often content to go back to the cool air-conditioning of his house to read or watch TV.

The longest hours during spring training are put in by the manager and the coaches. They arrive earlier in the morning than the players in order to be sure they have their assignments straight for the day and to go over points of emphasis and review how they think players are progressing. The managers also have to deal with the media, which for New York teams is no small task.

For all intents and purposes, Joe Torre wrote the book on how to handle the media. During the spring he actually does two sessions each day because his office simply isn't big enough to accommodate all the print and radio and TV people who want to talk to him at the same time. As a result, he will do one session with print and radio and then a separate one with TV.

Additionally, there are always people who need extra time once the formal session is over—a question here, five minutes there, do you have any time early tomorrow? Torre almost never says no. If he does say no on a given day, it is always with the promise that he will do it the next day or the day after. If someone insists they are fighting a deadline, he'll figure out a way to answer a question or two. No question seems to bother him, even when he's asked about his job security, which during 2007 was an almost-constant topic.

"I guess at this point in my life [Torre turned sixty-seven in July of '07], the good news is I can stop mid-anecdote and pick up again where I left off without any trouble," he said one morning, sitting in the empty dugout while his players stretched. "Everyone talks about pressure here. Pressure to me is having a team you don't think can compete. We always have a team that can compete. I get paid very well [$7 million a year] to do something I really enjoy doing. I really don't have a lot to complain about."

Torre has the luxury of having won four World Series and six pennants as the manager of the Yankees. He knows that whenever he stops managing, his place in the Hall of Fame is now assured. As a player he was a borderline Hall of Famer. In eighteen big league seasons, he hit .297, with 2,342 hits, 252 home runs, and 1,185 RBI—numbers that aren't quite worthy of the Hall of Fame but aren't that far off. If you add his managerial record, there's no doubt he belongs in the Hall.

Willie Randolph, Torre's Mets counterpart, has a total of six World Series rings—two he won as a player with the Yankees in 1977 and 1978, and four he won as one of Torre's coaches between 1994 and 2004. Randolph was also an excellent player—he had 2,210 career hits in his eighteen big league seasons and was a very good second baseman. It took him a while to get a shot to manage. For a number of years he was interviewed frequently, never hired. Often he felt as if he were being interviewed so that a team could claim it had at least considered an African American for the job.

"It did get frustrating after a while," he said. "I thought I was ready to manage and that I would do well, given a chance. It took a long time for me to get a chance."

His chance finally came when the Mets fired Art Howe in October 2004 after two disastrous seasons in New York. Randolph, the kid who had grown up in Brooklyn, had played most of his career with the Yankees but had played for the Mets in 1992, his last big league season. The Mets couldn't help thinking that Randolph's New York background, combined with his experience in the Yankee organization, would be a good thing.

They were right. Like Torre, Randolph doesn't often show a lot of emotion during games—one of the complaints about him among fans during his first season was that he hadn't been thrown out of a game—but he is extremely intense. He was also well organized and ran a training camp that had little wasted motion and produced a team that played much more fundamentally sound baseball than Howe's teams had. The Mets were 83–79 in 2005 and then ran away with the National League East title in 2006, with ninety-seven victories.

Although Randolph, who was fifty-two at the start of the 2007 season, still referred to himself as a "young manager," he was also an established manager, having put his imprint on what was now a winning team that began the season with high expectations.

"I think after last year, it's not unreasonable for us to say that our goal is to be in the World Series this year," Glavine said one afternoon in early March. "A lot of things can happen, especially with injuries, but we know we're good enough to do big things if we stay healthy and play up to our potential."

The biggest question mark in the Mets' camp was the starting pitching. Pedro Martinez had undergone shoulder surgery in the fall and was not expected to be back before August. Orlando Hernandez ("El Duque") listed October 11, 1969, as his birth date, but there wasn't a soul in the clubhouse who believed he was under forty. Oliver Perez and John Maine had both shown potential down the stretch the previous season, but whether they could be consistent, every-fifth-day starters was a question mark. The fifth starter? It could be Mike Pelfrey, who had pitched a total of twenty-one innings in the major leagues; it could be Humber, who was probably a year away; or it could be any one of several reclamation projects in camp, including Jorge Sosa, Aaron Sele, and Chan Ho Park, who had once signed a five-year $65 million contract with the Texas Rangers. He had won a total of twenty-two games during the duration of that contract, which might explain why teams are reluctant to give pitchers five-year contracts for big money.

The only sure thing was Glavine. He would turn forty-one a week before the season began, but no one doubted that he would take the ball every fifth day and start at least thirty times and pitch at least two hundred innings before the season was over. In eighteen full seasons in the majors, he had started fewer than thirty times just twice—and in those two years he started twenty-nine times—and he had never pitched fewer than 183 innings, pitching more than two hundred innings thirteen times.

Glavine was Mr. Reliable. "If there's one thing that Tom and I have done well through the years, it's take the ball every fifth day," said Greg Maddux, who in twenty-two years has been on the disabled list once—one more time than Glavine. "You can shrug at that, but it's a bigger deal than people think, especially when pitchers get older. Look at the staff Tom's on now: who can they absolutely count on every fifth day—one guy. That tells you it isn't as easy as it looks."

Mussina has had a few more physical problems than Glavine, but his record for consistency and reliability is close to Glavine's. Through 2006 he had made five trips to the disabled list—two of them in 1998—and had started at least thirty times in eleven of fourteen complete seasons. In nine consecutive seasons, he pitched at least 200 innings—including years of 243 and 238 innings—and pitched 197 innings in 2006, even though he had a stint on the DL because of a groin injury. He had also won at least eleven games in every year of his fifteen-year big league career, an all-time record.

"You're talking about two guys who figured out how to pitch at an early age," said Detroit Tigers manager Jim Leyland. "As they've gotten older, they've adjusted with time, learned what works and what doesn't work, and adapted. The great ones are always a step ahead."

Or, as Ron Darling, who pitched for the Mets, Expos, and Athletics during an eleven-year big league career put it: "When they were young, you knew they'd have long careers because even when they had great stuff, they pitched as if they didn't. They always used their minds. When you get older, the mind stays even if the stuff doesn't."

And so, as the full squads reported and the calendar turned to March and the first exhibition games, the Mets and the Yankees were full of questions about their pitching staffs. But both knew they could rely on Glavine and Mussina to take the ball whenever asked. Because, as Maddux put it, that was what they had always done.

10

Starting Over

WHEN PITCHING COACHES PUT TOGETHER their rotation for spring training, who pitches when has nothing to do with who deserves the first start or who the opponent might be. The only factor that really matters is when a pitcher is supposed to make his first regular-season start.

"Basically you take that day and count backward," Glavine explained. "You might tweak it a little bit because of travel, but that's about the only way it might change."

Veterans usually do not like to make long trips in spring training. So, if the Mets, who train on the east coast of Florida, were scheduled to play on the Sunshine State's west coast on a day that Glavine was supposed to pitch, they might move him back a day or they might put him in a split-squad game. (Some days, teams play two games; when that occurs a starting pitcher will almost always pitch the game at home.)

Glavine's first regular-season start in 2007 was scheduled for opening night in St. Louis. The Mets and Cardinals were officially opening the season on Sunday night, April 1.

Once Major League Baseball began its season on the first Monday in April with one game in Cincinnati—birthplace of the original professional team in 1869—and what was called "The Presidential Opener" in Washington, D.C. Time and travel and television had changed all that. There had been no baseball in

Washington for thirty-three straight opening days before 2005, and by the time it returned, baseball was opening on Sunday night to accommodate ESPN, or, on occasion, Japan. The 2008 season began in Japan with a two-game series between the Boston Red Sox and the Oakland Athletics. What could be more traditional than a 5:30 a.m. first pitch?

Glavine wasn't concerned with tradition, just getting ready for April 1. Before he had left for Florida, he had talked on the phone with Mets pitching coach Rick Peterson about his spring schedule. The only question was whether Glavine wanted his normal four days of rest before St. Louis or if he wanted an extra day to take a deep breath before beginning the season. Glavine opted for the extra day.

"One thing Rick has done the last couple of years is roll me back a day during the season when we have an off-day," he said. "I think that's helped me. At first I didn't really like it because I'm such a creature of habit, but now I think that extra day here and there helps me, especially late in the season."

Mussina was scheduled to start the Yankees' third game of the season on Thursday April 5 in New York against the Tampa Bay Devil Rays. Chien-Ming Wang, who had won nineteen games the previous year, would get the Opening Day start, followed by the prodigal son, Andy Pettitte. Then would come Mussina, Kei Igawa, and Mussina's pal, Carl Pavano. Joe Torre and pitching coach Ron Guidry liked the idea of going right-left-right-left-right, and the rotation played out in that order.

"It really doesn't matter to me whether I go first, second, third, or fourth, as long as I go," Mussina said. "I've never been the Opening Day starter here, and that's fine with me. Based on last year, Wang deserves to start first."

Mussina almost always calls Wang either "Wang" or "Wanger," even though his name is pronounced "Wong." He does it on purpose: "I want to see if anyone corrects me," he said. "I just do it for fun. I know how to say his name."

In fact, Mussina had become something of a mentor to Wang. Even though Wang didn't speak that much English, he and Mussina had figured out how to communicate. "We talk our own language," Mussina said. "It's called pitcher." Frequently, Mussina would talk to Wang about how to grip certain pitches or how to pitch in specific situations. Unlike Hideki Matsui, Wang does not speak to teammates or the media through an interpreter because he believes he will learn English faster that way.

Mussina also calls Alex Rodriguez by a name no one else on the team uses: "Rod." To everyone else he is "A-Rod" or "Alex," but to Mussina he's just "Rod."

"I think he calls me that because I'm the only one on the team who likes him," Rodriguez says, laughing.

"Or it could be the other way around," Mussina quips, which Rodriguez doesn't deny, even though Mussina laughs when he says it.

Mussina is an observer, and even though he and Rodriguez are teammates, he has spent a good deal of time observing Rodriguez in the clubhouse, on the field, and when he is dealing with the media.

"There is no question in my mind that at times, especially in postseason, he's trying too hard," Mussina said one day, early in 2007 spring training when the whole, "Will A-Rod opt out [of his contract] or won't he?" issue came up again. "One of the hardest things to learn in baseball is how not to try too hard. That's why the saying 'Try easier' exists. There are some situations where Rod needs to try easier. You can almost see him squeezing the sawdust out of the bat at certain moments.

"Think about what he walked into when he came here. He's the highest paid player in the history of baseball, so he's already got that hanging over his head, and now it's hanging over his head in New York. But that's not the hard part for him. He's immediately told he has to change positions because there can only be one man on any team, and our *man*—correctly—is Jete," known to most as Derek Jeter.

"So here's the message that goes out to Rod from day one here going forward: 'You have been the best player in baseball for the past ten years. There are some people who believe you are the best player in the history of the game. But you are no Derek Jeter.'

"Think about that for a minute. Wouldn't you be a bit confused?"

Mussina didn't think very much or very often about the so-called Jeter-Rodriguez feud. "Look, it's easy to be someone's friend when you only see them four or five times a year," he said. "When you're on the same team, you're together seven, eight months a year, almost every day, in a confined space. You see the other guy's flaws up close. In that sense, it's a little bit like being married.

"But there's also the issue of being the *man*. Like I said, there can only be one in a clubhouse, one on a team. One of them is the captain. One is the shortstop. The other one hits fifty home runs a year and may get to eight hundred before he's done. So which one is the man?

"In the eyes of the fans, it will always be Jeter, because no matter what Rod does he'll never have as many rings as Jeter. If he wins one, Jeter will have five; if he gets two, Jeter will have six. It's almost like being someone's little brother—no matter how old you get, you aren't going to catch up with your big brother. I'm not making excuses for Rod—the guy makes huge money, and people expect him to perform, especially in New York—but I can see where all of that weighs on him sometimes."

IN THE PAST TWELVE YEARS, the Yankees have again become America's baseball team, the team everyone either loves or hates. They have a larger national following than any other team (and are despised more nationally than any other team), and even their exhibition schedule in ten thousand–seat Legends Field—renamed George M. Steinbrenner Field in 2008—is sold out.

Mussina's first outing of the spring would come in the Yankees' third exhibition game, which was at home in Tampa against the Pittsburgh Pirates.

Saturday, March 3, was a chilly, windy day on the west coast of Florida. It was overcast and felt more like a day to go to a football game than to a spring-training baseball game. Mussina rolled his eyes when he saw the weather.

"First five days we were down here this spring, the temperature never got above sixty," he said. "The day the position players reported it was eighty. I actually think this is about me. Whenever I pitch in the spring, wherever I pitch, bad weather follows me: rain, wind, snow—you name it. About the only thing I haven't seen at some point is pestilence."

This is typical Mussina humor: biting and sarcastic. To the untrained ear it can sound like whining, but if you look closely you will see just the trace of a smile sneaking across his face as he's talking. Early in the season a member of Mussina's fan club—he has one that is based in Montoursville but still holds an annual get-together when the Yankees are in Baltimore—sent him a T-shirt. It said: "National Sarcasm Society...Like We Need Your Support." Mussina wore it proudly around the clubhouse.

The plan for a pitcher the first time he pitches in an exhibition game is to throw about thirty pitches, or two innings. If he throws twenty-four pitches in two innings, he will not go out for a third inning; he will go straight to the bullpen and throw a few extra pitches. If, on the other hand, he only has one out in the second inning and has thrown thirty-five pitches, he will probably come out.

"If you're at thirty-five pitches, and you've only gotten four outs, that means you're struggling to begin with," Mussina said. "It's okay to go a few pitches past thirty, but not too many, especially early in the spring and especially if the weather is cold."

Glavine, always the golfer, likes to refer to his planned pitch count as "par." In his spring debut against the Cardinals, he was three under par, pitching two hitless innings. The Cardinals' only runner came when an early-spring changeup slipped, and Glavine hit a batter. Other than that, the outing was everything you would want for the first time out.

"The hardest part about the first time you pitch in the spring is walking into the dugout after the first inning and sitting down while you're at bat," he said. "You simply haven't done that for five months — pitched, sat for a while, and then gotten up and pitched again. It doesn't sound like a big deal, but it can be, especially when you're a little older. It's easy to get stiff, especially if the weather is a little bit cooler. It's okay to do it once, but the first time you don't want to do it twice — no matter what your pitch count is."

So, at three under par, Glavine threw another dozen pitches in the bullpen and headed for a warm shower.

Mussina's first outing wasn't quite as smooth. Perhaps it was a harbinger of some kind, but when he trotted to the mound after the playing of the national anthem, there was no ball there waiting for him. Once he was able to get a ball and throw his warm-up pitches, his first at bat of the exhibition season lasted nine pitches before Pirate leadoff hitter Andrew McCutcheon, having fouled off four straight 2–2 pitches, punched a single past Derek Jeter.

"Not exactly an ideal start when you're only supposed to throw thirty pitches," Mussina said afterward. "You use up nine of them and don't even get an out."

He got an out two pitches later when catcher Jorge Posada threw out McCutcheon trying to steal second. Seven pitches later, Mussina was out of the inning, helped by a nice running catch in right field by Kevin Thompson on a slicing line drive hit by National League batting champion Freddy Sanchez. Aided by Posada, Mussina had gotten through the inning on eighteen pitches.

In an ideal world, a pitcher will average no more than fifteen pitches per inning. That would add up to 135 pitches over nine innings, but very few pitchers are around for nine innings these days, and they are almost never around for more than 120 pitches. Most pitching coaches begin to get relief pitchers warmed up when a pitcher closes in on one hundred pitches.

Mussina wasn't thinking about anything approaching one hundred pitches on the first Saturday in March. His hope was to get through the second inning with fewer pitches than he had needed in the first. He did, but not without some damage. With one out, Brad Eldred, the Pirates' young, massive (six-foot-five, 275 pounds) first baseman hit a 3–2 Mussina fastball about five miles over the left-field fence. Mussina escaped without further damage, having thrown a total of thirty-four pitches.

"Well, at the very least, my home-run pitch is in midseason form," he said, smiling, not long after leaving the game.

During spring training, when starting pitchers leave the game, they will usually speak to the media soon after. Mussina will put ice on his shoulder—he ices for twenty minutes after pitching— and take care of his media responsibilities while icing. Then he will shower and go home. Very few starting pitchers are still around at the end of an exhibition game.

"There are times, to be honest, when I don't even know the final score," Mussina said. "At this time of year, it's just not relevant."

WHAT WAS RELEVANT FOR BOTH GLAVINE AND MUSSINA was that they had come through their first outings unscathed— Eldred's home run aside. "During the spring, all you're really try- ing to do is get in your work and try to get a little sharper each time out," Mussina said. "You really don't worry about results. I had a game last year in Lakeland [against the Tigers] where I gave up ten runs. I wasn't happy about it, but it really didn't matter. What would matter is if you notice a drop in your velocity, or, as you get closer to April, if you're having trouble locating your pitches."

Glavine doesn't even worry about his velocity very much. To him, there just isn't that much difference in whether his fastball is at 86 or 82 miles an hour or someplace in between. "What's important is location and how I control my changeup," he said. "Ideally, I'd like it to be eight to ten miles an hour slower than my fastball. If I've got that going for me, I figure I'm in pretty good shape."

Both pitchers would increase their par to forty-five pitches for their second outing, assuming neither was feeling any pain after their first. "The hardest inning of the year sometimes is the second inning of the first exhibition game," Glavine said. "It's not really a big deal, but it's a test. I felt as if I came through that test in good shape."

Mussina's second outing was in Orlando, against the Braves. The biggest challenge he could see in that game was making sure he could find the ballpark. "Never been there," he said. "We don't go over there more than once a year usually, and it's never been my turn."

When veteran pitchers go on the road, they are given the option of driving rather than taking the team bus for the simple reason that there's no need for them to hang around when they're finished pitching. Mussina safely navigated his way up I-4, found the correct Disney exit, and was safely parked in the players' lot by ten o'clock.

The Braves have trained at Disney World since 1998, moving north and west from their longtime spring home in West Palm Beach, which they shared for years with the Montreal Expos. The Ballpark at Disney World is typical both of Disney—very efficiently run, sparkling clean, and expensive (ticket prices range from $14 to $22.50 for games that don't count)—and of the new spring-training facilities that have sprung up all over Florida and Arizona. Long gone are the days of rickety old parks and tiny spring-training clubhouses.

Most spring-training games are sellouts these days. Spring training has become big business. On a warm, sparkling day, Mussina was matched against Tim Hudson. Had it been a regular-season game, theirs would have been a marquee pitching matchup.

The Braves' string of Division titles had ended in 2006 when they had finished a miserable 79–83. They were hoping to prove that season had been a fluke in 2007. Already though, they had taken a serious hit: Mike Hampton, the talented, but oft-injured pitcher, had learned that he would need knee surgery.

"They're telling us two months, but I don't really believe that," Bobby Cox, who had managed the Braves since 1990, was saying before the game. "Breaks my heart. He had really looked good."

At sixty-six, Cox was nearing the end of a remarkable run as Braves manager. In 2007 he would break the all-time record for ejections as a manager, but as he sat in his office, feet up, there was never any sign of the intense Cox who sat on the bench keeping up a steady stream of commentary directed at the home-plate umpire.

"They've just made the strike zone too small," he said. "Some of it was Questech; some of it's just the way guys umpire now. Guys like Tommy [Glavine] and [Greg] Maddux really have had to adjust. I would guess that's true of Mussina too because he's that kind of pitcher now. The great ones do that, though; they make the adjustments."

He shook his head, getting nostalgic for a moment. "You know why I miss Tommy and Greg so much?" he said. "It isn't just because they were great pitchers; it's because they would do anything to help the team win. I mean anything. I remember a few years ago when John [Smoltz] got hurt; within ten minutes they were both in my office. 'Skip, if you need us to go short [on three days' rest], just say the word, we're ready.' Nowadays, if you asked a young guy to go short, the next call would be from his agent saying his client can't possibly risk his arm by doing that. Those guys would pitch with the other arm if you asked them to."

Once upon a time, pitchers routinely pitched on three days' rest. It was not uncommon to see them pitch on *two* days' rest in postseason. In the 1965 World Series, both Sandy Koufax and Jim Kaat pitched Game Seven on two days' rest. Koufax pitched a three-hit shutout and won 2–0. In 1967, Jim Lonborg pitched Game Seven for the Red Sox on two days' rest, and the next year both Denny McLain and Mickey Lolich pitched on two days' rest in Games Six and Seven for the Detroit Tigers.

"I think a lot of it has to do with what your arm and your body are conditioned to do," Glavine said. "Do I think pitchers today could go on three days' rest on a regular basis? Absolutely. Especially with all the modern training techniques we have, and," he paused to smile, "some of the extra help [that is, steroids] guys have gotten the last ten or fifteen years. But it isn't what we've been conditioned to do throughout our lives. These days kids are on pitch counts in high school, and you almost never pitch on three days' rest at any level of the game."

Pitching changed in 1969 for two reasons: following the 1968 season when Carl Yastrzemski led the American League in hitting with a .301 average and Bob Gibson pitched to an ERA of 1.12 for the St. Louis Cardinals, the mound was lowered from fifteen inches to ten inches. Run production had gone down so far in '68—which became known as "The Year of the Pitcher"—that something had to be done to level the playing field for the hitters. So, baseball literally leveled the mound, or at least lowered it so that pitchers didn't appear to be standing on Mount Everest from the batter's box.

The 1969 season was also an expansion year in baseball: the Montreal Expos and San Diego Padres joined the National League, and the Kansas City Royals and Seattle Pilots joined the American League. For the first time ever, the leagues were split into divisions—six teams in each—and there was a round of playoffs prior to the World Series, the so-called League Championship Series.

It was a whole new beginning for baseball as it celebrated its hundredth season.

But the biggest story in the game that year was the New York Mets. The Mets had been an expansion team in 1962, created to take the place of the Dodgers and Giants, who had fled New York for Los Angeles and San Francisco. The Mets were historically bad, going 40–120 their first year and losing more than one hundred games in each of their first four seasons, before finally breaking through in 1966 with a 66–95 record.

But in 1968, the Mets hired Gil Hodges as manager. They also started piecing together a remarkable young pitching staff, anchored by future Hall of Famer and three hundred–game winner Tom Seaver. By 1969 they had a rotation that included Seaver, Jerry Koosman, Gary Gentry, Nolan Ryan, and Jim McAndrew. Koosman was the elder statesman of the group at twenty-six. Wary of the fact that the youngsters were throwing off the lower mound and not wanting to risk their arms, pitching coach Rube Walker decided to put them on a five-day rotation, giving them each four days' rest between starts. When Ryan had to leave the team for a few weeks in August for military reserve duty (not at all uncommon for ballplayers in those days), Walker plugged veteran Don Cardwell into the rotation rather than trying to pitch any of the young pitchers on short rest.

The Mets went from 73–89 in 1968 to 100–62 in 1969 and caught the Chicago Cubs in early September en route to winning the first National League East title. They then swept the Atlanta Braves in the League Championship Series and stunned the heavily favored Baltimore Orioles in five games in the World Series.

Two pitchers on that staff are in the Hall of Fame—Seaver and Ryan, who became a star after the Mets foolishly traded him to the California Angels in 1971. Koosman pitched for more than twenty years. Among the youngsters, only Gentry and McAndrew did not become great pitchers.

Sports is like anything else: people copy success. Walker's model, the five-man rotation, soon became the norm in baseball. These days, no team would even consider a four-man rotation for any extended period of time.

Glavine and Mussina have each pitched on three days' rest a handful of times in their careers. It is so unusual that each time it has happened it has been noted in the bios provided in their teams' media guides. Glavine actually did it twice in 2003, which in this day and age is almost historic.

Joe Torre, who came up to the majors as a catcher, can still remember Birdie Tebbetts starting for the Braves twice on two days' rest in the 1957 World Series, a team his older brother Frank Torre played on.

"We've conditioned pitchers—and all players really—differently. Guys don't go to the mound thinking about a complete game anymore; they go out thinking they want to get to the seventh inning. The silliest stat in baseball history may be the 'quality start.' You pitch six innings and give up three runs and that's considered a quality start. If you do that over an entire year, that's an ERA of 4.50. When I played, if you had an ERA of 4.50 you got sent down. Now, you've had quality starts.

"It's not just pitchers, though; it's every position. Now we've got coaches who position the infielders and the outfielders on every play. What does that do? It ensures the players aren't thinking on their own out there. You've got exceptions—Jeter's certainly one—but most guys are constantly looking into the dugout for someone to tell them what to do. What's the thing guys do worst? Run the bases. Why? Because they can't look into the dugout for instructions. Sure, they can look at a coach, but for the most part you're on your own and you have to react instantly.

"What's changed the most by far, though, is the pitching. I think Bob Gibson had thirty complete games or something like that [actually twenty-eight in thirty-four starts] in 1968. What's the stat on Cy Young? He won five hundred eleven games, and four sixty-nine were complete games. Okay, that's a long time ago, but even in the '70s and '80s you basically had one guy in the bullpen you depended on. Guys like [Goose] Gossage and [Bruce] Sutter and [Sparky] Lyle routinely pitched two and three innings to get a save. Now you've got a seventh-inning guy, a set-up guy, and a closer. Your starter gives you six good innings, he's done his job.

"I remember when Roger [Clemens] got his three hundredth win a few years ago. We knew, he knew that when he got it, he was going to be sitting in the dugout watching Mariano [Rivera] close it for him. The same will be true of Glavine this year, unless something crazy happens. His job—almost every starter's job—is to get to the seventh inning. Period."

The story that backs Torre up better than any other dates to 1985 when Seaver was trying to win his three hundredth game in Yankee Stadium, pitching for the Chicago White Sox. It was a hot August day, and Seaver carried a 4–1 lead into the eighth inning. With two out, Seaver put men on second and third. Dave Winfield, then very much in his prime, walked to the plate.

Carlton Fisk, another Hall of Famer, was catching. He called time and trotted to the mound to talk to Seaver.

"How you feeling?" he asked Seaver, who was forty.

"Gassed," Seaver said. "I think I'm done."

"That's really too bad, Tom," Fisk said. "Because you're about to win your three hundredth game, and there's no f—— way you're coming out of this game."

Seaver took a deep breath, struck out Winfield, and retired the side in the ninth. In all, he threw 146 pitches that day. Twenty-two years later, it probably would have taken four relievers to get the last four outs.

A couple of statistics reveal how pitchers' expectations have changed. Early in 2007, Johan Santana, the Minnesota Twins' two-time Cy Young Award winner, pitched the sixth complete game of his big league career. One of the people calling the game from the TV booth that night was Bert Blyleven, who pitched from 1970 to 1992 for a number of teams and won 287 games. In 685 starts, Blyleven pitched 242 complete games, sixty of them shutouts!

Compare that to Glavine, who began 2007 with fifty-five complete games and twenty-four shutouts in 635 career starts, and Mussina who had pitched fifty-seven complete games and had twenty-three shutouts in 475 starts. It wasn't that Blyleven was a better pitcher than Glavine or Mussina—his career ERA of 3.31 was only slighter lower than Glavine's 3.46 and Mussina's 3.63. He simply pitched in a different time, even though he had only retired in 1992.

"I'm sure if we went to the mound thinking we had to pitch complete games, there would be a lot more of them," Mussina said. "Realistically, you know when you get close to a hundred pitches they're going to have the bullpen up. There are some nights where I'll have thrown sixty pitches the first three innings. At that point all I'm really trying to do is hang in there through six to give the team and the bullpen a chance. The days when they'll let a guy stay out there for a hundred fifty pitches or until his arm falls off are long gone."

These days a manager usually goes to the mound only to make a pitching change. When a pitcher needs a pep talk or a chance to catch his breath, it is usually the pitching coach who comes out.

"Sometimes when Gator [Ron Guidry] comes out, all he says is, 'Let's just take a break here for a second; I'm here to give you a little time,'" Mussina said. "Other times he'll have a specific suggestion about tactics or maybe he'll see something I'm doing wrong. Most of the time he's just out there to give me a break when he thinks I need it."

Torre almost always comes to the mound to make a change, but on occasion he will come out to ask a pitcher if he thinks he can get a batter out or to look him in the eye and ask him if he's okay.

"I've had to learn when I'm going out to ask a question to make sure I trot to the mound," he said. "When I was first managing the Mets, I went out one day to ask Jerry Koosman if he thought he could get one more batter out. I got to the mound and he handed me the ball. Well, that kind of answered my question, but I think as soon as he saw me come out, he took himself out of the game mentally because he thought I was coming to get him. Now, the guys know if I trot out there, I'm going to ask them a question."

Managers usually have a system or a code they use with their catchers to get their opinion without directly asking them what they think. The last thing a catcher wants to do is tell a manager that his pitcher needs to come out, especially since most pitchers don't want to come out.

"The only guy I would ever let talk me out of taking him out was David Cone," Torre said. "He was such a tough guy, especially in a tough situation. I remember in '98 we were playing Cleveland in the playoffs, and we had a big lead, but he had the bases loaded. [Jim] Thome was coming up, so I went out there and he said to me, 'Skip, I'll get this guy.' I believed him, so I left him in and he got him on a pop-up. Next guy hit a grand slam. Fortunately, we still won the game, but I told David later I should have been more specific. He told me he'd get Thome, but I never asked him about the next guy."

Torre will always look at Jorge Posada as he walks to the mound to get an idea of what he's thinking. "If he doesn't say anything, I'm figuring he thinks the guy is done," he said. "If he says something like, 'We're okay; we'll get this guy,' that means he thinks the guy has something left. After I hear that, then I'll look the pitcher right in the eye to see what I get back. Then, I make my decision."

On occasion, Torre will change his mind before he gets to the mound. Pitching in Detroit in May 2006, Mussina carried a shutout into the ninth inning but lost it with two outs because of an error. Figuring the shutout was over and with Mussina's pitch count right at one hundred, Torre took a couple of steps out of the dugout to bring someone in to get the last out with the Yankees leading 6–1.

"I heard Moose shouting at me the minute I got out of the dugout: 'What're you doing? Go back! Let me finish this!' I turned around and went back. If it had been two-one, it might have been different, but at six-one I understood."

That was Mussina's only complete game of the season. A few years prior to that, Mussina had given up six doubles in an inning during a game in Texas. When Torre came out to the mound to get him, Mussina looked at him and said, "What took you so long?"

Torre had no plans to go to the mound in Orlando in spring 2007. Mussina was scheduled to throw forty-five pitches, which everyone hoped would take him through three innings. His second start was similar to his first: it wasn't awful, but it wasn't brilliant.

Mussina gave up another home run, this one to Jeff Francoeur (a free swinger who Glavine also had a lot of trouble with), and threw a lot of breaking pitches, most of them curve balls. His pitch count was close to perfect: after struggling in the first inning when he gave up a run and needed twenty pitches, he only needed twelve pitches in the second inning and eleven in the third, meaning he finished the day at two under par on his pitch count. His control was excellent — thirty-two strikes in forty-three pitches — and he was on his way back up I-4 by three o'clock.

The best part of his postgame session with the media was when someone asked him his favorite spring-training question: "Are you where you want to be right now?" Mussina smiled and gave his favorite spring-training answer: "I'm in Florida pitching for the New York Yankees. I'm exactly where I want to be."

11

Getting Serious

AT NO POINT IN SPRING TRAINING does a pitcher worry about wins and losses. But there does come a time when he wants to feel as if he can throw close to one hundred pitches if necessary and that his stuff and his control are rounding into shape.

"You really start to pay attention about your third start," Tom Glavine said. "Most years you're going to start no more than six times, so when you start to push toward mid-March you realize Opening Day is only a couple weeks away. You need to see progress from that point on. If you don't, that's when you start to worry."

Glavine's third start of the spring came on March 11 against the Florida Marlins. He had pitched well again in his second start, against the Houston Astros, but had come in four over par, in part because he had some trouble with his control. Nothing major, especially early in the spring, but with only three starts left after the game against the Marlins, there was an air of things getting just a little more serious prior to the game.

"It's not like a real game; heck, I don't even know who they'll bring with them right now," he said, sitting in a half-empty clubhouse a couple of hours before game time. "I would think they'd bring [Miguel] Cabrera; I hope they'll bring him, but you never know. I'll certainly take a look during BP to see if he's here."

Cabrera was the Marlins' best hitter, and Glavine liked the

160

idea of testing himself in his third start. The plan was for him to pitch four innings or throw sixty pitches. If he came in under par after four innings, he would finish up in the bullpen.

The clubhouse was relatively empty because the Mets were playing two games, sending a split squad to Lakeland to play the Tigers. Teams will do this about a half-dozen times during spring training to try to get more players into games, and, just as important, to give as many pitchers as possible the innings they need. Glavine was pitching at home in part because he had seniority and, given a choice, would not make the three-hour drive to Lakeland, and because the game he was pitching would be on TV in New York on a Sunday afternoon and the Mets wanted to put their best foot forward. Aaron Sele, trying to make the team as a nonroster player, was pitching the other game.

Although Tradition Field is located in an area dominated by strip malls and fast-food joints and is no more than a mile from the parking lot known as I-95, it is a pleasant ballpark with a little more than seven thousand seats and picnic seating on a hill beyond the right-field fence for people who are more interested in the sun than the ballgame.

When Glavine trotted to the mound at 1:09, he was given a warm round of applause. The days when Mets fans did not truly consider him one of their own were long gone.

Like most pitchers, Glavine's warm-up routine before every inning is identical. He will throw three fastballs, two cutters, two changeups, and a fastball aimed at the outside corner for a right-handed hitter. It hasn't always been exactly like that—Glavine only started throwing a cutter two years earlier—but it is always that way now.

Glavine looked just as impressive starting out against the Marlins as he had against the Cardinals and Astros. He had to battle Hanley Ramirez, the Marlins' young, rising-star shortstop, but finally got him to pop to Jose Reyes at short on a 3–2 pitch.

Glavine thought he had Ramirez struck out on a 2–2 pitch, but umpire Jerry Meals didn't give him the corner. Ramirez fouled one fastball off on 3–2 before popping out.

That brought up Aaron Boone, who had made a nice comeback after the knee injury that had ended his career in New York. Boone had played in Cleveland in 2005 and 2006 and then signed with the Marlins as a utility infielder for 2007. He was now thirty-four, but with his long brown hair looked several years younger. Boone flied to right on an 84-mile-an-hour fastball. That brought up Cabrera, who had made the trip.

"My first real challenge of the spring," Glavine said. "Not because I hadn't faced good hitters the first two times I pitched, but by now the hitters have played seven or eight games and are starting to get in a groove."

Cabrera's a free swinger, and he didn't waste time trying to work a count on Glavine. Glavine's first pitch was a fastball, and Cabrera hit it sharply right at third baseman David Wright. The Marlins were gone on eleven pitches. At that point in spring training, Glavine had pitched six innings and hadn't given up a run.

That finally changed in the second inning. After Glavine had gotten the first two outs, right fielder Jeremy Hermida doubled, and second baseman Jason Wood singled to put the Marlins up 1–0. Glavine could live with that. He hadn't expected to go the entire spring without giving up a run.

The third inning, however, was a good deal more frustrating. The two teams had agreed to play the game using the designated hitter since the Mets were a little bit shorthanded because they were playing with a split squad. This will tell you how informal spring training can be. The two managers just decided before the game to use the DH, informed the umpires, and that was it; the DH was in play in a National League game in a National League park.

"Disappointing," Glavine said. "Would have been my first at bat of the spring."

So, instead of facing pitcher Sergio Mitre to start the third, Glavine faced shortstop Zach Sorenson, who singled. Two pitches later, with Sorenson going, Ramirez hit a ground ball to second baseman Jose Valentin. Distracted by Sorenson, Valentin booted the ball, putting men on first and second. Glavine threw strike one to Boone and then let an inside fastball get away, plunking him in the ribs.

Now, the bases were loaded, and Glavine was angry. "There is nothing more pointless in baseball than getting annoyed with a guy for booting a ball," he said. "He didn't do it on purpose. I will only get upset if someone isn't playing hard. Hosy just made a mistake, and then I compounded it with a really bad pitch."

Up came Cabrera. Bases loaded and a hitter who annually drives in well over a hundred runs at the plate. Glavine won the battle. Or seemed to. After Cabrera had hammered a 2–1 pitch deep but foul, Glavine got him to hit a little pop-up behind second base. Valentin went back and for a split second seemed to have redeemed himself for his error with a running, over-the-shoulder catch—only the ball hit the bottom of his glove, and he dropped it. The official scorer correctly ruled it a single since it would have been a superb play. Everyone moved up a base, and the Marlins led 2–0.

"Again, nothing you can do," Glavine said. "If Hosey makes the catch, it's a great play. I threw a good pitch, Cabrera's strong enough that he got it over the infield, and they get a run. It was just one of those innings that we all have. I was just glad it was happening in March."

Even in March, no pitcher wants to see an inning unravel. Glavine was able to get the next two hitters, Josh Willingham and Miguel Olivo, to fly out to right field. But the runners moved up both times, extending the Marlins lead to 4–0. As if to punctuate the futility of the inning, David Wright kicked an easy ground ball by Hermida before Glavine finally got Jason Wood to ground to second for the final out. When Valentin fielded the ball cleanly and threw it to Carlos Delgado without incident, the normally gentle spring crowd let out a derisive cheer.

Glavine understood. "Bad baseball is bad baseball," he said. "People paid to see the game. We weren't very good in that inning."

Of course that's what spring training is for—getting the kinks out. Glavine sailed through a one-two-three fourth and then headed to the bullpen to finish his day since, even with the troubles in the third, he had only thrown forty-nine pitches—eleven under par. Only two of the Marlins' runs had been earned, and the key play of the third inning had been Valentin's inability to corral Cabrera's pop-up.

One person who wasn't the least bit unhappy was Rick Peterson. "If you look at it from my point of view, that was vintage Tom Glavine," he said. "Think about it: his defense lets him down on three plays; he throws the one bad pitch that hits Boone; and yet, we're still in the game, and he comes back the next inning and gives us a one-two-three. You can't just look at numbers in pitching. You have to look at how the numbers came about. He's pitching really well. I feel great about him right now."

ACROSS THE STATE, Mike Mussina wasn't quite as sanguine about how his own spring was going. His first two outings had been okay—not especially sharp but not nearly bad enough to warrant concern.

His third start was at home against the Cincinnati Reds. The first batter of the game, Brandon Phillips, hit Mussina's first pitch deep into the left-field bleachers. Three games, three home runs, this one to the first batter—someone Mussina had never seen before in his life. "I couldn't even tell you his last name," he said a month later, recalling that evening.

The time for making jokes about having his home-run pitch in midseason form was now past. As Glavine had pointed out, the third start of the spring is when things start to get serious because when you're finished, half your spring training starts are over. To begin the third start of the spring by giving up a home run, "on a belt-high fastball, right down the middle," Mussina said, was not good.

The rest of the night—the Yankees were now starting to sprinkle some night games into their schedule—didn't go much better. Mussina gave up another run in the first—aided by an error by second baseman Robinson Cano—and a third run in the third. He was done after that, having thrown fifty-seven difficult pitches. Joe Torre and Ron Guidry decided there was no point putting anyone through a fourth inning of what they were all seeing.

"At that point, I wasn't at all happy with myself," Mussina said. "There comes a point where you need to start seeing improvement and progress as the spring moves along. I wasn't seeing it at all. I couldn't locate my breaking pitches, and my fastballs were up a lot—the home run was a perfect example. My velocity still wasn't where it needed to be either.

"What made it tougher was that it took me by surprise. I'd felt good coming into spring—I was healthy; there was just no apparent reason for it. After a while you start to question yourself a little bit: 'Maybe I'm not throwing it as well as I thought I was.' But you really can't do that. You have to convince yourself that today is going to be better than yesterday, even if you can't put a finger on why. You have to go back to your side sessions and really work. Maybe you weren't concentrating as hard as you thought because everything seemed easy. You look for something, and you tell yourself it's there; you just have to find it."

After the third outing Mussina worked hard in the bullpen trying to get his breaking pitches to go where he wanted them to. He slowed down, just a tiny bit, between pitches to make sure he was completely focused before he threw the ball. One of the biggest differences between veteran pitchers and young pitchers is that the veteran often sees his bullpens as an opportunity rather than as a chore. It isn't just something you do between starts because the pitching coach says you should do it; it's something you look forward to, especially when you aren't pitching well, because it represents a chance to find something that will make your next start better.

"It can be mechanical," Mussina said. "Maybe it's just a tiny little change you make in your motion or the way you stand on the mound before you pitch. Sometimes you make a change so small, it really doesn't change the way you're throwing but you think it does. And if you think it does, that can be as helpful as something that does actually change the way you're throwing.

"I never change my routine. I throw five fastballs, five sinkers, five curves, five changeups, five sliders. Then I throw three of each out of the stretch and finish with one of each from the windup and three fastballs—four-seamers away—to finish up. I don't keep throwing one pitch until I get it right. I know there are guys who do that, but that can get too frustrating. I keep throwing, and I hope if I don't start out well that I'll get better. Maybe Ron or [bullpen catcher Mike] Borzello will say something to me while I'm throwing, or maybe they'll say something afterward to give me something to think about or to work on the next time I throw."

When he's struggling, Mussina will talk to a lot of different people, looking for answers. He respects Guidry, not only as someone who was a successful pitcher but as someone who was a successful *Yankees* pitcher. "There is a difference," he said. "Mel [Stottlemyre] was the same way. They know what it's like to pitch in Yankee Stadium and in New York. That helps."

He will also talk to Torre as an old catcher who knows a lot about pitching. But the person he talks to most often is Mike Borzello.

Borzello was never a successful pitcher for the Yankees or for any other team. He grew up in Los Angeles, going to Dodger games with his dad, who had played baseball as a kid and as an adult, though never professionally. He also saw a lot of Lakers games because his mother's sister was married to Rudy LaRusso, a standout player for the team in the 1960s.

He was a good infielder who went to college thinking he might have a chance to get drafted, and did, in the thirty-first round, by the Cardinals. Two years into his professional career, he began to understand the realities of the minor leagues. He was playing A-ball, and the pitching coach was Hub Kittle, who had pitched in the major leagues for many years.

"One day we're sitting around talking before a game, and Hub says to me and a couple of the other guys, 'Look around here; how many guys on this team do you think have a chance to play in the big leagues? One, two, three maybe? So why are the rest of you here? So that those guys can have games to play.'"

Borzello thought there might be a ray of hope when the Cardinals decided to make him a catcher. He wasn't keen on it at first but came to enjoy the position. "I found that I liked having the game in front of me and being in on every pitch," he said. "I was lucky because Dave Ricketts was the Cardinals' minor league catching instructor, and he was the absolute best. Everything I know about catching, I learned from him.

"But even after the switch, I realized I was never going to be more than an organization player, and I started thinking I wanted to do something else."

An organization player is the kind of player Kittle was talking about — someone who bounced around the minor leagues making sure that the organization's prospects had teammates to play their games with. Borzello, a bright guy with a college degree, found himself tiring of the long bus rides and the pay, which had gotten to $1,100 a month at the start of 1995, his fifth year as a pro.

He got to Double-A ball briefly — in Little Rock, Arkansas — and started to hear people telling him he would make a good manager or coach at the minor league level. "They wanted me to go to the South Atlantic League," He said. "I'd been there. Some of the bus trips are fifteen hours. I decided to go home, even though I knew I'd miss the game."

Back in Los Angeles, a friend of his from the local CBS TV affiliate got him an interview at CBS for a job reading potential scripts. He was hired and liked the job, even though a lot of what he read was awful. "It was fun," he said. "Interesting. And I wasn't riding any buses."

He was happily ensconced reading scripts in February 1996 when he got a surprise phone call from Bob Watson, whom he had met during spring trainings with the Cardinals. Watson had just become the Yankees' general manager. Joe Torre was the new manager.

"They were looking for a bullpen catcher," Borzello said. "Joe remembered me from spring training and so did Bob. Watson said to me, 'Why don't you come on down here?' I was skeptical. Was this for a week? Was it a tryout? I figured it was the Yankees and guys that I liked. I decided to go down and see what it was about.

"I got there and they said, 'Can you throw BP?' I said I could. Then they asked me to catch [John] Wetteland who had that nasty sinker. I must have done okay because the next thing I know they're offering me a job."

Bullpen catcher may not sound like a glamorous job, but when you are part of any major league team, much less the Yankees, the life is a lot different than riding buses in the minor leagues. Borzello enjoyed what he was doing right away. Mel Stottlemyre was the pitching coach, and he kept giving Borzello more and more responsibility.

"I learned a lot working with guys like David Cone and Jimmy Key," he said. "They were such pros. They knew exactly what they needed to do to get ready or to fix things. They liked input — honest input. In that way, they were a lot like Mussina."

When Mussina came to the Yankees in 2001, he was assigned to play catch early in the season with Brian Boehringer. But Boehringer was released, leaving Mussina without a catch partner. Borzello was assigned to take Boehringer's place, and he and Mussina quickly became friends.

"What I learned early with Mike, as with most good pitchers, is that if they ask you if something's good and you say yes and it's not, they know," Borzello said. "You tell them yes when the answer is really no, and they won't ask you again. So, my tendency is to tell them exactly what I really think right from the start. Mike liked that. He always asks me what I think because he knows I'll give him an honest answer."

Borzello isn't just Mussina's bullpen catcher, he is his best friend on the team. They are the same age and have similar interests: '80s music and TV shows, old cars, and pitching. What's more, Mussina feels comfortable that Borzello isn't likely to leave the team while he is still there.

"You have to be careful about how close you get to guys on a team," he said. "It's the nature of the game. This is my seventh year here, and how many guys are left from when I got here? [Derek] Jeter, [Jorge] Posada, Mo [Rivera], and that's it. I'm the only starting pitcher from that year who is still around. Borzy's not going anywhere — certainly not as long as Joe is in charge and probably even after that. So, there's an extra level of comfort that the guy isn't going to get traded, leave as a free agent, or get cut. He's here."

Because Borzello had worked with Mussina for considerably longer than Guidry, who became the pitching coach in 2006 after Stottlemyre left, he would often see things or tell Mussina things that Guidry might not. After the Cincinnati start in March, Borzello didn't think there was any reason to panic.

"Sometimes you do need to kick him in the butt," he said. "But a lot of times you have to remind him how good he is. For a guy who has done as much as he's done for as long as he's done it, he can lose confidence quickly."

Mussina and Borzello will often talk at length after an off-day bullpen session. Their conversation can be about anything from the quality of Mussina's breaking pitches to his location to his game plan. Often Borzello will question him about how he pitched to specific hitters and why he threw certain pitches.

After working hard with Guidry and Borzello between starts, Mussina pitched against the Pirates for the second time that spring. Since the Pirates train in Bradenton, a relatively short drive from Tampa, they play the Yankees frequently during March.

Right from the beginning, Mussina felt better on the mound than he had since he first arrived in Florida. He was throwing "strike one," which most pitchers understand is a key to success. There are all sorts of statistics that prove a pitcher is far more successful when a count begins 0–1 to a batter than when it begins 1–0. Batters know this too, so they are often looking for a fastball over the plate on the first pitch. The best pitchers can throw strike one without grooving it.

One of the notable exceptions to the strike-one rule is Glavine. "He may be the only pitcher, certainly one of the few, who is better when he's down one and oh," Tigers manager Jim Leyland said. "Most pitchers down one and oh, you think you're getting a fastball; if they get you oh and one you tend to think breaking pitch. Glavine's got that great changeup that he'll throw on any count, so you never know with him if he's going to throw that or a fastball. I think he almost prefers one and oh because then he's got the hitter trying to outthink him, and most guys aren't smart enough to do that."

Mussina is more typical—strike one is key for him. Against the Pirates, he threw strike one to four of the first six hitters and got all six of them out, three of them on one or two pitches. "I had better velocity and location," he said. "I got some first-pitch outs, and I got my breaking pitches over. It wasn't as if it was spectacular, but it was better. That's what I needed to see—improvement. I had to stop running in place."

The only inning in which he was in any trouble was the third, when he gave up two one-out singles but pitched clear. He left after five innings, having allowed three singles and no runs. He pitched ahead of the Pittsburgh hitters almost the entire night.

"At this point in his career, it's really all about location," Joe Torre said. "He's got all these different pitches he can throw; the question is *where* is he going to throw them? When a pitcher gets older, especially one who was once consistently in the nineties but isn't anymore, there's a tendency to be afraid to pitch to contact. You do that, you end up pitching behind a lot, and that's no good. Mike sometimes forgets that it's okay to let the hitters hit the ball. That's why there are eight guys on the field behind him—to catch balls that are hit. I'd rather see him give up a home run with nobody on and then get three fly-ball outs than see him walking guys or pitching three and one all the time. That will catch up with anyone sooner or later."

Intellectually, Mussina understands all this. But sometimes, standing on the mound, knowing his fastball might top out at 90 but is more likely to be in the 87- to 89-mile-an-hour range, he gets a little bit bat shy.

"You know you can't pitch from behind," he said. "No one can on a consistent basis. But if you see a couple of balls go four hundred feet or you're giving up line drive after line drive, you do get a little bit nervous about throwing white on white too often. If you're throwing ninety-five or more, maybe you can get away with it. The rest of us can't."

The Pittsburgh game relaxed Mussina a good deal. "It was important to see improvement, and I did," he said. "I didn't have to worry that I was just spinning my wheels. I was getting closer to where I needed to be the first week in April."

April was now two weeks away. Mussina would have two more starts before the season began. The first would be against the Toronto Blue Jays, and the second would be against the Blue Jays' Triple-A team, for the simple reason that no one saw any need for

him to make the drive to Lakeland, where the Yankees were playing on March 30, the day Mussina was scheduled to make his last
spring start.

Mussina stayed behind and pitched for the Trenton Thunder,
the Yankees' Triple-A farm team. His opponent was longtime
major league journeyman Tomo Ohka, best known for getting
himself traded by the Washington Nationals for yelling at manager Frank Robinson, when Robinson, one of the game's all-time
great players, came to the mound to take him out of a game.

Ohka hardly looked ready for prime time, giving the Thunder
seven runs in less than five innings. Mussina was just the opposite. He pitched seven shutout innings, gave up four hits, nudged
his pitch count up over eighty for the first time all spring, and pronounced himself ready to start the season.

"I better be ready," he said. "I seriously doubt if I ask them to
push the start of the year back a week or two that they'll do it."

He smiled and, without being prompted, added: "Am I where I
want to be? I sure hope so, because I really don't have any choice
in the matter."

AFTER THE SLOPPY GAME AGAINST THE MARLINS, Tom Glavine
came back five days later to face them again. This time both he and
his fielders were far more efficient. Glavine pitched five innings —
that spring, he had gone two innings, three innings, four innings,
and five innings, which is pretty much a perfect start for a pitcher —
and this time the only inning he was in trouble was the fourth when
he got wild for a moment, walking two and hitting a batter. But he
pitched out of the jam and ended up with five shutout innings.

"Sometimes I'll walk a guy, even if it means putting someone
in scoring position, rather than give in and throw him a pitch he
might hit for extra bases or out of the park," Glavine said. "Walks
really don't scare me. Throwing a pitch that's over the plate on
three and one does."

Glavine's approach to pitch counts—as Leyland points out—is often different than the norm. He throws more balls than most good pitchers. In fact, he is almost at the top or near the top of the standings in the now closely tracked ball-to-strike ratio. In other words, he throws far more balls than most pitching coaches would like to see.

"Ideally, you'd probably like a two-strikes-to-one-ball ratio, or something close to that or even better if possible," Glavine said. "But sometimes I just can't pitch that way. I'm just not going to give in to the hitter because the count is three and one or even three and oh and throw him a fastball he can hit."

"Not giving in" is a mantra among pitchers. It means you don't give a hitter a fastball over the plate in order to try to throw a strike when you are behind in the count. Most pitchers talk about not giving in, but few are as stubborn about it as Glavine. In fact, when other players talk about him, that is almost invariably the first thing they bring up: "You know he's never going to give in." Glavine is as apt to throw a changeup on the outside corner on 3–0 as he is on 0–2.

"The only time it creates a problem for me is if I'm having control problems on a given day and it drives my pitch count up," he said. "I don't want to get in a situation where I throw sixty pitches the first three innings because then I know it's going to be a battle to go six. At times, it can be a delicate balance."

Glavine's fifth start of the spring should have come on March 21 against the Dodgers in Vero Beach, which is about 30 miles north of Port St. Lucie on I-95, a fairly easy trip, especially midmorning, for a 1:05 game. But Willie Randolph and Rick Peterson asked him to stay home that day to pitch in a simulated game. Their reasoning had little to do with Glavine.

"They were trying to make decisions on guys," Glavine said. "Aaron Sele, Chan Ho Park, Jorge Sosa, Mike Pelfrey all needed some innings, and they wanted to see them pitch in game conditions a couple more times before they decided who to bring north and who they wanted in the rotation to start the season. I just needed work, so staying home and pitching in a simulated game was no problem for me."

Simulated games can take several forms. The kind Glavine pitched in involved his throwing about eighty pitches over six innings. No formal score was kept, and Glavine's "team" didn't come to bat. Instead, he simply sat in the dugout for about ten minutes after every three outs, the way he probably would in a real game.

That left Glavine with one final start before the opener. It was at home against the Dodgers. Glavine pitched six innings and, in his last inning of the spring, finally got knocked around a little bit: five hits produced three runs. It was the only time other than the sloppy Sunday game against the Marlins that he gave up any runs at all. Even after giving up those runs, he finished the spring with a sparkling ERA of 2.25.

"I think I probably got a little careless, let my mind wander a little that last inning against the Dodgers," he said later. "Maybe the thought crossed my mind for a second that this might be my last inning ever in spring training. I didn't do a lot of that during the spring, but on occasion those thoughts would cross my mind: 'Is this the last time?' Or maybe I'd just had enough of pretend baseball, which in the end is what spring training is. The wins and losses don't matter; neither do the stats. You're just trying to get ready for the real thing."

Glavine was ready. The real thing was six days away.

Mussina as a member of the USA Baseball Junior
National Team in 1986. *(Courtesy of Mike Mussina.)*

Mussina as a college sophomore, with Stanford coach Tom Dunton.
(*Courtesy of Mike Mussina.*)

The brothers Mussina—Mark and Mike—with their mom,
Eleanor, shortly after Mike was called up to the Orioles in August
of 1991. (*Courtesy of Mike Mussina.*)

Mussina throwing a breaking pitch; notice the form is perfect.
(*© New York Yankees.*)

Mussina shows off his six-time Gold Glove skills. (© *New York Yankees.*)

For a competitor, there is nothing worse than just watching. (© *New York Yankees.*)

A Glavine Family Christmas: Jonathan, Mason, Tom, Chris, Amber, and Peyton. (*Courtesy of Tom and Chris Glavine.*)

Tom and Chris Glavine at the White House one week before he rejoined the Braves. (*Courtesy of Tom and Chris Glavine.*)

Glavine always makes it look easy on the mound. *(Photo by Marc Levine. Courtesy of the New York Mets.)*

Glavine shows his three hundred–victory pitching form. *(Photo by Marc Levine. Courtesy of the New York Mets.)*

Peyton, Tom, and Mason together in uniform. *(Courtesy of Tom and Chris Glavine.)*

Tom and son Mason surrounded by photographers after the Number had finally been named. *(Photo by Marc Levine. Courtesy of the New York Mets.)*

12

Real Baseball

IF THE DAY PITCHERS AND CATCHERS report for spring
training is the most romanticized in baseball, Opening Day is not
far behind. There is, for example, no such thing as "opening
day"—capital letters are required. Teams that will play in front of
half-filled stadiums almost every day of the season will sell out on
Opening Day. Fans who may not show up again for the rest of the
season, unless perhaps their hometown team makes postseason,
will show up on Opening Day.

On Opening Day, everyone has hope. Even the Pittsburgh
Pirates.

Of course, Opening Day, like everything else in sports, has
changed considerably since the days when presidents threw out
the first pitch in Washington, D.C., and no one played in the
National League before the Cincinnati Reds.

Once, it was unheard of for Opening Day to be Opening
Night, but nowadays it happens on a regular basis. Four of the fifteen openers played during the first three days of the 2007 season
were played at night, and three more were played in the late afternoon to accommodate television.

The Mets-Cardinals was a game set up strictly for television,
specifically ESPN, which liked to take advantage of the fact that
Sunday was a rest day during college basketball's Final Four, and
there was no serious competition for viewers. Generally speaking,

players really don't care where or when Opening Day or Opening Night falls. Their major concern is the weather. Having just come from the warmth of Florida or Arizona, they know their bodies will be in for a shock when they come north in early April. This is especially true for pitchers because the most difficult thing to do in cold weather is to keep your fingers moist, which is critical when pitchers try to feel the baseball and grip it to throw a specific pitch.

"Being cold isn't so bad," Tom Glavine said. "Not being able to feel the baseball is very bad. It affects every pitch you throw."

On especially cold days, pitchers will keep a hot-water bottle with them in the dugout and wrap their pitching hand around it between innings. Often, they don't remain in the dugout when their team is up, instead racing back to the clubhouse to keep warm. This is more difficult to do in the National League, where pitchers hit at least once every three innings and frequently more often than that. On especially cold days, pitchers are also allowed to back off the mound and lick their fingers to keep them moist — something not allowed when the weather is warmer.

The Mets and Cardinals got lucky on Opening Night in St. Louis. The game-time temperature was a balmy seventy-two degrees, although there was a brisk seventeen-mile-an-hour wind blowing out to right field. For the Mets, the most difficult part of the evening was what came before the game: the Cardinals unveiling their World Championship banner while most of the 45,429 in the new Busch Stadium celebrated. The Mets couldn't help feeling that they could easily have been unveiling that very banner when they got home the next week.

The Mets had gone through the postseason without two of their top-three starting pitchers — Pedro Martinez and Orlando Hernandez — and had still come within one victory of the World Series. They had lost Game Seven of the National League Championship Series to the Cardinals when their best hitter, Carlos Beltran, had taken a called strike three from rookie reliever Adam

Wainwright, with two outs, the bases loaded, and the Mets trailing 3–1 in the bottom of the ninth.

That's why there was a strong sense of "this is our year" in the Mets clubhouse. The players believed they had lost to the Cardinals with one hand — or perhaps more accurately, two arms — tied behind their backs. Martinez still hadn't returned, but Hernandez had, and with most of the 2006 team intact, there was no reason to believe that 2007 would not be their year.

Opening Night certainly did nothing to dispel that feeling.

Glavine was matched against Chris Carpenter, who had won twenty-one games and the National League Cy Young Award in 2005 and had come back from injuries to win fifteen more in 2006. Which was why the last thing Glavine expected was to walk to the mound in the bottom of the fourth inning with a 5–0 lead.

"Of course I got the whole thing started," he joked.

In a sense, he had. He had led off the top of the third with a single, and, even though he had been forced out at second by Paul Lo Duca, his hit started a two-run inning for the Mets.

On the mound, Glavine was pretty close to cruise control. Adam Kennedy tripled with one out in the bottom of the third, but Carpenter bunted into a fielder's choice at the plate trying to get Kennedy home. It wasn't until the sixth inning that the Cardinals began to get to Glavine even a little bit. A pinch-hit single by Skip Schumaker was followed by an RBI double by David Eckstein that made it 5–1. Then Preston Wilson, the ex-Met, singled, but Beltran cut Eckstein — and the potential for a big inning — down at the plate with a perfect throw from center. That play loomed large when Glavine walked Albert Pujols — a classic example of an intentional though technically unintentional walk — and then very unintentionally hit Scott Rolen to load the bases.

That brought up catcher Yadier Molina, whose two-run home run in the ninth inning of Game Seven of the NLCS had been the difference between the two teams a little more than five months earlier. He hit the ball hard but lined it right at Jose Reyes.

End of inning, end of the night for Glavine. He had thrown eighty-nine pitches, twenty-three of them in the sixth, and he and Rick Peterson agreed that was plenty for Opening Night. The bullpen took over and produced three scoreless innings, and the Mets won 6–1.

It was about as good a start to the season as Glavine or the Mets could have hoped for: Glavine had been effective and so had the bullpen. As a bonus, Glavine had been on base twice with a single and a walk, and the Mets had taken a little of the joy out of the Cardinals' celebration of their 2006 title. The win made Glavine 5–3 in season openers, and, most important, it made him 291–191 for his career—nine wins away from pitching Nirvana.

Glavine's victory got the Mets off to a rolling start. They went on to sweep all three games in St. Louis, which sent them to Atlanta in as good a frame of mind as possible. Which was important. Because there was no place in baseball more difficult for the Mets or for Glavine.

Opening day for the New York Yankees was far more traditional than the Mets' Opening Night in St. Louis. To begin with, it was at Yankee Stadium, generally considered the most historic venue in sports. In 1999 when *Sports Illustrated* had, as part of its end of the millenium compilation, selected the twenty most historic venues in sports, Yankee Stadium had been ranked number one.

It was so historic that it was going to be torn down. For years, Yankees owner George Steinbrenner had insisted the Yankees needed a new ballpark. He had talked about moving to New Jersey and to downtown Manhattan. He had insisted at one point that people were afraid to go to games in the Bronx at night. Then the team got good again, and attendance in the Bronx shot up to about fifty thousand people per game—day or night.

Still, Steinbrenner, like a lot of owners in sports, wanted a monument to himself. Yankee Stadium, which had opened in 1923 and been refurbished in 1974 and 1975 (the Yankees played those two seasons in Shea Stadium), was still a wonderful place to watch a baseball game. But it didn't have nearly as many luxury boxes as Steinbrenner wanted, and luxury boxes are the yin and yang of most owners' existence today. Attendance is nice; hundreds of luxury boxes is much nicer. What's more, Yankee Stadium would always be "The House That Ruth Built." The New Yankee Stadium would be, as the first ten pages of the Yankees 2007 media guide reminded everyone, "The House That George Built."

"It's just hard to believe that in two years this place won't be here anymore," Joe Torre said. "I know why the new place is needed, but there's just so much history here."

Monday, April 2, 2007, would be the eighty-third—and second-to-last—Opening Day in Yankee Stadium. The Yankees' Opening Day pitcher would not be Chien-Ming Wang as had been planned. He had torn a hamstring in what should have been his second-to-last spring training start and would be out for a month. Andy Pettitte was nursing a sore back, so Torre didn't want to move him up a day. Mike Mussina's schedule had been set up for him to pitch on Thursday, so it was impossible to move him up three days. The same was true for Kei Igawa. That left just one man who could take the ball on Opening Day for the Yankees: Carl Pavano.

"It's ironic, isn't it?" Mussina laughed. "Actually, after Wanger got hurt, I thought to myself, 'It makes sense for Pavano to pitch. He's healthy. He wasn't supposed to go until Saturday, so it falls right for him in terms of rest, so why not?' I even brought it up to Ron [Guidry]. Maybe it will be the start of something good for him."

Pavano was sharp for four innings, while the Yankees built a 3–1 lead, but the season did not start auspiciously for the Yankees' two biggest stars: Alex Rodriguez dropped a foul pop in the first inning, and Derek Jeter booted a ground ball in the second. A-Rod's first at bat produced a strikeout and the first boos of the season.

Pavano sailed into the fifth before things began to come apart for him. The Devil Rays scored four times in the fifth, and Torre had to go and get him, with one man out and three runs in. The Yankees got him off the hook when Rodriguez singled, stole a base, and scored in the seventh to take the lead at 6–5 and then hit a two-run home run in the eighth to silence the boos. The Yankees went on to win 9–5, and, at least for one day, all was well in "The House That Ruth Built and George Was About to Tear Down."

Things did not stay that way for long. Wednesday's game — most teams have a day off after Opening Day — was rained out. That meant Mussina would be pushed back to pitching on Friday against the Orioles instead of the final game against the Devil Rays on Thursday.

"I know people talk about me being a creature of habit, and it's true," he said. "I like to pitch on the fifth day, and at times I've had trouble adapting when I have to wait a day. In this case, the plan was for me to pitch on my sixth day, which at the start of the season, especially going from hot weather to cold, isn't a bad thing. It's also easier if it's planned. I can plan my off-day schedule knowing I've got an extra day."

Another extra day was not part of the plan. "I know how it sounds when you say it, but when you go a week between starts, it feels like forever. Sometimes you wonder if you'll even remember how to pitch when you get out there."

Pettitte pitched the second game against the Rays and wasn't much better than Pavano, although once again the Yankee defense was awful. After three errors on Monday, the team made three more on Thursday, on a cold night, and Pettitte was gone with no one out in the fifth, having given up four runs — only two of them earned. The Rays went on to win 7–6.

Two games into the season, the Yankee bullpen had already pitched nine and two-thirds innings. That was not what Torre or Guidry had in mind. Since the team was scheduled to play three days in a row against the Orioles, they were counting on Mussina to pitch deep into the game and give the bullpen a chance to catch its breath.

It didn't come close to happening that way. Mussina's season began like this: a lead-off double in the gap by Brian Roberts, a bunt single by Melvin Mora, and a two-run double by Nick Markakis. Orioles 2, Yankees 0. The game was not yet four minutes old.

It was, to be fair, a miserable April night. The temperature at game time was forty-one degrees, and with the windchill the temperature was closer to freezing. It was overcast and dank, and Mussina had trouble getting loose in the bullpen and clearly didn't feel comfortable when he got to the mound.

"It's always been tough to pitch in cold weather, but it's tougher now than when I first came up," he said. "After the strike [in '94], they changed the baseballs. You could feel it when you put them in your hands. They're slicker now, tougher to grip, and they're wound tighter. Much tighter."

How does he know that?

"A year or so after the strike, we were sitting around during a rain delay, talking about how different the baseball felt in your hands," he said. "For some reason, I had kept a couple of balls in my locker from before the strike. We went and got one and cut it open. The inside of the ball just lay there; I mean literally just laid down on the table. Then we opened up a poststrike ball — it was as if the thing was alive. It literally stood up on the table next to the other one that was just lying there."

Other pitchers confirm Mussina's suspicions. "During the strike

I worked out at home with a bunch of balls I'd brought home with me," said Ron Darling. "When we came back, the ball felt different in my hands. I took a couple home and compared the stitching. It's much tighter on the new balls — and the balls are slicker. It makes a big difference, especially when the weather's cold."

Mussina, who describes himself as a "paranoid, conspiracy theorist," believes that Major League Baseball thought home runs were an important part of bringing the game back after the strike. That's one reason many believe baseball turned a blind eye toward steroid use. It also explains, Mussina believes, the slicker, more tightly wound baseballs; the much smaller strike zones of recent years; and, clearly, the smaller ballparks being built all around baseball.

"Consider this stat," Mussina said, reeling off numbers as he often does. "In 1992 my ERA was 2.54, and I finished third in the league. In 2000 my ERA was 3.79, and I finished third again. What does that tell you?"

Warming up on a frigid night, Mussina knew he was going to struggle to control his breaking pitches. He went through his bullpen routine and walked to the mound. Like Glavine, he never varies the eight warm-up pitches he throws when he is on the mound: two fastballs, a sinker, a curve, a changeup, a slider, another sinker, and, finally, just like Glavine, a fastball to the outside corner for a right-handed hitter. "That's the pitch I want to feel coming out of my hand before I start to pitch for real," he says.

The ball never felt good coming out of his hand that night.

"It doesn't matter what the conditions are," he said later. "There are no excuses. You have to pitch in the conditions that exist. The other guy is pitching in the same conditions. Hitting isn't easy when it's that cold either. I just wasn't very good."

One of the reasons the New York media had come to respect Mussina was that he didn't make excuses. If it had been Randy Johnson pitching that night, he probably would have talked about how tough it was to feel the baseball in the cold and how unfair it was to play baseball in such lousy weather.

Mussina knew the weather was lousy. But he also knew he was lousy. He managed to make it through four innings — giving up three more runs in the third after the Yankees had tied the game at 2–2 — and another in the fourth. He had one good inning, the second, and that was it. Pavano had gotten one out in the fifth on day one; Pettitte had pitched to two batters in the fifth on day two. Mussina never made it to the mound for the fifth on day three. Torre decided eighty-four pitches and six earned runs was enough for one night.

"On the one hand, you know it's just one start and there's no season longer than a baseball season," Mussina said. "On the other hand, we really could have used a good start that night, and I didn't come up with it. That's a bad feeling. I had a chance to pick the team up and instead I let it down. No one likes doing that."

Back in the clubhouse he sat in front of his locker for a few minutes, stewing. Then he went to ice and watch the rest of the game. This was not the way to start the season, for him or for the rest of the starting staff.

"I try not to take it home with me," he said. "Especially when my family is in town, which they were that weekend. The trip home in the car is my time to let the frustration seep out of me so that when I get home I'm not in a bad mood for my kids."

Mussina almost never listens to the radio or to tapes or CDs in the car. Unless there is a specific reason to listen to the radio, he drives in silence, trying to get his mind to leave the ballpark behind. He does have XM radio, though. Why? "It came with the car," he said.

His second start would be in Minnesota. That was good news. No matter how cold it might be outside, the game would be played inside the Metrodome. The conditions would be perfect. Mussina was 20–5 lifetime against the Twins. The chances that his second start would be considerably better than his first appeared to be excellent.

———

THE FOLLOWING AFTERNOON, Tom Glavine walked into the visitors' clubhouse inside Atlanta's Turner Field and headed straight to the computer a few feet from the door to make certain his request for thirty tickets had been taken care of by the Mets.

After five years, he had gotten over the initial shock of walking into the Braves' ballpark and turning left to go to the visitors' clubhouse instead of right to go to the home clubhouse. He always needed to come up with a lot more tickets in Atlanta than in any other road city for the obvious reason that it was still his home. The best part about the Mets' three trips a year to Atlanta was that he got to stay at his house.

The news on the field during his first four years as a Met had not been nearly as good. Put simply, the Braves had hammered him most of the time, especially during his first two years in New York.

"Even on those rare occasions when I did pitch well, things just didn't seem to work out," he said. "I'd be lying if I said it didn't bother me."

Glavine had pitched considerably better against his old team in 2006. He had started against them three times and had gone 1–1 with an ERA of 3.32. Even so, the no-decision had perhaps been his most frustrating day of the season: the Sunday in Atlanta when he had been staked to a big lead and Willie Randolph had pulled him after four innings, with the lead down to 8–6. The Mets had gone on to win, but Glavine had not gotten the win, and it had produced his first — and only — real blowup with Randolph.

Glavine's numbers against the Braves were awful: he was 3–9 overall, with a 5.68 ERA. In Atlanta, the numbers were worse: 2–5, with a 6.70 ERA.

"I think at first it was just us knowing him so well," Bobby Cox said. "Then, after a while, it became mental. He expected us to light him up, and we did. But ever since he started pitching inside, he's been tougher on us. We've gotten lucky a couple of times. To be honest, when we face him, I want us to win two-one. I don't like to see Tommy embarrassed, but I like seeing us lose even less than I like seeing him embarrassed."

This matchup, five days into the season, was about as big a deal as an April baseball game can be. To begin with, the Mets were undefeated, having routed the Braves 11–1 the previous night in Atlanta's home opener. The Braves were 3–1, having started the season with a three-game sweep of the Phillies in Philadelphia. The season was less than a week old, and already it was beginning to look as if the Braves and Mets would be dueling for the lead in the National League East all year.

"I'm not sure we can stay with them," Cox said, perhaps trying to put some early pressure on the Mets. "There are really no holes in that lineup at all."

Opposition hyperbole aside, the Mets' everyday lineup certainly appeared to be outstanding. It started with shortstop Jose Reyes, who had emerged as a star in 2006 and at the age of twenty-three was considered by many the best lead-off hitter in baseball. "He may be the best lead-off hitter I've seen since Rickey Henderson," Cox said, dropping the name of the sport's best ever lead-off hitter. "I mean, what can't he do? He hit nineteen home runs last year — that should improve. He stole sixty bases [actually sixty-four]. He's gotten more patient [his walks had almost doubled in 2006], and he can really play the position. The kid is great."

The kid playing next to Reyes on the left side of the infield was just about as good. David Wright was twenty-four and already had two one hundred–RBI seasons behind him. He was bright and outgoing and got more female fan mail than anyone else on the team.

Reyes and Wright were both the face and the future of the franchise. Both had been signed to long-term contracts the previous summer and were being compared favorably to the older

Yankee duo of Derek Jeter and Alex Rodriguez, both lock Hall of Famers.

Surrounding them were veterans like first baseman Carlos Delgado, who had failed to drive in at least one hundred runs only once in the previous nine seasons (and that had been in 2004 when he had driven in ninety-nine runs in Toronto, while missing thirty-four games with injuries). Delgado was also one of the team's unquestioned clubhouse leaders, a thoughtful, stand-up person who had engendered some controversy because of his decision several years earlier to stay inside the clubhouse during the playing of the national anthem — a silent protest against the war in Iraq.

Carlos Beltran, the quiet center fielder, had hit forty-one home runs and driven in 116 in 2006, after playing poorly in 2005, the first year of the seven-year, $119 million contract he had signed that winter. The Mets had signed Moises Alou to play left field during the off-season. Alou had been oft-injured throughout his career, but when healthy he was still a very solid, consistent hitter. Shawn Green, the right fielder, was showing signs of age but had also been a hundred-RBI man four times in his career. Paul Lo Duca, the everyday catcher, was a four-time All-Star who had hit .318 in 2006. Jose Valentin, the second baseman, was coming off a career year too, having hit .271, with eighteen home runs.

If there was any question mark at all surrounding the Mets, it was age. Every starter other than Wright and Reyes was at least thirty: Alou was forty; Valentin and Lo Duca were thirty-five; Delgado almost thirty-five; Green thirty-four; and Beltran was about to turn thirty. Older players can be injury prone, and there is no way of knowing when they will start to lose their skills or, in some cases, lose them all of a sudden.

The pitching staff was also old: Glavine was forty-one, and even though Orlando Hernandez claimed to be thirty-seven, no one in the clubhouse believed him. "I'm not saying he's old," Glavine joked, "but he does get mail from AARP."

Pedro Martinez was thirty-five and wouldn't pitch for most of the season. Billy Wagner, the closer, would be thirty-six at mid-season. There was some youth with Oliver Perez and John Maine, both in the rotation at twenty-five, and Mike Pelfrey at twenty-four. But the pitchers the Mets would probably rely on most in September and October were all a lot closer to the end of their careers than the beginning.

"You can look at it one of two ways," Willie Randolph liked to say. "We're old or we're experienced."

For four games the Mets had looked experienced and very good. They were hitting; the starting pitching had been superb; and they were, it appeared, sending an early message that they were still the team to beat in the National League East. Opening the series in Atlanta with a one-sided win was a very good sign.

The second game of the series would be a 3:55 p.m. start for the benefit of FOX TV, which had decided to move back its Saturday game-of-the-week starting times to the late afternoon in the hope that it would attract more viewers coming in from Saturday activities. A cold front had engulfed the entire East Coast, and it was hardly a beautiful day for baseball: the game-time temperature was forty-one degrees, with whipping winds making it feel a good deal colder than that.

"Definitely a two T-shirt day," Glavine said in the clubhouse. "If I could wear more and still get my arm around to throw the ball, I would."

Watching Glavine and his old pal John Smoltz prepare to pitch was a good way to get a sense of how different their personalities are. Glavine is hardly different on a day he is pitching than on a day he is not. He will come in, change, go into the training room to get his arm worked on, and then relax in front of his locker, watching whatever is on the clubhouse TV or chatting with anyone who is around. About an hour before the game is to start, he will retreat into the training room with Peterson and that day's catcher—usually Lo Duca—to go over the other team's hitters.

Smoltz, who loves to talk and tell stories most days, is completely hyper on the day he pitches. "My best friend might walk in
the clubhouse, and it's possible I wouldn't recognize him," he likes
to say.

On this particular day, Smoltz was bouncing from one locker
to another in the Braves clubhouse looking for a second T-shirt
that would fit him properly. Pitchers normally do not like to wear
any extra clothing because it may affect their pitching motion.
But they also need to work up a sweat, and on a cold day that can
be difficult. Smoltz darted from locker to locker, saying repeatedly, "I need something that's comfortable."

If someone had suggested he sit down and relax like Glavine,
Smoltz would have looked at him as if he had just dropped in
from Mars.

Not only was it a difficult day to pitch, it was also a difficult
day to field. The wind made it tough, as did the slanting, late-
afternoon sun. Smoltz gave up a home run to Lo Duca in the first
inning, but the Braves got it right back when Delgado dropped a
perfect throw from Valentin on a routine Kelly Johnson ground
ball to start the bottom of the inning.

"Believe it or not, he lost the throw in the sun," Glavine said
later. "I don't think I've ever seen that in my entire life—a first
baseman losing a throw from second base in the sun. But it was a
very strange day."

Glavine eventually walked the bases loaded before getting out
of the inning on a Jeff Francoeur RBI ground out and another
ground out by Brian McCann—Delgado was able to handle both
throws. It was 1–1 after one. What was troubling for Glavine was
that he had already thrown thirty pitches.

Throughout his career, Glavine has had difficulty in the first
inning. It is something he has never completely figured out. At
times he has tried throwing fewer pitches in the bullpen, more
pitches in the bullpen, and warming up a little earlier or a little
later. "Sometimes it's just a matter of getting used to the mound,"

he said. "The mound on the field is always different than the bull-pen mound so you have to adjust. Sometimes I just struggle with my control early, or maybe I'm trying too hard. One way or the other, I always try to get off to a good start. It just never seems to be easy for me."

A lot of great pitchers are more vulnerable early than late. As the old baseball saying "You better get him early" suggests, once a good pitcher gets in a groove, it is often hard to get him out of it. Glavine was a perfect example.

He fell behind 2–1 in the second inning on a solo home run by Matt Diaz, the Braves' young left fielder, but then settled in, retiring seven of the next eight. Smoltz worked out of trouble in the third, then gave up a single to Alou and a double to Green, with two outs in the fourth. A lot of players—most—would have scored on the Green double, especially with two men out, but Alou is slower than the bureaucracy in Washington, so he had to hold at third. The Braves opted to walk Valentin intentionally, so they could pitch to Glavine with the bases loaded.

"I *so* wanted to drive the ball someplace for a couple of runs," Glavine said. "Obviously they did the right thing pitching to me, but a hit in that situation off of Smoltzie would have been sweet."

Glavine is not one of those athletes who tries to claim that all games are the same or that he doesn't feel extra butterflies in certain situations. Pitching against Smoltz, especially in Atlanta, was absolutely a big deal to him. They had faced each other only once previously. That had been in 2005, shortly after Glavine went through his pitching makeover. It had been one of Glavine's rare good starts against the Braves. He had left a 1–1 game after seven innings, only to see the bullpen give up a run in the eighth, allowing Smoltz to win the game 2–1.

"To say that it doesn't feel different to go out there and pitch against him would be silly," Glavine said. "He's one of my best friends; we were teammates all those years. The last thing I want to do is lose to him. You walk into the ballpark for a game like this — it does feel different. A win means a little more; a loss stings a little more."

Smoltz had come up in the second after Diaz's home run and had pushed the count to 2–1. Glavine then threw him a hard slider, which Smoltz hit weakly off the end of the bat back to Glavine. In the cold, hitting the ball that way stung Smoltz's hands, and he yelled in pain as he dropped the bat.

"Why'd you have to throw me a slider?" he yelled at Glavine, half joking as Glavine easily threw him out at first.

"Because I needed to get you out," Glavine yelled back, not joking at all.

Now, Smoltz needed to get Glavine out. Trying very hard to give himself a lead, Glavine swung late at a good Smoltz fastball — even in the cold, Smoltz was still getting his fastball up to 95 and 96 miles per hour — and popped it to third. Opportunity gone.

The Mets did tie the score in the fifth when Reyes walked and stole second and Beltran singled him home. They had a chance to take the lead in the sixth when Glavine sacrificed Green to second and Reyes walked again with two out. But Smoltz struck out Lo Duca with a 96-mile-an-hour fastball on his 118th pitch of the game to keep the score tied.

"The only way I can get a win at that point is if we get to Tommy in the bottom of the inning," Smoltz said later. "Because there was no way with that pitch count Bobby [Cox] was letting me come out for the seventh."

Glavine had thrown ninety-two pitches through five innings, struggling to throw his breaking pitches over the plate. Smoltz was having the same problem. Each was having difficulty getting a feel for the baseball in his cold, dry hands.

Andruw Jones, one of the few Braves left who had been a Glavine teammate, began the sixth with a double to left after Glavine thought he had struck him out on a 2–2 changeup that plate umpire Randy Marsh deemed to be outside. "Sometimes baseball is a game of inches," Glavine said later. "On that play it was a game of an inch — or less."

Francoeur, who often gives Glavine trouble because he doesn't try to outthink Glavine but just swings at what he sees, hit Glavine's 2–1 fastball hard to right, so hard that Jones had to hold up at third. The hit came on Glavine's 103rd pitch of the day. He knew he was on a very short leash at that point. "I was hoping to maybe get through the inning somehow and give our guys a chance to get to their pen in the seventh."

It didn't happen, in part because the defense let him down. Valentin did make a good play on a McCann line drive for the first out. Not wanting to throw a fastball to Craig Wilson, a dead fastball hitter, Glavine kept missing with his changeup to fall behind 3–0. When he did throw a fastball, Wilson, with the green light from Cox, crushed a line drive to right that was just foul. Glavine wasn't going to throw him another fastball. He missed with another changeup, and the bases were loaded. Randolph came to the mound. Diaz was up next and he had already homered. But Glavine convinced Randolph to let him try to finish the inning, pointing out that he didn't feel that tired because of the cold weather.

Randolph's decision to leave Glavine in looked like a good one when Diaz hit a fly ball to right that would probably have been a sacrifice fly, except that Green, fighting the wind, dropped it. Jones scored to make it 3–2, and everyone moved up a base. That was it for Glavine, whose pitch count was now at 113 — fifty-seven of those pitches balls. It was one of the few times in his career that Glavine could remember throwing more balls than strikes in a game.

Pedro Feliciano came in for Glavine, and the Braves scored twice more before the inning was over to make it 5–2. The Braves bullpen held on from there, and Atlanta won 5–3, meaning both teams were now 4–1.

The loss was tough to take for Glavine because he had hung in on a tough day, giving up only four hits but being done in by his wildness—especially on his breaking pitches—and the Mets' defense. Only two of the five runs charged to him were earned.

"If you figure you're going to have thirty starts in a year, you probably think there will be ten times when you're so good you should absolutely win and ten times when you're bad enough that you clearly deserve to lose," he said. "The ten in the middle probably decided your season. That was one of those ten. I was good enough to win with some help, bad enough to lose without it. Unfortunately that was one of those days when I didn't get the help I needed. Plus, Smoltzie made some big pitches when he had to." He smiled. "I would expect nothing less from him."

The Braves won the next day to end week one in first place. There were only twenty-five weeks left in the season. The teams would meet again—fifteen more times to be exact—and so would Glavine and Smoltz.

The Yankees finished their first week of the season 2–3, without a starting pitcher reaching the sixth inning. Kei Igawa, the $46 million Japanese pitcher, managed to make it through five innings in his Yankee debut but gave up seven runs in the process. An Alex Rodriguez grand slam in the ninth rescued the Yankees that day, but they lost to the Orioles in their next outing, with starter Darrell Rasner failing to get out of the fifth.

But, as always seemed to be the case, Minnesota was like a health spa for the entire team. Carl Pavano became the first starter to win a game with seven solid innings on Monday, and Andy Pettitte pitched six shutout innings the next night, as the Yankees won 8–2 and 10–1. It was left to Mussina to complete the sweep.

The night started out well enough. There was still snow on the ground outside, but it was seventy degrees inside the Metrodome as Mussina warmed up, and he felt comfortable, much more so than before the Baltimore game. He was going on his normal fifth day, and that felt good too.

He gave up a walk in the first inning and a double to Torii Hunter in the second but easily pitched out of both innings. "I felt much better than in New York," he said. "I had something on the ball, and my location was about a hundred percent better."

Luis Rodriguez led off the third inning for Minnesota. On the first pitch he threw to him, Mussina felt something grab inside his left leg. He knew he'd done something but hoped it was minor. Rodriguez singled to right. Then, Alexi Casilla, the weak-hitting shortstop who was batting ninth, also singled. Mussina was fairly certain at that point he had done something to his hamstring. Like any pitcher, he'd had hamstring injuries before. A hamstring injury can be fairly mild, a pull that can be fixed with some heat, or it can be very serious and keep a pitcher out for months.

Mussina decided to try one more batter before he told anyone he was hurt. Maybe — not likely but maybe — it would somehow loosen up. On his third pitch to Luis Castillo, he knew better. He couldn't land without feeling pain, and as a result he was pushing his pitches rather than following through the way he needed to.

He walked off the mound and waved at Ron Guidry in the dugout. Guidry trotted out to meet him.

"What's up?" he asked.

"I hurt myself," Mussina answered. "Hamstring."

"How bad?"

"I can't pitch."

By now, Torre and assistant trainer Steve Donahue had followed Guidry out of the dugout.

"What's up?" Torre asked Guidry.

"Hamstring," Guidry answered. "He can't pitch."

Mussina walked off the field while Torre signaled for reliever Sean Henn to start warming up. Since Mussina had left with an injury, Henn had all the time he needed to get ready.

As he eased onto the training table to let Donahue feel around the back of his leg, Mussina's mind was racing. A hamstring, he knew, could be a bad injury. But it didn't hurt, he thought, that much. He didn't think he'd torn it, just pulled it enough that he couldn't land on it.

"On the one hand, it's your second start of the season and you know you're probably looking at the DL," Mussina said. "On the other hand, it isn't your shoulder and it isn't your elbow. It's a hamstring and it's April. It isn't exactly how you want to start your season, but it's early. If you only miss two weeks, you're back before April is over."

If you only miss two weeks.

Sitting on the training table in Minneapolis, with snow falling outside and the DL looming, Mussina knew one thing for sure: he was *not* where he wanted to be.

13

A Cold Spring

THE YANKEES WAITED A FEW DAYS before deciding whether to put Mike Mussina on the disabled list. They had this luxury because baseball rules allow a team to place someone on the DL retroactive to the date when he last played, regardless of when they actually decide to make him inactive.

There are two disabled lists: one that requires a player to be out at least fifteen days, and another that requires him to be out at least sixty days. The sixty-day DL is generally used only for long-term injuries and for players who are out for the season.

Mussina was fairly certain when he walked off the mound in Minnesota that he was looking at a stint on the DL but was certainly willing to wait a few days to see if the hamstring would loosen up more rapidly than he expected. "Nothing to lose by waiting," he said. "They can wait until they need someone to pitch in my spot before making a decision. But a hamstring isn't something you want to take a chance with and really hurt yourself. My goal, realistically, was to come back in as close to fifteen days as possible."

That would be on April 26. The Yankees waited three days to see how Mussina was feeling. He flew with the team from Minnesota to Oakland and tried to throw lightly in the bullpen on Saturday. It only took him a few pitches to know there was no way he could think about trying to throw hard. The next day he was placed on the DL. Chase Wright, a twenty-four-year-old lefty who had spent the 2006 season pitching in A-ball, was called up to take his spot in the rotation. It was the sixth time in seventeen big league seasons that Mussina had been forced to go on the DL.

"Which, if you think about it, is pretty good," he said.

True. But not as good as Tom Glavine, who was truly a medical marvel, having never been on the DL. He had missed a few starts over twenty years but had never been out long enough to merit the DL.

Glavine had come out of the start in Atlanta disappointed but feeling fine physically, even after throwing 113 pitches. The Mets came home from the first week on the road with a 4–2 record, a good start, although one sullied by the fact that the two losses had come in Atlanta to end the trip.

"It would have been nice to reestablish our superiority on those guys right away," Glavine said. "We had the chance to do it after Friday night but didn't. Still, it's a long season."

If someone could find a way to get every American to chip in a dollar each time a baseball person says "It's a long season," or "There's still a lot of season left," there would be no reason for the government to collect taxes. Baseball people talk about how long the season is in February, and they talk about it in September. When the New York media was getting impatient about Pedro Martinez's return one evening, Mets general manager Omar Minaya shook his head and said, "Hey, fellas, it's a long season. We've got a lot of baseball left to be played." That was on September 2.

The Mets' first homestand—of the long 2007 season—was against the Philadelphia Phillies. The Phillies were off to a brutal beginning, having started 1–5. Already there was talk that Charlie Manuel might be the first manager to lose his job that spring.

Glavine was scheduled to pitch the third game of the series, against Jamie Moyer. This was, to put it mildly, an intriguing matchup. To begin with, Glavine was the youngster of the two, since Moyer was forty-four. In fact, according to the Elias Sports Bureau, Glavine-Moyer represented the oldest combined age of two starting left-handers in a game in Major League Baseball history. Only Elias can come up with stats like that.

Beyond that were the obvious similarities between the two. When Moyer and Glavine watched each other, they might as well have been looking into a mirror. Glavine was a soft-tossing lefty; Moyer tossed even softer. His fastball almost never cracked 80 miles an hour, but, like Glavine, he had been keeping hitters off-balance for years with a great changeup and pinpoint control. Batters constantly walked to the plate knowing they could crush both pitchers, then walked away wondering why they had just rolled out to shortstop. They were masters of "the comfortable oh for four." A hitter almost never saw a pitch he couldn't hit and at the end of the night would be oh for four without ever feeling uncomfortable at the plate.

Moyer is an unabashed fan of Glavine. For years he carried a tape of Glavine's performance in Game Six of the 1995 World Series with him wherever he went. "To me that game represented as close to a perfect performance by a lefty who has a style like mine as I had ever seen," he said. "It wasn't so much the results, which were obviously great, but the way he pitched that game. The way he stood on the mound, his mechanics on every single pitch, his release point.

"I always say that I can watch a pitcher release a ball and, without looking, tell you where the pitch went and how it broke or didn't break. That night, every pitch he threw was a good pitch—regardless of what the hitter did or, in most cases, didn't do with it. That game was what I was striving to achieve for years."

Moyer no longer carries the tape because several years ago, in a game in St. Louis, he finally pitched a game he thought was comparable. "When I look at that tape now, that's what I want to be every single time I pitch," he said. "But Glavine was the model for me. Even now, I love to watch him pitch. I think I learn something every time I watch him."

Moyer is a remarkable story. He had been drafted by the Chicago Cubs in 1984 out of St. Joseph's University—hardly a baseball power—and made it to the big leagues in 1986. But he hurt his arm in 1989 and was released by the Texas Rangers at the end of the 1990 season. That led to several years of wandering in the baseball hinterlands. He spent 1991 in St. Louis and was released again at the end of that season. The Cubs re-signed him, then released him before the 1992 season began. He finally signed a minor league contract with the Detroit Tigers in May and spent that year pitching in their minor league system, where he began to develop his changeup. At the end of that season, he signed with the Baltimore Orioles and made it back to the big leagues for good in 1993.

In Baltimore he became friends with a veteran pitcher named Jimmy Key and a young pitcher named Mike Mussina.

"We spent hours talking about pitching," Moyer said. "We would talk about it in the clubhouse, in the bullpen, in the outfield during batting practice. We talked about how you set up hitters, about improving your mechanics, about how to have a good bullpen. I mean everything. I never got tired of listening to those two guys. What's really too bad is you don't see young pitchers do that anymore. Everyone's got an iPod or a cell phone going all the time. There's very little talking in baseball anymore."

Sitting in a comfortable chair, Moyer gestured around the Phillies clubhouse. Sure enough, several players were sitting in their lockers talking on cell phones; several others stared into space with headphones on. The only person who appeared to be having a conversation at that moment was Moyer—with a reporter.

"Talking to Key was great back then because he'd been at it for so long," he continued. "Mussina hadn't been, but it didn't matter. Even then when he was very young, he really understood the art of pitching. In a way, I think I learned how to pitch from those two guys, not just how to throw but how to think on the mound and off the mound. In those days, Moose could throw hard, but that wasn't how he won. He won because he was always a step ahead of the hitter. Sort of like Glavine, only from the right-hand side."

Sort of like Moyer. After three years in Baltimore, Moyer signed with the Red Sox for the 1996 season. At that point he was in the midst of a very ordinary career: he was thirty-three years old and had a big league record of 59–76. He had started to see improvement in Baltimore but was still learning to throw his changeup where he wanted with consistency. He pitched well in Boston, going 7–1 through the first half of the season, but was sent to Seattle in what appeared to be an unremarkable trade deadline deal for Darren Bragg.

In Seattle, Moyer became a star. Over the next ten years he was 145–81 for the Mariners, including twenty-win seasons in 2001 at the age of thirty-eight and in 2003 at the age of forty, when he was 21–7 with a 3.27 ERA. He and his wife, Karen, the daughter of former Notre Dame basketball coach and ESPN commentator Digger Phelps, established the Moyer Foundation to raise money for kids at risk. The foundation has raised almost $10 million, and Seattle is still home during the off-season for the Moyers and their six children.

With the Phillies trying to make a late run in 2006, they traded for Moyer, bringing him to the team he had rooted for as a little boy. He had pitched well, going 5–2, but the Phillies — as always seemed to be the case — had come up short of making the playoffs, their thirteenth straight year without a postseason appearance. Moyer knew the end was near but still felt he could get batters out enough to contribute.

"I won't have to ask anyone to tell me when I'm done," he said. "The hitters will tell me. That's how baseball works."

The night of Thursday, April 12, was hardly one for two senior citizens of baseball to be out trying to pitch. It would be forty-four degrees when Glavine walked to the mound, with the wind whipping through Shea Stadium so hard that it brought back memories of the New York Jets and Joe Namath playing on this same field on cold, windy, late-fall afternoons.

Only this wasn't an afternoon. "This will be worse than Atlanta," Glavine said, pulling on the requisite extra T-shirt and sipping hot coffee in the clubhouse. "Because it's night, it will only get colder as the game goes on. It will be almost impossible to feel the ball."

Glavine hadn't pitched much better against the Phillies in his Mets career than he had against the Braves. He had been 24–10 against the Phillies while in Atlanta but was 2–7 against them as a Met, with an ERA of 5.27. Beyond that, his ring finger had started to feel cold while playing against the Phillies the previous August. What's more, even though the Phillies were off to a terrible start, the Mets had reason to want to hammer them early and often. During spring training, Jimmy Rollins, the Phils' talented shortstop had said, "I think we are the team to beat in the National League East."

That comment rankled the Mets since they had finished twelve games ahead of the Phillies the previous season and saw no evidence that they weren't at least twelve games better than the Phillies again. "It would be nice to make him eat those words," Glavine said. "And there's no reason why we can't do it."

At that moment, Rollins was hitting .250 and the Phillies were 2–6. So far, so good, as far as the Mets were concerned.

As always, Rollins led off for the Phillies. On 2–1, Glavine threw what he thought was a perfect changeup. Rollins laid off, and plate umpire Ed Montague—one of Glavine's favorite umpires—called the pitch a ball.

"Perfect example of why it's important, especially at this point in my career to get the close pitch," he said. "If it's two and two, I can throw any pitch I want to throw. At three and one, I really don't want to start the game by walking Rollins because there's a decent chance he's going to steal second and then you feel like you're in trouble right away. So, I threw him a fastball and got a little more of the plate than I wanted to get."

The pitch also didn't have much on it—the radar gun clocking it at 79 miles per hour, as Glavine tried to get his velocity up in the cold. Rollins jumped on the pitch and hit it into the left-field bullpen. "Nice start," Glavine joked later.

Before the inning was over, Glavine had walked the bases loaded. Fortunately, he got Wes Helms to strike out on a 3–2 changeup, and walked to the dugout relieved but not exactly thrilled after another thirty-pitch first inning. "Right away the chances of going deep into the game are pretty much gone after an inning like that," he said. "But at least it was only one-nothing."

The weather wasn't any better for Moyer, and he was quickly in trouble too, giving up singles to Jose Reyes and Paul Lo Duca and an RBI single to Carlos Beltran, to tie the game at 1–1, with no one out and runners on first and third. But, as veteran pitchers will do, Moyer took a deep breath and found a way out. He struck out Carlos Delgado and got David Wright to ground into a double play.

Rollins hit another home run in the second, this time on a 3–2 changeup that left Glavine kicking at the mound. The Mets got one back in the second and then took a 4–3 lead in the fourth when Reyes singled two runners home with two men out. The reason the runners were both in scoring position? Glavine had sacrificed with one out, laying down a perfect bunt.

"Perfect example," he said, "of why every pitcher should know how to bunt."

Glavine managed to get Rollins to ground to shortstop the third time he came up, and fought his way through six innings without giving up any more runs. Moyer also made it through six before both old men headed for well-deserved ice packs for their arms and hot showers for their aching bodies.

"You see in a game like that why Tommy is Tommy," Rick Peterson said. "Five outs into the game he's given up three runs and two home runs. And then he puts his head down and that's it for the night. A lot of guys under those conditions, with the start he had, throwing fifty pitches [actually forty-nine] the first two innings, don't make it to the fourth. He hangs in there through six and gets a win."

The final was 5–3, the Mets bullpen again pitching well behind Glavine, giving him his 292nd win. Moyer took the loss and remained at 217 wins. In all, not too bad for a couple of pitchers who were more likely to hit a dozen home runs apiece than throw a single pitch at 90 miles per hour before season's end. Glavine hit 86 a couple of times over the course of the evening; Moyer hit 80 — once.

"Slow, slower, slowest," Mets' closer Billy Wagner joked. "But they get people out."

Twenty years after arriving in the major leagues, they both still got people out.

By the time the Mets and Phillies met for two more games a week later at Citizens Bank Park in Philadelphia, it appeared likely that Charlie Manuel wouldn't make it out of the month of April as Phillies manager.

Both teams had only played twice since they had met in New York as the awful April weather continued in the East. The Mets had been rained out of the last game of their series against the Washington Nationals, and then both teams had watched it rain all day in Philadelphia the next day. That made the two-game series into a one-game series.

The Phillies decided to move Moyer back a day so that Freddy Garcia, one of their big free-agent acquisitions who had started the season on the DL, could make his 2007 debut. The Mets opted not to move anyone back, meaning Glavine would pitch the one game in Philadelphia, and Orlando Hernandez and John Maine would pitch the two games in Miami against the Marlins.

"We need to ask Glavine if he's not being a little bit of a prima donna not moving back a day," WFAN's Christopher Russo said on the air that day to his partner Mike Francesa. "Might be better for the team if he pitches in Miami, wouldn't it?"

Actually it might have been better for *Glavine* to pitch in Miami, where the temperature would be about forty degrees warmer than in Philadelphia. Rick Peterson had come to Glavine after the rainout and informed him that he and Randolph wanted him to take his turn in Philly. Hernandez was very delicate, and they didn't want him to pitch in the cold weather.

"Which was fine with me," Glavine said. "I was planning on pitching in Philly, and I was mentally ready to pitch in the cold again. But I wouldn't have minded being pushed back at all."

The reason Russo and Francesa got a chance to ask Glavine about the rotation was because WFAN paid him $35,000 a year to appear weekly with their afternoon drive duo, who had, arguably, the most popular local sports talk show in the country. It is now commonplace for broadcast media outlets to pay athletes and coaches to appear regularly on the air, but WFAN must have the largest pay-the-jocks budget in the country. In addition to Glavine, the station paid both local managers, Joe Torre and Willie Randolph, to appear on a weekly basis, and it also paid a number of local pro football players and coaches for appearances. Glavine didn't mind going on with Russo and Francesa, especially when it gave him a chance to correct a misconception, because unlike some talk-show hosts they *would* ask him the question rather than talk behind his back.

Having explained to WFAN's listeners why he was pitching that night, Glavine went out to pitch. In a way, it was an ideal night to pitch because, even though it was again frigid and windy, the wind was blowing straight in from left field. With the Phillies playing horribly, and the weather just as bad, the crowd in Citizens Bank Park was tiny—far smaller than the announced 27,058.

Attendance figures can be deceiving, especially early in the season when the weather's bad or late in the season when a team is out of contention. Major League Baseball announces the number of tickets sold, which means that season-ticket holders who stay away or those who buy a ticket but don't show because of bad weather or a bad team are counted as being there.

There were probably no more than fifteen thousand fans in the park when Garcia, wearing a red glove, walked to the mound. Before he could throw a pitch, the umpires made him return to the dugout to change gloves — the red was too distracting for the hitters. He returned with a bright blue glove, which was somehow deemed to be less distracting.

Apparently the glove didn't distract Moises Alou, who twice hit balls through the wind into the left-field bleachers, the first time with David Wright on first base, the second time leading off the sixth inning. Carlos Beltran added an RBI double in the fifth, and that was plenty for Glavine who pitched what was becoming a typical game for him: six innings, 103 pitches (exactly the same number as five days earlier), five walks and a hit batter, and six hits. He pitched into trouble, then he pitched out of trouble.

The first inning was typical: Shane Victorino doubled to left, and Chase Utley walked. That brought up Ryan Howard, the 2006 National League MVP and one of baseball's best hitters with men on base. Glavine's first pitch was an outside fastball that Howard hit right back at him. Always prepared to field his position, Glavine grabbed the ball and turned it into a one-six-three double play. End of threat.

In the third inning, Glavine did something that very few pitchers, if any, would think of doing. He intentionally, though technically unintentionally, walked Howard, with a 2–0 lead and the bases loaded.

"Let's put it this way," he said. "No way was he going to see a fastball with the bases loaded. I would rather let him drive in one with a walk than four with a homer."

And so Glavine threw five changeups and one curve ball, which was way outside, and walked in a run. Then he got Pat Burrell to ground out to end the inning.

It helped Glavine that the Phillies grounded into three double plays. That allowed him to pitch six shutout innings. He also got a hit and scored his first run of the season in the fifth. "I'm not as fast as I used to be," he said. "But I can still move a little when there's a run to be scored."

The only bad moment of the night for Glavine came in the fifth inning. Shawn Green had doubled with one out and moved to third on a Valentin ground out. Glavine came up. As a pitcher will always do in a situation with a runner on third, Glavine stood outside the batter's box for a moment checking with third-base coach Sandy Alomar Sr. to see if anything—a squeeze bunt perhaps—had been called by Willie Randolph from the dugout.

Nothing was on. Glavine took a rip at the first pitch and was stunned to see Green barreling down the third-base line. A squeeze bunt had been on, but Alomar had given Glavine a sign that indicated nothing was on and Glavine swung away. Green was easily thrown out, which was a lot better than what might have happened if Glavine had somehow hit a line drive in his direction.

Signs get changed all the time in baseball. Since stealing signs is considered part of the game, teams constantly change their signs. In doing so, players have to be reminded that what might have been a bunt sign last week is now a take sign. In every set of signs, there is one sign that indicates to a player that something is on or that, no matter what comes after this, nothing is on. Glavine had seen the sign that indicated nothing was on. Alomar had given it inadvertently, forgetting for an instant that the signs had been switched.

"It happens a couple times a year," Glavine said. "We were lucky I swung and missed and lucky that, in the end, it didn't affect the outcome of the game. As it turned out, it was just embarrassing."

The signs between a pitcher and a catcher are different than base-running signs, which involve things like touching one's face, wiping a hand across the shirt, or touching the bill of one's cap. A catcher will put down fingers—which can be a problem if a pitcher is at all nearsighted—to suggest to the pitcher what he wants him to throw. The standard signs are one finger for a fast-ball, two for a curve, three for a changeup or a slider, and, if a pitcher has a fourth pitch—say a cutter in Glavine's case—that might be four fingers.

But there are times when those signs change too. When a runner gets to second base, signs almost always change because the runner might see a sign and relay it to the hitter. Normally, the catcher will give two signs: the first one will be the indicator. If he puts down one finger, that means the next sign the pitcher sees is the pitch he wants him to throw. If he puts down two fingers first, that means the second sign he sees is the pitch he wants. It can get more complicated than that. A catcher can give a double indicator, meaning that the second sign he puts down—say a two followed by a three—is the sign indicator. In that case, the third sign that follows the indicator is the pitch that's called.

Glavine is fairly simplistic about signs because he rarely shakes off his catcher. "Maybe once a game he'll do it," catcher Paul Lo Duca said. "If you have experience catching Tom, you have a good idea what he wants to throw, and he doesn't worry all that much about what he's throwing as much as *where* he's throwing it."

Mussina is different. His catcher, Jorge Posada, knows that his sign is nothing more than a suggestion to Mussina, who will probably shake him off about 50 percent of the time—not unusual for an experienced pitcher who throws as many different pitches as Mussina does. When there's a runner on second base, Mussina insists on a completely different set of signs from the indicator through the actual pitch call. "He's as careful with a runner on second as anyone I've ever worked with," Posada said.

"That's part of Mike being Mike; he doesn't leave anything to chance."

The Mets were able to joke about the missed sign in Philadelphia because no one was hurt, and they went on to win the game 8–1. Things were a lot worse for the Phillies. Not only did they lose, but after Glavine struck out to end the inning, the Phils threw the ball around the infield, forgetting that Glavine had just made the third out. Not one of the nine men on the field made a move for the dugout.

At game's end, while the Mets prepared to head for Miami with an 8–4 record, the Phillies clubhouse was not a happy place to be. The team was 3–9, and Charlie Manuel got into a shouting match with a radio reporter who wondered what in the world was wrong with a team that was supposed to be a contender.

There were no shouting matches in the Mets clubhouse. Glavine was now 3–1, and his ERA after four starts was 2.70. He had only one complaint at that moment: "Is the temperature ever going to hit fifty?" he asked.

It was still April, and for Mike Mussina the month of April felt like a long season. When he began to do rehabilitation exercises on his leg, he was relieved to find that the injury wasn't serious. The team had done an MRI to be certain there was no tear, and once that had been confirmed he began working toward being able to get back on a mound, throw with some velocity, and land on the injured leg without feeling pain.

As it turned out, that took about two weeks. Which meant that his first goal—to return to pitching in the minimum fifteen days—wasn't going to be met.

"You can't rush these things," Joe Torre said. "You especially can't rush them with a thirty-eight-year-old. I know Moose wants to get back out there, especially with the staff struggling, but he's smart enough to know the point is to get him out there and keep him out there, not have him go out and hurt it again."

Mussina did understand that. He also understood the various steps in coming back from an injury because he had been there before. Once he was back on the mound throwing in the bullpen without pain, he could begin to plan a rehab start. Since he hadn't been out for that long, one would probably be enough.

A player can be placed on a rehab assignment for as long as thirty days. After that, if he isn't called up to the major league team, he must either be assigned to the minor league team or just remain on the DL and not play at all. That rarely happens. Most rehabs last no more than a week for a position player and a start or two for a pitcher.

Mussina was ready for his rehab start on April 27. The plan was for him to pitch for the Trenton Thunder in a game in Harrisburg, and then, if all went well, he would pitch the following Wednesday on his regular four days' rest in Texas.

"It feels fine right now," he said, sitting in the dugout at Yankee Stadium on the day before the planned rehab game. "But you really can't tell for sure until you really push it. Even the rehab game doesn't tell you for sure, but it should give you a pretty good indicator. At least you hope so."

There was one problem with the rehab plan: weather.

"We're trying to find a place where it isn't supposed to rain tomorrow," Torre said. "Right now, there's no place. Everywhere he could pitch, there's supposed to be rain."

Mussina couldn't help but roll his eyes when he heard the various weather reports. "Into my life rain always falls—especially when I'm supposed to pitch," he said, smiling. "I remember one spring it rained so much on days I was pitching that I started to think I was related to Noah. Right now, sitting here, I have no idea where I'm pitching tomorrow. I know it will be someplace, but the last thing I want to do is get on a plane, fly someplace, and not be able to pitch."

The alternative to flying someplace to pitch in a minor league game was to stay in New York and pitch a simulated game, either on the Yankee Stadium mound or, if it were raining in New York (which was predicted), in the bullpen. Neither Torre nor Guidry was terribly excited about that idea.

"I think you need to pitch in a real game of some kind," Torre said. "You just push yourself harder by instinct when there are fielders around, real hitters at the plate, and a scoreboard behind you. If there's anyone I would trust to know how hard he needs to push himself, it's Moose, but I'd much rather get him into a real game."

The decision was made *not* to make a decision until after that night's game against the Toronto Blue Jays. Mussina's return was very much under the radar at that moment anyway. The Yankees were floundering at 8–12 and had called up twenty-year-old phenom Philip Hughes, who had been scheduled to spend the season in Triple-A.

On the same day that Mussina had gone on the DL, Carl Pavano had also gone on the DL. After his impressive outing in Minnesota, he had reported some tightness in his right forearm. The so-called tightness would eventually lead to season-ending surgery. Chien-Ming Wang had made his first start of the season two days earlier, but with Pavano gone and Mussina not back yet and the rookies who had been given starts all struggling, the Yankees were desperate enough to push up Hughes's schedule by several months.

While Mussina was studying weather reports, Torre sat a few feet away in the dugout going through his daily meeting with the media, who surrounded him at the start of batting practice each day with microphones, TV cameras, and notebooks. Getting close enough to Torre to actually hear him was so important that some media members would take up spots near where Torre always sat twenty minutes before he was due to arrive.

One of the Japanese reporters asked Torre the day's opening question: "Joe, is there panic in the locker room at this point?"

"Absolutely," Torre replied, deadpan. "That's the way we always do things around here."

With Hughes making his debut and a series with the Red Sox—who already had a five-and-a-half game lead—beginning the next day, the subject of Mussina's rehab start was not front-page (or, in New York, back-page) news. Which was fine with Mussina.

"The less questions I'm asked right now the better," he said. "Because until I get on a mound and try to throw hard, I really don't have any answers."

He wasn't nervous about the rehab start because there was really nothing to be nervous about. "Either I'm good enough to pitch next week or I'm not," he said. "It isn't as if I have to prepare mentally. This is all physical. The mental part will come again when I can actually pitch in a game."

Hughes was unimpressive that night, and the Yankees lost again, this time 6–0. After the game Torre studied the weather reports and made a decision.

"Nothing looks good," he told Mussina when Mussina came into his office to check in before driving home. "The last thing we need is for you to *not* pitch tomorrow because if you're healthy we need you to pitch Wednesday."

Mussina knew that. "I really think I can find out what I need to find out if I stay here and pitch a simulated," he told Torre.

Reluctantly, Torre agreed.

"If we hear something different about the weather, I'll call you in the morning," Torre said. "Otherwise, let's do it here early tomorrow afternoon."

Mussina woke up the next morning to find it raining hard. There had been no change in the weather report for any of the cities where he might go to pitch. He arrived back at Yankee Stadium at 1:30, and, with the rain still coming down steadily, he walked under the stands along with Guidry; Ramon Rodriguez, the number two bullpen catcher; and pitching instructor Rich Monteleone, to the Yankee bullpen in right field.

Mussina warmed up as if he were about to pitch in a game, throwing to Rodriguez, while Guidry stood behind him watching. After Mussina had thrown about thirty pitches, Monteleone stood in at the plate as a batter, and Mussina began to pitch to him. There were differences between this and a real game, of course: Monteleone didn't swing at any of his pitches, and there was no umpire calling balls and strikes, although Mussina made a mental note about where his pitches were going, and Guidry made a point of noting location.

He threw about twenty pitches, mixing them up the way he might in a game. Then he sat down for about ten minutes to simulate the wait he would have in the dugout while his team was at bat. He pitched the second "inning" from the stretch, then sat down again. The third inning was from the windup, then one more inning—after another break—from the stretch. In all, he threw about sixty-five pitches. He was a little bit tired when he was finished, but there was no pain in the hamstring. He had made a point of focusing on trying to throw hard, trying to imagine a batter swinging at his pitches. He told Guidry he felt fine. He was ready to pitch on Wednesday in Texas.

"Joe's right. Being out in the bullpen with no one around, and a hitter who isn't swinging at your pitches isn't the same as pitching in a game," Mussina said. "But I wasn't really trying to find out that day if I had good stuff or location, even though I was aware of both. I was trying to find out if I could pitch, sit for a while, pitch again and sit again, and not get stiff or tight or feel pain in my hamstring. I was able to do it, and that's what was important.

"I didn't feel relieved; I just felt more like, 'Okay, let's go. Let's get this season on track.'"

Once Torre got the report on Mussina's performance in the bullpen, he penciled him in to start the next Wednesday in Texas.

That would be May 2 — a month into the season. The first month had been a complete washout for Mussina: two starts, six innings pitched, six runs allowed, and a record of 0–1. By the time he took the mound in Texas, the Yankees' record would be 11–14.

Not exactly the start anyone had envisioned. But, in case you've never heard it before, it's a long season. It had certainly been a long month.

14

Spring in New York

TOM GLAVINE FINALLY GOT HIS WISH when the Mets came home from Florida. The Braves were in town for three games, and after one more cold, miserable night on Friday, the weather finally broke. The sun came out on Saturday, the temperatures went up, and more than fifty-five thousand people showed up for the second game of the series, which the Mets won, after Tim Hudson had pitched the Braves to a win in the opener.

All of which set the stage for Sunday afternoon, April 22. It was Smoltz versus Glavine again, a rematch of that frigid Saturday in Atlanta two weeks earlier—only this time the temperature was seventy degrees when Glavine walked to the mound, there was a light breeze and no humidity, and Shea Stadium sparkled as much as a forty-three-year-old dowager stadium can sparkle.

The Mets were 11–5; the Braves 11–6. Glavine was 3–1; Smoltz 2–1. It was about as perfect a day for baseball as you could possibly hope to see.

Glavine threw his warm-up pitches, Kelly Johnson stepped into the batter's box, and the crowd settled in. Glavine threw a fastball that caught a little more of the plate than he planned, and Johnson jumped all over it. The ball disappeared over the right-field fence before many in the crowd even knew Glavine had thrown the first pitch.

"He had struck out four times the day before," Glavine said

213

later. "He's a guy who will generally take strike one anyway. I'm thinking he isn't going to come out flailing after a four strikeout day. But I gave him a pitch that was too good *not* to swing at. Bad mistake.

"It's sort of like stepping into what you think is a hot shower, and it's ice cold. You kind of jump back and go, 'What was that?' It's a shock. You have to take a deep breath and say, 'Okay, that's not exactly ideal, but that's all they get.'"

Glavine did just that. In fact, he retired the next eight batters he faced before Johnson got a two-out single in the third. Glavine gave up another single to Edgar Renteria but then got his ex-teammate Chipper Jones to strike out looking. He was settled in.

The problem was it appeared possible that one run might be all Smoltz would need. He retired the first six Mets before Shawn Green singled, leading off the third, and Jose Valentin reached on a Chipper Jones error. That brought Glavine up in a bunting situation. Smoltz threw two fastballs at 96, and Glavine fouled both off, which really annoyed Glavine. On 0–2 he got the bunt down, but Smoltz pounced on it and got the force play on Green, another of the Mets' slow-footed base runners, at third.

He was even more upset a moment later when Reyes hit a ground ball that would have scored a run had he moved the runners up. Instead, Glavine was forced out at second, and Paul Lo Duca grounded out to end the threat.

Smoltz finally cracked a little in the fifth when Green hit his first pitch of the inning into the Mets bullpen to tie the game at 1–1. The Mets threatened for more when Reyes singled and Lo Duca doubled, but bad luck and good pitching kept them from taking the lead. The bad luck came when Lo Duca's shot in the right-center-field gap bounced over the wall for a ground rule double. If the ball hadn't gone over the fence, Reyes could have scored running backward. Instead, he had to stop at third. Smoltz then struck out Carlos Beltran looking, bringing back some not-so-fond memories of Beltran's final at bat of 2006.

Glavine walked to the mound to start the sixth, frustrated. "In a game like that you figure you're only going to get so many chances," he said. "Smoltzie was really dealing the first four innings, so I was thinking the fifth might have been our best shot to get him. You see a ball bounce over the fence the way Paulie's did, and you kind of flinch and start to wonder, 'Is this going to be one of *those* days?'"

Glavine was wondering that even more in the sixth. The inning began innocently enough: Glavine struck out Renteria, and then Beltran ran down Chipper Jones's line drive on the warning track. But Andruw Jones singled to left on a ball that just got past David Wright at third base. Brian McCann then slammed Glavine's first pitch into the right-field corner, and Green had to make an excellent play in the corner to hold Jones at third.

Up came Jeff Francoeur and out to the mound came Rick Peterson. When Peterson comes to the mound it is for one of six reasons:

• To counsel the pitcher on something he might be doing wrong: overthrowing, something in his mechanics, or pitch selection.
• To give the pitcher a rest: "Sometimes you just need to catch your breath," Glavine said. "Rick will come out and say, 'I'm just here to give you a few seconds to relax.'"
• To ask the pitcher if he still thinks he can get people out or if he's tired. Unlike some pitchers who think admitting to being tired is a weakness, Glavine is always honest. "If I'm gassed, I say so," he said. "What's good about that is that Rick knows I won't lie to him, so if I say I'm okay, he usually believes me. Sometimes he'll tell me I'm wrong but not usually."
• To stall so the bullpen can get ready when a pitcher runs into sudden trouble. Although the Braves' threat had been sudden, and Glavine had thrown ninety-one pitches, that's not what this visit was about.

• To simply stand on the mound and wait for the umpire to come out to break up the meeting so Peterson can tell him he's doing a lousy job of calling balls and strikes. Technically, arguing balls and strikes means automatic ejection, but Peterson will chance it on occasion. In eight years as a major league pitching coach, he has been ejected twice. "Sometimes he'll come out and stand there with his arms folded and just say, 'Hang on a minute; I'm not here to see you,'" Glavine said. "Then the umpire comes out, and he'll let him have it."

One of Peterson's tricks is not to look at the umpire when he's letting him have it. In fact, more often than not, he will direct his comments to Glavine: "I'll say something like, 'You just keep throwing the ball where you're throwing it, Tommy. Those are good pitches. This guy is too good an umpire to keep missing pitches the way he's been missing them.'"

• To discuss specific strategy on the next hitter.

That last item was Peterson's purpose as he jogged to the mound with Francoeur approaching the plate. Those who watch Peterson regularly know instantly when he has come out to talk strategy because he won't put his arm on the pitcher's shoulder, which is what he does when he has come out to soothe or counsel or stall. The question was whether to pitch to Francoeur or walk him intentionally and pitch to Matt Diaz with the bases loaded.

It was not a righty-lefty question since both are right-handed hitters. It was more about who Glavine felt more comfortable pitching to at that moment. Francoeur has more power, but Diaz is a better hitter for average. Glavine's control had been excellent all day, but pitchers do occasionally tighten up a little with the bases loaded and get behind in the count, forcing them to groove a pitch to keep from walking in a run. Beyond that, Glavine remembered the home run Diaz had hit against him in Atlanta fifteen days earlier. He opted for Francoeur.

"Francoeur is a free swinger, which means he might get a hit off a good pitch, or you might get him out on a bad one," Glavine said. "My thought was to pitch to him and not give him anything especially good to hit. If he walked, fine, then I'd deal with Diaz."

Francoeur didn't walk. Glavine threw him two changeups, hoping he would bite on one, but he took both, the second for a strike. He then worked outside with two fastballs. On the second, Francoeur leaned across the plate and hit it right up the middle into center field, scoring both runners. The Braves were up 3–1.

Glavine was angry with himself. "I didn't second-guess pitching to him," he said. "And it wasn't a bad pitch. But it was a little too good, especially in those circumstances, against a hitter who will go get a pitch, which is what he did. I'm standing there thinking we should be up in this game at least two-one and now we're down three-one, and it's probably my last inning. I was pissed."

He calmed down long enough to pick Francoeur off to end the inning but still walked into the dugout steaming. The last thing a pitcher wants to do after his team has either gotten him even or put him ahead is give runs right back, especially with two outs. Glavine had violated two cardinal rules of pitching on a day when he thought his opponent might not give up any more runs.

That, however, proved not to be true.

The Mets quickly loaded the bases with one out on singles by Delgado and Alou and a walk to Green. At that point Bobby Cox, convinced that plate umpire Paul Emmel was squeezing Smoltz, got into a heated argument with Emmel. More often than not, Cox gets ejected for arguing balls and strikes, almost always in defense of his pitcher. He got, as the saying goes, "his money's worth" with Emmel before leaving, still gesturing angrily just in case Emmel was not completely certain that he was unhappy.

As soon as Cox was gone, Jose Valentin ripped a single to left to make it 3–2, Alou's lack of speed forcing him to stop at third. The good news for Glavine was his team was rallying. The bad news was that, with the bases loaded, Willie Randolph sent Julio Franco up to pinch-hit for him. Glavine understood. Smoltz was on the ropes, and Randolph had to go for the knockout. Still, he had only thrown ninety-five pitches and had hoped to go one more inning.

"I hadn't seen the seventh inning yet," he said. "I felt like I had plenty left. But there was no choice in that situation."

Franco flied out to short right field, failing to advance the runners. But Reyes made up for that, hitting a line drive into the right-field corner. All three runners scored. Reyes was jumping up and down on third base clapping his hands, and the Mets led 5–3. Shea Stadium rocked with noise. A moment later Lo Duca singled to left to make it 6–3, and, remarkably, Smoltz was gone. No one was more shocked than Glavine.

"To me, Smoltzie seemed locked in, which is why I was so upset when I gave up the two runs in the top of the inning," he said. "I thought at that point my job was to try to keep it at one-one and hope we could get to their bullpen — that it was that kind of game. But baseball is completely unpredictable that way. There were a couple pitches John wanted that he didn't get, and then Hosey [Reyes] just crushed that pitch. If you think about it, that was about the fifth or sixth time in two games we needed a big two-out hit, and he was the first one to get it."

Smoltz conceded later that he probably let Emmel's strike zone get to him a little bit. "That's not an excuse," he said. "In fact, that's on me. As a pitcher you have to overcome that stuff. Especially when you're as experienced as I am. You can't sulk. You have to get outs."

That's easier said than done. Both Glavine and Mussina agree that as they've gotten older, they have become more short-tempered with umpires, particularly when they don't get a key pitch that they think is a strike. "It's about margin of error," Mussina said. "When I was younger, if I threw a two-and-two pitch that I thought was strike three, I felt fairly confident I could come back and get the guy on the next pitch. Now, I'm not as certain. I haven't got as many really good pitches in me per game as I used to have. And, when the next pitch becomes a hit, which it seems to a lot nowadays, I really get angry."

Both Glavine and Mussina have reputations among umpires as "pros." They don't argue often, and when they are upset they don't show it in a way that "shows up" the umpire. Major league umpires are obsessed with not being "shown up." If a catcher argues balls and strikes without turning around, he is likely to get away with it. If he turns around or takes off his mask, he's probably gone. If a pitcher walks off the mound shouting at an umpire, he's probably going to be in trouble. If he says something walking off the mound at the end of an inning without pointing a finger or being obvious, the umpire will frequently let it go. Especially if he knows the pitcher was right.

"Sometimes I'll come in the dugout, and Paulie [Lo Duca] will say to me, 'The ump said he missed that one,' referring to a pitch I was upset about," Glavine said. "Once I hear that, I'm not going to give the guy a hard time about that pitch. It's over. Umpires make mistakes; so do pitchers." He smiled. "Of course we pay a higher price for our mistakes. But if someone says, 'I got that one wrong,' they aren't going to have any trouble with me."

Mussina is the same way. Like Glavine, if he walks down off the mound to say something to an umpire, that means he is really angry. "I worked the plate for him probably forty or fifty times," said Rich Garcia, a retired umpire who now works evaluating umpire performances. "He was always a pro. In fact, if he walked up behind me right now and started talking I would have no idea who it was because I'm not really sure I ever heard his voice. Occasionally you could see in his body language that he didn't like a call—and when he got upset it was probably because you missed one—but I don't ever remember him actually saying anything."

Or, as one current umpire put it: "If Tom Glavine or Mike Mussina gives you a hard time, you probably deserve it."

Whether Emmel deserved a hard time from Smoltz or Cox

was hard to say, but Smoltz was clearly affected by his strike zone. "I had great control that day," he said. "Check the numbers."

The numbers bear him out: ninety-eight pitches, seventy-one strikes. By comparison, Glavine, who didn't walk anyone, threw fifty-nine strikes in ninety-five pitches.

If Glavine had been home watching the game, he undoubtedly would have empathized with his pal. But he wasn't in a very empathetic mood in the bottom of the sixth. "My only disappointment was that we didn't get to him for four or five more," he said.

Glavine was smiling as he walked up the runway to the clubhouse after Beltran popped up to end the Mets' sixth. At that moment, he thought he had stolen a win. "When you get pinch-hit for because you're behind, you know the odds of getting a win that day aren't great," he said. "If you win two or three of those a year, you've been very lucky. After we scored the five and got Smoltzie out, I thought maybe I had stolen one. You tell yourself 'Don't count the win yet,' but mentally, with a three-run lead and the bullpen pitching well, I think I was counting the win."

While Glavine headed for the training room to put ice on his arm, Ambiorix Burgos took over. Burgos had been picked up in what would turn out to be a disastrous off-season trade with the Kansas City Royals (Brian Bannister, the pitcher traded for Burgos, ended up being an effective starter, while Burgos found himself back in the minor leagues). He got the first two outs in the seventh but then gave up a pinch-hit double to Scott Thorman. Randolph decided to go lefty-lefty at that point and brought Scott Schoeneweis in to face Kelly Johnson, who had already homered and singled off of Glavine in a lefty-lefty matchup.

Schoeneweis promptly walked Johnson, bringing Edgar Renteria to the plate with the tying run. Glavine wasn't thinking in those terms as he sat on the training table staring at a TV set. "I was thinking, 'Let's get this guy and not let Chipper or Andruw come up with men on base,'" he said.

He got his wish — sort of. Renteria launched a 1–1 pitch over the left-field fence to clear the bases, tie the score, and ensure that Glavine couldn't be the winning pitcher. Icing his arm, Glavine felt as if someone had punched him in the stomach. A moment later, he got a text message from his wife, Chris, who frequently sends messages when he has come out of a game. It was succinct. "DAMMIT," it said.

A few minutes later, Schoeneweis came into the clubhouse looking sick. A Duke graduate who had beaten cancer while in college and gone on to a solid major league career, Schoeneweis had been signed by the Mets during the off-season to give them another left-handed arm in the bullpen. He and Glavine had become friends quickly. Both liked to play golf, and both had interests that tended to range beyond box scores.

"Tom, I'm so sorry," he said, seeing Glavine.

"Hey, Scott, no worries," Glavine said, trying to sound casual. "It happens. We'll get 'em the next time."

At that moment Schoeneweis wasn't thinking about the next time. Like all the Mets relievers, he felt extra pressure whenever he came into a Glavine game with a lead.

"Anytime you come into a game, you want to pitch well," Schoeneweis said. "But any of us would be lying if we said we weren't aware of what Tom is trying to do. Any time he has a lead, you want to be sure you don't blow it for him because that's an opportunity gone. When Renteria went deep, I just felt sick to my stomach. What makes it harder is knowing who Tom is. I knew he would never give me a hard time about it, that, in fact, he'd try to boost my spirits about it. That's Tom. He's just the kind of teammate you don't ever want to let down, but especially not when he's so close."

It's worth noting that Schoeneweis never mentioned the number three hundred. It had almost become code in the Mets clubhouse not to specifically talk about three hundred wins. Glavine had simply stopped saying it. He would talk about "the goal I'm trying to reach" or "where I'm trying to get to" or "what it is I'm hoping to get done here." But he never said he was trying to win three hundred games. The relief pitchers had picked up on that. It had become "The Number That Must Not Be Named."

"We all feel this every time Tom pitches," said Billy Wagner, the closer, who lockered next to Glavine and drove with him to the ballpark most days. "Look, it's entirely possible he may be the last guy to do this. We all want to be a part of it; we all want to help him get it done. But with that comes extra pressure. I know if he can't pitch a complete game, there's nothing in the world I want more than to have that ball in the ninth inning when he gets to that doorstep. But if I somehow blow it . . ." He shook his head. "Don't even want to think about it."

Schoeneweis had no choice but to think about it that day. Glavine was fully aware of the pressure the relievers were feeling. His three closest friends on the team were the three guys most likely to be put in a position to either fail or succeed with his three hundredth win on the line: Schoeneweis, Wagner, and Aaron Heilman, who had become the team's set-up man.

"What you really don't want to do is sit around and talk about it," Glavine said. "But it does become the elephant in the room. We all know it's there. In theory, if I pitch well, getting ten wins should not be a problem. But you don't want it to linger. You don't want it hanging over the team's head. You want to get it done and then focus on the pennant race and nothing else. But I think we all know it isn't a subject that's going to go away. When you think you've got one and then you lose it, everyone feels it. Not just me — everyone. I know that, I understand it, and I also know that, realistically, there's nothing I can do or say except pitch well and win seven more games."

That was how many wins Glavine needed after the Braves went on to win 9–6 on that sparkling Sunday. They had now won four of six from the Mets to start the season and had jumped into first place. There weren't a lot of smiles in the Mets clubhouse late that afternoon.

"You hate to blow any lead," Willie Randolph said.

Especially to the Braves. Especially with Glavine seven outs away from number 294.

ACCORDING TO THE TOM GLAVINE THEORY OF PITCHING, there are ten starts a year (if you are a successful starting pitcher) that you should absolutely win.

Glavine had one of those ten starts in Washington, six days after the lost game against the Braves.

Only he didn't get the win. The reason, in the minds of all the Mets, was an umpire named Tony Randazzo.

Umpires come in all shapes and sizes and, perhaps most important, personalities. More than any other officials in sports, they are given the independence to call a game in almost any manner they wish when working home plate. That's been reined in to some degree by Questech in recent years and by Major League Baseball telling them to call the "high strike." The strike zone, top to bottom, is supposed to be from the letters across the batters's jersey to the top of the batter's knees. The upper part of the zone had crept so far down in the late 1990s that hitters were taking belt-high pitches, and umpires were calling them balls.

Even now though, umpires have distinctly different strike zones — so much so in fact that players scout them. Some umpires have wider plates than others, and some will give pitchers the low strike, something that makes Glavine very happy. "When I see a guy giving me the low strike early, I know I've got an excellent chance to have a good night if I'm even decent," he said. Umpires also have different styles: Some make a strike call instantly; others take their time. Some make their calls loudly; others can barely be heard.

In 2007, there were sixty-nine full-time major league umpires, ranging in experience from Bruce Froemming, who was in his thirty-seventh season (Froemming had been around so long that players occasionally asked him what the weather was like on the day Babe Ruth hit his 714th home run), to Lance Barksdale, who was entering his fourth full season. Umpiring is a little bit like being appointed to the U.S. Supreme Court: once you are in the majors, it will take an act of God or Bud Selig—God being more likely to intervene—to get an umpire fired.

Randazzo is one of the least experienced umpires in the majors, even though he was in his eighth big league season. He had been one of twenty-four umpires brought to the majors in 1999 when twenty-two umpires had resigned as part of their union's attempt to force the owners to give them a new contract. MLB had accepted the resignations, and it had taken a court battle of several years for some of the umpires to get their jobs back.

In the meantime, Randazzo and twenty-three others were promoted, either at the start of 1999 or midway through that season. During that period, MLB had changed the way umpires worked, doing away with the tradition of American League umpires and National League umpires as part of the changeover in the way all of MLB was run. Now, there are no longer league offices or league presidents. Everyone reports to the commissioner of baseball.

The crew assigned to work the Mets-Nationals series in Washington the last weekend in April was led by Larry Vanover, a fourteen-year veteran umpire, though a relatively inexperienced crew chief. The home plate umpire for the second game of the series was Greg Gibson, another member of the class of '99. Randazzo was at first base, Charlie Reliford at second, and Vanover at third.

It was a cool, comfortable Saturday night in Washington, and Glavine was matched up against the Nationals' Jerome Williams, who had struggled mightily in his first three starts, much the way the rest of the Washington staff had. The Nats were in their third season in Washington, D.C., since Major League Baseball had abandoned Montreal following the 2004 season. Perhaps more important, they were in their final season in RFK Stadium, a decrepit relic that had been built at the start of the "multipurpose" stadium era. It had housed bad baseball teams — the expansion Washington Senators from 1962 to 1971 — and had been home to the Washington Redskins until 1996, when the team had moved to suburbia, into perhaps the worst-planned stadium in sports history. From 1996 to 2004 RFK existed for two reasons: to give the local Major League Soccer team, D.C. United, a home and to be available if the day ever came when Major League Baseball returned to Washington.

Baseball had finally come back in 2005, and the Nationals' first season had been a huge success. The team had been a surprising 81–81 and even spent some time in first place in early summer. Attendance was more than 2.7 million, and MLB was going through the lengthy process of finding the team an owner — something the franchise had not had for five years, beginning in Montreal. In 2006, Washington real estate mogul Theodore Lerner had been selected as the team's owner. The team had not played as well, and Hall of Famer Frank Robinson had been fired as manager at the end of the season.

Now, the Nationals were in full rebuilding mode. Stan Kasten, the man who had hired John Schuerholz and Bobby Cox in Atlanta, was the new team president. Manny Acta, a former Mets coach, was the manager. And most of the pitchers were like Williams: very young, inexperienced, and trying — without much success — to learn on the job.

At twenty-five, Williams was one of the Nationals' more experienced pitchers, having pitched two full seasons in San Francisco and part of two others with the Cubs. He had a big league record of 23–24 coming into the season, but his ERA as he walked to the mound on a cool, comfortable night with a crowd of just under thirty thousand in attendance, was 6.25. On the surface, this was a pitching mismatch.

Baseball, however, isn't played on paper. Williams kept walking hitters and then pitching out of trouble. Through six innings he had walked six, given up one hit, and left five men on base. Glavine was better. He had given up just three hits through five innings. In the sixth, with one out, Williams came to bat. Glavine quickly got ahead of him 1–2 and almost struck him out on a changeup that he barely fouled off.

If Williams had struck out it would have been the twenty-five hundredth strikeout of Glavine's career. "Which isn't too bad for a soft-tossing lefty," Glavine joked. "I was glad he fouled the pitch off. I didn't want twenty-five hundred to be against a pitcher."

He got his wish because Williams crushed the next pitch, a fast-ball Glavine got careless with and left over the plate. "For a minute I thought he'd hit it out," he said. "Which would have been both bad and embarrassing. I was actually relieved when it hit the fence."

Williams had hit the ball off the bottom of the left-field fence. He was so surprised to have hit the ball that far that he spent some time at the plate admiring his work before jogging to first, turning what should have been a double into a single.

Grateful for that break, Glavine faced lead-off hitter Felipe Lopez. He promptly got him to hit a ground ball to shortstop, the proverbial tailor-made double-play ball. Reyes flipped the ball to Damion Easley, who relayed it to Carlos Delgado for the inning-ending six-four-three. Glavine took a step off the mound toward the dugout, then stopped in disbelief. Tony Randazzo had his arms spread, palms down, giving the safe signal.

Glavine uses less profanity than about 99.9 percent of the athletes on earth. If he says he's "pissed off" about something, that is enough to turn heads. Now though, seeing Randazzo's call, he began walking in the direction of first base screaming. "*What? What?* Are you fucking kidding me?!"

He was halfway to first base before he realized that he was screaming. Seeing his pitcher screaming at the top of his lungs while walking toward an umpire and his first baseman also yelling in dismay, Willie Randolph sprinted from the dugout. A manager comes out at a moment like that for several reasons. First on the list is making sure none of his players—especially his starting pitcher—gets ejected. Hearing Glavine screaming the f-word got Randolph moving instantly, because umpires are very sensitive to that word. In fact, one of baseball's unwritten rules is that if you say "motherfucker" to an umpire, you are automatically ejected. Umpires and players call it the magic word. Glavine hadn't said the magic word, but Randolph wasn't taking any chances.

Beyond that, when a call is missed that clearly, a manager has to go out to show support for his players. There is no way a base umpire is going to change a call like that once he's made it. Nevertheless, a manager has to go out and protest so his players know he's backing them and to make sure the next close call is likely to go his team's way. As in, "You owe us one." Good umpires never give anyone a "makeup" call. But not everyone is a good umpire.

"I used to say to coaches, 'I owe you one, but I'll never pay you back,'" said Hank Nichols, a great college basketball referee who works as an evaluator of umpires for MLB. "You make one mistake, fine. You should try never to make it two."

Randolph got to Randazzo with Glavine still several steps away, standing with his hands on his hips, still jawing, but a bit calmer now that his manager had arrived. According to Randolph, the first thing he said to Randazzo was "Just tell me you missed it, and I'll go back in the dugout."

Randazzo adamantly insisted he had the call right, that Lopez had been safe.

"You're joking, right?" Randolph said. "You have to know you missed that one."

Umpires don't miss safe or out calls on the bases very often. A play involving a force—no tag needed—is about as easy a call as an umpire can make. As long as he is in position and can see the runner's foot hit the bag and hear the ball hit the glove, he shouldn't miss very often. The most famous missed call at first

base was in Game Six of the 1985 World Series, when Don Denkinger called Jorge Orta safe at first, leading off the bottom of the
ninth inning for the Kansas City Royals. The St. Louis Cardinals
led the game 1–0 and were three outs from winning the World
Series. Orta was out by about a step. Denkinger called him safe,
and the Royals scored two runs, won the game, and then won
Game Seven the next night (11–0, the Cardinals completely failing to show up) and their first and only World Series title.

Since then, all truly bad calls at first base bring up Denkinger's
name. This call wasn't anywhere close to being as critical as Denkinger's, but Randazzo had missed it just as badly. His reaction to
Randolph wasn't much better than the call. He started shouting
at Randolph that he had the call right all the way.

"That's when I went off," Randolph said the next day. "Look,
umpires miss calls. They're human. I make mistakes every day.
But at least admit you missed it. Don't start shouting at me that
you didn't. While he was screaming, he bumped me. That's when
I really got angry."

The argument grew heated quickly, and Randazzo ended up
throwing Randolph out of the game. By now, all the Mets were
angry. After Randolph left, Glavine had to get his mind off the
call and back on the game.

"Something like that happens, you have to pitch through it,"
he said. "On the one hand, Randazzo blew the call. On the other
hand, it's up to me to get the third out, get in the dugout, and cool
off. I didn't do it."

He hung a changeup to Ronnie Belliard who smashed it into
the gap in left-center field. Lopez scored easily, and the Nationals
led 1–0. Glavine was now officially pissed. He was pissed at Randazzo and pissed at himself. He got the third out of the inning
and walked off the mound barking angrily at Randazzo.

"I was staring at him to see if he would look at me and say anything," he said. "He didn't look at me. I started to say something
else, to really get on him, but I caught myself. You have to think

about the next time he's behind the plate and you're pitching. Do umpires hold grudges? Of course they do. I'm not questioning their integrity; I'm just saying it's human nature. A guy has given you a hard time in the past; you remember it. Maybe subconsciously you don't give him borderline pitches. You have to be aware of stuff like that. I really wanted to go at him because the whole notion that everyone in the park knew he'd missed it but him really got to me. But I held back. I had to.

"I would say the number of times I've done that in my career is less than five," he said. "I would love to know what he thought when he looked at the tape after the game."

Umpires are required to look at tape after games, especially of controversial calls. There is a DVD machine in every umpire's locker room, and they are given a DVD of the game as soon as it is over.

The Mets were able to tie the game in the seventh, but their mini-rally forced Glavine out of the game. With runners on second and third, acting manager Jerry Manuel had to put in a pinch hitter for Glavine to try to get the runs home. He got the tying run in when Nats pitcher Jesus Colome—who had replaced Williams when he hurt his foot at the start of the inning—threw a wild pitch to pinch hitter David Newhan. But with Easley on third with the go-ahead run, Newhan grounded out.

Glavine had thrown eighty-four pitches, meaning he had at least another inning in him or perhaps two on a cool, comfortable night. He had given up one run—with some help from Randazzo—and had been in control the entire evening. Yet, he headed up to the clubhouse after Newhan ended the inning, with no chance to get a win.

"I felt like I had studied to take a test, had gone in and aced it, and then someone came up and said, 'We gave you the wrong test; you have to take it again in five days,'" he said. "Some nights you know you were lousy and you deserve to get beat. Other nights you were okay and it could go either way. But when you pitch the way I pitched that night, and you come away with nothing, at least in part because an umpire blew an easy call, that's frustrating."

The game ended up dragging on for four hours before the Mets won it in the twelfth, aided by another blown Randazzo call in the ninth, that helped them tie the game. "Give the guy credit," Mets TV announcer Gary Cohen said. "He had three calls to make that night, and he missed all three."

The first had come in the fifth inning when Randazzo had called Easley and Reyes out on back-to-back dazzling plays by Zimmerman. Reyes's call was close; Easley's was not. "I probably should have gone out then," Randolph said the next day. "Maybe if I had said something in the fifth, he'd have gotten it right in the sixth." Good umpires will let players and managers know when they know they've made a mistake. "I remember in Baltimore when I was playing, Steve Palermo threw me out because he thought I was getting on him about a check swing from the dugout," Randolph said. "It wasn't me though, it was [Bucky] Dent and [Graig] Nettles. But he nailed me.

"In those days George [Steinbrenner] was involved in everything. When he heard what happened he wrote a letter to [American League president] Lee McPhail and got everyone on the team to sign it, saying that it was Bucky and Graig, and Palermo got the wrong guy. I got a letter of apology from McPhail, and when I saw Palermo he told me he was sorry, that he'd made a mistake."

Frequently when an umpire misses a pitch or two, he will send word to a pitcher through his catcher that he missed a call. "The older guys, the ones who are more secure about themselves tend to be that way," Glavine said. "Randy Marsh, Tim McClelland, Ed Montague, John Hirschbeck—guys who are usually right—will tell you when they know they got one wrong. Once they do that, there's nothing left for you to say."

It can go both ways. Earlier in the month, when Glavine had pitched against Jamie Moyer, Montague had ruled that a Moyer pitch had hit David Wright in the foot. Moyer didn't see it hit him or hear it, so he argued with Montague adamantly. "When I got in the clubhouse and saw the tape, I saw Ed had it right," Moyer said. "He confused me a little because he didn't give the sign you usually give for a hit batsman, but he had the call right. I picked up the phone, called the umpire's room, and said, 'Hey, I'm sorry I gave you a hard time. I saw the tape. You had it right.'"

Like Glavine, Moyer was thinking about the next time he pitched with Montague behind the plate. "True," he said. "But it was also the right thing to do."

If Randazzo regretted what had happened, he never let either Randolph or Glavine know. "Haven't heard from him," Randolph said the next day. "And I don't expect that I will."

The fact that the Mets won the game was a little bit soothing for Glavine, but not getting a win when he had pitched so well was aggravating. "If I'm being honest, I want to get this done in part because I want it to happen but also so it can be off the table for everyone," he said. "A night like tonight just sets it back at least another five days."

Glavine was 3–1 as April came to an end. He could easily have been 5–1. The bullpen had blown one game, and Tony Randazzo had helped blow another.

15

Back on Track

IF GLAVINE WAS FRUSTRATED with three wins in April, he at least had the luxury of knowing he was pitching well and he was healthy. Mike Mussina had neither as May began. He had pitched two games, lost one, and gone on the disabled list after pitching a grand total of six innings to an ERA of exactly 9.00.

The good news was that he had felt good while pitching the simulated game in the bullpen on April 27. Torre scheduled him to return five days later in Texas. Mussina had to wait six days because, naturally, it rained.

The rainout was rescheduled for the next day as a day-night doubleheader because the Yankees were not scheduled to return to Texas again during the season. Day-night doubleheaders are a pox on baseball. They exist for the sole purpose of allowing the owners to squeeze out every last possible dollar from the paying public. In the old days, a rainout was made up with a doubleheader — one admission, two games. Nowadays, the owners want separate admissions, even though the afternoon game usually draws a tiny crowd since it is not on the original schedule.

When a rainout occurs and is rescheduled as a day-night, Joe Torre always gives the pitcher who was supposed to pitch the previous day the option of pitching day or night. Some prefer to get the start over with and pitch during the daytime. Mussina will usually opt for the night game.

"I don't like pitching in an empty, quiet stadium," he said. "I would rather have people cheering against me and making *some* kind of noise than pitch when no one is there. Those afternoon games of day-nights tend to be very quiet."

Andy Pettitte pitched the afternoon game in front of a crowd that could have been counted on several hands. But, not long after the Yankees had won that game 4–3, it started to rain again. "I'm thinking, 'You have to be kidding,'" Mussina said.

Fortunately the rain abated this time and the game started forty minutes late. The delay — twenty-four hours or forty minutes — didn't seem to bother Mussina. He retired the Rangers one-two-three in the first inning, only his second one-two-three inning of the season. He started the second by striking out Sammy Sosa before Hank Blalock singled. That led nowhere and the Yankees then staked him to a 2–0 lead in the top of the third.

"I felt great," Mussina said. "It was a good night to pitch, not too hot at all, especially for down there. I mean it can be in the eighties and humid in May, and it felt more like seventy. I was glad to get the first inning out of the way and do it quickly. My control was surprisingly good from the start. When you haven't pitched for a while, the thing you worry most about is your control. I wasn't throwing as hard as I normally would be in May, but that was to be expected. My location made up for it most of the time."

Only in the fourth did the Rangers mount any kind of rally. Sosa, making a comeback after a year out of baseball, singled with one out. Blalock doubled and Sosa, who at age thirty-eight could be timed on a sundial when running the bases, stopped at third. Ian Kinsler scored him with a sacrifice fly to make it 2–1, but Mussina got Brad Wilkerson to pop out to end the inning. He then retired the Rangers one-two-three in the fifth.

"By then I was pretty gassed," Mussina said. "You go twenty-two days without pitching, it's hard to get your stamina back. I couldn't run at all while I was out because it was a hamstring so my conditioning wasn't what it should be. Plus, when you haven't actually pitched, the act of getting on the mound in game conditions is completely different than throwing in the bullpen or a simulated game or even a minor league game. Your arm strength just isn't there. I hadn't thrown that many pitches, but I was tired."

Ron Guidry and Torre had watched Mussina closely throughout the game. He wasn't on a strict pitch count, but he was very much on a "don't push him too hard" leash. When Mussina walked to the dugout after the fifth and sixty-four pitches, Guidry walked over to him.

"How you feeling?" he asked.

"Tired," Mussina answered.

Guidry nodded. "That's what I thought. We're going to get you some help. Good job."

If Mussina had said he felt fine, Guidry probably would have told him he was done for the night anyway.

"When you're working with a guy like Moose, you expect him to be honest, because he's too smart to try to be macho, especially the first game back," Torre said later. "But if he had wanted to keep going, we weren't going to let him. There was just no sense in it, even if he had said he was okay."

Mussina was both happy and relieved: happy that he had pitched well; relieved that he had been pain free. He figured the odds that he would get a win leaving the game up 2–1 after five innings weren't great, but that wasn't what this start was about. "It wasn't a struggle in any way, and it could have been after three weeks," he said. "I walked up to the clubhouse thinking if I somehow got a win that would just be a bonus because when you come out up one run with four innings to go you certainly can't count on a win."

He got one though, even though it took five Yankee relievers—including closer Mariano Rivera—to get to the finish line. The only run the bullpen gave up was a home run to Mark Teixeira in the eighth by the ever-erratic Kyle Farnsworth. In the meantime, the Yankees had tacked on three more runs against the Texas bullpen, and the final was 5–2 — Mussina's 240th career win.

"Number one for this year is a lot more important than that right now," he said. "At some point, even though you tell yourself it's early and there's no need to panic, you *do* start to panic a little. Is this just a three-week injury, or is it the beginning of the end? It's always there in the back of your mind when you get to this point in your career. It isn't something you lie awake in bed and worry about at night, not often anyway, but when you aren't throwing well or when you get hurt, you can't help but wonder just a little. Getting to pitch and to pitch well felt very, very good."

Mussina had to wait the extra day again before his next start. Since he and Pettitte had pitched on the same day, Torre opted to start Pettitte a day before Mussina, partly because Pettitte was pitching well but also because Mussina was still rebuilding arm strength. The opponent was the same: Texas, this time in Yankee Stadium.

Mussina went six innings and got up to eighty-five pitches. The Yankees made life a little bit easier for him by scoring four runs in the first. As in Texas, Mussina only had one difficult inning. This time it was the third. Wilkerson led off with a home run to make it 4–1. Nelson Cruz doubled and Chris Stewart walked. For some strange reason Kenny Lofton then bunted. Exactly why Lofton would choose to bunt or why manager Ron Washington might order him to bunt with two men on, no one out, and the team three runs behind with a chance for a big inning, no one knew for sure. But Mussina wasn't complaining.

The runners moved to second and third, but the potential momentum of the inning was lost. Mussina got the dangerous Michael Young to ground to second — Cruz scoring — and then got Teixeira to fly to left. Inning over, lead intact at 4–2. The Yankees added two in the fourth and cruised from there.

Mussina still felt strong when he came out. "I thought I could go another inning," he said. "Gator [Guidry] came over to me after the sixth and said, 'Good job. You're done.' For a second I thought about trying to talk him into another inning. There are times when I'll do that. But I knew he was probably right—there was no sense pushing it past eighty-five pitches the second time out.

"As an older pitcher, you have to be aware of your limits. There are times now where I really think I can go one more inning or get one more batter, and by doing so I'll blow up a good game. That's the thing about pitching—you can be good for an entire game, and one or two hitters can ruin the whole thing for you. It's not like hitting where you can be terrible the entire night and then be a hero with one swing. In pitching, if you're terrible, you're terrible, and you usually get knocked out early. But there are other times where you're actually pretty good, and you end up looking terrible because of a mistake or two. The way our starters had been going, there was no point in taking a chance on turning a good outing into a bad outing."

Mussina's return to the rotation could not have come at a more critical time for the Yankees. His April provided a pretty good summation of the starting staff's April. A lot of it had to do with injuries: Mussina and Chien-Ming Wang had started a total of four times and had combined to be 0–3 in April. Carl Pavano had started twice and was now gone, as far as everyone was concerned, for good. Kei Igawa, the $46 million man, had simply been awful, throwing home-run pitch after home-run pitch. His performance was best described by longtime radio play-by-play man John Sterling, who, searching for something—anything—positive to say about Igawa, came up with: "Well, if he would stop giving up home runs all the time, he might be a pretty good pitcher."

Only Andy Pettitte among the five projected spring starters had pitched well in April, and, naturally, he had been the pitcher the Yankees hadn't scored any runs for. He was 1–1 at the end of the month, even though his ERA was under 3.00.

The injuries had forced the Yankees to parade an array of rookies and inexperienced pitchers to the mound: Darrell Rasner, Chris Britton, Tyler Clippard, Matt DeSalvo, Chase Wright, and Colter Bean had all been called up and been used as starters and middle relievers. The decision to call Philip Hughes up before the end of the first month of the season made it pretty clear how desperate the situation had become.

Mussina's first start in Texas had come in a series that had given the Yankees both hope and a bit of despair. Hughes, in his second start, had been brilliant in the opener, pitching no-hit ball into the seventh inning. But he had strained a hamstring in the seventh, far more seriously than Mussina had strained his in Minnesota, and was placed on the sixty-day disabled list two days later. After the rainout, Pettitte and Mussina had both pitched well in the doubleheader. That made three straight good starts — a 2007 team record — but with Hughes on the DL, the Yankees were forced to start Igawa again when they came home to play the Seattle Mariners.

The Yankees did everything they could to back up Igawa. They scored five runs in the first inning and three more through the fourth. It wasn't enough. Igawa was knocked out after giving up back-to-back hits to start the fifth. Colter Bean came in and got out none of the four hitters he faced. The Mariners ended up scoring eight runs in the inning and won 15–11. Igawa had given up eight runs in four innings plus two batters, and his ERA went to 7.63. His next stop would be Tampa to work with the Yankees' minor league instructors on his "mechanics." The loss dropped the Yankees to 12–15, six and a half games behind the Red Sox.

The next day, Pettitte called a meeting of the pitchers. This was not the kind of pitchers' meeting that is always held on the first day of a series to go over the opposition's hitters. This was to talk about what was going on with the pitching staff. Every-one crowded into the video room in a corner of the clubhouse to talk.

Player meetings in baseball are rarely emotional, and it isn't often that anything especially brilliant or revealing is said. This meeting was no different. Pettitte was the right person to call the meeting and start it because he was the one pitcher on the staff who had pitched well. His point was simple: What we're doing isn't good enough. Yes, we've been injured, and yes it's early (it is, of course, a long season), but this was unacceptable.

He was talking, for the most part, to the starters. The bullpen hadn't been great, but it had the excuse of being overused because of the starters' incompetence.

Mussina, the other veteran in the room, also spoke. He pointed out that he hadn't been much use to the team in April but went on to talk about what was expected when you pitched for the Yankees. "I've been on teams that began circling days on the calendar trying to get the season over with from the All-Star break on," he said. "Believe me, it's not fun. And it really wouldn't be fun around here. We're expected to win here. That can be tough, but it's what's expected. We have to pitch better — all of us. It's that simple. The guns in the lineup can hit a million home runs, but we still have to pitch well for us to win."

Near the end of the meeting, Torre and Guidry came into the room. They told the pitchers they had confidence in their ability to get the job done. Wang and Mussina were finally healthy, and Pettitte had pitched well. With Igawa gone, the fourth and fifth starters were now Darrell Rasner and Matt DeSalvo, another call-up from Triple-A. Unsaid was the fact that help might be on the way in the form of Roger Clemens, who the team was trying to sign for his annual June unretirement.

"On the face of it, a meeting like that isn't going to do that much," Mussina said. "But I think Andy was right to call it. We were wallowing a little bit. Look, realistically, it was easy to see why we'd been so bad. We were running guys out there who had been sent to the minor league camp in mid-March. There was a reason they were sent down: they weren't in our top five as starters. Some weren't even close to that. Now, we put them in Yankee uniforms and say 'Go out and win.' It's a lot easier said than done.

"But we all needed a little kick in the butt—from ourselves—because it's too easy to use injuries as an excuse. Or bad weather, which we'd had plenty of. It doesn't matter. In the end, you have to perform. That was what I tried to say and what Andy said: we have to be better than this, regardless of the circumstances. We all knew that, but it wasn't a bad thing to get together in a room and just say it."

Coincidence or not, the starting pitching began to improve after the meeting. Wang was superb that night, getting his first win of the season, and Rasner and three relievers pitched a combined 5–0 shutout the next night. There were still rocky days: Wang got bombed in the finale of the Texas series after Pettitte and Mussina had both pitched well.

A week later, the team went into Chicago with a 17–19 record and Mussina scheduled to pitch the opener. Naturally, the game was rained out, creating another day-night doubleheader. This time, Mussina opted for the afternoon game because the weather report for the night game wasn't good, with temperatures expected to be in the forties. As it was, the temperature for the afternoon game was fifty-six degrees. The announced attendance was 30,953, but it looked like about twenty-five thousand of those were season-ticket holders who didn't come to the game.

"I felt like I was throwing batting practice in the first inning," Mussina said. "There just wasn't anyone there. No noise, nothing. I almost asked some of the guys in our dugout to get on me so I'd be hearing something."

Mussina didn't pitch badly in the empty stadium formerly known as New Comiskey Park before a phone company paid to have its name plastered all over the building, but he didn't feel comfortable the whole day.

"It was one of those days you have as a pitcher where nothing feels quite right," he said. "It's hard to explain. You don't feel quite right in the bullpen, and you walk onto the mound and your first thought is, 'Have I ever done this before?' The ball doesn't feel quite right in your hands, and you just aren't confident throwing your pitches. You can get by on a day like that, and I almost did it — but not quite."

Being pushed back an extra day didn't help. Mussina was already scheduled to pitch on his sixth day because the Yankees had a day off on Monday between their series in Seattle and the one in Chicago. That meant that once again it had been a week since he had started. Even worse, he had warmed up on Tuesday before the rainout and had gone through all his game-day routines.

"The bottom line is we're paid a lot of money to pitch well, not to make excuses," Mussina said. "But it does throw you off when you go through all your game-day routines and then have to go through them the very next day. It doesn't mean you can't pitch well; it just makes it a little bit harder — at least for me."

Mussina got through the first three innings without giving up a run and with only two scratch singles. But with one out in the fourth, he got behind Paul Konerko 3–1 and threw a white-on-white fastball that Konerko crushed for a home run and a 1–0 White Sox lead. In the meantime, the Yankees were struggling to score against the immortal John Danks, who had come into the game with an ERA of 5.63. They finally scored a run in the fifth to make it 1–1. Mussina gave up a run in the fifth and was saved from a big inning when Melky Cabrera went over the fence to keep Juan Uribe's two-out, one-on drive in the ballpark. Instead of trailing by at least three runs, the Yankees were down just 2–1.

They tied it again in the sixth, but the tie lasted five pitches. Mussina got into another bad count—3–1 again—to A.J. Pierzynski, and the catcher launched another long home run to put the White Sox up 3–2. A double by Jermaine Dye, a hit batsman, and an RBI single by Joe Crede, and Torre was on his way to the mound.

"That was one of those days where I turned what looked like a bad day into a pretty good one and then let it all get away in the sixth," Mussina said. "The Pierzynski home run was really what did me in because he hit a pretty good pitch. It was a sinker on the outside corner, and he took it to the opposite field. Sometimes you have to give the other guy credit. On the other hand, I kept pitching in bad counts, especially in that inning. I simply couldn't locate my fastball, and bad counts and bad location usually add up to bad things."

Mussina relies heavily—more so than Glavine, because Glavine loves to throw his changeup even on bad counts—on getting ahead of hitters. "There's a reason why oh-and-one and one-and-two are called pitchers counts," he said. "It isn't coincidence. If I'm pitching two-and-oh and three-and-one a lot, you can be pretty sure that isn't going to be a good day. There are exceptions of course, but on a percentage basis it's pretty consistent. I never got comfortable in Chicago. I was happy with myself for giving them five pretty good innings—thanks to Melky. But the sixth was awful. Depressing. I felt like I had taken a step backwards."

The Yankees split the last two games in Chicago, dropping their record to 18–21. On the day they lost the final game in Chicago 4–1 with Matt DeSalvo starting the game, the Red Sox swept a doubleheader in Boston from the Tigers. It gave them a nine-and-a-half game lead.

"If we were playing well, we'd be three or four games back," Mussina said. "As it is, we have a long way to go—either to get to them or to get to the wild card."

The season was only seven weeks old, and already the dreaded "wild card" phrase was being heard in the Yankees clubhouse.

The team flew to New York after the final game in Chicago. But they were not heading to Yankee Stadium to play. Instead, they would cross the Triboro Bridge into Queens and spend the weekend at Shea Stadium.

The timing, for the Yankees, could not have been worse.

16

Subway Series I

Tom Glavine and Mike Mussina arrived at Shea Stadium on Friday afternoon, May 18, within minutes of each other. Glavine walked through the old ballpark's players' entrance, turned right, and walked down the curving hallway to the home clubhouse. Mussina went the opposite way, turning left to walk to the visitors' clubhouse.

Literally and figuratively, they were going in opposite directions.

Glavine was wired, excited by what was to come during the next three days. Mussina was tired, depressed by what was going on and dreading the next three days, even though he would not be pitching.

"I love these games," Glavine said, sitting in front of his locker. "I think the whole Subway Series thing is awesome. I walk in here when we play these games—or when we play at Yankee Stadium—and I'm tingling. I'm sure Cubs–White Sox is great and Angels-Dodgers or Giants-A's, but there's nothing quite like this. I mean, just look around. This is a big deal."

The Mets clubhouse was packed. Every member of the New York media appeared to be at Shea, along with a lot of out-of-town media. Fox would televise the Saturday game and ESPN the Sunday game, so a lot of their people were milling around too.

Because Shea Stadium was built in 1964, the home clubhouse is relatively small—not as big as the visitors' clubhouses are in most of the new parks built in the past fifteen years. The visitors'

243

clubhouse at Shea isn't as small as the one at Fenway Park or at Wrigley Field, but it is very small, especially for a Subway Series.

"It's a pain in the neck," Mussina said, looking at the masses packed into the visitors' clubhouse. "The whole weekend is a pain in the neck. People don't understand. We play big games with a lot of media attention all the time. In a sense, we're used to it, and that's okay. But you walk in here, and everyone's looking for a back-page story or wants to know what you ate for breakfast."

He paused and smiled. "Froot Loops."

A few feet from where Mussina stood putting on layers of clothing because the weather outside was miserable, Yankees utility man Miguel Cairo was on his hands and knees, laying down masking tape across the entryway to the players-only section of the clubhouse — the hall that led to the training room and the players' dining area.

"Miggy," Mussina asked. "What in the world are you doing?"

"These guys," Cairo said, gesturing at the horde of media. "Some of them are coming over and trying to look into the eating room. I'm putting down a boundary they can't cross."

"Good thing to worry about, Miggy," said Joel Sherman, a *New York Post* columnist who was also observing Cairo. "You guys are eighteen and twenty-one and ten games out, and you're worried about where we're standing. Good priorities."

Cairo glared at Sherman, who glared back.

A Yankee employee walked around the room informing anyone who would listen that Kei Igawa had thrown nineteen pitches from halfway up the mound that day in Tampa as part of his "retooling" project.

Mussina couldn't resist. "Nineteen pitches from halfway up the mound?" he said. "I guess he must be on the Pavano plan."

No one had seen Carl Pavano for weeks since he had been placed on the sixty-day DL, but Mussina insisted that his car was still at Yankee Stadium. "It's parked right next to mine," he said.

Hearing that, one could not help but think of the classic *Sein-*

feld episode in which George Costanza leaves his car in the Yankee Stadium parking lot for days, and George Steinbrenner
decides he must be dead. Steinbrenner drives to the Costanzas'
house in Queens and tearfully informs Mr. Costanza when he
answers the door that he has terrible news: "George is dead."

Mr. Costanza, played brilliantly by Jerry Stiller, looks at Steinbrenner and says, "Ken Phelps for Jay Buhner? What were you
thinking?!"

No one thought Pavano was dead, except as a pitcher for the
Yankees.

To call the Yankees clubhouse tense would be a vast under-
statement. That day, Jason Giambi, the team's on-again, off-again
slugger, had been quoted in *USA Today* as saying, "I shouldn't
have used that stuff," an obvious reference to steroids. He had
then gone on to say that Major League Baseball "owed fans an
apology" because of what had happened in what was now becoming known as "the steroid era."

Having the story break on day one of the season's first Subway
Series set off a heightened media frenzy. Writers, radio reporters,
TV reporters, and camera people were ringed around Giambi's
locker awaiting his arrival when Mussina first walked into the
clubhouse.

"What's up with that?" he asked.

Someone tossed him a copy of *USA Today,* which he read.

"Honestly, I don't get it," he said a little later while Giambi was
no-commenting reporters on the story. "I mean, is there anything
in here that we didn't already know? I guess to outsiders, since
almost no one has admitted to doing steroids, it's a big deal. In
here, where we all know guys have done steroids, this really isn't
news." Mussina pulled on a jacket and said, "I need some air —*any*
air"— and headed for the dugout.

Mussina was far more concerned about reports that general
manager Brian Cashman and manager Joe Torre might lose
their jobs if the Yankees didn't perform well over the next six

days: three games with the Mets and three at Yankee Stadium with the Red Sox.

"To be honest, no knock on Cashman at all, but something happening to Joe would affect us all a lot more because he's the guy we work with day in and day out," Mussina said. "I know how this business works, especially here, but, my God, is it Joe's fault that we've started six different rookie pitchers this year and we aren't even at Memorial Day? Is it his fault I got hurt and Wang got hurt?"

He paused and sat silently for a minute, staring at the rain and the tarpaulin while the dugout heaters hummed overhead. The game-time temperature that night would be a balmy fifty-two degrees, with the wind making it feel more like forty-five. It would only get colder as the night wore on.

"It feels like it's been November all season, except for about a week," Mussina said, staring up at the dugout heaters. "I can't remember seven weeks like this since I got here. In Baltimore I went through three years like this, and it wasn't any fun.

"The fact is, we just haven't been a very good team. Part of it is the starting pitching; although we've been better since Andy called that meeting. It's more been about doing the things good teams do. Good teams get a runner in from third with less than two out most of the time. Good teams move a runner one way or the other. Good teams turn one-run innings into three-run innings, not the other way around. Good teams make a play in the field when they really need it.

"We haven't done that very much. Everything has been a struggle. In some ways, my season is a lot like the team's: I've been bad, I've been hurt, I've gotten a little better, then I've slid back. I know I have to be better, and I know we have to be better.

"There's nothing more deceiving in baseball sometimes than a pitcher's won-lost record. Look at Andy and look at me. I'm two and two and he's two and three, but there's no comparison in the way we've pitched. He's been good almost every time out. I've had two decent outings, and that's it. My ERA is almost three runs a game higher than his, and we have the same number of wins.

"The worst I ever pitched in the big leagues was in 1996, and that's the closest I ever came to winning twenty games. If I hadn't given up one run in eight innings my last start, my ERA would have been over 5.00. In 2001, my ERA was 3.15 and all my numbers were better than Roger [Clemens], but he was twenty and three.

"Right now, though, there isn't much deceptive about our numbers. We're what—eighteen and twenty-two? We've played to that record. That doesn't mean we aren't better than that, but we better start playing like we can supposedly play pretty soon. I figure it will take ninety-three to ninety-five wins to at least get a wild card. Do the math. That would mean going seventy-seven and forty-five the rest of the way to win ninety-five. Are we capable of that? Yes. But we better not dig the hole very much deeper."

Mussina was genuinely concerned that Torre might get fired. "I really don't want my manager to get fired," he said, his voice a lot softer than usual. "Not only would it be unfair, it would hurt the ballclub. People really don't know just how good Joe is."

Mussina had battled with Torre on occasion during his seven years with the team, but he had the utmost respect for him.

"Because he always looks calm on the bench, people don't think he's intense," Mussina said. "But he is. When we aren't playing well, he lets us know. Once or twice a year, he'll walk in after a game, and, instead of going to his office, he'll just stand in the center of the clubhouse. Those of us who have been around awhile know that means he's really upset."

Mussina remembered exactly where and when that had happened in 2006. "We were in Washington, and we weren't playing well. We had a big lead on Saturday, blew it, and lost the game. But I think what really got to him was Shawn Chacon."

Chacon had helped save the Yankees' season in 2005 after

coming over in a trade from the Colorado Rockies. But he had pitched poorly in '06, and, even with a big lead that day, couldn't get out of the fifth inning.

"Joe went to get him with two outs in the fifth, when he was one out from qualifying for a win. But he'd blown most of the lead by then. Still, he flipped the ball to Joe and made it clear he was upset to come out.

"In the clubhouse, Joe started talking about playing well as a team, not as individuals. He didn't raise his voice, but he was clearly angry and looking right at Chacon.

"At first Chacon is looking back at him. Joe keeps talking, never really raises his voice but is getting hotter and hotter, and he takes a step in Chacon's direction. At first, Chacon took a step toward Joe. Then he stopped and looked down. Joe finally says, still looking right at Chacon: 'Does *everyone* understand?' Chacon just nodded kind of weakly. The message was clear."

Two weeks later, Chacon was traded to Pittsburgh.

Mussina stared at the rain for a while longer and finally said: "It's just not much fun around here right now."

THINGS COULD NOT HAVE BEEN more different than it was with the Mets at that moment.

They had finished April a solid 15–9 and were now 26–14 and in first place, after going 5–2 on a trip to Arizona and San Francisco and following that up by taking two of three from Milwaukee and three of four from the Cubs on the current homestand. The previous day they had rallied with four runs in the ninth for a 6–5 win over the Cubs and were riding high coming into the Subway Series as the only first-place team in town.

"It feels like we're starting to become the club we all expected we could be," Glavine said. "We've had some ups and downs, but lately we've been a lot more solid. The feeling in here is very up."

Glavine was pretty up himself, even though his pitching had

been a little bit uneven in May. After the "Tony Randazzo" game in Washington, he had pitched in Arizona in the first game of a seven-game road trip. He hadn't been awful, but it had probably been his worst outing of the season. He'd given up four runs in six innings, three of the runs coming on home runs: a two-run shot by Chris Snyder in the fifth, and a solo shot by Orlando Hudson in the sixth after the Mets had tied the game at 3–3. Glavine left in the seventh for a pinch hitter. The Mets won 9–4 after scoring six runs in the ninth, but Glavine was long gone by then.

"It was one of those games where there were a few pitches you'd like to have back," Glavine said. "Obviously the home runs, but I just wasn't as sharp as I had been—certainly not close to what I'd been in Washington. It was one of those games in the middle—I could have lost, I could have won; I ended up with a no-decision.

"I really didn't feel all that sharp early, so I was glad to at least give the team six innings and not force the bullpen to go out there early. In all, it wasn't bad, but it wasn't great. I was glad we won. Still, that made three straight starts without a win for me: the Atlanta game where I thought I was going to win; the Washington game where I probably should have won; and this game where I could have won. You definitely don't want to go down the road feeling like it's hard to win games. Not this year anyway."

The Mets pulled into San Francisco in the midst of Barry Bonds Mania. While the rest of the country viewed Barry Bonds's assault on Henry Aaron's all-time home-run record as something between a bore and a pox, in San Francisco Bonds was viewed as a heroic figure. Glavine had always had great respect for Bonds's ability but found it hard to find any joy in his chase of Aaron.

"I guess I try to take the view that he's innocent until proven guilty," he said. "Although the circumstantial evidence out there is kind of hard to ignore. If he did it [Glavine paused as if trying to keep a straight face], he's certainly not the only one. He's just the most talented."

Glavine had always pitched pretty well against Bonds. He

had given up four home runs to him through the years and had learned—or so he thought—to stick to fastballs away and changeups when pitching to him. "Last thing I always say when we go through their lineup is 'No sliders to Bonds,'" he said. "He crushes my slider."

Glavine pitched the middle game in the San Francisco series. Barry Zito, who the Giants had signed to a seven-year, $126 million contract the previous winter—beating the Mets for him in a bidding war—won the opener against Oliver Perez, and Glavine faced rising star Matt Cain in the second game.

Right from the start, Glavine felt like he was going to have a good night. Brian Runge was the home-plate umpire, and the first knee-high pitch Glavine threw was called a strike. He threw another, and it was a strike too. Then he threw one a little bit lower, and it was also a strike.

"Any time an umpire is giving me that low strike, I know I have a chance to pitch a good game," he said. "Not only is that a good pitch for me and a tough pitch for a hitter, but it gives me a lot of confidence knowing I can go there and probably get a strike call."

It also helped that for one of the first times all year, the Mets bunched some runs for Glavine early, getting three in the first and another in the second, to stake him to a 4–0 lead. It was the first time since opening night in St. Louis that Glavine had a lead like that early in the game. It was a perfect night to pitch—warm without a lot of breeze (rare in San Francisco)—and Glavine felt as if he were on cruise control.

Until Bonds came up in the fourth.

"Paulie [Lo Duca] put down slider," he said, laughing about it later. "I don't shake my catcher off very often. I started to but then I thought, 'He's thinking Barry takes the first pitch a lot, and he'll lay off a slider, especially if I keep it away a little bit.' So I figured what the heck, let's try it.

"Mistake."

Bonds didn't lay off the slider. Instead, he hit it about nine hundred feet into the night. Glavine had to laugh while Bonds circled the bases. "I guess he can still hit my slider," he said. "Thank God no one was on and I had a four-run lead. Otherwise I would really have been kicking myself. I'd gotten him out on a changeup in the first; I should have kept throwing the changeup until he hit it."

That turned out to be all the Giants got. Glavine scattered six other hits, walked only one, and struck out five. For the first time all season, he started and completed a seventh inning, throwing 105 pitches. The bullpen finished up. Glavine was 4–1, and the Number That Must Not Be Named was only six away.

His night wasn't over when the game finished. Somewhere between Arizona and San Francisco, it had been decided by several members of the team's leadership—Lo Duca, Carlos Delgado, David Wright, Billy Wagner, and Glavine—that the team needed to do something as a bonding exercise.

More often than not when teams do something like this, it is to break a losing streak or to try to get some kind of run going in a pennant race. This was neither of the above, just a sense within the clubhouse that even though they were 19–11 when they arrived in San Francisco, they needed to do something to catch fire, to get on a roll, to put some distance between themselves and the rest of the National League East.

The bonding mechanism selected? Buzz cuts, given in the clubhouse by various teammates.

"Sometimes having everyone look ugly can bring you together," Glavine said.

Glavine had been allowed to escape the razor until after he pitched. But with the win secured, he had to endure the razor. This was bad on two levels: the first and far less important one was the surprising amount of gray that showed up when layers of his mostly brown hair fell away. The second and far worse was when photos of him taken right after the razor had done its work made their way to the Internet.

"Different world," he said. "In the old days I would have had a few days to work on an explanation speech."

That speech would have been delivered to one Christine Glavine of Alpharetta, Georgia, whose eight-year-old son, Peyton, was receiving his First Holy Communion that Saturday. Mrs. Glavine's husband had been given permission by his employer to take the day off to fly to Atlanta to be there for their son's big day.

And now this.

"Are you kidding me?" she screamed on the phone. "Do you realize that you look like a complete dork? Do you know that your son's First Communion is Saturday, and you are going to walk in there looking like a complete and utter dork? How could you do this?"

"Team bonding?" came the meek reply.

"Team bonding my a———. You couldn't tell your teammates your son was counting on you to *not* look like a dork on Saturday?"

If there was ever an example of an athlete taking one for the team, this was it. Glavine knew his wife was half angry, half amused, and that she understood jock rituals pretty well. He also knew that he did kind of look like a dork, and she was not happy about that.

The Glavines are a religious family. Both Tom and Chris went to church with their parents every Sunday as kids and try to make it to church every Sunday they can, given Tom's travel schedule eight months a year. Glavine is not one of those athletes who wears his religion on his sleeve. He will never say he won or lost a game because of God's involvement. He talks about the role religion plays in his life only when asked about it, and even then he low-keys it.

"I'm not an evangelist," he will say. "But religion is important to me. I don't talk about it, and I don't try to tell anyone else what they should or shouldn't do. But it's been a part of my life for as long as I can remember."

Which would make the First Communion of one of his children an important day. And now, he would show up looking like a dork.

"In life and in baseball, sometimes you just gotta do what you gotta do," he said, laughing. He was not amused when the gray hairs were pointed out to him. He could live with being a dork. A gray-haired dork, not so much.

THE GLAVINE FAMILY SURVIVED the buzz-cut episode, and Peyton's First Communion went well. Two days later, Glavine was back in New York to pitch against the Chicago Cubs, a team that had spent millions of dollars on new players during the off-season. The Cubs were hoping that their investments might make it possible for them to avoid extending their string of seasons without a World Series title to ninety-nine. With the Red Sox winning a world title in 2004 and the White Sox in 2005, there was no one close to the Cubs anymore when it came to World Series futility.

Whether it was the new haircut or the gray hairs or the Cubs' improved lineup, Glavine started poorly, giving up four runs in the first two innings. His control, which had been so good since the weather had begun to warm, had deserted him. With two out in the first, he gave up a run when Alfonso Soriano doubled and third baseman Aramis Ramirez singled him in. "That wasn't surprising," Glavine said. "I think he's hitting about .700 against me for his career. He kills me."

Glavine got into more trouble in the second when he walked Mark DeRosa—a former Atlanta teammate—and gave up a double to Angel Pagan. But he seemed close to getting out of it when pitcher Jason Marquis came up. He promptly fell behind Marquis 3–1 and came in with a fastball, not wanting to walk the pitcher and face the top of the order with the bases loaded. Marquis lined a single up the middle scoring two runs, then scored himself on a two-out Cesar Izturis double.

"Just bad pitching," Glavine said. "The weather had gotten cold again [it was sixty-one when the game started, but wind gusts of more than twenty miles an hour made it feel a lot colder], and I had trouble getting into a rhythm. I couldn't locate my breaking pitches early. The good news was that I was able to hang in there for six innings when it looked like I might not make it out of the second."

"Classic Tom Glavine," Rick Peterson said. "Everything was a struggle for him that night, but he still gave us a chance to win the game. If you want to know why people in baseball respect him so much, it's a game like that, when nothing is easy, but he still hangs in there and stops the other guys when he absolutely has to stop them."

The Cubs didn't score again after the second. The Mets chipped back with two in the fourth and two in the sixth to tie it. They even had a chance to get Glavine a win. With two outs in the sixth and Lo Duca on second base with the go-ahead run, Willie Randolph sent David Newhan up to pinch-hit for Glavine. A hit would give the Mets the lead and give the bullpen a chance to make up for the Braves game three weeks earlier. But Newhan struck out. The Mets did win the game but not until the bottom of the ninth.

Three days later, the Mets staged a classic four-run ninth-inning rally to steal the last game of the series from the Cubs, arriving at Shea on a high for day one of the first Subway Series. "Is it cold outside?" Glavine asked. "I'm not sure any of us have noticed. Of course if it's cold tomorrow, I guess I'll notice since I'm pitching."

The Mets won the opener that night 3–2, Oliver Perez out-pitching Andy Pettitte. Wagner, who had been lights-out all year, closed it in the ninth for his tenth save. His ERA for the season was a minuscule 0.50.

"People tell me all the time, 'Well, you can't be perfect,'" Wagner said. "I always ask them, 'Why not?'"

Wagner was an improbable baseball star. He was listed at five foot eleven but didn't look that tall. And yet, a couple of months shy of turning thirty-five in July, he could still throw into the high 90s, and he had been one of the game's best closers for ten years with the Astros, the Phillies, and was now in his second year with the Mets. The save in the opener of the Yankees series was the 334th of his career, putting him in the top ten of the all-time saves list.

He and Glavine had become close friends, very much an Odd Couple. Wagner was from southern Virginia and had the drawl to prove it. Glavine was from New England. Wagner would say just about anything to anyone; Glavine almost always measured his words. Glavine's locker was the one farthest from the clubhouse door in New York, a few steps from the safety of the training room. There was an empty locker next to his, and Wagner's was the next one down. The two of them shared the empty space, a veteran's perk.

There were four people on the Mets who almost never ducked the media, and their lockers were all around Glavine's: Wagner on one side, with reliever Aaron Heilman next to him. Paul Lo Duca and David Wright were on the other side of Glavine, in the next row over. Wagner, Lo Duca, Heilman, Scott Schoeneweis, Wright, and Carlos Delgado were the players on the team Glavine was closest to—each for a different reason.

Glavine played golf with Heilman and Schoeneweis. Wright was young and bright and always looking to learn from the veterans, so he often reached out to Glavine on how to handle off-field situations. Wright really didn't need that much help because his instincts were good. "Sometimes I think I should be asking him for advice," Glavine said. "He walked in here in 2004 and handled himself like he'd been in the majors for ten years from day one."

Delgado was like that too—someone who had been a leader on every team he had played on: in Toronto, in Florida, and now in New York with the Mets. He was especially important as an influence on the young Hispanic players on the team. Major League Baseball in 2007 is made up primarily of four groups: Caucasian

Americans, Hispanics, Asians, and African Americans, the last group's number dropping rapidly.

The Mets had no Asians on the team after Chan Ho Park was optioned to Triple-A, and when the season began they had one African American on the team—Damion Easley—until Lastings Milledge was called up at the All-Star break. The rest of the roster was a split between Hispanics and whites.

Rarely is race or ethnicity an issue in a baseball clubhouse. For one thing, the sport has been worldwide for so long now that hearing more than one language spoken is a given. The Hispanics tend to play cards with the Hispanics so they can yell at each other in Spanish, and the English speakers do the same. The Mets actually had some chess players on their team: Shawn Green and John Maine frequently stared at one another across a board before games. Heilman and Easley also played.

"We're like any team," Glavine said. "We get along better when we're winning than when we're losing. But I think there's a natural tendency for the younger Hispanic players to look up to Carlos [Delgado] because their backgrounds are similar and their experiences are similar. Plus, if he really needs to give one of them a talking-to, he can do it in Spanish. If Jose Reyes needs to talk to someone, the natural person for him to go to in my mind is Carlos. Now, if Jorge Sosa has an issue, he might come to me and want to talk pitcher to pitcher. It depends on the situation."

Lo Duca and Glavine talked most often as pitcher and catcher. But there was mutual respect between the two. Glavine appreciated how hard Lo Duca had worked to make himself into a catcher. He had done very little catching until his fourth year in professional baseball, when the Dodgers had told him he was being sent from Double-A ball to A-ball to learn how to catch.

"My problem had been that I really didn't have a position," Lo Duca said. "When I was in college [Arizona State] my position, to be honest, was hitter. That's the reason I was drafted so low—I didn't have a position."

The Dodgers drafted him in the twenty-fifth round of the 1993 draft after he had hit .446 at ASU and driven in eighty-eight runs in a seventy-five-game season. He had bounced around in the minors until the decision to make him a catcher. Mike Sciosia, now the Angels' manager, was then the minor league catching instructor for the Dodgers and taught him the position. Lo Duca proved an eager student. Even so, he was still splitting time between the major leagues and Triple-A as late as 2000, before having a breakout year with the Dodgers in 2001, at the age of twenty-nine, when he hit .320 with twenty-five home runs and ninety RBI in his first full big league season.

He was a three-time All-Star when the Mets got him from Florida in return for two minor leaguers during one of the Marlins' periodic salary dumps. He had been an All-Star for a fourth time in 2006, even though he had gone through a very public divorce and been the subject of rumors that he had a gambling problem. In spite of all that, he was still the most outgoing player in the clubhouse, the one guy guaranteed to be wandering around before a game willing to talk to anyone. He loved catching Glavine.

"You can't ask for an easier guy to catch," he said. "He almost never shakes me off, which, as a catcher, makes it easier to call the game because you aren't constantly worried that you're calling the wrong pitch. He never blames anyone but himself for a mistake. When I called that slider against Bonds in San Francisco, I started to say something in the dugout, and he just waved me off and said, 'I threw a bad pitch; forget it.'

"I'm not sure people understand how much everyone on this team wants to see Tom get to three hundred." (As a nonpitcher, Lo Duca was allowed to utter the number.) "I can't even begin to tell you how much that night will mean to *me*. If I have a broken leg that night, I'm catching. There's no way I'm going to miss being a part of that."

Wagner, the person Glavine talked to most often on the team, felt the same way about the Number and often said he would probably tackle any other pitcher sent out to pitch the ninth inning that night. Most days, he and Glavine drove to Shea together. Wagner had gotten very good at reading Glavine's game-day moods. "When he's really nervous, he can't stop talking," he said. "Most of the time, I'm the talker. But if Tom's really wired before a game, I may not say a word from Greenwich until the Triboro Bridge."

According to Wagner, Glavine was quite talkative on the drive in prior to game two of the Subway Series. He knew that, even in weather worse than the night before—raw, rainy, and windy—Shea would be sold out and the game would be on national TV. Plus, he had only won once in his last five starts—although he hadn't lost—and he wanted to get back on track and moving in the direction of, as he put it before the game, "the place I'm trying to get to."

You know, *that* place.

It was raining at game time, one of those 3:55 starts for the benefit of Fox. Even so, the place was almost full, the no-shows among the 56,137 who had bought tickets remarkably minimal, given the weather.

As was often the case, Glavine struggled in the first inning, although this time he had help. His favorite umpiring crew was in town. Tony Randazzo was working first base—"Of course, where else would he be?" Glavine joked before the game. Larry Vanover, the crew chief, was behind the plate. It took one batter—Johnny Damon—for Glavine to feel as if he was being squeezed.

"I threw two pitches to Damon that I thought were strikes that were called balls," he said. "I'm out there thinking, 'Oh boy, here we go.' The last thing I need against that lineup is a guy with a postage-stamp strike zone." Damon walked.

Glavine did strike out Derek Jeter before Hideki Matsui singled. He pitched carefully to Alex Rodriguez—who already had fifteen home runs—and walked him on a 3–1 pitch he thought had caught the corner. Very quickly he was in trouble—bases loaded, one out.

"You have to take a deep breath and stay calm in those situations," Glavine said. "You tell yourself that you're one good pitch from being out of the inning. You don't think about the alternatives."

Glavine threw a good pitch to Jorge Posada, a slider down and in, and Posada chopped it to Reyes. The ball was hit slowly enough that even with Posada running, Reyes and Easley couldn't turn the double play. They forced Rodriguez while Damon scored to make it 1–0. But Glavine got Bobby Abreu to fly to Carlos Beltran in center to stop the bleeding right there.

Watching from the dugout, Mussina could see that Glavine was getting squeezed by Vanover. He was happy to see his team load the bases, but, as a pitcher, he could relate to the frustration he knew Glavine was feeling. "I was hoping we'd score ten on him," he said. "But I could see he wasn't getting anything from the home-plate ump. Obviously as a pitcher you relate because you've had days like that too."

The day soon got better for Glavine and much worse for the Yankees. Darrell Rasner, their latest number four starter, lasted two batters. Reyes led off with a single. Then, on Rasner's ninth pitch of the day, Endy Chavez hit a shot up the middle that ricocheted hard off Rasner's pitching hand. Chavez reached first while Reyes sprinted around to third. Clearly hurt, Rasner tried to throw four warm-up pitches, but the pain was overwhelming. As it turned out, he had fractured his index finger. The next day he joined Pavano on the sixty-day DL.

Mike Myers, who normally came into a game late to get out a batter or two, had to come in to relieve. He got Beltran to fly to center, with Reyes scoring, and struck out Delgado. But he got a 3–2 fastball up to David Wright, and Wright hit one of the longest home runs ever seen at Shea Stadium. It flew over the left-field bleachers and landed about 460 feet from home plate. The Mets led 3–1.

Pleased to be leading, Glavine walked to the mound to throw his warm-up pitches for the second inning. As he crossed the foul line, he heard Vanover calling his name.

"Hey, Tom," Vanover said. "You just keep throwing the pitches you were throwing in the first inning, and you'll be fine."

Glavine was stunned. In twenty years in the big leagues, he had never been told by an umpire during a game that pitches that had been called balls were actually strikes, which was what Vanover was doing.

"It shocked me," he said. "I mean, occasionally an umpire will adjust his strike zone during a game, but not often. You have to understand what they're giving you on a given day and adjust. But I had never had an ump tell me to keep doing what I was doing after an inning in which I walked two and was behind in the count. I was pretty amazed."

He might still have been in shock when Robinson Cano blasted his second pitch of the inning over the right-field wall to cut the margin to 3–2. But from that point he settled down, began throwing strikes—at least according to Vanover—and shut the Yankees down for the next five innings.

"He did make an adjustment after the first inning," Glavine said. "Nothing big, but the close pitches that had been balls in the first inning were, for the most part, strikes after that. I was happy about it, but I also thought, even if it seemed strange, that the guy deserved credit for maybe thinking he was a little off in the first inning and adjusting. It's no different than giving up a couple of runs early and thinking maybe you need to change something."

While Glavine was breezing, the Mets were pummeling the Yankees' overworked bullpen. Glavine helped build a fourth run with a sacrifice bunt in the second, and Wright hit another home run, this one a two-run shot in the third, to make it 6–2. By the time Glavine walked out to start the seventh, he had an 8–2 lead.

He knew he was on a short leash at that point. He had thrown ninety-nine pitches—twenty-seven of them in the long first inning—and with a six-run lead Willie Randolph and Rick Peterson weren't going to push him very far past one hundred pitches. "I would have liked to have gotten through that inning just because I wanted to go seven and not six," Glavine said. "But after [Josh] Phelps got the hit, I knew Willie was coming to get me."

Phelps had singled on an 0–1 pitch. That made 101, and Randolph figured the bullpen could handle a six-run lead for nine outs. He brought in Scott Schoeneweis, hoping to get him through the eighth inning unscathed and give Wagner the day off. It didn't work out quite that way. Schoeneweis gave up one run in the seventh, which wasn't a big deal since the lead was 8–3.

Glavine, icing his arm in the clubhouse, didn't feel any tension as he walked from the training room to the couches in the middle of the clubhouse to watch the eighth.

Alex Rodriguez led off with a home run. Then Posada homered. It was 8–5. Abreu walked, and Randolph waved in Pedro Feliciano. Getting just a little bit nervous, Glavine walked into the coaches' conference room, which wasn't that far from his locker. He felt bad for Schoeneweis, who he knew was pitching on a bad leg he had not said anything about publicly. But right now his concerns were more immediate. Feliciano gave up a double to Phelps that made it 8–6 and brought Derek Jeter up with the tying run.

Glavine decided to try the training room again. Maybe a little time in the whirlpool would change the Mets' luck. It worked. Jeter grounded to third. Then the Mets scored two runs in the bottom of the eighth to extend the lead back to 10–6. Taking no chances, Randolph brought Wagner in to pitch the ninth, even though it was not a save situation. (If a pitcher starts an inning and the lead is more than three runs, he cannot be credited with a save.) Wagner didn't care if it was a save situation. He just wanted to get Glavine the win. Glavine wasn't taking any chances either. He stayed put in the whirlpool, even though he was getting kind of warm.

Wagner retired Matsui to start the inning, and Glavine felt himself relaxing. Then Rodriguez and Posada singled. Glavine unrelaxed. Abreu hit a roller in front of the plate and Wagner pounced on it.

"First base!" Glavine heard himself scream.

But Wagner was a little off-balance when he picked up the ball and decided his best chance for an out was Rodriguez, charging for the plate. He tried to throw the ball to Lo Duca and threw it past him. Glavine heard himself screaming again: "No, Billy, no! Not there! Get the out at first!"

Too late. Rodriguez scored, Posada went to third, and Abreu reached first. Once again the tying run was at the plate, with the score now 10–7. That was it for Glavine. "I couldn't watch anymore," he said. "I walked back into the coaches' room and turned the TV off. I told the guys to come in and tell me what happened."

Fortunately, it didn't take that long. Wagner jacked his fastball up to 98 and struck out Cano for the second out. Then, with the rain coming down hard, he struck out Phelps to finally end the game.

"We won ten-seven; Billy got the last two outs," one of the clubhouse kids reported to Glavine.

"About time" was his answer.

Wagner appeared a moment later, carrying the game ball with him. Glavine thanked him but couldn't resist a question. "What the hell were you doing throwing the ball home?" he asked.

"I couldn't get turned around to first," Wagner answered sheepishly. "Probably should have just held it."

"Probably right," Glavine answered. "Good job anyway."

Wagner smiled. "Five to go."

Glavine nodded. He was now 5–1 on the season. "Five to go," he said.

17

Drought

THE YANKEES MANAGED TO SALVAGE the last game of the Subway Series the next night, young Tyler Clippard (who, not surprisingly, had been nicknamed "The Yankee Clippard") outpitching John Maine, who didn't have a nickname but had pitched very well all year. The win allowed the Yankees to limp back to the Bronx with a 19–23 record, still ten and a half games behind the Red Sox, who came into town riding high at 30–13.

For once, the Yankees had their pitching set up exactly the way they wanted it: Chien-Ming Wang would pitch the first game, Mike Mussina the middle game, and Andy Pettitte the finale.

"If we can't get something done with the three of us pitching, I don't know when we will," Mussina said.

Before Wang outpitched Tim Wakefield in the opener, there were still rumors swirling that Joe Torre and Brian Cashman were in trouble. That win seemed to quiet things down for the moment. Mussina was matched against Julian Tavarez the next night.

Unlike Glavine, Mussina has never been especially bothered by the first inning. Like Glavine — and most quality pitchers — he has absolutely no clue what's going to happen once he reaches the mound, regardless of how he warms up. There is, however, one key difference in his warm-up. Glavine is going to throw fastballs and changeups 80 to 90 percent of the time, mixing in a cutter, a slider, and a curve, no matter how he feels in the bullpen. "If my change isn't good, I just have to hope it will get better by the time the game starts," Glavine said.

Mussina's warm-up, in contrast, is more like an audition for his pitches. Because he throws so many different pitches — fastball, curve, slider, changeup, sinker, cutter — with almost equal effectiveness at different times, he uses his warm-up to decide which pitches he thinks will work best on a given night.

"He creates his game plan while he's in the bullpen," said Mike Borzello, who has warmed up Mussina before games for seven years now. "He doesn't pitch off scouting reports very much. He's aware of what hitters have done off him in the past; he knows who is a dead fastball hitter, who likes the ball down, things like that. But for the most part, he comes out of the bullpen thinking, 'My slider's good today; I'll throw it more.' Or if he doesn't think his curve is sharp, he may only use it as a waste pitch [a pitch thrown way off the plate on a pitcher's count like 0–2 or 1–2, just to show it to the batter] that night."

Mussina is also more apt to worry about a shaky warm-up than Glavine, although he understands that the way you warm up frequently has nothing to do with the way you pitch.

"It's not as if there's anything you can do," Mussina said. "And I've had games where I was awful in the bullpen and pitched well. I remember pitching a one-hitter in Texas once when I literally didn't throw a single strike in the bullpen. You just walk in and go with whatever you think you have that night."

The bullpen before a game is not a place to make adjustments. "Ron [Guidry] will usually just hand me a towel when I'm done and ask me how I feel. If the answer is 'Lousy,' there's not much to be done at that point."

On the night of May 22, Mussina walked to the mound to face the Red Sox feeling quite unsure about what was to come. He hadn't been at all happy with the way he had felt in his last outing in Chicago, but a quiet ballpark certainly wasn't an issue this night: Yankee Stadium was packed and as loud as it gets during the regular season, just as it always is with the Red Sox in town.

It took four batters for Mussina to get that sinking feeling about his night and his season. He struck out Julio Lugo to start the game, eliciting a huge roar from the crowd, which wanted to see the Yankees build on the modest two-game winning streak they had started at Shea Stadium.

Kevin Youkilis, one of those players who always seem to be on base in critical situations for the Red Sox, singled to right field. That brought Mussina to what is arguably the most dangerous twosome in baseball: David Ortiz and Manny Ramirez.

When Yankee fans think of the Red Sox, dating to the 2004 series when the rivalry changed forever after Boston came back from a 3–0 deficit to win the American League Championship Series, they think of Ortiz hitting big home runs. Ramirez is the no-doubt future Hall of Famer on the team, but Ortiz is the more feared clutch hitter. Mussina pitched Ortiz carefully, but he lined a single to right, putting men on first and second with one out.

Up came Ramirez, who grew up in the Bronx and has always hit well in what was his home team's ballpark as a kid. Ramirez is difficult to pitch to under any circumstances because he hits for average as well as for power, and, even though left field in Yankee Stadium is much more difficult to reach than right field, his power is such that if he gets a pitch to hit, it really doesn't matter what direction the ball goes, it's going out.

"What makes Manny tough is that he's patient," Mussina said. "He doesn't go up there flailing. You're going to have to throw him a decent pitch. If you don't, he'll take the walk. At that point in the game, I really don't want to walk him because then the bases are loaded for [J.D.] Drew and [Mike] Lowell. Either way, I've already put myself in trouble by letting Youkilis and Ortiz get on. Especially Youkilis. The way you want to pitch to Ortiz and Manny in an ideal world is two outs and nobody on or leading off. That way, worst case, if they take you deep, it's just one run."

Mussina quickly got behind Ramirez 2–0, hoping he might swing at a breaking pitch off the plate. "Now I'm in a bad place," he said later. "Bad things happen on bad counts. There aren't many counts in the world worse than two and oh to Manny with runners on base."

He tried to throw a fastball on the corner, but the pitch strayed a little too close to the white, and Ramirez jumped on it. The ball disappeared into the left-field bullpen in the blink of an eye, and six minutes after throwing his final warm-up pitch, Mussina was down 3–0.

"It's a little bit of a sick feeling," he said. "You've got a packed ballpark; it's the Red Sox; we're already in a deep hole; we really kind of need to sweep them to get ourselves on a roll. And I walk out there and put us down three-nothing right away."

It could have been worse. After Drew grounded out, Lowell doubled, and catcher Jason Varitek, another Yankee killer, singled. Lowell had to hold at third though, and Mussina managed to get center fielder Coco Crisp on a grounder to first to keep the margin from growing.

"I actually had a chance to salvage the night after that," Mussina said. "Three's not good, but you're still in the ball game. And it wasn't as if [Josh] Beckett was pitching for them." (Beckett is the Red Sox ace.)

Julian Tavares, who was pitching, is a career journeyman, a fifth starter at best. But he breezed through the first three innings and didn't give up a run until the fourth. By then Lowell had homered to lead off the fourth, and the single runs the Yankees scored in the fourth and the fifth sliced the margin to 4–2.

Still, Mussina was hanging in, and the Yankees were in the ball game when Mussina started the seventh. "At that point I had taken what started out as a bad night and given us a chance to make it a good night," he said. "That's what you have to do when you have a first inning like that. Your goal becomes 'Get to the seventh or the eighth, and hold them where they are.' I had almost done that. Then I screwed up and walked Varitek to start the seventh and pretty much ruined everything."

Actually he almost pitched himself clear after the Varitek walk. Crisp hit into a force, and Dustin Pedroia, the rookie second baseman, flied to right. Mussina was one out away from giving his team seven innings, after a shaky start, and a chance to rally against the Boston bullpen. But Crisp stole second, and Lugo singled him home to make it 5–2. Then the ever-pesky Youkilis doubled into the gap in right center, and Lugo, running all the way with two outs, scored to make it 6–2. That was Mussina's ninety-ninth pitch of the night. He never threw the hundredth. Torre brought in Mike Myers, who promptly gave up an RBI single to Ortiz to make it 7–2. The Red Sox won 7–3.

Mussina was now officially disgusted with where his season was going. He could live with a lost April, but now it was almost the end of May and he was 2–3 with an ugly ERA of 6.52.

"You get to a point where you say, 'I know I'm a better pitcher than this, but where is it?' " he said. "It wasn't as if I was getting crushed every time out, but I wasn't good. You're not looking to be mediocre or barely okay. You're looking to be good."

Mussina is never afraid to ask for help or suggestions. As it happened, that week, ex–Yankee pitching coach Mel Stottlemyre was visiting. John Flaherty, the former backup catcher who was now a Yankee broadcaster on YES—the Yankee-created TV network—was also around. Looking for different voices and opinions, Mussina asked each of them what they thought might be the problem. At the same time, he was still talking to Guidry and Borzello and Torre, seeking as much input as he could find.

"What you really hope for in that situation is that they all say the same thing," he said. "Maybe they see something in your motion, and they say, 'Do this,' and you feel better. That wasn't the case this time."

In fact, he got five different answers from five different people: Stottlemyre thought his location was off, that he was missing his spots by trying to be too fine; Flaherty thought he needed to throw more fastballs early in counts to get ahead and set up hitters for his breaking pitches; Borzello thought his velocity hadn't come all the way back to where it needed to be after the hamstring injury; Guidry thought he needed to work on his mechanics, most notably from the stretch; Torre thought he was "pitching away from contact," afraid to throw strikes because he didn't have enough confidence in his stuff.

Five different answers but, in a sense, all the same: because Mussina didn't have confidence in what he was throwing, he was pitching away from contact and frequently getting into bad counts as a result.

"You have to remember who you are," Torre told him. "You didn't win two hundred forty games without having good stuff. Trust it and you'll be fine."

Mussina took in all the advice and decided that everyone was right. "Which meant I just had to go out there and go with what I had and believe it was good enough."

Simple as that sounds, this was a constant issue with Mussina: not so much believing in himself—he knew he was a good pitcher—but in remembering what he had done to make himself a good pitcher.

"Sometimes he listens too much to outsiders," Borzello said. "He spent some time with [ex–Orioles teammate] Todd Frohwirth earlier this month, and Todd said something to him like, 'You have to remember you're thirty-eight, not twenty-eight.' All of a sudden he thinks he has to be a completely different pitcher. I told him that was bullshit, that what he had was plenty good enough if he'd just throw it with some confidence."

Mussina went to the mound five days later to face the Los Angeles Angels of Anaheim (perhaps the silliest name in the history of sports) on a sparkling Sunday afternoon. The Angels had been the Yankees' jinx team dating back to the 2002 playoffs, when they had beaten the Yankees in four games and gone on to win their first World Series. They had also knocked the Yankees out of the playoffs in 2005 and were the only team in the American League with a winning record against them in the Joe Torre era.

The weekend in New York had been like most Angels-Yankees series. The Angels had won the first two games, and Mussina now had to face John Lackey, their best pitcher, in the finale.

The first pitch Mussina threw was a 91-mile-an-hour fastball to leadoff hitter Reggie Willits. He proceeded to strike out the side in the first inning and walked off to calls of "Mooooose," which sound like boos if you don't know what they are. They were like music to Mussina's ears at that moment, not having heard them all season.

The Yankees went ahead 1–0 in the second inning, when Wil Nieves, the seldom used backup catcher, lined a two-out RBI single to center to score Bobby Abreu. Nieves was in the lineup because Torre liked to give Jorge Posada one day off a week, and he had kept him in the lineup throughout the Boston series and for the first two days of the Angels series. Coming into the game, Nieves was one for twenty-six for the season.

Mussina is not a pitcher who worries about who his catcher is. Some pitchers don't like throwing to certain catchers or prefer a specific catcher. Years ago, Steve Carlton was so insistent that he pitch to Tim McCarver—first with the Cardinals and then with the Phillies—that McCarver liked to joke that when he and Carlton died they would be buried sixty feet, six inches apart. When Randy Johnson was with the Yankees, he had preferred pitching to Flaherty, so Posada's off-days almost always coincided with the days Johnson pitched.

Mussina was comfortable pitching to Posada. The two had worked together for seven years, and Posada, who has almost no ego as a catcher, was perfectly comfortable with Mussina shaking him off. "With some pitchers, you call pitches," he said. "With Mike and some others, you make suggestions."

Mussina also liked throwing to Nieves, for the simple reason that he was smaller than Posada and provided a naturally lower target for him. He also liked him personally. At twenty-nine, Nieves was the classic journeyman ballplayer. He had made it to the major leagues with San Diego in 2002 for twenty-eight games and a year earlier had been in six games for the Yankees. Making the team in 2007 as the backup catcher was the highlight of his baseball career. He was, without question, the friendliest person in the clubhouse. Three weeks after the Angels game, on Father's Day, he made a point of asking each male member of the media if he was a father. If he was, Nieves wished him a Happy Father's Day and said he was looking forward to being a father someday himself.

The second inning RBI was the fourth of his big league career and his first in five years. More important to Mussina, it gave him a lead to work with. In the fourth, the lead became 2–0 when Robinson Cano doubled with one out, Doug Mientkiewicz was hit by a pitch, and Nieves again drove in a run with a base hit.

"Those hits were huge," Mussina said. "Because you really aren't expecting Wil to pick up your offense. What was too bad was we couldn't build anything else out of it."

The Nieves single put men on first and second with one out and the top of the order coming up. But Melky Cabrera grounded into a double play to snuff the possibility of a big inning. "A guy like Lackey, you only get so many chances," Torre said later. "We had a couple chances to pounce on him early and didn't."

Mussina continued to pitch like, well, the old Mike Mussina. He gave up a run in the fifth when he struggled, giving up four singles, but was bailed out by a double play. He came back with a one-two-three sixth and walked to the mound in the seventh up 2–1, knowing he was being watched closely by Guidry and Torre, having thrown eighty-five pitches on the first hot day of the year. His goal was to get through the seventh and hope the setup guys could work the eighth and give the ball to Mariano Rivera for the ninth.

He started fine, getting Gary Matthews Jr. looking at a good curveball. On a 3–2 pitch to Casey Kotchman, he threw a changeup he thought might be strike three. Plate umpire Jim Wolf didn't see it that way and called ball four.

"It wasn't like he missed it," Mussina said. "It was a close pitch, and he just didn't give it to me. That's the biggest difference with Questech. Once, a veteran pitcher, if he could throw to a certain spot, even if it was a ball or two off the plate, he got the call. Now, most of the time, you don't get that pitch anymore."

Instead of two outs and no one on, Kotchman was on first with one out. Torre decided ninty-five pitches was enough for Mussina. As he walked to the mound, the crowd booed, thinking the hook was a quick one.

"I had two thoughts: one, that it was warm and Mike hadn't been stretched out very much yet," Torre said. "Two, though, was more important: this was the best he'd pitched all year. I wanted to make sure he left the mound with a good feeling. I didn't want to leave him in too long and have a bad inning mess up the confidence he'd built by pitching so well."

Mussina wasn't surprised to see Torre. "I pretty much knew going out for the seventh that if someone got on that was going to be it," he said. "I didn't have a problem with it."

He left to a standing ovation, his first of the season. Mussina walked off the mound, head down, and crossed the first-base foul line. A couple of steps across it, hearing the cheers, he paused for a moment, then stopped and took off his cap and waved it to the crowd in thanks.

"I was thinking to myself as I left the mound, 'Was I good enough that I should tip my cap?'" he said. "Believe it or not, I think fans are often too generous with us. I've had games where I leave leading seven-five, and they give me an ovation. I don't deserve it. I'm leaving with the lead because the guys scored a lot of runs, and I'm ahead even though I wasn't very good. I don't like to tip my cap when that happens because I just feel the cheers are undeserved."

Mussina decided his performance that day—six and one-third innings; six hits, all singles; one run (to that point); one walk; and six strikeouts—merited doffing his cap. When his family is in the stands, he will always wave his cap in their direction at that moment because if he doesn't his sons get upset with him for waving to fifty-five thousand people but not to them. Jana and the kids were home that day, so he settled for the fifty-five thousand.

"It felt good to go out and pitch well," he said. "I wasn't limping along; I had good stuff; I had good location; I didn't pitch away from contact. I felt good about myself."

The icing for the day would have been to get a win. Scott Proctor, who had been the closest thing the Yankees had had to a decent setup man in 2006 and 2007, came in to take his place. The notion of getting a win didn't last very long. Proctor instantly gave up a double to Howie Kendrick, which moved Kotchman to third. Then he completely lost the plate, walking Mike Napoli to load the bases and then Erick Aybar—after Aybar fouled off seven pitches on 2–2—to tie the game at 2–2. Mussina, who had accepted congratulations from his teammates and then headed to the clubhouse to ice, saw the tying run trot in from third as he was wrapping the ice packs around his shoulder.

"Well, at least there wasn't any suspense," he said, forcing a laugh. "Sometimes when you come out in the seventh or eighth, watching those last few outs can be torture, especially in a close game. When you pitch well, you would really like to get a win. Obviously there are times when you don't pitch that well and you get a win, but when you're in the clubhouse and you're up two-one, you aren't thinking about those days. I didn't even have my ice pack on before I knew I wasn't getting a win."

Not long after that, the team's chances of winning were pretty much gone. Proctor walked Chone Figgins and left to loud boos, the Yankees now down 3–2. The Angels tacked on another run and completed the weekend sweep with a 4–3 win.

The loss dropped the Yankees to 21–27, putting them twelve

and a half games behind the Red Sox after climbing to within nine and a half by taking two of three in their series with the Sox earlier in the week. That brief moment of brightness seemed a long way off in the quiet postgame clubhouse. Even John Sterling, the longtime radio play-by-play man who could usually find hope in a leadoff single with the team down 5–0, sounded despondent. During a sponsored postgame bit, "the highlight of the week," Sterling played the last out of the Wednesday-night victory over the Red Sox, which climaxed with his trademark, "the Yankees winnnnnn." Coming out of that piece of tape, Sterling said quietly, "It seems like forever since I've had a chance to say those words."

He brightened a moment later though, adding, "At least today there was some hope for the future, and it came in the form of one Mike Mussina."

THINGS WEREN'T NEARLY as dreary in Met-ville. Even after losing the last game of the Yankees series, the Mets were a snappy 28–15 and had a two-game lead on the Braves as they headed to Atlanta for the third of the six three-game series they would play against the Braves during the season. The only real negative in the first quarter of the season had been the Braves taking four of the first six games against the Mets.

"We handled them pretty well last year [winning eleven of eighteen]," Glavine said. "We need to show them we can do the same thing this year."

They didn't exactly do that in the opener, going down 8–1. But they bounced back behind a superb pitching performance by Oliver Perez to win game two 3–0. That gave them a chance to tighten up the season series if they could win game three. It was a pretty good pitching matchup: Tom Glavine versus John Smoltz, act three for the 2007 season. In four years, Glavine and Smoltz had matched up once as starters. Now they were doing it for the third time in seven weeks.

The game had a little more juice than usual, as if it needed it. Smoltz had turned forty nine days earlier: "I'm exactly a century away from my goal—to play on the Senior PGA Tour," he said, referencing the golf tour that one has to be fifty to play on. Someone pointed out that he probably meant a decade away. "Hey, I'm forty," Smoltz said. "My mind isn't as sharp as it used to be."

His pitching certainly was. He was off to a great start, with a 6–2 record and an ERA of 2.58. In his last start in Washington, he had been hit on the hand by a line drive and had been frightened that he might be hurt. But it had turned out to be a broken pinky on his nonthrowing hand. "It hurts like hell," he said. "But it doesn't bother me when I pitch."

The six wins had put Smoltz at 199 for his career. If you added the 154 saves he had accrued during his four seasons as the Braves' closer, it seemed very likely that a 200th win would make Smoltz a Hall of Fame lock. Only Smoltz and Dennis Eckersley had won at least 150 games (Eckersley had won 197) and saved more than 150 (Eckersley had saved 390). Smoltz had missed all of the 2000 season after Tommy John surgery, and large chunks of both 1998 and 2001 with injuries. And yet he had come back to pitch well, first out of the bullpen and then as a starter again.

"I think if Smoltzie gets to two hundred wins, when you factor in the saves and his postseason record, there's no way they can keep him out," Glavine said. "I'm rooting like hell for him to get to two hundred. Just not against me."

Smoltz was probably most proud of his postseason record because it was the one place where he had clearly outshone his old buddies Glavine and Greg Maddux. He had won more postseason games than anyone in history, going 15–4. By comparison, Glavine was 14–16 and Maddux 11–14.

"I think that's the thing that's most special to me," Smoltz said. "If you look closer, the four games I lost could have been wins. One was one to nothing to Andy Pettitte in Game Five of the '96 World Series. Another was two to one. Postseason is a completely different kind of baseball than regular season. Tom and Greg are very good at getting guys to give up at bats because [hitters] aren't mentally tough enough to deal with everything they bring to the table. In postseason, no one gives up an out. Everyone is focused on every at bat because it's so important. There are no easy outs for a pitcher. I think because I've been more of a power pitcher than they are, I've been able to adapt to postseason a little bit better."

But Smoltz, for all his success, felt as if he had taken a backseat to Glavine and Maddux through the years. "I think they took turns at the steering wheel while I was in the backseat," he said. "Part of it was they never got hurt and I did. They had multiple twenty-win seasons and multiple Cy Young seasons; I had one of each [1996]. It never bothered me; it's just the way it was."

Glavine knew that Smoltz would savor getting win number two hundred against him in Atlanta, with the crowd rooting him to the finish line on every pitch. "I knew going in I'd have to pitch really well to have a chance," Glavine said. "I would have been shocked if John was anything less than great that night."

Smoltz was just that. Glavine was almost as good. The two players who had been thorns in his side in April continued to be troublemakers in May. Leadoff hitter Kelly Johnson, who had opened the game at Shea with a first-pitch home run, singled to start the game and ended up scoring on a sacrifice fly by Jeff Francoeur. Glavine had to pitch clear of a two-men-on, two-out situation (typical Glavine first inning) but did so and trailed 1–0. Then Matt Diaz, who had led off the second inning the last time Glavine faced the Braves in Atlanta, again led off the second inning with a home run on a 2–0 pitch, and the Braves were up 2–0.

"It occurred to me then that if I didn't hold them right there, we had no chance at all," Glavine said. "Smoltzie was dealing."

Glavine did hold them there. The Braves didn't score again, but Smoltz didn't need them to. He was in trouble only twice. In the third, Glavine singled with one out and Jose Reyes followed with another single. Then Carlos Beltran got an infield single with two outs to load the bases for David Wright. Smoltz reached back and threw a 96-mile-an-hour fastball past Wright to get out of the inning unscathed.

The Mets had one more chance against Smoltz in the seventh when Shawn Green and Ruben Gotay both singled with one out. Glavine had already thrown 110 pitches to get through six innings (throwing thirty-one in the first hadn't helped), so Willie Randolph went to his bench for David Newhan, sending him up to hit for Glavine. Newhan grounded into a force play. So did Reyes.

That was it for Smoltz: seven shutout innings, a 2–0 lead, and a standing ovation as he came off; the crowd knew that after 101 pitches he wouldn't be back to pitch the eighth. His bullpen finished for him, but not before closer Bob Wickman made it interesting in the ninth. A single by Carlos Delgado, an error by Johnson on Green's ground ball, and a sacrifice bunt by Gotay put the tying runs in scoring position with one out. But Wickman got pinch hitter Julio Franco to tap back to him (Delgado scoring), and Reyes popped the first pitch he saw to Edgar Renteria. Game over: Braves 2, Mets 1.

Smoltz and Atlanta rejoiced. Glavine was, to use his word, pissed. "I was proud of John and happy for him to get two hundred," he said. "But I really didn't want to spend the rest of my life hearing from him how he beat me to get to two hundred. I was pretty steamed going through the postgame interviews and getting dressed. Once I got out of the ballpark, I was okay. I called him on the way home and left him a message telling him I was proud of him. He called back a while later and we had a good talk."

Glavine smiled. "It didn't make me feel any less pissed off to talk to him."

Someone suggested that perhaps he could get even by winning his three hundredth against Smoltz. "Oh God, I hope not," he said. "We don't see them again until mid-August. If I haven't gotten it by then, I'll be a wreck."

He was 5–2 and pitching well. There was no reason to believe the Number would not be reached before August.

Even so, Glavine's next outing was discouraging. It followed a pattern that was becoming familiar: an early struggle, followed by several innings of strong pitching with little run support. In this case there was *no* run support.

The San Francisco Giants were in town and that meant the Barry Bonds Circus would draw a lot more media attention than anything Glavine or the Mets were trying to accomplish. The Mets had gone to Florida after the Atlanta series and swept the Marlins, meaning they came home with a 32–17 record and a four-and-a-half-game lead that was widening, it seemed, on a daily basis.

The Giants were awful. Barry Zito, their big free-agent acquisition of the winter, was pitching to an ERA of just under 5.00. The team was old and cranky and overwhelmed by the Bonds Circus. Bonds had gotten into the habit of doing one press conference at each road stop. Exactly why anyone wanted to talk to him was a reasonable question to ask, but no one seemed able to resist. He was like the scene of an accident.

The Giants had announced that Bonds would speak to the New York media on the first day of the series. But Bonds changed his mind, deciding to push it back until Wednesday, leaving a lot of camera crews and columnists looking at one another before game one on Tuesday. The Mets won that night 5–4 in twelve innings. The losing pitcher for the Giants was ex-Met Armando Benitez, who among fans had set some kind of unofficial record for blown key games during his time in New York. Beating Benitez to start a homestand put everyone in a good mood.

It didn't last. Glavine began the next night by getting two quick outs in the first inning. It looked as if, for once, he might have a low pitch count in the first. Wrong. Rich Aurilia beat out an infield single in the shortstop hole, and Bonds, who had deigned to speak to the media *and* play in the game that day, singled to center. Glavine then walked catcher Bengie Molina after thinking he had struck him out on a changeup. Now it looked like a familiar Glavine first inning: bases loaded, two out. Pedro Feliz singled to center, driving in both Aurilia and Bonds. The Giants led 2–0, and Glavine had spent thirty-one pitches by the end of the inning.

Still, that didn't seem like a disaster given how poorly Zito had been pitching. But it was apparent from the first that the Zito who had been the most highly sought free-agent pitcher of the off-season had decided to show up for at least one night. His curveball, the classic twelve-to-six that starts at a batter's shoulder and ends up at his feet, was as good as it had ever been, and he was throwing it for strikes. He had the Mets flailing right from the start.

The Giants widened their lead in the third, although the inning was not without an amusing moment: After Aurilia led off with a single, Bonds hit a ground ball to first base. Once, Bonds was a great base runner, an excellent base stealer. Now, he would lose to a fast racewalker. Seeing Carlos Delgado field the ball cleanly, Bonds flipped his bat away and *walked* about twenty feet down the first-base line, as the Mets easily turned a three-six-three double play. They probably could have completed the play twice more, and Bonds still wouldn't have been at first base.

The double play prevented a big inning. Molina singled right afterward, and Feliz tripled to score him. That was it for the Giants, but it was more than enough. Glavine and Zito each pitched seven innings, each threw 122 pitches, and each threw seventy-seven strikes. The difference was that Glavine gave up the three runs. That was the final: 3–0.

Once again, Glavine was not unhappy with the way he had pitched but with the result—for him and for the team. He had been 3–1 on April 17 after his first four starts. Since then he had started eight games and gone 2–2, even though his ERA during that stretch was a very respectable 3.55. He had pitched at least six innings in every one of those starts and had given up three or fewer runs in six of them; four runs in the other two. It was not hard to make the case that he could have easily won six of those games rather than two if he'd had some run support.

If you left out the Yankees game in which the Mets had scored eight runs with Glavine on the mound, the team had scored eighteen runs in seven games behind him, an average of 2.7 runs a game, which wasn't going to be enough to win very often.

Every season, almost every baseball team has one pitcher it always seems to score a lot of runs for and one pitcher for whom it never seems to score runs. Glavine was very aware of that fact. "I just hope this is a blip and not a trend," he said. "I gotta believe that it is."

18

Bumps in the Road

THE BLIP CONTINUED FOR GLAVINE in his next start. The Phillies were back in town, but they looked like a very different team than the one the Mets had faced in April. Since their dreadful 4–11 start, they had gone 24–18 and were within a game of .500, although they still trailed the Mets by eight games. Manager Charlie Manuel had not been fired, although it still appeared that he was just one more losing streak from being out of work.

"We knew in April they were a better team than what we saw," Mets manager Willie Randolph said. "Getting them at home now, this is a good chance for us to make a statement within the division."

They hadn't made that statement to the Braves, who were three and a half games back and 6–3 against the Mets. There didn't seem to be any reason, though, not to make it to the Phillies.

Game one was a familiar matchup: Glavine versus Moyer. Old versus older. Slow versus slower.

Both were superb. Glavine actually set the Phillies down one-two-three in the first, the first time in five starts that the opposition hadn't scored in its first at bat. "I felt like someone should present me with a game ball or something," he joked.

The Mets scored two off of Moyer in the second and might have had a bigger inning than that. After Paul Lo Duca had

280

singled in two runs, Glavine extended the inning with two outs by singling to right, moving Lo Duca to third. But Jose Reyes, who had been so hot early in the season, grounded into a force play, and the Mets settled for two. Then Glavine quickly gave the two back in the third—on another two-out rally.

"That's bothersome," he said later. "You have to finish innings. In the San Francisco game, all three runs I gave up were with two outs, then I did it again in that inning against the Phillies."

What made it more frustrating was that it would be many innings and hours before either team would score again. Glavine and Moyer each left after seven innings, with the score tied at 2–2. The Phillies won the game 4–2 in eleven innings. The blip appeared to be turning into a trend.

It was now June, and, in theory at least, Glavine could have already had the ten wins he needed to get to *the* Number. Instead, he was still halfway there and wondering when he might win again. To make matters worse, the Phillies swept the series and crept to within five games of the Mets. The only good news was that the Braves were swept by the Marlins so they gained no ground.

The Phillies series closed out a disappointing homestand. The Mets had gone 3–6, and Glavine had pitched twice, gone 0–1, and given up five runs in fourteen innings. The next road trip would be difficult: three games in Detroit against the Tigers, three in Los Angeles against the Dodgers, and three in Yankee Stadium against the Yankees. Since Glavine would pitch on Sunday in Detroit and the following Saturday in New York, he would be facing lineups—both good ones—with a designated hitter rather than a pitcher. That wouldn't make things any easier.

"We'll get to use a DH in those games too," he said. "Maybe that will help."

Maybe. Except that Glavine had gotten two of the eight hits the Mets had managed against Moyer and was hitting .292. Only

Jose Reyes had a higher batting average at that moment. Not having Glavine batting might not be such a good thing.

WHILE GLAVINE WAS PITCHING WELL and not winning games, Mike Mussina was pitching better—and not winning games.

The Angels game, even though it had not resulted in a victory, had given him a confidence boost. It had reminded him that Mike Borzello was right—he still had the pitches to be successful as long as he didn't pitch from behind, which he had been doing on a regular basis prior to that game.

The Yankees flew straight from New York to Toronto after the final game of the Angels series. With their record 21–27, the team held a meeting prior to the opener against the Blue Jays. Then they went out and lost 7–2.

"Guess that shows you just how much team meetings mean," Mussina said. "Of course, if we had won that night, we all would have said that the meeting really focused us. Good pitching focuses you. We just weren't getting enough of it."

Andy Pettitte pitched well—and lost—the next day, before the Yankees escaped Toronto by winning the finale. From there, it was on to Boston for three more with the Red Sox, who had now built their lead to thirteen and a half games—bringing back memories of 1978 when they had led by fourteen and a half in July, before being caught by the Yankees in September en route to the Bucky Dent playoff home run in October. Except there was no reason to believe in early June 2007 that this Yankees team had any chance to match what the 1978 team had accomplished.

Chien-Ming Wang outlasted Tim Wakefield in the opener in Boston, which sent Mussina to the mound against Curt Schilling in game two for another Saturday Fox TV broadcast. It was warm and overcast in Boston when the game started, and the weather got worse as the game wore on.

Both pitchers were solid early, but the Red Sox broke a 1–1 tie in the fourth on a David Ortiz walk, a Manny Ramirez double, and a Kevin Youkilis walk that loaded the bases. Mike Lowell singled one run in, and then Jason Varitek grounded into a double play to score another run. Soon after that, it started to rain quite hard, and the umpires ordered that the tarpaulin be put on the field.

Often after a rain delay, a manager will change pitchers, especially if the starting pitcher is older. Trying to warm up a second time in the same day can be difficult, and sometimes a pitcher will go back out without being completely loose and pitch poorly. Pitchers hate rain delays. They lose their rhythm and their feel for the game, and they can't ice their arms if they're going back in to pitch. This time, though, both pitchers came back out after the delay because it lasted only twenty-nine minutes.

"Much longer than that, and it's probably too tough," Mussina said. "But half an hour isn't that much longer than sitting through a long inning in the dugout—except you get extra warm-up pitches after it rains. I told Joe I thought I was fine to go back out. It was warm [eighty-one degrees and humid], so it wasn't hard to work up a sweat again."

Schilling didn't fare so well after the delay. He got through the fifth but gave up four runs in the sixth, giving Mussina a 5–3 lead going into the bottom of the inning.

"In that situation you *have* to go out there and put up a zero," Mussina said. "Your guys have just turned the game around for you. Your job is to keep it right there. I failed pretty miserably."

He worked Lowell, who was having a fabulous season, to 3–2, then hung a breaking pitch that Lowell hit over the Green Monster. That made it 5–4. The crowd was still cheering Lowell when Varitek hit an 0–1 pitch to dead center field for another home run. Torre was out of the dugout almost before Varitek's shot landed.

"Not good," Mussina said. "I really felt okay going into the inning. They had dinged me a little in the fourth, but I felt like I was going along pretty well and now we had the lead. If I get through one more inning there, I think we've got a shot. I didn't get through one batter."

The Red Sox ended up battering the Yankees bullpen and winning the game 11–6. It was a discouraging loss in many ways. "We win the first game; if we can win that one, we've got Pettitte going the next night, and maybe we can sweep them and put a dent in their confidence a little," Mussina said. "I go out in the sixth and get blown up and we lose. That was a loss that really hurt for a lot of reasons."

The Yankees did come back to win the last game on an Alex Rodriguez home run in the ninth but headed for Chicago still way back and still six games under .500. They won two of three in Chicago before Mussina pitched the finale against ex-Yankee Jose Contreras.

This time, he was the Good Mussina, much as he had been in New York against the Angels. He breezed through six innings, allowing only two hits. The Yankees weren't much better against Contreras but managed to scratch a run in the fourth for a 1–0 lead. Mussina entered the seventh clinging to that lead.

Jim Thome led off the inning with what amounted to a swinging bunt. The ball dribbled toward second baseman Robinson Cano but was hit so slowly that Cano, playing practically in right field against Thome, couldn't make the play at first base. Then Paul Konerko singled to left, and Thome made it all the way to third. Mussina took a deep breath. He knew he had to bear down to try to get out of the inning without giving up the tying run.

He walked back onto the mound and was about to look in for a sign when, out of the corner of his eye, he saw someone pop out of the Yankee dugout. "I figured it was [Ron] Guidry," he said later. "My first thought was, 'Okay, he's coming out here just to give me a breather before I pitch to [A.J.] Pierzynski.'"

When he looked up though, it wasn't Guidry walking toward him; it was Torre. He wasn't jogging either, the way he would if he was just coming out for a consult. In fact, he was waving his arm in the direction of the bullpen, signaling for Mike Myers to come in to the game.

Mussina was stunned. He didn't know his pitch count at that moment (it was seventy-nine), but he knew it was low. It was a warm evening in Chicago — eighty-six degrees at game time — but he felt fine. And he was pitching well. It wasn't as if either ball in the inning had been hit that hard. This wasn't Boston; balls were not flying over fences. And yet, there was Torre, walking up onto the mound, hand extended, waiting for Mussina to hand him the ball.

Which he did. Mussina would never show up a manager or a pitching coach on the mound, especially Torre. The only time in his career he could ever remember being angry enough to say something to a pitching coach had been in Baltimore when one of his many pitching coaches there — he thinks it was Bruce Kison but isn't absolutely sure — came out to the mound and said, "You have got to start throwing better pitches."

To which Mussina replied, "No shit. Thanks for the encouragement."

More often than not, Mussina is likely to be funny when someone comes to the mound to get him. But now he said nothing, simply handed the ball to Torre and walked off. "I was a little bit in a state of shock," he said. "I just couldn't believe he came and got me that quickly."

Mussina walked into the dugout, received congratulations from his teammates, and went up the runway to the clubhouse. He had just walked inside, planning to "ice and sulk," when he heard cheers coming from the field and from the clubhouse TVs. Pierzynski had singled off of Myers to tie the game. "Took even less time to lose the chance for a win than the Angels game," he said later with a wry smile. "At least this time we won."

The Yankees scored three in the eighth and six in the ninth to turn the game into a rout, but it was Scott Proctor who got credited for the runs and the win. That was disappointing. What really hurt, though, was the quick hook.

Torre knew Mussina was upset. "It isn't as if he's hard to read," Torre said. He knew why and understood why. "It was purely situational. We needed a strikeout, and Myers had struck Pierzynski out four times in five at bats. After that I was hoping to get Proctor in to get a ground ball or another strikeout and maybe get out of it with the lead. It had nothing to do with the way Moose was pitching."

Mussina read those comments in the newspaper the next day back in New York but wasn't really assuaged. Torre didn't expect him to be. The next day when the two passed in the clubhouse, Torre said, "Do we need to talk?"

"Yeah, I think we do," Mussina said.

They walked into Torre's office and sat down. "You thought I took you out too fast," Torre said. "It was situational."

"I read that," Mussina said. "What bothers me is the feeling that I've lost your confidence. You didn't think I could get out of the inning. I know I haven't pitched well this year, but if you don't trust me to get out of a jam anymore that really bothers me."

Torre understood. He knew he was dealing with a pitcher with a great deal of pride who had pitched out of a lot of tougher jams than the one in Chicago. "All I had to do was think back to '03 [Game Seven against Boston] for a perfect example of that," Torre said. "I told him again it had nothing to do with losing confidence or trust in him. I still feel very confident with the ball in his hands. I just thought the inning lined up better with Myers coming in for Pierzynski. As it turned out, I was wrong and I was right. Myers didn't get Pierzynski, but Proctor got the next three. Maybe Moose would have done as well or better, but I had to do what I thought was best for the club. We were in a tight game that we badly needed to win. But I understood his frustration."

Mussina felt a little better after he and Torre talked. "I'd be lying if I said it didn't still bother me," he said a couple of days after the game. "I hear Joe and I know he's always honest, but in the back of my mind I can't help but wonder if a year ago, same situation, he doesn't let me pitch out of it. If your manager doesn't trust you, that's a problem."

Six days after the game in Chicago, Mussina finally got his third win of the year against the Arizona Diamondbacks. The Yankees staked him to a 7–1 lead in the fourth inning, and he breezed into the eighth inning. The only glitch came in the sixth when Conor Jackson hit a two-out home run to make it 7–2. This time when Torre came to get him, he had no problem with taking the rest of the night off.

"At least I got you tired this time," Torre said, referring to the fact that Mussina had thrown 101 pitches. Mussina laughed. The lead was safe, he had pitched well—there was no hesitation when he doffed his cap—and for the first time in a month he was a winning pitcher.

"I'd almost forgotten what it was like," he said. "It was nice, really nice, to pitch with a lead and feel like one bad pitch wasn't going to ruin the whole night. I gave up the home run to Jackson and I wasn't happy about it, but it wasn't as if the whole night was ruined because of it. I just had to get the next guy out."

Which he did. The win was the Yankees' eighth in a row. They had won the last three in Chicago, swept the lowly Pittsburgh Pirates, and had now won a pair against Arizona to get to 32–31, the first time they had been over .500 since early April.

Mussina was 3–3 for the season, halfway through June. Not what he had planned for or hoped for, but it was where he was. Whether he liked it or not.

MUSSINA'S CATCHER in the win over the Diamondbacks was Wil Nieves. It was the fourth straight time he had been the catcher with Mussina on the mound.

Torre hadn't planned to make Nieves into Mussina's personal catcher, and Mussina had never requested it. But it had evolved into that, even though Nieves was hitting just .122. Twice with Nieves behind the plate, Torre had used Jorge Posada as the DH to keep his bat in the lineup—he was hitting over .340.

"It was something we just sort of fell into," Torre said. "It was Wil's day to catch when Moose pitched against the Angels on the last Sunday in May. As it happened, he pitched his best game of the year, and Wil got two hits. The next Saturday in Boston, it was a day game after a night game, and that's usually a good time to give Georgey [most of the Yankees call Posada "Georgey," even though the correct way to say his name is "Hor-hay"] a day off from catching. Moose wasn't great that day but he was okay, and I thought the rain was a factor too. He had a nice rapport with Wil. So, I decided to just go with it that way for a while and see what happened. When he pitched well in Chicago and then again against Arizona, I figured we'd just ride it that way for a while."

Mussina was fine with the change. "One of the things that made it different for me was that Wil was only catching one game a week," Mussina said. "That meant his focus was different. Jorge is catching six times a week. He basically has a few hours to prepare for each game mentally. Wil had four or five days. That meant he spent extra time on the hitters, and when we would sit down and talk he would have ideas and thoughts on what we could do different from the last game and what the next lineup's weaknesses might be. That's not a knock on Jorge at all, it was just a fact created by their roles being so different."

New York being New York, the Mussina-Nieves-Posada "triangle" became a story. Michael Kay, the Yankees' longtime TV play-by-play man, who also hosted a radio show, wondered on air exactly what Mussina had done to deserve a personal catcher. Although Mussina gets along with most of the media now, he and Kay had never repaired the bad start they had gotten off to in 2001. Others who got along better with Mussina wondered how Posada felt about the whole thing.

Which was a legitimate question to raise. Posada had been one of the best catchers in baseball for most of ten years. He was part of that core of players—along with Derek Jeter, Mariano Rivera, Andy Pettitte, and the now-retired Bernie Williams—Yankees who had come up in the organization and had been part of the four Yankees World Series titles in five seasons between 1996 and 2000. He had become the full-time catcher in 1998 and had improved steadily both as a hitter and as a catcher since then. In 2007, with his thirty-sixth birthday in August and his contract up in October, Posada was having his best offensive season ever.

What's more, he was very much a part of the team's heart and soul. Jeter was the captain, the unquestioned leader in the clubhouse, but Posada was probably a close second. He was completely respected by all his teammates, and the pitchers enjoyed throwing to him, even though he could get angry with them at times.

"Sometimes you have to kick someone in the butt," he said. "Other times you have to stay calm. It's part of my job to know what's best for each guy."

Posada was from a baseball family. His dad, Jorge Sr., had grown up in Cuba but had escaped the country as a young man by stowing away in the bottom of a cigar boat that was bound for Spain. "Things had gotten so bad there he felt he had no choice," Jorge Jr. said. "No one was working, there was no food, nothing."

From Spain, Jorge Posada Sr. eventually found his way to Puerto Rico, where he found work and started a family. He had played baseball as a kid and loved the game and became friends with Pat Gillick, who at the time was working for the Yankees. When Gillick became the general manager in Toronto, he hired Posada as a scout. Jorge Jr. played everything as a kid—"No one believes me when they see me run now, but as a kid I ran track, and I was pretty fast," he said, laughing—but always knew that baseball was the sport his dad wanted to see him play.

"I actually liked basketball better when I was young," he said. "But I liked baseball too. We got the game of the week down there on Saturdays and then the Cubs on WGN and the Braves on TBS.

My dad really pushed me to play baseball. He never had a chance to live out his baseball dreams, so he wanted to be sure that I did."

He was a good enough high school infielder to be recruited by many of the top college baseball programs in the United States, and though he had planned to go to Miami or Florida State or the University of Florida, he had to regroup because his SATs were 730, and at the time he needed 800 to get a scholarship. He thought he would go to Miami Dade Community College, one of the top junior-college programs in the country, but his dad didn't think going to school in Miami was a great idea.

He was scouting for the Braves by then, and one of the other scouts told him that Calhoun Community College (in Decatur, Alabama) had a very good program and a very good coach. The coach, Fred Frickie, called Jorge and offered him a scholarship. Posada wasn't sure.

"To be honest, I had no idea where Alabama was," he said. "I asked him if the weather there was hot. He said yes, so I said fine."

He was there for two years (and it *was* hot) and had signed a letter of intent to play at Alabama when the Yankees took him in the twenty-fourth round of the 1990 draft. "They offered me $35,000 to sign, which was a lot of money and a lot more than you usually offer to someone drafted that low," he said. "I decided to take it and see what happened."

It was during his second year in the organization that the team decided to make him a catcher. Major league teams are always looking for players with arms strong enough to catch who can also hit because good hitting catchers are hard to find. The Yankees saw that potential in Posada and sent him to the Instructional League in the fall of 1991 to learn how to catch.

It was a slow process. He only caught part-time in Greensboro in 1992, but the next year he was a full-time catcher. "I think I had thirty-eight passed balls," he said. "I felt like I spent the whole season chasing balls to the backstop. I simply had trouble follow-ing the arc and the movement of the breaking pitches. I mean, it was tough enough trying to hit those pitches, but catching them, wearing the mask—it was all new and it was hard. It was embar-rassing. But I was determined to get better at doing it."

His work paid off in a move up to Triple-A Columbus in 1994, but he broke an ankle that summer. "It set me back, and it slowed me down," he said, smiling. "Until then I still ran pretty well. Peo-ple who have seen me since I got to the majors don't believe me when I tell them that."

His first invitation to a major league camp was in 1995, and he still remembers arriving at seven o'clock every morning—"I thought I was an eager beaver," he said—and checking Don Mat-tingly's locker. "His clothes were already there, and he was out on the field. It struck me that it probably wasn't a coincidence that the hardest worker on the team was also the best player."

Posada had brief stints in the majors in '95 and '96 and was with the team throughout postseason in '96. Joe Girardi, the incumbent catcher, kept telling him, "I'm just holding the job for you."

Girardi became his mentor. "He would tell me, 'Don't ever lose a job because someone works harder than you.' He taught me how to work out and how to be tougher. He showed me how to use video and showed me things about the game I wasn't seeing. He studied lineups; he would look at every at bat of a team's previous game against a particular pitcher. He taught me about how to learn things from watching a guy's feet.

"For example, if Jim Thome comes up and spreads his feet extra wide, he's trying to go up the middle. If he closes his stance, he's trying to pull. That affects the pitches I'm going to call. Joe was the one who taught me to look for things like that. I still talk to him [Girardi, who will manage the Yankees in 2008, was a Yankee broadcaster in 2007] whenever I get the chance."

Since 1997, Posada has been the Yankees' starting catcher. He has been an All-Star five times and has won the Silver Slugger Award as the best hitter at his position five times. He was thrilled when the Yankees signed Mussina because he knew firsthand how tough he was to hit. But learning to work with him was a major adjustment.

"At first I had no clue," he said. "It seemed as if whatever I was thinking, he was thinking the exact opposite. I think he must have shook me off on every pitch for the first two months. As a catcher, you don't want a guy shaking you off all the time because you worry that they might be a little bit tentative if they don't think you're in agreement. We talked about it a lot—at first it did no good. By June, we started to know how the other guy was thinking, and things went much better after that. I began to get a better feel for him and that helped us both. Since then, I think we've worked well together."

Posada was too much of a pro to throw a fit over a pitcher preferring another catcher. He also knew this situation was different than it had been two years earlier when Randy Johnson had gone to Torre and all but demanded that John Flaherty be his personal catcher after he'd broken out of a slump and pitched well on a day Flaherty was catching. "That was tough, especially in the playoffs," Posada said. "I want to catch every game in postseason."

That was a long way from happening here, and Posada knew that Mussina hadn't gone to Torre because both Mussina and Torre had told him that. "I told Mike that he had turned on me, but I knew it wouldn't last, that he's just having a fling," he said. "Wil and I talk all the time about how to call the game. Sometimes he'll look into the dugout, and I'll try to help him out. I know Mike is comfortable with him. In some ways, it's easier for him because he can control the game more easily. Wil is less likely to disagree with him than I am, and maybe, right now, that's what Mike needs."

The real issue was Nieves's bat. Everyone agreed he caught a good game and he had a reasonably good arm. But, the two hits in the Angels game aside, the days he caught, it was almost as if the

Yankees were putting a National League lineup on the field with Nieves in the role of pitcher.

"For now it's fine," Torre said. "We'll just ride with it. If we get to postseason, then we might have to make some decisions. Right now, we're a long way from anything like that."

THE HOT STREAK that put the Yankees over .500 coincided with the Mets' first real slump of the season. After their 3–6 home-stand, the Mets headed for Detroit to face the defending American League champion Tigers in their first non-Yankees interleague series of the season. The Tigers had added Gary Sheffield to an already potent lineup in the off-season and were battling the Cleveland Indians for first place in the American League's Central Division.

The teams split the first two games of the series, the Mets breaking their four-game losing streak on Friday, before losing on Saturday. The rubber game featured the old man, Glavine, against the kid, the Tigers' twenty-two-year-old rookie, Andrew Miller.

Things could not have started much better for the Mets. David Wright hit a three-run homer off Miller in the first. The three runs were one more than the team had scored for Glavine in his three previous starts combined.

"Maybe I just couldn't stand prosperity," he joked later.

The Tigers got one run back on a Sheffield shot to left field in the first inning, the good news being that no other runs scored because Glavine had retired the first two Tigers. They got a second run back in the second when Ivan Rodriguez walked and Brandon Inge singled him home. It was the Rodriguez at bat that really began the trouble for Glavine. Twice, he threw changeups he thought were strikes. Twice, Tim McClelland, the home-plate umpire, called balls. McClelland is considered one of the best ball-and-strike umpires in the game by most.

He is very tall, which may help him see the plate better since he looks almost straight down as the ball crosses the plate. The only complaint players have with him is that he is maddeningly slow when making his strike calls, seeming to move in slow motion to get his right arm up.

On this day, he and Glavine were not seeing the strike zone the same way. It got worse in the third inning when Placido Polanco led off with a double. Glavine retired the next two hitters and then faced Omar Infante. Twice, he thought Infante had been struck out. Twice, McClelland said he hadn't been. Infante walked, and Glavine stalked off the mound, took the return throw from Lo Duca, and snapped the ball angrily into his glove. He didn't say anything, but his body language made it clear he thought he was being squeezed.

"That would be an accurate reading," Glavine said later. "Tim is a good umpire. I just thought he had a real small strike zone for me that day. I'm not sure why."

Instead of being in the dugout still leading 3–2, Glavine had to face Rodriguez, a very solid hitter even at thirty-five. He promptly tripled in both runners to put the Tigers ahead 4–3, and now Glavine was really upset. He got the last out of the inning and stalked to the dugout, frustrated. His pitch count had skyrocketed, in large part, he believed, because of McClelland's strike zone, and he knew that getting through six innings would be very difficult.

As it turned out, he didn't make it through five. The next inning was his worst of the year: a Placido Polanco single, a Sheffield RBI triple, an Infante bunt single to drive in Sheffield, a double by Rodriguez, and a two-run single by Sean Casey made it 8–3 Tigers and sent Glavine to his earliest shower of the season. It was the first time all year he had allowed more than four earned runs. Aaron Sele came in and gave up a home run to Inge to make it 10–3 and closed the books on Glavine's day: eleven hits and nine earned runs in four and one-third innings.

"It certainly wasn't pretty," he said. "The balls and strikes didn't help, but I wasn't good either. You have to pitch through things like that, and I didn't. It was my first really bad day of the season."

No one felt worse about it than Rick Peterson. He was just as convinced that Glavine was getting squeezed as Glavine. "I should have gone out and said something, even if I got thrown out for doing it," he said. "Tim's a good umpire; maybe he would have adjusted if I'd gotten into it—I don't know. Tommy deserved a better fate."

Peterson has only been ejected three times as a pitching coach. "The first time was in Oakland when I told Bob Davidson he was calling the game as if he'd just fallen off a turnip truck," he said. "I've actually said worse to umpires and not been ejected. My only regret is that I didn't send him a bag full of turnips the next day. I wish I'd said something to Tim. As it turned out, whatever I did wouldn't have made things worse."

Glavine was now 5–4. He would next pitch the following Saturday against the Yankees in Yankee Stadium. He had not won a game since beating them at Shea in May. It would be exactly four weeks since that game when he faced them again.

19

F—— the Process

THINGS HAD CHANGED considerably during the four weeks that had passed since the first Subway Series. The Mets had gone 8–13 since the Yankees had departed Shea Stadium and arrived in the Bronx, having lost five straight games—including being swept by the Dodgers in Los Angeles—and nine of their last ten. The Yankees had used their win in the final game at Shea as a springboard to a 15–8 run and were coming off sweeps of the Pirates and Diamondbacks in interleague series and had won nine in a row.

"What's not to love about interleague play?" Mussina joked.

The Mets still led the Braves by two games and the Phillies by five—largely because neither had played very well of late either—and the Yankees still trailed the sizzling Red Sox by eight and a half, but the moods in the two clubhouses had shifted dramatically.

"I think we're all just a little bit frustrated right now," Glavine said in the visitors' clubhouse in Yankee Stadium on Friday afternoon. "We know what kind of team we have here, and we've been waiting to get on that big hot streak we know we're capable of having. It just hasn't come yet."

In fact, the Mets had yet to piece together a five-game winning streak all season. They managed to end their losing streak in the opener thanks to Oliver Perez, who had become a major Rick Peterson reclamation success story. Perez had come to the Mets

296

the previous July as a throw in to a trade-deadline deal general manager Omar Minaya had made in order to acquire relief pitcher Roberto Hernandez. Perez had been a rising star in 2004 at the age of twenty-two, when he went 12–10 on a bad Pittsburgh team and pitched to an ERA of 2.98.

He had completely fallen apart after that. His ERA had doubled the next year, and he had been sent back to the minors. The Pirates were more than happy to part with him as part of the Hernandez–Xavier Nady trade. He had actually been the Mets' game-seven starter in the NLCS in October and had pitched well, allowing just one run in six innings, even though the Mets lost the game.

"If you were a stock, I'd buy you now," Peterson had told Perez during spring training. "Because you have the ability to be worth a lot—especially to yourself—by the end of this season."

Peterson's prediction was turning out to be true. Perez pitched seven and a third shutout innings against the Yankees, lowering his ERA to 2.93 in a 2–0 Mets win. The victory stopped the Mets' bleeding and the Yankees' winning streak and set up a matchup the next afternoon between Glavine and twenty-two-year-old Tyler Clippard.

For the first time in anyone's memory, a Mets-Yankees Saturday game was not broadcast on Fox. Even so, Bill O'Reilly, the right-wing talk-show host, was at the game. He turned up in the Mets clubhouse, glad-handing players until a security guard asked him if he had a credential for the clubhouse. O'Reilly's response was something along the lines of "Don't you know who I am?" Whether the guard did or did not know who O'Reilly was and whether that would have caused him to remove O'Reilly more quickly or more slowly, no one knows. O'Reilly was asked to leave, which galled him.

What apparently galled him even more was the sight of his archenemy, MSNBC's Keith Olbermann, walking around the clubhouse unimpeded. There was a reason for that: Olbermann, who had begun his career in sports and still cohosted an hour-long segment of *The Dan Patrick Show,* then on ESPN radio, actually covered sports, so he had a credential. That didn't much matter to O'Reilly, who complained loud and long to Yankee officials, demanding that Olbermann's credentials be removed. They weren't.

Glavine probably would have been happier if he had just left with O'Reilly. His day was at least as miserable. As in Detroit, the Mets scored early for him, staking him to a 2–0 lead on a David Wright RBI single in the first and a home run by Ruben Gotay in the second. Once again, Glavine couldn't stand the prosperity, even though he breezed through the first. The Yankees tied it in the bottom of the second, and the Mets went back ahead 3–2 in the third. Glavine immediately gave up a two-run home run to Alex Rodriguez in the bottom of the inning to make it 4–3. Then Ramon Castro answered with a two-run home run in the fourth to make it 5–4, until Derek Jeter hit a two-run home run to make it 6–5.

It was now the Mets' turn to hit a two-run homer in the fifth. At the rate things were going, the game was going to end up finishing on ESPN's *Sunday Night Baseball.*

But the Mets missed their turn, failing to score. The Yankees did not. Posada led off with a double that knocked Glavine out — his shortest outing of the season — and the Yankees ended up scoring two more runs in the inning, making it four consecutive innings in which they had scored two runs.

Glavine was disgusted with himself, frustrated with the results, and angry at home-plate umpire Bruce Froemming.

Froemming was in his thirty-seventh and last year as a major league umpire. He had umpired more games than any man in history and had survived as long as he had because he had a self-deprecating sense of humor and most of the time managed to take his job seriously without taking himself seriously. He'd even survived a controversy several years earlier, when he had asked some players to autograph items for him—an absolute no-no if you are an umpire, for obvious reasons.

Froemming had once been one of the better ball-and-strike umpires in the game. That was no longer the case. Players had noticed that Froemming had developed a flinch when working the plate, moving backward just a tiny bit as the ball was delivered. "If you're moving, even just a little bit, it's hard to see the ball as it crosses the plate," said Mussina, who watched closely from the dugout that day. "I felt for Tom because I know how important it is to have your good pitches called strikes. He wasn't getting it, and it forced him to change the way he pitched. I guess there's a reason why this is Bruce's last year."

Glavine liked Froemming but at that moment could only wish he had retired a year earlier. When Peterson came to the mound to talk to Glavine in the fourth inning, he let some of his frustrations tumble out. Peterson understood. "Tom wasn't great by any means," Peterson said the next day. "But Bruce was the worst possible umpire for him to have behind the plate right now."

Glavine was upset because he felt two umpires he had liked through the years—Tim McClelland in Detroit and now Froemming—had forced him to throw strikes he didn't want to throw. "Look, if they'd given me every single pitch I thought I deserved, I might still have gotten bombed in those games," he said. "I wasn't good. But it isn't like I can afford to throw the ball over the plate. I can't. They weren't giving me pitches I thought should have been strikes. Pitchers and hitters are in a nonstop battle for a few inches one way or the other. If a guy throws ninety-five, he may not need those few inches. If you throw eighty-five, you need them. When I didn't get those few inches those two days and I had to throw pitches where I didn't want to throw them, I got hurt."

Two games had yielded eight and one-third innings of pitching and sixteen earned runs. That jacked Glavine's ERA from a more than respectable 3.36 to 4.67.

All of that didn't make for the happiest of Father's Days, although being with his family was a good distraction. His parents and Chris's parents were down for the weekend, and they all went to a good Italian restaurant for dinner on Saturday night and took the kids to brunch on Sunday. "Father's Day may be the only day of the season when it's a break to play at night," he said. "I had most of the day with the family."

The one present Glavine would have liked to get for Father's Day was an answer to why he had pitched so poorly in back-to-back outings. Part of it, he knew, was the rhythm of the season. "No one goes through an entire year without a bad stretch of some kind," he said. "I've had them every year of my career. It's like the old baseball saying about bad teams having winning streaks and good ones having losing streaks.

"When you're going through a streak like this it's certainly no fun. You're frustrated, and you do wonder on occasion if you'll ever get another out or feel good on the mound again. You know that's not the case, but there are times when it feels that way."

Pitching poorly in the Subway Series didn't make things any easier for Glavine. When the Yankees are playing the Mets, even the U.S. Open golf championship, which is the big story of the weekend everyplace else in the sports world, takes a backseat. Sunday's stories on the game were quick to point out that Glavine hadn't won a game in a month. No one knew that better than he did.

"The thing is, I haven't pitched poorly for a month," he said. "I've pitched poorly twice. Before that I pitched well but didn't get any wins. People are acting like it's been a month since I pitched well."

When Glavine walked into the clubhouse on Sunday afternoon it was, naturally, packed. The clubhouses at Yankee Stadium are bigger than the ones at Shea, but not much. The visitors' clubhouse is narrow, and there aren't a lot of places for players to hide from the media. The dining area in the back of the room is off-limits, but anyone can walk to the door and stick his head in to talk to someone. No one on the Mets was taking the Miguel Cairo approach and putting tape down to mark the off-limits area, so Glavine dressed quickly and found a spot as far from the door to the dining area as he could so he could watch the golf tournament in semipeace.

After a while he got up to walk to the training room. He was in the hallway leading there when he ran into Peterson. "How are you feeling?" Peterson asked.

"Been better," Glavine answered.

Peterson had been trying to decide whether to talk to Glavine that day or wait until the team got back to Shea the next day to begin a series against the Minnesota Twins. It would be easier at Shea; they could just go into the coaches' room in the back of the clubhouse and talk, but if Glavine was stewing, he preferred to do it sooner rather than later. Seeing the look on Glavine's face, Peterson decided sooner—even in a hallway—was better.

As he always did with a struggling pitcher, Peterson reminded Glavine about "the process." He wasn't that far off, he told him. The umpires certainly hadn't helped matters the last two games, and he'd been facing good lineups where there really wasn't any margin for error. There were things they could work on when he threw his bullpen the next day, and it probably wasn't a bad thing that there was an off-day Thursday, which meant he would get an extra day of rest before pitching against Oakland on Friday.

"With Tommy, you know you're saying a lot of things he already knows," Peterson said. "There isn't anything in baseball he hasn't been through. I just want to make sure he doesn't get too focused on results when they haven't been good, because I know and he knows those results aren't who he is. There was nothing seriously wrong with the way he was pitching, nothing that couldn't be corrected fairly easily."

Glavine leaned on the wall while Peterson talked, and listened. He liked the fact that Peterson never seemed to lose his cool or get upset; in many ways it was a nice change from the in-your-face approach he had dealt with during his years in Atlanta with Leo Mazzone. But right then, right at that moment, in the visitors' clubhouse at Yankee Stadium, knowing people were again questioning whether he could still get hitters out, and that many of those people were standing a few yards away waiting to talk to him, Glavine really didn't want to talk about the process or how many clubs he had in his bag when he went to the mound.

"I hear you, Rick," he said finally, when Peterson paused. "But right now, the way I feel, to be honest, is fuck the process; I want to win a fucking game."

Peterson got it. "I know, Tom," he said. "So let's go out tomorrow and figure out how to win one."

That was good enough for Glavine. He squared his shoulders and prepared to enter the Lion's Den.

HE HADN'T EVEN REACHED his locker before he saw trouble. A camera crew from one of the local New York TV stations was waiting. Glavine had noticed the camera and cameraman and the reporter holding a microphone when he had darted from the dining area to the training area. Maybe, he thought, they're just waiting for someone—anyone. Now, it was apparent they were waiting for him.

"Tom, have you got a minute?" came the query as he approached.

Ninety-nine times out of one hundred—no, nine hundred ninety-nine times out of one thousand—Glavine's answer would have been "Sure, I'm okay until we go out to stretch."

Now he looked at the TV reporter, microphone in hand, a friendly smile on his face, and said, "What's it about?"

The reporter, probably a little bit surprised at the cool in Glavine's voice, said, "Well, you know, I'd just like to talk about pitching, I guess. About your pitching and what's been going on the last month."

As much as Glavine didn't want to talk at that moment, he probably would have sucked it up and done it if not for the words "what's been going on the last month." As soon as he heard them, Glavine stiffened. "Look," he said evenly, gazing into his locker as if the treasure of the Sierra Madre might somehow be buried inside, "I don't want to be a jerk, but today, I'm really not up for that. I'm really sorry. I just don't think that's a conversation I want to have right now."

The reporter wisely waited to see if Glavine would say anything else. Sometimes, especially when dealing with a good guy, reporters know that silence is the best way to get someone to change his mind. Not this time. "I understand," the reporter said, sticking his hand out. "Maybe some other time?"

"Almost any other time," Glavine said. "I appreciate your patience."

Which he did.

"You see, that's what's tough about playing in New York sometimes," Glavine said a few minutes later, as the room was clearing with players headed to the field for stretching and batting practice. "The perception is I've pitched poorly for a month because I haven't won in a month. The fact is I've had *two* bad outings. That's it. So, if I go on camera and the guy asks me something about a lost month, and I answer by saying it's really only been a bad week and I was pitching well before then, I just didn't get any runs, it sounds like I'm throwing my team under the bus. Even if I just say, 'I was just unlucky for a few starts,' people will read into that.

"So, my other option is to say no, which I probably haven't done five times in my career, and then the guy may think I'm a jerk. Fortunately, he seemed like a good guy, and he didn't get mad. But it's still hard.

"The best thing for me to do would be to win a game." He smiled. "Of course, to do that I need to stay with the process."

Stay with the process. And win a fucking game.

FIVE DAYS LATER, Glavine had stuck with the process and walked to the Shea Stadium mound on a breezy, cloudy, but comfortable early-summer Friday night to pitch against the Oakland Athletics. The A's had last visited Shea Stadium in 1973 for the third, fourth, and fifth games of the World Series, which they ultimately won in seven games. Their presence in the building brought up two of the better trivia questions in baseball history, one related to the 1973 World Series, the other strictly related to the A's:

Question one: What did the Mets' leadoff hitter do in the first inning of Game Three in each of the Mets' first three World Series? *Answer:* Hit a home run. Tommie Agee had done it against the Orioles in 1969; Wayne Garrett had done it against the A's in 1973; and Lenny Dykstra had done it in Fenway Park against the Red Sox in 1986.

Question two: Who was the last American League Most Valuable Player that was a switch hitter? *Answer:* No, not Mickey Mantle. It was Vida Blue—the A's pitcher who was the MVP in 1971 after winning twenty-four games. The DH didn't come into play until 1973, so Blue, a switch hitter, came to bat on a regular basis throughout his MVP season. He was 12 for 102 at the plate, a batting average of .118, but he did switch hit and he did win the MVP that year.

Glavine wasn't much concerned with history or trivia as he took the mound that evening. During his two bullpen sessions that week, he had worked hard on the mechanics of his delivery, trying to be sure he wasn't coming across his body with his arm as he let go of the ball. "If you do that, you're flying open toward the plate," he said. "It's just like in golf. If you're too open, the ball will go sideways. You want to feel as if you're following straight through in the direction of the plate. It means you have more power, and on your breaking pitches the ball will move from side to side or down, the way you want it to, rather than going in just about any direction when you're too open."

He and Peterson had also decided he needed to work a little bit faster. Glavine has always pitched fast, but Peterson thought he was working a little more slowly, especially when he wasn't feeling confident about the pitch he was about to throw. "Hitters see that," Peterson said. "It gives them more confidence, makes them think you're concerned. Let's be a little bit faster in between pitches, not give them time to feel comfortable."

Glavine has always believed that body language is an important part of pitching. "If you show frustration, the hitters see it," he said. "If your shoulders droop or if you're acting like you can't get a break, they can tell. It empowers them. But if you catch the ball, look in for a sign, and get set to pitch again without showing them anything, it says to them, 'This guy wants to pitch; he's fired up.' I needed to let the hitters know I wanted to pitch."

As Glavine warmed up for the first inning, he still felt like he was coming across his body a little bit in spite of all the work in the bullpen. Through the years he has moved the spot he pitches from on the rubber more and more toward the third-base side because, as a left-hander, he believes he is less likely to come across his body while aiming for the outside corner against right-handed batters from there.

To use one of Peterson's beloved golf analogies: if you're hitting the ball too far to the right, aim left. By standing on the third-base side, Glavine almost has to aim left to get the ball to the outside part of the plate against righties. Even though he pitches inside far more now, his bread-and-butter pitches are still fastball outside and changeup outside.

"Throwing the ball a little bit differently against lefties isn't really that difficult," Glavine said. "On a percentage basis, the number of pitches I throw where I want the ball to go to my right [across his body] is pretty small compared to the other way."

Most pitchers move around the rubber during their career, searching for the best release point they can find. In a game where inches always matter, the decision on exactly where to pitch from isn't a small one. Mussina, who has always pitched inside and outside throughout his career, has always felt comfortable smack in the middle of the rubber. That's where most pitchers start out as kids. Some never move. Others experiment. Glavine has always been an experimenter, although he settled on the third-base side years ago in Atlanta.

After his third warm-up pitch prior to the first inning, still feeling as if he was pulling his pitches a little bit from left to right, Glavine decided to try something on the spur of the moment. When Paul Lo Duca tossed the ball back to him, Glavine caught it, and then, before throwing his next warm-up pitch, moved a few inches to his right, putting himself almost on the corner of the rubber on the third-base side. The shift was three, perhaps four inches.

"It was something I'd done a few times in the past," he said. "I decided to give it a shot and see how it felt because I just didn't feel the way I wanted to feel at that moment."

His five remaining warm-ups felt good. He didn't feel as if he had to exaggerate his motion to the left anymore in order to drive straight down the mound in the direction of the plate. "It just felt better right away," he said.

Whether by coincidence or not, he had an easy first inning. That was good, but he didn't get too excited because he hadn't had any trouble against the Yankees in the first inning either. The Mets gave him a quick 1–0 lead on what had come to be known as a "Reyes run." The shortstop led off with a bunt single to third base and reached second when Eric Chavez threw the ball away. He scored a moment later on a Carlos Beltran single. Reyes was leading the National League in stolen bases, and letting him reach first base was almost like giving up a double because of his baserunning ability.

The lead was a brief one. Shannon Stewart, the A's second hitter in the second, crushed a 1–2 fastball into the left-field bullpen to tie the score at 1–1. "Normally you give up a home run, you tell yourself, 'Okay, it's one bad pitch, let's move on and finish the inning,'" Glavine said. "At that moment, though, I was still a little shell-shocked because of the two games I'd pitched leading up to that one. The thought 'Oh God, not again' did cross my mind."

Glavine doesn't panic often, and this was no exception. He got out of the inning with no further damage, and the game settled into a pitching duel between Glavine and A's starter Lenny DiNardo. Oakland had been a consistent contender for years under the much ballyhooed leadership of general manager Billy (Money Ball) Beane. Bob Geren was the new manager in '07, and once again they were a solid club. They arrived in New York with a record of 39–32, a half game better than the Mets, who had slid to 38–32.

It was Glavine who helped get the lead back. He led off the bottom of the third with a double down the left-field line. Reyes sacrificed him to third, and he scored on a sacrifice fly by Lo Duca to make it 2–1. "Pure speed run," Glavine joked. "I did it all with my legs."

His pitching arm was now firmly in command. After Stewart's home run, he didn't give up a hit until back-to-back one-out singles in the fourth. Here some luck came into play. Bobby Crosby hit a wicked shot toward the middle that Reyes somehow got to, scooped on a short hop, and turned into a spectacular double play.

"That ball was hit so hard, if Hosey doesn't make the play he made, it's probably in the gap and they score two and take the lead," Glavine said. "He makes a play, we're out of the inning, and the whole game changed right after that. That's just the way the game is: some nights you're better than what you get, other nights you aren't quite as good. If Hosey doesn't make that play, who knows how the rest of that inning goes."

Instead, Glavine settled into a groove, and the Mets broke the game open in the sixth with five runs after Shawn Green had homered in the fifth to make it 3–1. Glavine again contributed with his bat during the big rally. With two down and a man on second, Geren opted to walk rookie left fielder Carlos Gomez to pitch to Glavine.

Standing in the on-deck circle, Glavine turned to the dugout with a big smile on his face. "Obviously they haven't done a very good scouting job," he said. "Don't they realize how hot I am?"

He actually was hot with the bat, having had hits in four of his previous five at bats, including the double in the third. His batting average was well over .300 at that point. He continued hot, with an RBI single that made the score 8–1. Reyes followed with a shot into the left-center-field gap.

"As soon as I saw where the ball was going, I knew I had a problem," Glavine said. "The ball was too well hit for me to not try to score. I hadn't run that hard for that long in a while."

Maybe if he hadn't been wearing his jacket, Glavine would have been okay. Years ago, pitchers routinely put on jackets to run the bases, the thought being that they wanted to keep their pitching arms warm. Nowadays, a lot of pitchers are never on base because of the DH, and, more often than not, when a pitcher does reach, he eschews the jacket. Glavine is old-fashioned enough that with a little chill in the air he had put on the jacket.

"Bad aerodynamics," he said. "Slowed me down."

He was out at the plate on a bang-bang play. He had no choice but to try to score, though, since Reyes was practically running up his back by the time he got around third. "I'm just not as fast as I used to be," Glavine said.

That was perhaps the only disappointment of the night. Coincidence or not, the two changes—working more quickly and moving a few inches on the rubber—yielded positive results.

Even after his long run, Glavine set the side down in order in the seventh and breezed through the eighth. He had thrown 109 pitches through eight innings, and Randolph and Peterson decided to let him start the ninth with a 9–1 lead to see if he might be able to get through it quickly and get a complete game.

"I knew the deal was one batter gets on, and I'm done," he said. "I was okay with it."

Chavez led off the inning with a single, and Aaron Heilman came in to finish. The Mets breathed a deep sigh of relief. Glavine had his first win in five weeks, his sixth of the season, and the 296th of his career. Four away from the Number felt like a lot closer than five away had.

"I felt like I'd been running in mud for a while," he said. He smiled. "Rick was right. The process worked."

And he finally got a f—— win.

20

Road-Trip Blues

DURING THE FIRST NINE DAYS of interleague play, it appeared that National League baseball was exactly what the doctor had ordered for the Yankees. They swept the Pirates and the Diamondbacks and then won two of three from the Mets, winning the final game of the second Subway Series 8–2, behind Chien-Ming Wang, who, after missing almost the entire first month of the season, was now 8–2.

Things were very much looking up. Wang, Andy Pettitte, and Mike Mussina were all pitching well. Pettitte had hit a slide early in June but had bounced back with a 7–1 win against Arizona the day after Mussina's solid performance against the Diamondbacks. What's more, help had arrived. The Yankees had melodramatically announced the return of Roger Clemens on a Sunday afternoon in early May, signing him to a contract that would pay him about $1 million a start.

Clemens had made his 2007 debut in the Pirates series, pitching effectively enough for an almost-forty-five-year-old coming out of retirement for the nineteenth time, in a 9–3 win. With a rotation of Wang, Pettitte, Mussina, and Clemens, the Yankees could plug almost anyone into the fifth spot until Philip Hughes was healthy enough to return to the rotation.

"Right now we feel like anybody we run out there, we're going to have a chance to win the game," Mussina said. "It wasn't that way in April and May."

The Yankees headed west after the Mets series, their record 35–32 and seemingly headed north. They had a nine-game trip: three games in Colorado and then three in San Francisco to wrap up interleague play, followed by three against the always-mediocre-at-best Orioles in Baltimore. There was no reason to think the hot streak wouldn't continue.

Except it didn't. Mussina pitched the opener in Colorado against the Rockies and didn't pitch badly. He gave up scratch runs in the third and fifth and a home run to catcher Yorvit Torrealba in the sixth but was outpitched by Josh Fogg in a 3–1 loss. The notion that the Yankees would go into Colorado and be held to one run seemed all but impossible. Coors Field had been baseball's launchpad for years because of the thin air in Denver. MLB had taken the audacious step in 2002 of putting baseballs in a humidor before games to keep them moist so they wouldn't fly so far, and scoring had come down but not so much that one would expect the Yankee lineup to be shut down by Josh Fogg.

The opening game proved to be a harbinger. Jeff Francis beat Pettitte the next night 6–1 in a game that was close until late, and the Rockies completed the sweep the night after with a 4–3 win over Clemens. The last thing in the world anyone would have believed could happen in Colorado was that the Yankees could have Mussina, Pettitte, and Clemens all pitch well and lose. Even less probable was the team scoring just five runs in three games against the Colorado pitching staff.

The Yankees managed to win the opener in San Francisco before blowing a ninth-inning lead the next day to lose in thirteen. That set up Mussina against Noah Lowry, the rapidly improving Giants lefty, in the finale.

From the beginning, the day was a struggle for Mussina. It wasn't as if the Giants were lighting him up. "It was just that everything was hard," he said later. "I didn't have very much confidence in my pitches."

His struggles may have been defined best by the way the Giants ran the bases. Almost everyone who reached first base stole second base about five seconds later. Poor Wil Nieves had no chance. Mussina was so locked in on trying to deal with the hitter at the plate that he seemed to forget about runners on first.

Barry Bonds, of all people, started the parade. Bonds had once been a feared base runner, but the combination of his change in body type, aching knees, and age (almost forty-three) had virtually brought him to a halt as a runner. Most of the time he didn't even bother to run out ground balls, and he simply jogged after any ball in the outfield that was more than two or three steps out of his range. About the only time he ran with any enthusiasm was when a pitcher failed to pay attention to him, and he could steal a base by running at three-quarter speed instead of half speed.

After Bonds had singled to start the second in a scoreless game, he immediately stole second. Ryan Klesko walked, and both runners moved up on a ground ball. A Pedro Feliz sacrifice fly scored Bonds, and then Guillermo Rodriguez doubled Klesko in to make it 2–0. Two innings later, Nate Schierholtz led off with a single and—you guessed it—stole second. Trying desperately to make a play, Nieves overthrew the ball, and Schierholtz ended up on third. The Giants then executed a squeeze, Lowry bunting, Mussina fielding, and Schierholtz scoring to make it 3–0.

That was all the Giants needed as it turned out. Mussina pitched out of further trouble, giving up five hits, walking three, and allowing five steals. The fact that he only gave up the three runs in his five innings was a tribute to his toughness with men in scoring position. That he had to come out after five innings was the result of having thrown 105 pitches by the time he got the last out in the bottom of the fifth.

"That's just not good enough," Mussina said. "You have to be able to give your team more than five innings. The three runs were okay; it was good that I hung in there and didn't let the game get out of hand. But you can't be over a hundred pitches before the end of the fifth inning. You have to pitch more efficiently than that."

Watching his friend from the bullpen as he always did, Mike Borzello was discouraged. In May, he had thought Mussina's unwillingness to go after hitters was strictly a product of his arm strength not being all the way back after the stint on the disabled list. Now though, it was late June and Mussina was still pitching scared.

"He just didn't want contact," Borzello said. "There's a reason why there are eight other guys out on the field with you. You can't pitch behind in the count all day long because you're afraid to throw the ball over the plate."

Mark Mussina, watching on television, felt the same way. "He had gotten to the point where he was afraid to give up home runs," he said. "He wasn't giving up that many home runs, but he wasn't giving himself a chance to pitch deep into games because he was afraid to throw strikes."

One of the reasons Mussina and Borzello are friends is that Mussina knows Borzello will tell him what he thinks. On the flight home that night, Mussina sat down with Borzello to ask him what he thought about his performance that day.

"You were bad," Borzello said.

"Well, I wouldn't say I was good," Mussina said. "But three runs in five innings isn't all that bad."

"No, it's not," Borzello said. "But your pitching was *bad*. What's made you a really good pitcher is having confidence in your stuff. You've always known if you throw your pitch where you want to throw it you're going to get outs. You didn't pitch that way today. You pitched scared. No one can pitch well that way."

Mussina didn't exactly love hearing Borzello's words, but he knew he was right. He had always had so many pitches in his arsenal that if one was off on a given day — or even two — he had other options. Back home, Mark, who had started charting every pitch Mike threw in 1994, noticed a pattern developing. "Fastball away, fastball away, fastball away," he said. "That was all he was doing. There was one game in that period where forty-four of the first fifty-one pitches he threw were fastballs. After the game I heard Joe [Torre] say, 'He just needs to have more confidence in his fastball.' I said, '*What?!*' He's throwing eighty-seven percent fastballs, and Joe thinks he isn't showing enough confidence in his fastball?"

Torre wasn't talking so much about how many fastballs Mussina was throwing but *where* he was throwing them. Much like Glavine in 2003 and 2004, Mussina had fallen into the habit of only throwing outside, although for a different reason. Glavine, who had never been a hard thrower, believed he had to stay away from hitters to be successful and had been successful that way for years — before Questech and the Mets came into his life.

Mussina had thrown a good deal harder than Glavine when he was younger, and now he couldn't do that anymore. Most of his fastballs were in the 86- to 88-mile-per-hour range, and he topped out at 90. Mussina knew he needed to adapt but was having a tough time doing it.

"There's nothing harder than being able to throw hard when you're young and waking up one morning and finding out you can't throw that hard anymore," said Ron Guidry, who had thrown very hard as a young pitcher but had been able to win twenty-two games at the age of thirty-five after he could no longer blow batters away. "Your mind tells you that you should still be able to do certain things, but your body won't let you do it. Accepting the fact that you need to pitch differently is half the battle — maybe more."

Glavine had needed to reinvent himself as a pitcher in 2005. What Mussina was going through wasn't all that different. And it was every bit as difficult.

THE SUNDAY LOSS IN SAN FRANCISCO dropped the Yankees under .500 again at 36–37. They flew east to Baltimore, hoping a series against the Orioles would be a cure-all as it had frequently been in the past ten years when the once-proud Baltimore franchise had become little more than a laughingstock, owner Peter Angelos changing general managers and managers the way George Steinbrenner once had while his team went through one losing season after another.

The Orioles had already fired another manager, Sam Perlozzo, early in 2007, and replaced him with minor league–lifer Dave Trembley. At the same time they had revamped their front office, hiring Andy McPhail, who had successfully put together teams in Minnesota and Chicago. The hiring of McPhail was viewed in baseball circles as a step forward for owner Peter Angelos, who had frequently refused to give final say on trades and signings to his general managers. Most people believed McPhail wouldn't have agreed to come to Baltimore unless he was given complete control by Angelos.

His hiring was, the long-suffering fans in Baltimore hoped, a long-term solution. Short-term, the Orioles still weren't very good. They were 32–43 when the Yankees got to town and headed for another ninety-loss season. Their gorgeous ballpark, Oriole Park at Camden Yards, had become known in recent years as "Yankee Stadium South," because so many Yankee fans made the short trip from New York to snap up tickets they couldn't get for sold-out games in New York. The Orioles had drawn well over three million fans on a regular basis after first moving in to Camden Yards in 1992, but their attendance had been in free fall in recent years, as each hopeful April turned into a wait-till-next-year July. Even the presence of the Yankees didn't fill every seat, although crowds of close to forty thousand showed up — considerably higher than the usual average of under thirty thousand.

The Yankees always seemed to play well in Baltimore. The 2006 season had been typical: even though they were only 5–4 against the Orioles in New York, they were 7–3 in Baltimore. The small dimensions of the ballpark played to their power, and the fact that half the crowd was on their side most nights didn't hurt either.

But they were at the tail end of a long road trip and not playing well. It showed the first two games: a 3–2 loss and a 4–0 loss. In the second game, Clemens was outpitched by Baltimore lefty Erik Bedard, who was becoming one of the best pitchers in the game.

Prior to the second game, Torre decided to send Mussina home to New York a day early, meaning he would miss the final game of the series. Managers will often send a starting pitcher to the place where he is going to pitch next a day or two early so he can be rested for his start, but more often it happens when a coast-to-coast trip is involved or during postseason. The Yankees' trip from Baltimore to New York was the shortest they would make all season—other than when they played the Mets at Shea Stadium. But with the third game at night and bad weather in the forecast, Torre decided to send Mussina home early.

"If you think about it, it makes sense," Mussina said. "Best-case scenario we're going to play a three-hour game, which means the earliest we get to the airport is between eleven thirty and midnight. We land at twelve thirty, have to bus to Yankee Stadium to get to our cars, and by the time we're home it's two o'clock. That's *if* the game doesn't run long or if there's no rain."

Mussina was long past feeling any qualms about coming back to Baltimore in a visiting uniform. He had expected boos when he first left to sign with the Yankees, but they hadn't been nearly as loud as what Glavine heard when he left Atlanta. Many, if not most, Oriole fans knew that Mussina had signed with the team once for a hometown discount and had been willing to sign in the spring of 2000 for five years at $60 million, considerably less than the $88 million for six years he got after the season from the Yankees.

What's more, the presence of all the Yankee fans frequently drowned out any boos he might hear. "Actually, it doesn't sound much different than the old days when they used to yell 'Mooooose,'" he said, smiling.

On this trip, he heard no boos since he wasn't scheduled to pitch. As it turned out, Torre's notion that getting Mussina home and to bed on Thursday would be good for him proved to be a smart one. The teams played a long game that came to a halt because of rain after the Yankees had scored four runs to take an 8–6 lead in the top of the eighth inning. The umpires waited until almost midnight before suspending the game—since the Orioles hadn't gotten a chance to bat in the eighth and the game was official (having gone more than five innings)—meaning it would be completed the next time the Yankees came to Baltimore. It was three o'clock in the morning by the time the bus pulled into Yankee Stadium.

Mussina was sound asleep.

GLAVINE WAS SLEEPING a lot better too, after his performance against Oakland. The A's were the Mets' last interleague series— 2007 was a year in which the AL East played the NL West, and the NL East played the AL West—meaning the Yankees were in San Francisco when the Mets hosted the Athletics, and the St. Louis Cardinals came into Shea for their only scheduled visit of the season after the Mets had completed their sweep of the A's.

The Cardinals were a far different team than the one that had upset the Mets in the NLCS the previous October. They had been rocked by injuries, controversy, and even death. The death had occurred in May when relief pitcher Josh Hancock slammed his SUV into the back of a tow truck that was working on a disabled car. He died almost instantly. An autopsy determined that he had been drunk at the time of the accident, which led MLB and the players union to ban all alcohol from major league clubhouses. For years, many players routinely drank a beer or two (or more) in the clubhouse after games.

The Yankees and the Mets had already banned alcohol before the Hancock accident. Mussina, as the Yankees' player rep, took part in a conference call with other player reps a few days later, in which it was decided to formally ban all alcohol from clubhouses. "It probably should have been done long ago," Mussina said. "But after this, it's pretty much a no-brainer."

Hancock hadn't been drinking in the Cardinal clubhouse; he'd been in a bar. But MLB and the union had to let the public know that drinks weren't being handed out like candy bars inside their stadiums after games.

Hancock's death came less than two months after Cardinals manager Tony LaRussa had been charged with DUI during spring training, when he fell asleep at the wheel of his car at a stoplight. LaRussa was an icon in St. Louis, especially after winning the World Series. He had been a major league manager since 1979 and had enjoyed success with the White Sox, the Athletics, and the Cardinals, regularly making the postseason, even though the 2006 World Series was "only" his second world championship — the first having come in 1989 in Oakland during the "earthquake" World Series.

But while LaRussa was seen as one of baseball's best managers and smartest people, there were also those who found him to be arrogant and difficult. Probably everyone on both sides of the argument was right: LaRussa was a great manager, was extremely smart, was arrogant, and could certainly be difficult. His DUI was cause for glee in some circles, especially among those who liked to mockingly call him "the Genius," a phrase that had followed him since he had been featured in a bestselling George Will book on baseball that had portrayed him as one.

All of LaRussa's brilliance was going to be needed to keep the 2007 Cardinals afloat. The pitching staff was in tatters, with Chris Carpenter, the 2005 Cy Young Award winner, out for the season; closer Jason Isringhausen hurt; and others who had pitched well at the end of 2006 not pitching nearly as well. Slugger Albert Pujols had been on the disabled list, as had starting shortstop David Eckstein.

The Mets had very little concern for the Cardinals' troubles when they came to town. "Talking about revenge is silly," Glavine said. "There's nothing we can do to change what happened last year. They went to the World Series and won. That chance is gone. But it's still nice to go out and beat them."

The Cardinals limped into Shea Stadium with a 33–39 record, although they were still in contention in the National League Central because no one was playing very well. In 2006, the Cardinals had won the division with eighty-three victories—the Mets won ninety-seven—and it was beginning to look as if eighty-three to eighty-five wins would be good enough to win the Central again.

LaRussa was a big Glavine fan. "Don't misunderstand, when he pitches against us I want to beat his butt," he said. "But I've been around the game long enough to appreciate the kind of competitor he is and to appreciate the way he's carried himself through the years. He's one of those guys who you can say without hesitation is good for the game. When he wins three hundred, I'll be standing up somewhere and applauding."

Glavine was focusing on 297 when he took the mound in the third game of the series. The teams had split eleven-inning marathons in the first two games, and the weather had turned miserably hot and humid. It was ninety-three degrees when Glavine threw his warm-ups, with the skies getting darker by the minute. "One of those nights where you want to get a lead early and get through five fast," Glavine said.

He knew of what he spoke. The Mets did get an early lead when David Wright hit a two-run home run with Paul Lo Duca on first base in the bottom of the first. From there, Glavine worked quickly and efficiently. With one out in the second, Scott Rolen hit a soft line drive over shortstop for a base hit. No one realized it at that moment, but it was the Cardinals' final hit of the night.

Glavine was full of confidence coming off the game against Oakland, and against the weak-hitting St. Louis lineup he was dominant. After Rolen's hit, he gave up a two-out walk to shortstop Aaron Miles. But he got Brendan Ryan to ground to shortstop and then got the Cardinals one-two-three in each of the next four innings.

The Mets weren't doing a lot more against winless (0–10) St. Louis starter Anthony Reyes (no relation to Jose), but it didn't matter. When Glavine got Ryan Ludwick for the final out of the sixth inning and his thirteenth consecutive out, it was pouring, and plate umpire Mark Carlson ordered that the tarp be brought out to cover the field.

The umpires waited almost two and a half hours before calling the game. When they did call it, Glavine had his first official complete game of the season and a one-hit shutout. Of course if Glavine hadn't given up the hit to Rolen and if the game had been able to continue, the question then would have been whether Glavine would have gone out to pitch the seventh inning.

Traditionally, pitchers don't come back after a long rain delay, especially older pitchers. The only exception to that rule would come if a no-hitter was involved. Glavine had never pitched a no-hitter — the closest he had come was taking one into the eighth inning in 2004 against the Colorado Rockies — which wasn't all that surprising. More often than not, no-hitters are pitched by power pitchers, frequently power pitchers with control problems, who keep the hitters off-balance by throwing very hard, often in the wrong direction. Nolan Ryan, who exploded all records for no-hitters by pitching seven of them (Sandy Koufax is next with four), is the career leader in both strikeouts and walks.

A pitcher like Glavine, who isn't going to strike out a lot of people, is far less likely to get twenty-seven outs without surrendering a hit. The more batters make contact, the more likely someone is to poke the ball someplace where it can't be caught. "Realistically my chances for a no-hitter at this point in my career are pretty slim," he said. "My chances early in my career weren't all that great either."

What would he have done had he been pitching a no-hitter and the game had resumed after the delay? "I'm pretty sure Rick [Peterson] wouldn't have wanted me to go out there again," he said. "Too risky."

But a no-hitter? "I guess we would have at least talked about it," he finally conceded. "It's probably a good thing it wasn't an issue."

Far more remarkable than Glavine having not pitched a no-hitter is the fact that the Mets — in forty-six seasons of baseball — have never had a no-hitter. This is a team that had Tom Seaver pitch for it, Nolan Ryan (briefly), Dwight Gooden, and Jerry Koosman. The first two are power pitchers in the Hall of Fame; the third would be there if he hadn't blown up his career with drug use; and the fourth was a borderline Hall of Famer who was a dominant pitcher when young and with the Mets.

Seaver pitched five one-hitters while he was a Met, including coming within two outs of a perfect game in 1969 against the Chicago Cubs. An obscure outfielder named Jim Qualls, who was in the lineup that night only because the regular center fielder Don Young had made a defensive blunder the day before, broke it up with a solid single to left-center. Seaver, who finally did pitch a no-hitter after being traded to the Cincinnati Reds, always called that his *im*perfect game. Gary Gentry, another young power pitcher on that 1969 team, pitched two one-hitters for the Mets. Ryan pitched one, as did Gooden. Remarkably, Steve Trachsel, whose only real place in baseball lore is as the pitcher who gave up Mark McGwire's sixty-second home run in 1998, pitched two one-hitters for the Mets.

In all, there have been twenty-three complete-game one-hitters in Mets history. Technically, Glavine's was the twenty-fourth, but a six-inning one-hitter hardly resonated with him. What did was the win, his seventh of the season. He was now three wins away with three starts left before the All-Star break.

"Boy, would it be nice to go away for a few days with that part of the season behind me," he said. "It probably isn't realistic, but it would sure be nice."

What was most important was that he was pitching well again. Since the two bad games against the Yankees and Tigers and the slight adjustment on the rubber, he had pitched fourteen innings, given up one run—the home run by Shannon Stewart in the Oakland game—and had won twice.

"It's always a relief when you come out of a little slump," he said. "Because you know then it was only a slump."

MUSSINA WAS IN A LITTLE SLUMP of his own. He had lost twice on the western road trip, and, even though he hadn't pitched horribly in either game, he knew Borzello's succinct analysis of the game in San Francisco—"You were bad"—was accurate.

Well-rested, he went to the mound against the Oakland Athletics on Friday night, June 29. It was exactly a week since Glavine had gotten back on track against the A's. The Athletics had come into Shea Stadium playing good baseball, but the trip to the East Coast had not gone well. After being swept by the Mets, they had gone to Cleveland and lost three of four. Tired at the end of a long trip, they were probably just what the doctor ordered for a pitcher trying to find himself again.

Mussina was in control from the start. He had worked in the bullpen during the week on locating his pitches, on making sure he could hit his spots so as not to fall behind in too many counts. He knew he couldn't afford to pitch behind and that he had to stop worrying about giving up home runs and pitch to contact more often.

"The thing about Moose is, he's smart," Joe Torre said. "That sounds simplistic, but there are some guys who are book smart but not baseball smart. Moose is both. He knew what happened in San Francisco, and he couldn't go out and pitch like that and expect to have any kind of real success. So, he adjusted. That's what guys who don't have overpowering stuff have to do: make adjustments all the time. He did that."

As is often the case, getting out of trouble in the first inning proved key. There's no better example of how important it is to get to a good pitcher early than Glavine, who gives up almost half his runs in the first inning. But it is true of all good pitchers.

"The first inning you often aren't completely comfortable on the mound," Mussina said. "It takes a while to get yourself to feel exactly the way you want to feel in the game. You throw thirty to forty pitches in the bullpen, then you only get eight warm-ups on the mound. That's why a lot of times if you see a guy who is good get through a tough first inning, he settles down and pitches well. When you're on the bench facing someone good and you get men on in the first, you automatically think, 'Better get him now because there might not be another chance this good.'"

That was certainly the case with Mussina against the A's. With one out in the first, he walked Shannon Stewart, with Oakland's two best power threats, Nick Swisher and Jack Cust, coming up. Stewart promptly stole second, which put him into scoring position. "The inning can go either way at that point," Mussina said.

It went his way. He struck out Swisher with a fastball that hit 90 and got Cust to fly out to Hideki Matsui in left. Threat averted. The Yankees then scored twice in the bottom of the inning, and Mussina felt a surge of confidence.

"Remember in my last two outings, we'd scored a total of one run while I was pitching," he said. "Going out to the mound with a two-oh lead after that felt more like ten-oh. I had to remind myself what it was like to pitch with the lead."

He relearned the art quickly. All night long he was around the plate, allowing the A's to put the ball in play. He worked ahead of hitters and only walked one batter. Of the twenty-one outs he got, eighteen came on balls that were put in play; he struck out three. He completely shut down Oakland until the seventh inning, when

Eric Chavez led off with a double, and Mark Ellis singled, Chavez stopping at third.

It was Mussina's first jam of the night. He got out of it immediately, getting Dan Johnson to hit the ball right back to him. Quickly, he turned it into a one-four-three double play, allowing Chavez to score to make it 2–1. Bobby Crosby flied to center, and the inning was over. Torre and Guidry decided right then, even though Mussina had only thrown eighty-four pitches — his most efficient performance of the season — that they wanted to let the bullpen get the last six outs.

"When a guy's been struggling, and he goes out and pitches that well for that long, you want to make sure he walks away with a good feeling," Torre said. "He had started to look a little bit tired in the seventh, even though he did a good job pitching out of trouble. I thought getting him out was not only the best way to win the game but the best way to make sure he went into his next start with some confidence."

Torre was proven correct, although it wasn't easy. He brought in the always-flammable Kyle Farnsworth. There was no enigma on the Yankees quite like Farnsworth. He could throw harder than anyone on the team, often reaching 98 on the radar gun. But he was maddeningly inconsistent, frequently walking batters at crucial moments, then giving up a key hit — often a home run — to give up a lead.

Plus, it was never his fault. When the media would try to ask him about a poor outing, he would snarl and say it was somehow their fault (shades of Carl Pavano?) and that he really didn't care what anyone other than his family and friends thought of him. He didn't include his teammates in that speech or the team that was paying him $7 million a year to pitch considerably better than he had pitched.

Farnsworth coming into a 2–1 game in the eighth was about as sure a bet as Wall Street in November of 1929. He started the inning by getting Jason Kendall on a ground ball back to the box, but then promptly gave up back-to-back singles to Shannon Stewart and Mark Kotsay. Icing his arm in the clubhouse, Mussina couldn't help thinking another chance to get a win was about to go by the boards. Torre got Mariano Rivera up but had to let Farnsworth pitch to one more batter while Rivera got warm.

Most of the time in key situations, Farnsworth would do one of two things: give up a home run (and blame it on the media) or get a strikeout. This time, he struck out Nick Swisher. Torre wasn't going to push his luck. He strolled to the mound as slowly as possible and waved Rivera into the game.

If Rivera is not the greatest closer in the history of baseball, he is certainly part of the conversation. He has probably pitched in more crucial situations than any relief pitcher in history, becoming a critical part of the Yankee bullpen in 1996 when Torre moved him from the starting rotation to being a two-inning setup man for then-closer John Wetteland. Torre called that decision "the Formula"—Rivera in the seventh and eighth and Wetteland in the ninth—and saw it as the key to the Yankees taking control of the American League East en route to their first World Series title in eighteen years.

Wetteland was allowed to leave as a free agent after that season, and Rivera has been the closer ever since. He entered the 2007 season with 413 saves, which put him fourth on the all-time saves list. Beyond that, he had a staggering thirty-four saves in postseason play, a number put in better perspective by the fact that Hall of Famer Dennis Eckersley had fifteen.

Of course Rivera had been given more postseason opportunities than any other closer in history, having been on a team that had been in the playoffs all ten years that he had been closing games. Still, he had proven himself in the clutch so many times that when he failed—in the 1997 Division Series against Cleveland, the 2001 World Series against Arizona, and the 2004 American League Championship Series against Boston—it was man-bites-dog news.

Rivera was now thirty-seven, and the first half of the season had been a struggle for him. On the rare occasions when he'd had a chance to close a game in April, he had pitched poorly. He had started to pitch better as his chances to pitch increased, but he still had only nine saves as he jogged in from the bullpen to try to bail out Farnsworth.

Seeing him come in, Mussina breathed a sigh of relief. Rivera might not be the sure thing he had once seemingly been, but he was still about as good as it got. And Mussina would rather have him in the game than Farnsworth. So, clearly, would Torre, who had more or less reinvented the closer's role as Rivera's manager. In the 1980s, Tony LaRussa had changed the game by making Eckersley strictly a three-out closer. Eckersley never came into the game before the ninth, and he almost always came in to start the ninth, regardless of how well the starter—or whoever pitched the eighth—was pitching.

Baseball people copy success, so other managers began using their closers to get three outs and three outs only. Torre changed that with Rivera. If he felt he needed a win badly enough, he would bring Rivera in during the eighth, sometimes even to start the eighth, especially in postseason. Frequently the Yankees set up postseason games to use whoever they had to in order to get through the seventh and try to get the ball to Rivera with the lead because they were almost certain he would get the final six outs.

Now, needing four outs, Rivera struck out Jack Cust. He got two quick outs in the ninth, before one of his cutters got away and he hit Dan Johnson with a pitch. But he made up for that by striking out Bobby Crosby to end the game, giving Mussina his fourth win of the season.

"If you had told me before the season that on June 29 I'd get my fourth win and Mo would get his tenth save, I wouldn't have believed you," he said. "But right now it feels like a big deal. It's been a long three months for all of us. I just hope this is the start of a good run for all of us. We could certainly use it."

The Yankees were 38–39 after the win and in third place, eleven games behind the Red Sox. That same day the Mets went into Philadelphia and swept both ends of a day-night double-header to up their record to 45–33. They had a four-game lead on the Braves and a five-game lead on the Phillies, who dropped back into third place at 41–39 after being swept.

Driving into the stadium the next morning, Mussina switched on the radio, which he will do on occasion just to hear what people are saying. "I like to know what they think about what I know," he said with a smile.

The discussion centered that morning on the Mets. Would Pedro Martinez be part of the postseason rotation? If so, would he pitch Game One or would Tom Glavine pitch Game One? Could John Maine and Oliver Perez be relied on in October?

Mussina laughed. "We're not even at the All-Star break yet, and people are setting up postseason rotations for the Mets," he said. "And us? We don't exist anymore. All I could think was 'Wow, these guys really don't get baseball.'"

And since neither the Mets nor the Yankees had quite reached the halfway point of their seasons, there was still a lot of baseball yet to play.

21

Limping to the Break

THE FOURTH OF JULY is a line of demarcation in Major League Baseball. It always falls almost exactly halfway through the season, and, history shows, teams that are in first place on the Fourth of July very often are in first place when the season ends.

The six division leaders on July 4, 2007, were the Red Sox, Indians, and Angels in the American League, and the Mets, Brewers, and Padres in the National League. If the season had ended that day, the wild cards would have been the Tigers in the American League and the Dodgers in the National League.

The Yankees certainly hoped their first half wasn't an indication of how their season was going to turn out. They reached the halfway point of their schedule at 40–41 after Chien-Ming Wang beat the Minnesota Twins 8–0 on July 3 at Yankee Stadium. Their second half began at home on July 4 with two-time Cy Young Award–winner Johan Santana pitching for the Twins against Mike Mussina.

Mussina had traditionally pitched very well when facing an opponent's top pitcher. Even though pitchers will point out that they are facing the other team's lineup, not the other pitcher, they are fully aware of who the other starting pitcher is every time they take the ball.

"You have to be aware of it," he said. "If you're pitching against a guy like Santana, you know going in that if you give up more

328

than a couple of runs you probably aren't going to win the game. It can affect the way you pitch in a certain situation. If you're down one-nothing, and they have men on first and third, you might try to get a pop-up or a strikeout rather than a double-play ball because you don't want to concede that run. I think it actually makes me pitch better because I know I have less margin for error. It isn't as if you're trying any harder; it's just that you're a little more focused."

Glavine agrees and adds one other factor: "Certain games, you just have more adrenaline going to the mound," he said. "It can be for a variety of reasons, but knowing you're facing a top pitcher is certainly one of them."

In many ways, the Twins were the anti-Yankees. They were a small-market team that had actually been targeted for extinction by MLB in 2001 when the owners had decided that contraction was one way to make up for their expansion mistakes (see Tampa Bay and Miami). The Twins, owned by Carl Pohlad, who was more than willing to be contracted, and the Montreal Expos, who had no owners, were the targets.

Both clubs survived in large part because the players union fought for the jobs that would have been lost, and the Twins blossomed into a good team thanks to the shrewd leadership of general manager Terry Ryan and manager Ron Gardenhire. They had reached the playoffs four times in six years, although they were having a tough time in a strong division in 2007, trailing both the Tigers and the Indians, with a record of 42–40 on the Fourth of July.

Mussina's concerns about not falling behind Santana quickly became reality in the first, when the normally reliable Derek Jeter opened the game by kicking Jason Bartlett's routine leadoff grounder. If that wasn't frustrating enough, Bartlett ended up scoring when 2006 AL MVP Justin Morneau sliced a ball softly down the left-field line that landed about two inches fair before bouncing into the stands for a ground rule double.

The only reason Bartlett was on second, at least in Mussina's mind, was that plate umpire Adrian Johnson (an umpire brought up from the minor leagues to replace a regular ump who was on vacation) had called a 2–2 fastball he had thrown to Joe Mauer a ball when Mussina was convinced it was a strike. Mauer had won the American League batting title in 2006 and had a reputation for having a good eye. Umpires are frequently influenced by who is at the plate, just as they are often influenced by who is pitching. When Ted Williams, who probably had the best batting eye of any hitter in history, was playing, it was often said that umpires never called a borderline pitch to him a strike because they figured if Ted Williams thought the pitch was a ball, it must be a ball.

Mauer took the 2–2 pitch, and Johnson figured it must be a ball. On 3–2, Bartlett was running and reached second base on Mauer's ground ball to Jeter. If Mauer had struck out, Bartlett would have been on first when Morneau doubled and would not have been able to score because the ball bounced into the stands. Mussina might have escaped the inning without giving up a run. Instead it was 1–0.

"When you have an inning like that, when you're throwing pretty well and you know you're up against Santana, you do think, 'Oh God, is it going to be one of those days?'" Mussina said later. "You have to pitch through it, but you wouldn't be human if you didn't notice it."

Mussina didn't let it affect him. He was almost flawless over the next few innings, and Santana, while good, was human. Hideki Matsui hit a long home run off him in the second inning to tie the score at 1–1. Then in the fourth, the Yankees had a real chance to take control of the game. Jeter led off with a double, and, after Alex Rodriguez grounded out and Matsui walked, Andy Phillips singled to score Jeter and give the Yankees a 2–1 lead. After Robinson Cano popped out, Kevin Thompson walked to load the bases with two out.

Which left Joe Torre with a decision to make. Wil Nieves, who was now locked in as Mussina's personal catcher, was due up next. Nieves was hitting .120, and his chances of getting a hit off Santana, realistically, were close to zero. Managers rarely pinch-hit in the fourth inning of a game, especially for their catcher, because most teams only carry two catchers these days. If something happens to the second catcher, you are forced to go to someone who only catches in emergencies—for the Yankees it would have been utility man Miguel Cairo—and that can be a disaster.

That said, as Mussina had noted, you sometimes have to approach a game differently with a Santana on the mound. You only get so many chances most days against a first-class pitcher, and this could be the Yankees' last best chance to really get to Santana. The bold play would have been to hit Jorge Posada for Nieves and go for broke. Torre played it conservative. Nieves flied to right. As it turned out, they never threatened Santana again, even in the seventh, when Torre *did* pinch-hit Posada for Nieves.

By then, the game had unraveled. The Twins had scratched another run in the sixth when Bartlett had singled, stolen second, and then scored on back-to-back ground-ball outs. That tied it at 2–2. "At that point I'm not thinking in terms of getting a win," Mussina said. "Realistically, I just want to hold on long enough so we can get into their bullpen and maybe get the win that way."

He couldn't do it. Torii Hunter led off the seventh with a ringing double, and left fielder Jason Kubel, hardly one of the Twins' bigger threats, hit Mussina's next pitch into the right-field bleachers to make it 4–2. Mussina exited right then and there, frustrated that a good day had turned into a bad one, and the Twins went on to win 6–2.

This was an ifs and buts game, but the bottom line was still another loss. In sixteen years in the major leagues, Mussina had never won fewer than eleven games in any season. Midway through the 2007 season, he was 4–6. And his team, one game past that midway point, was now 40–42 and twelve games out of first place.

THE METS AND TOM GLAVINE had no such issues on the Fourth of July. They were in first place, and Glavine, in spite of taking a loss two days earlier against the Colorado Rockies, felt good about the way he was pitching.

There were, however, some signs of cracking in the foundation, even though the Mets were leading the Braves by four games and the Phillies by five.

It had started when Paul Lo Duca had been ejected from a game against the Oakland A's for arguing balls and strikes and then followed up his ejection by throwing equipment onto the field to let umpire Marvin Hudson know just what he thought of his work. Naturally, he was suspended (two games), and just as naturally he appealed the suspension. One of the sillier rules in baseball allows a player to keep playing while a suspension is under appeal. Why it takes more than twenty-four hours to determine whether to amend a suspension, no one understands. The circumstances are usually clear-cut; there is always videotape evidence; and there is no reason why the commissioner's office has to wait until a player is in New York to hear his appeal since conference calling is available anywhere, anytime, anyplace.

Things change slowly in baseball, so it is not the least bit uncommon for a player to trot out to his position on the same day MLB announces that he has been suspended. In the case of Lo Duca, his appeal dragged out long enough that it became something of a headache for the Mets, who needed to know exactly when they were going to have to call up a catcher to take his spot. Since a suspended player is not considered to be off the roster, someone would have to be sent down or released, and the question was who it would be and when it would happen.

As the appeal dragged on—three days, four days, five

days—Lo Duca was asked about it every day. Was he thinking about withdrawing the appeal and just getting it over with? Did he now regret his outburst? How much of a problem would it be if he was suspended on June 29 when the Mets had a day-night doubleheader and almost certainly needed two catchers?

Most days Lo Duca was the most cooperative guy in the clubhouse when it came to the media. He was outgoing, loved to talk, and enjoyed the give and take. But the whole suspension thing wore on him, and, finally, five days after the incident, he got angry. "Go talk to some of the other guys, will you?" he said. "There *are* other guys in here who speak English, you know."

It was a fairly benign blow-off, the kind you might expect from someone who has been asked the same questions five days in a row. But someone—not surprisingly not a regular beat writer—decided that Lo Duca had been firing some kind of ethnic slur, a comment about the number of Hispanic players on the team. Anyone who knew Lo Duca knew that wasn't what he was saying or anything close to what he was saying. The Hispanic players certainly knew it, but once it was in a New York newspaper *(Newsday)* it became a story.

When Lo Duca walked into the clubhouse at Citizens Bank Park in Philadelphia on the morning of the day-night doubleheader, he was instantly surrounded by every person wearing a press credential. He was angry. He said if people were going to misconstrue comments he made, maybe he would stop talking to the media completely. Things were bad enough that Mets PR director Jay Horwitz rounded up some of the Hispanic players to come to Lo Duca's defense.

That morning, most of the Mets were wearing brand-new T-shirts that had been created by several of the veterans, including Glavine, Billy Wagner, Carlos Delgado, and Lo Duca. The veterans were getting tired of all the doubts they perceived to be surrounding a team that was in first place and had been almost the entire season. So, to mock the doubters (the media), they had

T-shirts made up with a picture of Bozo the Clown. Under Bozo was the word "ENOUGH!" On the back of the T-shirt were the words: "There ain't a big top big enough for THIS circus."

The Yankees would have found the Mets' discomfort amusing. They dealt on an almost daily basis with questions about the future of their manager, general manager, and practically everyone in the starting lineup. The Mets were bridling over a few people wondering why they hadn't yet put together a five-game winning streak.

"I guess it's all relative," Glavine said, as he watched Lo Duca answer question after question. "But look at what Paulie's being put through. No one's better with the media than he is, and he's getting hammered for saying something he didn't say."

That much was true. But the T-shirts were a sign of a team feeling a certain amount of pressure. The Mets were supposed to win the East as easily in 2007 as they had in 2006 and then glide into the World Series. Real life is never that simple.

"I think there is a tendency to think because you win by twelve one year, you should win by twelve the next year," Glavine said. "I can tell you from experience, it doesn't work that way. But I do think we're all waiting for that hot streak to come. We know we're capable of it; we just haven't done it yet."

They weren't going to do it before the All-Star break. After winning the first three games in Philadelphia, they lost the finale and headed to Colorado and Houston for the last week before the break. Glavine was relieved to learn he hadn't made the All-Star team. There had been some talk that he might be invited since it was possible this would be his last year, and while he had not pitched *that* well, he had pitched solidly.

"I really hope they don't do it," he had said. "It isn't that it isn't an honor; it is. But I could use a few days off doing nothing. I wouldn't be excited to have to fly to San Francisco and then go straight back to New York. I've been in All-Star games [ten of them], and they're fun. But this year I could use the rest."

He was scheduled to pitch twice more before the break. After the series in Philadelphia, he opened against the Colorado Rockies and pitched five shutout innings. The problem was that he pitched a total of six innings, and in his one nonshutout inning (the third), he gave up six runs. Three scored on a home run by Matt Holliday, who was developing into one of the best hitters in the game. That was upsetting but understandable. The last two scored on a single by pitcher Jason Hirsh after Glavine had intentionally walked the number eight hitter to pitch to Hirsh.

"Boy, do you hate when that happens," he said. "A four-run inning is bad, but a six-run inning is a lot worse. After that, my job was to try to eat up a few innings to save the pen."

He did that, lasting through six innings, but the night and the series was lost. The Rockies, who had been picked by most people to finish fourth or fifth in the National League West, were starting to show signs of serious life. They had swept the Yankees, and now they had swept the Mets. That didn't necessarily make them contenders (they were still only 42–43) but there were some indications that they should be taken seriously.

"That's a good, young lineup," Glavine said. "Sometimes you think it's the ballpark, and in the past at times it has been. But I think those guys are good enough to hit just about anyplace. The question will always be their pitching."

The last loss in Colorado on the Fourth of July dropped the Mets to 46–37, still in first place but on a 13–20 slide during a five-week stretch. They still had a three-game lead going into Houston to play four games before the break, but there was a sense that the team had become fragile, that something wasn't quite right.

That feeling grew stronger in Houston. The Mets managed to end their four-game losing streak behind yet another strong performance by John Maine—who was 10–4 and All-Star worthy, even though he hadn't been selected—but were shut down the next night by the immortal Wandy Rodriguez in a 4–0 loss.

That wasn't the worst part of the night. That came in the eighth inning when Jose Reyes hit a routine ground ball to Mike Lamb at third base and decided not to bother running the ball out. As luck would have it, Lamb bobbled the ball but still made the play easily since Reyes wasn't running. That play so infuriated Randolph that he yanked Reyes from the game.

If it had been the first time Reyes had loafed or hadn't been paying enough attention on the bases it would not have been cause for serious concern. But it wasn't. It was starting to become a habit and that's what troubled Randolph. At his best, Reyes was as exciting as any player in the game. He was the best base stealer in the National League; anything he hit anywhere near a gap was going to be a triple, and he was a dynamic leadoff hitter who was hitting .310. He had MVP potential. Bobby Cox had already labeled him the best leadoff hitter he had seen since Rickey Henderson.

Randolph knew the Mets needed a fresh and eager Reyes in the second half of the season. He yanked him from a game that was lost, had a talk with him, and decided not to bench him the next night. "I hope," he said, "the message was sent."

Glavine pitched his final prebreak game the next night. Lo Duca was his catcher, having finally served his suspension the two previous nights. That was the good news. The bad news was the man standing behind Lo Duca: Glavine's pal Tony Randazzo.

"I couldn't believe it when we got to town, and I saw we had them [Larry Vanover's crew] again," he said. "It was as if they were following us around."

Once again Glavine pitched well, except for one inning. Only this time, he didn't see himself as solely responsible for the bad inning. Randazzo, in his mind, played a role.

With two down in the fourth and Hunter Pence on first base, Glavine struck out Carlos Lee to end the inning. Or so he thought. Glavine was a half step off the mound before he realized Randazzo hadn't put up his arm. His next pitch could have been a strike too, only it wasn't.

"At that point, I was hot," he said. "I just thought he had missed two pitches that he shouldn't have missed. I probably lost my focus a little against [Morgan] Ensberg, even though I shouldn't have."

Ensberg doubled in two runs. Really annoyed now, Glavine gave up a triple to Chris Burke, and the Astros led 3–0. "Really, it's on me that I gave up those runs," he said. "I let the two calls bother me more than I should. Plus, it didn't help that Ensberg is a good hitter. He actually hit a pretty good pitch. But if I strike Lee out, Ensberg is leading off the next inning, not hitting with two men on with me flustered."

Once again, Glavine got past his rocky inning and managed to pitch seven innings. By the time he left, the Mets had tied the score at 3–3, but, as had become part of a pattern, they couldn't quite push their way into the lead before he left the game. Glavine ended up throwing 106 pitches, only 58 for strikes. It was classic Glavine cliff-hanging. He pitched from behind all night but only walked one batter and gave the Astros nothing after the fourth.

"In the end, I pitched well, except for a couple of pitches in the fourth," he said. "I kept us in the game, which is a starter's job. But it was still frustrating to walk away with another no-decision when I had pitched well enough to get a win most nights."

It took the Mets another ten innings after Glavine left to score again. They finally won the game 5–3 in the seventeenth inning — after five hours and nine minutes — by scoring two runs in the top of the inning. By then, Glavine was showered and dressed and was sitting in the middle of the clubhouse wearing an old Houston Oilers football helmet he had found on the floor of the equipment room.

"I tried watching in the training room, in the clubhouse, in the sauna. I tried walking away and not watching. Nothing worked. Finally, I found the Oilers helmet and put it on. We scored two runs and won."

Maybe Glavine should have worn the helmet again the next day. The Astros scored eight runs early and went on to an 8–3 win. That sent the Mets off to the All-Star break with a record of 48–39 and a two-game lead in the National League East. A year earlier, they had gone to the break 53–36 with a twelve-game lead.

"This year we're in a race," Glavine said. "As long as we understand that and don't get frustrated by the fact that we aren't going to put this thing away in August, we should be fine. This is more normal than last year."

Glavine's first half had been extremely solid. He had started nineteen times, and his record was 7–6, with an ERA of 4.36. Those numbers, though, were somewhat deceiving. He'd had two truly awful outings, but in his other sixteen starts, he had pitched to an ERA of 3.02. In fourteen of his nineteen starts, he had given up three earned runs or less, and he had pitched at least six innings in all but three of his starts.

Statistics can be manipulated to suit any argument. What was clear about Glavine's first half, though, was that he had given his team a serious chance to win most of the time he pitched. It was also clear that, with any luck at all, he would have already reached the Number That Must Not Be Named. He had a 2–1 loss, a 3–0 loss, and four no-decisions, in which he had pitched six or seven innings and given up one, two, or three runs. If he had won half of those games, the Number Could Already Have Been Named — and celebrated.

"Yeah, but that's baseball," Glavine said. "This has been one of those years where I haven't really stolen any wins yet, so you have to figure that will come in the second half. What's good is that, overall, I've pitched well. I don't feel as if I've really gotten on a roll yet. It's been two good starts, then a mediocre one, then a decent one, with a few bad ones thrown in along the way. I still feel as if there's a hot streak in me." He smiled. "I guess you could say the same for the whole team. Maybe once I get this thing done, we'll all loosen up a little bit."

Tight is a relative word. While the Mets were feeling a bit baffled by their first half, the Yankees were simply frustrated. They managed to win three of their last four games before the break, even taking two of three from the dreaded Angels, but were still 42–43 heading into their three days off. They were ten games behind the Red Sox and eight and a half games behind the Indians for the wild card. It was the first time since Joe Torre had been the manager that the team had been under .500 going into the All-Star game.

"It's all very simple," Mussina said. "We've had injuries, which haven't helped at all. But we also haven't played good baseball. If we continue to play this way in the second half, we're in serious trouble. If we play like we know we can play, then we've got a chance."

Mussina would pitch fourth when the second half began, behind Pettitte, Clemens, and Wang. That would mean he would go eleven days between starts. "Not ideal," he said. "But that's the way it is. My job is to win more than four games in half a season. Period."

22

Good News, Bad News

LIKE ALL THINGS IN BASEBALL, the traditions that are associated with the All-Star break aren't what they used to be. This is an era, it is worth remembering, when the October Classic can end in November. It is an era when corporate names are plastered all over stadiums, often until the corporation is in bankruptcy. (Anyone remember Enron Field?) It is also an era when teams not only no longer play doubleheaders on Memorial Day, the Fourth of July, and Labor Day, but in some cases do not play on those holidays at all.

And, it is an era when the three-day All-Star break is four days for a lot of teams. In fact, in 2007, on the traditional post-All-Star break start-up Thursday, only twelve of the thirty teams were scheduled to play.

Two of those twelve teams were the Mets and the Yankees. Both returned from the break on the traditional Thursday, the Yankees traveling to Tampa Bay, while the Mets hosted the Cincinnati Reds.

The first day back after the All-Star break is usually a happy one for most teams. The three or four days off gives everyone a burst of energy. There is a sense of starting again, that a bad first half can be put behind a team or a player. John Sterling, the Yankees radio play-by-play man, put it concisely when he opened the pregame show from Tampa by saying, "It's time for the players on this team to start playing like the numbers on the back of their bubblegum cards."

The Yankees were the New York team in a deep hole, but it was the Mets who were acting as if they were in trouble. During the break, general manager Omar Minaya decided to shake up Willie Randolph's coaching staff. He had not been happy with the impatient approach of a number of the Mets' hitters during the 15–21 run that had led to the break.

So, he fired hitting coach Rick Down, a close friend of Randolph's, dating back to their days together with the Yankees. He replaced Down on the coaching staff with Rickey Henderson and then announced it would not be decided until the second day of the Reds series whether Henderson or Howard Johnson would be the hitting coach.

In the end, Johnson was given the hitters, and Henderson was assigned to Johnson's old spot at first base. If nothing else, the maneuvering raised some eyebrows in the clubhouse.

"We are in first place, aren't we?" said Glavine, whose day-to-day life was completely unaffected by the changes. "Usually, if you make changes like that in season, it's because the team isn't performing."

Bringing Henderson into the clubhouse on a daily basis had to be considered a gamble. On one hand, he was the greatest base stealer in baseball history and the most productive leadoff hitter in history. On the other hand, he had always been, to put it gently, an enigmatic clubhouse presence with all the various teams he had played on, including the Mets. Once, he had put down tape around his locker and declared the area inside the tape off-limits to the media. He was one of the first great third-person talkers. During card games in the clubhouse he would often say, "Rickey takes three." And frequently he had trouble remembering team-mates' names. Often he would refer to them by position or skill: "Hey, weak-hitting shortstop, what time is BP today?"

He had also been playing cards in the clubhouse during extra innings of a Mets playoff loss to the Braves in 1999, something most of the players in the 2007 clubhouse might not know about, but certainly something all Met fans and anyone with any connection to the team remembered.

No one was sure which Rickey would show up as a coach: the Rickey who could help make Jose Reyes even better, who could help everyone in the clubhouse run the bases better and hit better, or the Rickey who might encourage laziness and showboating.

Which brought up the subject of the other new arrival: Lastings Milledge had been called back up from Triple-A. Milledge was, arguably, the Mets' most talented young player. At twenty-two he had speed and power and could be spectacular at the plate and in the outfield. But he had proven himself remarkably immature a year earlier when called up, showboating constantly, and clearly having no idea what Glavine or Mussina meant when they said that being in the big leagues did not make you a big leaguer.

When he bridled at the tradition of rookies being forced to wear costumes for a late-season road trip—every team does it—Billy Wagner hung a large sign in his locker that said "Know Your Place, Rook."

The veterans on the team were less than amused with Milledge's notion that being part of rookie hazing was beneath him. "Actually, we were pretty mild with the rookies that year," Glavine said. "We only made them wear superhero costumes. It's been a lot worse in the past. I can remember the year my brother came up in September, they all had to wear belly-dancer-type costumes. Mike was dressed like Jeannie from *I Dream of Jeannie,* and we dropped all of them off two blocks from the hotel in Chicago and made them walk the rest of the way dressed in their outfits. Now *that* might have been something to complain about. Not this."

Now, Milledge was back, saying he had learned lessons from a year ago and just wanted to help the team. How that would work out with Henderson as one of his coaches was the subject of a good deal of speculation inside the clubhouse.

"I guess," Glavine said, "we'll just have to wait and see what we see."

Actually, what he should have said, given the changes on the team, was "Tom will just have to wait and see what Tom sees with Hall of Fame first-base coach and rookie outfielder."

GLAVINE WOULD PITCH third to start the second half, Rick Peterson thinking a couple of extra days off couldn't hurt. "It's a good idea," Glavine said. "To come back after not picking up a ball for three days and pitch has never worked that well for me. This way I get in the bullpen before I pitch, and I should be ready to go."

He was more than ready on a sweltering Saturday night after the teams had split the first two games of the series. The game started late because of ceremonies honoring Ralph Kiner, and a rain delay, but it didn't bother Glavine. He had none of his normal first-inning troubles, getting the Reds one-two-three on only twelve pitches. The second didn't start nearly as well: second baseman Brandon Phillips, who was having a career year, blasted a 2–2 fastball that drifted too close to the plate over the right-center-field fence, and the Reds led 1–0.

Glavine was superb after the Phillips home run. He didn't give up another hit until the seventh inning, a ground single by Ken Griffey Jr., and he had the Reds off-balance. He struck out five and made it look easy most of the night.

There was only one problem: Matt Belisle was pitching just as well. The Mets had a great chance in the third when they got three hits, but they failed to score because Reyes was thrown out stealing, and Carlos Delgado, still struggling with a .243 batting average, hit a fly ball to left, with two on and two out. In the sixth, the Mets finally tied the game at 1–1 when David Wright singled and stole second, then scored on a two-out Shawn Green single.

It stayed that way until the eighth. Glavine got the side in order and wondered if he might get to pitch the ninth. He had thrown 104 pitches, but it was a humid evening. "Great job," Peterson said when he walked into the dugout, offering his hand. Glavine knew that meant he wouldn't pitch the ninth. He understood, given the conditions and his pitch count, but he was disappointed. He had pitched his best game of the season, and now, unless the Mets could score in the bottom of the eighth, it would only produce another no-decision.

It looked like that was exactly what was going to happen when Mike Stanton, the ex-Met and ex-Yankee (who would be one of the players named in the Mitchell Report in December), quickly got the first two outs of the inning. The no-decision looked like an absolute certainty when Green hit a slicing drive to left field that most outfielders would have caught without too much trouble.

But Adam Dunn isn't just any outfielder. He got a bad break on the ball, lumbered over toward the line, and finally slid and hoped it might hit his glove as he was going down. It short hopped off of him while Green raced to second, with what had to be scored a double, simply because Dunn spent so much time circling it that in the end he had little chance to make the catch.

The reprieve brought Milledge to the plate. He had been given the left-field job after being recalled because Moises Alou was still on the disabled list. Milledge was two for eleven since his return, but he jumped on Stanton's first pitch and lined it cleanly into center field. Green scored to make it 2–1, and suddenly Glavine and the other veterans didn't think Milledge was that bad a guy after all.

Billy Wagner came in to pitch a one-two-three ninth, and, in what seemed like the blink of an eye, Glavine had an unlikely win, even though he had pitched brilliantly. "That's one where you walk out and feel like you might have stolen one," he said. "I pitched well, but with two outs and nobody on in the eighth, it certainly doesn't look like I have much chance to get a win."

Someone among the writers gathered around Glavine's locker after the game pointed out that he was now only two wins away from three hundred. Glavine winced. "Don't say it too loud," he said.

It was getting tougher and tougher not to.

THE NEXT AFTERNOON IN TAMPA, Mike Mussina was looking for career-win number 243, not a sexy number but an impressive one nonetheless.

The Yankees had won two of the first three games against the Devil Rays to get to .500 at 44–44, but no one was jumping up and down with excitement about that. The Rays were, arguably, the worst expansion team in baseball history. As bad as the Mets had been their first seven years, they had won a World Series in their eighth year. The Angels had needed forty-one years to win a World Series but had good teams along the way. The Astros had never won a World Series and hadn't played in one until their forty-fourth season but had plenty of playoff teams through the years.

The Rays had never finished at .500 since coming into existence in 1998. In fact, they had never won more than seventy games. And they played in what might have been the worst indoor ballpark ever created—worse even than the Kingdome in Seattle, best described by Sparky Anderson, who said, "It's the only place I've ever been where it is always overcast indoors."

Tropicana Field—another lovely corporate name—was even worse. It wasn't so much overcast as dark. Add in the fact that the team was always awful, and you hardly had a festive atmosphere. As in Baltimore, large chunks of the crowd were Yankees fans, the difference being that Camden Yards was a wonderful place to watch bad baseball, as opposed to "The Trop," which was a bad place to watch bad baseball.

The Rays had improved their hitting in 2007. They could score runs. They simply couldn't stop anyone from scoring, which was why they were their usual 35–55.

Mussina didn't mind coming to Tampa. For one thing, he got to sleep in the house he owned there. For another, he knew the chances that his team would score for him against the Rays' pitching staff were pretty good. His mound opponent was one Edwin Jackson, who came into the game with an ERA of 7.35. Naturally, though, at least in Mussina's mind, Jackson spent the first four innings pitching like Johan Santana, the Yankees going down quickly and quietly.

In the meantime, Mussina was struggling again: with his stuff, with his location, and with home-plate umpire C.B. Bucknor, another of the umpires hired during the 1999 purge, whose reputation for calling balls and strikes was, to put it politely, not good.

Mussina gave up two runs in the first and was instantly in trouble in the second, giving up a single to Ty Wigginton and a bunt hit to former Yankee catching prospect Dioner Navarro. Then he settled down and got Akinori Iwamura to pop to Rodriguez and thought he had Carl Crawford struck out on a 2–2 slider.

Bucknor called it ball three. Mussina already felt squeezed, and that call, on what Joe Torre calls "a bastard pitch"—because there's just no way to hit the bastard, really—made Mussina angry. Crawford grounded the next pitch into right field for an RBI single, and Mussina was off the mound, halfway to home plate, screaming at Bucknor almost as soon as the ball found the hole. This from someone who most umpires say never shows anger, except occasionally in his body language.

"That changes as you get older," Mussina said. "When you're older and you just aren't as good as you used to be and you know it, a guy misses a pitch like that and you find yourself thinking, 'I'll never throw this next pitch that well, and I'll bet this is going to cause a problem.'"

"I'm not even sure it's a conscious thought, but it's definitely there rolling around in your mind somewhere. When Crawford gets that hit to drive in a run when I had him struck out, I just lost it for a minute."

The very best umpires know when they've missed a call and will usually let a player vent for at least a moment afterward. Most umpires aren't that good, Bucknor included. And all of them hate being shown up. When Mussina came down off the mound yelling at Bucknor, Bucknor took off his mask and started walking toward Mussina. In seventeen major league seasons, Mussina has never been ejected from a game. This had that potential.

Fortunately, Nieves jumped in between his pitcher and the umpire. He was hot too, but he figured if someone was going to get ejected, better him than Mussina. His quick thinking gave Torre time to come out and take over the argument.

"It was over pretty quickly," Mussina said. "I was hot, really hot. But Wil and Joe got in there, and I realized that yelling at Bucknor wasn't going to make him get the call right. So, I went back to the mound and told myself it was three-nothing, and I needed to keep it there, that we were bound to score some runs sooner or later."

He did hold them there, although it wasn't easy. "The good news was they got a lot of hits off me [eleven], but they all ended up being singles," Mussina said. "I wasn't good, that's for sure, but I managed to hang in there and scratch my way through six innings."

He actually left with the lead because the Yankees finally got Jackson for four runs in the fifth, which put them ahead 4–3. Technically, Mussina produced a "quality start"—six innings pitched, three runs or fewer allowed. But it was nothing short of a miracle that the Rays had only three runs when he left.

The next day Mark Mussina called his older brother. "That may have been the worst quality start in the history of baseball," he told him.

"I wasn't great, that's for sure," Mike responded. "But I got through six because all the hits I gave up were singles."

"No," Mark said. "You got through six because they don't know how to run the bases. Think about it: you faced twenty-seven hitters and got fourteen guys out."

He was right. Mussina had given up eleven hits and walked two. In addition to three runners being thrown out on the bases, he had gotten B.J. Upton to ground into a double play in the fifth. That meant almost half the hitters he had faced had reached base.

"You could just see that he was struggling again," Mark said. "It worried me. He was so concerned with not giving up home runs that he wasn't coming inside *at all*. You can't pitch that way. Batters start diving over the plate, knowing the pitcher isn't going to drive them back at all. They have no fear of the inside pitch. I didn't say what I said to him to put him down or to make him mad, just to try to make him understand that what he was doing wasn't working."

Mussina understood. He didn't get the win that day because Ron Villone came in to relieve in the seventh and instantly gave up a two-run homer to Carlos Pena (another ex-Yankee farmhand, who would finish the season with 121 RBI) to put the Rays back in front. The Yankees rallied again to win 7–6, but Mussina ended up with a no-decision.

"Which is probably what I deserved that day," he said. "I hung in there, I got some outs when I had to, but I certainly wouldn't ever claim I pitched well or deserved a win that day."

Mussina had hoped the start in Tampa would be a springboard to getting the second half off to a good start. The team had won three of four and was over .500 at 45–44. But Mussina still had just four wins.

The Yankees went home from Tampa and promptly won the first three games of a four-game series against the Blue Jays, before Wang blew a 2–0 lead late in the finale, allowing Toronto to salvage the game 3–2. Still, with Tampa Bay coming to New

York for a four-game series, there was a strong sense in the club-house that the team was getting on a roll. They were now 6–2 since the All-Star break, and they had won nine of the last twelve.

The opener against Tampa Bay was the same matchup as the last game in Tampa five days earlier: Jackson versus Mussina. Once again, it was not unreasonable to think the Yankees would score early and often.

And, once again, it didn't happen that way.

In fact, Jackson completely shut down the Yankees over six innings, allowing just four hits before turning the game over to the bullpen. By then, the Rays had a 9–0 lead because Mussina and his bullpen had completely melted down.

It started innocently enough. Mussina gave up a first-inning single to Carl Crawford but struck out the side, hitting 90 with several pitches. "My velocity was good," he said. "My arm felt good. I felt fine warming up in the bullpen. There were really no warning signs."

He pitched a one-two-three second. Then came the third. Greg Norton led off with a single, and Navarro doubled to put men on second and third. Iwamura hit a sacrifice fly to left to score Norton, making it 1–0. "At that moment, I can't even tell you why I felt like I'd lost the game," Mussina said. "It didn't make sense. It was one-nothing. I just felt like we weren't going to score any runs."

He gave up an RBI single to Crawford to make it 2–0. Guidry trotted to the mound. It was strictly an "I'm here to give you a breather" visit. Mussina listened, sort of, while Guidry talked. Guidry wasn't trying to tell him anything, he was just waiting for plate umpire Scott Barry to come out and shoo him back to the dugout.

B.J. Upton stepped in. Crawford led from first. He had already stolen one base in the game, and Mussina didn't want to let him get into scoring position. "I was thinking about him more than the pitch," he said. "When I threw the pitch, it was a fastball right down the middle."

Any major league hitter can hit a fastball down the middle a long way, especially one at 87 miles per hour. Upton, a rapidly improving young hitter, proved that in spades. He hit a rocket that still appeared to be climbing when it finally crashed down three rows deep in the upper deck in left field. Players frequently reach Yankee Stadium's upper deck in right field, where it is only 314 feet to the seats in the lower deck, and the upper deck is almost directly overhead. In left field it is 365 feet, and the upper deck doesn't hang as far over the lower deck as it does in right field. It takes a mammoth blast to reach it.

"If you're going to give one up, it might just as well go in the upper deck," Mussina said, able to joke about the shot later — much later. "I told people Gator [Guidry] came out and said to me, 'Why don't you throw one down the middle and see how far this guy can hit it?' I certainly found out."

Upton's moonshot made it 4–0. Mussina didn't give up any more runs in the inning, but he walked the bases loaded before getting the last out on a ground ball to second by Norton, the tenth man to bat. Mussina had thrown forty-six pitches in the inning, which is half a game for some pitchers. It may not have been the worst inning of his career, but it had to be one of the longest.

"After Upton's shot, he didn't want to throw a strike," Joe Torre said the next day. "He was pitching scared. At the end of the inning, I just said to him, 'You have to trust your stuff more.' He goes out next inning and gets the side on eight pitches. You would hope that would tell him something."

Mussina didn't last much longer than that. He gave up doubles to Upton and Brendan Harris in the fifth, and came out, having thrown ninety-three pitches. The bullpen only made things worse, and after almost four hours the final score was 14–4.

Mussina was devastated. He'd had good nights, and he'd had

bad nights throughout the season, but this was really bad. This wasn't April, when the weather made it tough to pitch, and he wasn't coming off an injury. In fact, his arm felt as good as it had ever felt. He just couldn't get people out.

For one of the few times in his baseball career, he couldn't leave the game behind when he left the park. He was brooding. Usually the silence of the car relaxed him, allowed him to unwind. He always made a point of putting himself into "PG" mode before he got home, leaving the language of the clubhouse behind him by the time he walked in the front door.

"The only good thing was that it was a fast turnaround," he said the next morning. "It was midnight when I got home, and I had to get up and leave right away. My family really didn't need to be exposed to me right at that moment.

"I can leave physical things behind me, that's not a problem. But when it's mental, that's a lot harder. If you need to work on your mechanics in some way, you come to the park, work on them in the pen or something, and go home. If you're injured, you know what you have to do that day in terms of rehab or getting your arm ready to pitch again, and that's it, you go home.

"But when it's mental, you can't escape it. You can be playing with your kids, and you think about it. You can be in a restaurant with friends or lying in bed, and you think about it. It's just not any fun."

The Yankees and Devil Rays had one of those delightful day-night doubleheaders on Saturday, the second game making up the rained-out game from the first week of the season that had pushed Mussina's first start back a day, getting the season off on the wrong foot—a place where it had stayed for most of four months.

Mussina walked into the clubhouse the next morning looking as if a dark cloud was right behind him. A local reporter, someone he liked, who was working on a Cal Ripken story for the following weekend to coincide with Ripken's induction into the Hall of

Fame, asked Mussina if he could ask him a couple of questions about his old teammate.

Mussina sighed. "You know what, I'm really sorry; I just can't do it today," he said. "I'm so pissed off now, I don't even want to talk about Cal. Maybe tomorrow; I just can't do it today. I'm really sorry. I just have to figure out a way to pitch better."

That was really what was on his mind: how to pitch better. He knew it would be a long day for the rest of the staff and that, with two games to play, both Guidry and Borzello would be tied up all day. In fact, the schedule was so busy that Chien-Ming Wang, whose day it was to throw in the bullpen, would do his throwing during the first game because there was no other free time.

"He might even have to pitch an inning," Guidry told Borzello. Both knew why: Kei Igawa was the starter. If all went well, it would be his last start, since Philip Hughes was supposed to come off the DL the following week.

While Mussina was moping around the clubhouse, Torre and general manager Brian Cashman were having one of their periodic meetings in Torre's office. One of the topics for the day was Mussina. Cashman wanted Torre to know that if he thought moving Mussina out of the starting rotation was the right thing to do, he shouldn't let seniority or salary affect that decision.

"Don't be afraid to put payroll in the bullpen if you feel that's the right thing to do," Cashman said to Torre, referring to Mussina's $11.5 million salary.

Torre understood. At that moment, though, unless Igawa suddenly became a different pitcher, there were no alternatives to Mussina. The Yankees had Wang, Clemens, Pettitte, Mussina, and—they hoped—Hughes. Joba Chamberlain was tearing up the minor leagues, but the plan was to bring him to New York to set up Mariano Rivera, since no one else had been able to fill that role. Ian Kennedy was another possibility but probably wasn't ready.

"It wasn't as if we had reached the point of 'one more bad start and we're going to yank Mike,'" Cashman said later. "He was clearly struggling, though, so I wanted to let Joe know if he thought he had to make a move it should be based only on performance."

Mussina knew none of this. All he knew was that he needed to pitch better. The thought that he might be taken out of the rotation hadn't crossed his mind. He had made 491 major league starts without ever missing a turn for anything, except an injury.

As luck would have it, Saturday was the day the Yankee bats exploded. They scored seven runs in the first game and seventeen in the second, en route to a doubleheader sweep.

Wil Nieves caught the second game that night. Jorge Posada had caught Mussina on Friday night, in part because Torre didn't want Posada to catch both games on Saturday; in part because he knew the Yankees were trying to trade to upgrade the second-string catching spot offensively; and in part because Torre knew (as did Mussina) that in key games in September and in October (if the Yankees got there), Posada was going to be the starting catcher.

"It's no big deal to me at all," Mussina said. "I've thrown to Georgey for seven years. We're fine together." He did not blame his poor performance on Posada. "I did a good job of pitching poorly all on my own," he joked.

Nieves got two hits and drove in two runs in the nightcap of the doubleheader. When he walked into the clubhouse, Torre asked if he could see him in his office. It is never good, especially for a marginal player, when the manager asks to see you.

Torre told Nieves that the Yankees had traded a minor league pitcher to the Los Angeles Angels for backup catcher Jose Molina—one of three Molina brothers catching in the big leagues. The Giants' starter was Bengie Molina, and Yadier, the youngest of the three, was the starter in St. Louis. Molina would be flying to New York the next day. Nieves would be designated for assignment, which meant he could be released or sent to the minor leagues. Since the Yankees didn't know when Molina would arrive the next day, they needed Nieves to stick around in case Molina's plane was late so they would have a catcher available if something happened to Posada. Only when Molina arrived would Nieves officially be designated.

Mussina had left the clubhouse by the time Nieves finished with Torre. He'd been told about the trade and felt bad, very bad. "It's part of the game," he said. "You see guys come and go all the time. That's one of the reasons I don't get very close to other players that often. Just look at our team. I'm in my seventh year, and there are only four guys [Jeter, Rivera, Posada, Pettitte] who have been here longer—and Andy was gone for three years and came back.

"Still, when I heard about this, I felt for Wil. We'd spent a lot of time together. We were on the same schedule. He only caught the days I pitched, so we talked a good deal in between our starts. Plus, he's just a good guy."

When Mussina arrived in the clubhouse the next day, Nieves was saying his good-byes to people, still waiting for word on when Molina would arrive. This was the baseball equivalent of being strapped into an electric chair and then being told to hang on for a few hours until the executioner arrived from out of town.

Mussina walked across the clubhouse to talk to Nieves. He thanked him for all the work they had done together and wished him luck. Mussina is not an emotional person most of the time, but he felt emotional saying good-bye to Nieves. "We didn't hug," he said. "But I wouldn't have minded if we had."

It wasn't until 1:30—shortly after the game that day had started—that Molina reached Yankee Stadium. Wil Nieves took off his uniform, picked up his things, and left the clubhouse. His nameplate was gone by the time his former teammates came back inside following their win over the Devil Rays.

Soon after saying good-bye to Nieves, Mussina went to the bullpen with Guidry and Borzello for his normal between-starts bullpen session. He threw his usual battery of pitches to Borzello, and then the three men sat down on a bench in the bullpen and talked.

Both Borzello and Guidry thought they had noticed something watching Mussina throw out of the stretch. They thought he was leaning forward just a little bit as he came set, not standing up as tall or as straight as he normally did.

The three of them stood up, and Mussina walked back onto the bullpen mound without a ball. "Pick your leg up the way you do when you're going to deliver out of the stretch, and just hold it up in the air," Guidry instructed.

Mussina went into his set position, picked his leg up, and held it in the air. After a few seconds, he could feel himself starting to fall forward—not hard, not fast, but just a little. Guidry had him do it again. Same result.

"If you're in the correct position, if you're balanced the way you need to be, you should be able to stand on one leg until you get tired," Guidry said. Guidry's a left-hander and he's fifty-six, but he can still pick his right leg up off the ground from the set position and stand there and hold a conversation for as long as he feels like talking.

Mussina, at that moment, could not. Guidry and Borzello told him to set up again in the stretch and simply stand on the mound the way he did before lifting his leg. "Stand taller," Guidry said. "Try to feel like you're standing up as straight as you possibly can."

Mussina did as he was told. They worked on getting him to stand up straight and to focus on remaining as vertical as possible once he had gone through his stretch—still dipping down low the way he always did to peek between his legs—but then remembering to stand back up straight when he came set. Only after he had gone through that ritual several times, focusing on standing straight, much the way kids at a Catholic school are taught to sit up straight, did Guidry allow him to continue his motion to the point where he lifted his leg.

"Okay, now hold it," Guidry said when Mussina's leg was up in the air again. This time Mussina was able to hold his leg up—in his case the left leg since he throws right-handed—for as long as he wanted to hold it there.

"Do it again," Guidry said.

Mussina went through the entire stretch motion, pretending to look in for a sign, dipping in, then standing up again as straight as he possibly could. Each time, he was able to stay balanced on one leg. After thirty minutes, Guidry had him throw a few pitches to Borzello. He felt better delivering the ball from the stretch than he had in a long time.

"The key was we all believed we had found something," Mussina said. "The best work I did as a pitcher that day was when I never threw a pitch or even had a ball in my hands. When you're a pitcher at this level, the tiniest thing can make a difference. [See Glavine moving a few inches over on the rubber in June.] It's often the kind of thing that no one watching the game can see. If the average person watched me pitch my next time out, I seriously doubt they noticed any difference in my delivery. But there was a difference, just a small one, and it helped me feel more balanced. I can't even swear to you that I *was* more balanced. I think I was. But the most important thing is I believed I was, and if I got results that was all that mattered.

"The important thing that day was when we walked in from the bullpen, I felt we had found something. I believed I was going to pitch better. When you're pitching badly, you need to find something—anything—that gets you thinking the next start will be better. Because you always have to believe that. If you don't, then you're in serious trouble."

His next start would be in Kansas City on Wednesday. He would know then if the nonthrowing session in the bullpen had been worth the time and effort.

23

Hardball

As poorly as Mike Mussina had pitched against the Devil Rays, he looked like Cy Young that night compared to what he had witnessed the night before on television.

He had decided to stay up to see a few innings of Tom Glavine's start against the Dodgers in Los Angeles. Even though Glavine and Mussina didn't know each other well — and in spite of whatever Glavine may or may not have said about Mussina's contract in 1997 — there was a great deal of mutual respect between the two of them. Mussina was very much rooting for Glavine to get to three hundred wins as quickly as possible.

"I still remember when Roger [Clemens] was going through it," he said. "Every outing was a big deal, a media circus, especially after he got to two ninety-nine. I think it took him four tries before he got it, and he had this entire troop of friends and family following him around the country. I remember thinking he was going for one of the great milestones you can reach in baseball, and it was torture for him. I hope it isn't that way for Tom."

Most baseball players are night owls because of the hours they keep during the season. Since most games are played at night — the Yankees had fifty-two scheduled day games on their 162-game schedule — most don't get to bed until after midnight, whether at home or on the road, and many stay up considerably later than that since they typically aren't due at their job—the ballpark—until three o'clock the next day.

Mussina was single when he first got to the big leagues and would go out after games fairly often. Marriage, kids, and age have changed that. "For one thing, you get to a point where you don't want to wake up in the morning feeling lousy," he said. "Then, when you have kids at home, you want to get to bed so you can see them in the morning. I don't really go out on the road at all anymore."

In fact, according to Mike Borzello, there's nothing Mussina likes more than going straight to his hotel room, shutting the door, and either going to sleep or reading himself to sleep. "He never even turns on the TV," Borzello said.

"Sometimes I turn on the TV," Mussina said. "But not all that often."

On Thursday night, July 19, Mussina was home preparing for his start the next night against Tampa Bay. With the Mets not playing until ten, his kids were in bed by the time the game started.

"I didn't watch for long," he said the next day.

The pitching matchup certainly appeared to be a good one: Glavine versus Derek Lowe, the Dodgers' veteran lefty, who still had one of the better sinkers in the game. The Mets had started their weeklong West Coast swing by losing two of three in San Diego. They still led the division by two and a half games when they arrived in Los Angeles to play four games against the Dodgers.

Glavine, coming off his great performance in New York against the Reds, was brimming with confidence, thinking he was about to get on the run he had been waiting for all year. If he could win in L.A., he would get his first shot at the Number the following Wednesday, at home against the always-awful Pittsburgh Pirates. It was, potentially, an ideal setup: the chance to, as he would say, "do what I'm trying to do" in front of a home crowd. It would also be a lot easier logistically to go for the win at home since the plan was for about thirty family members and close friends to be on hand.

Going for 299 in L.A., the only family members in the ballpark were Chris and their two youngest sons, Peyton and Mason. The boys enjoyed Los Angeles and had come out for the long weekend to see some shows and to watch their dad pitch.

The evening started wonderfully. Glavine felt good warming up, and he had always pitched well in Los Angeles. Most people in the National League thought the Dodger Stadium mound was a tad higher than the standard ten inches, perhaps because the Dodgers were always a pitching-oriented team. True or untrue, Glavine usually felt very comfortable on the mound there.

As if they understood how important it would be to Glavine to get a win, the Mets bombed L.A. starter Derek Lowe for six runs in the first inning. When Glavine came up to bat in the inning, Ron Darling commented on the Mets broadcast that "there aren't a lot of feelings better for a pitcher than coming up to bat before you've thrown a pitch."

Glavine was certainly happy to have the runs. But he actually felt a bit queasy going to the mound in the bottom of the first, up 6–0. "There's a tendency to overthink," he said. "If it's nothing-nothing or if you're at home, you have this plan on how you want to pitch, and you aren't thinking score at all. You get that big a lead, you have to say to yourself, 'Don't change the plan; pitch like you would normally pitch.' Of course the minute you do that, you aren't thinking the way you normally think."

Glavine quickly gave two runs back, and it might have been more if Jeff Kent hadn't been thrown out at third on Luis Gonzales's two-RBI single, which made the score 6–2. After Matt Kemp homered for the Dodgers with one on in the bottom of the second inning, it was 6–4.

What's more, Glavine had already thrown fifty-two pitches, a good pitch count for four innings, an okay pitch count for three innings, a horrific pitch count for two innings. "At that point, my thought process was all messed up," he said. "I was thinking, 'Just get through five with the lead, and maybe I can get the win.' Not exactly a positive attitude."

He felt better after the top of the third when the Mets tacked on three more runs. Glavine was in the middle of the rally, drawing a walk against Lowe—who looked shell-shocked by that point—and scoring the Mets' eighth run. He had a comfortable 9–4 lead going out to pitch the third and reminded himself that he just needed to throw strikes and let his fielders do the rest.

"On paper," he said later, "it was a good thought."

It lasted one pitch: Kent, leading off, hit Glavine's first pitch (a strike, no doubt) into the pavilion in left-center field to make it 9–5. While Kent was trotting around the bases, Rick Peterson was on the bullpen phone getting Aaron Sele up. No one wanted to see Glavine come out of a game with nine runs already on the board, but, unlike a year ago in Atlanta, the Mets were in a serious pennant race, and Willie Randolph had to think first and foremost about winning the game.

"I saw Aaron get up," Glavine said. "I understood. I knew I was on thin ice if I didn't start getting outs."

He didn't. Gonzales singled. Then Nomar Garciaparra, once the hero of Boston but a forgotten man there since 2004, also singled. Paul Lo Duca came out to the mound to give Glavine a pep talk that both men knew was nothing more than a stalling tactic to give Sele more time to get warm. "At that point, I figured I was no more than two hitters away from getting yanked," he said. "Maybe less."

It was less. James Loney singled to load the bases, and Randolph had no choice. The tying run was coming to the plate; Glavine had now thrown sixty-eight pitches and retired six batters out of sixteen.

Glavine felt slightly sick to his stomach. Watching at home on

TV, Mussina felt his pain. "As a pitcher, that's just about your worst nightmare," he said. "Your team puts up a lot of runs for you, and you just can't get anybody out. You feel helpless. You find yourself thinking, 'Exactly when did I forget how to pitch?'"

As embarrassed as he felt, Glavine stayed in the dugout for the rest of the inning, the way he always did when taken out of a game, even though he wanted to run into the clubhouse and hide. Sele did a good job holding the Dodgers to one run after taking over in a bases-loaded, no-out jam. When the inning ended, Glavine sat in the dugout as if unable to move because he was still stunned by what had happened: two innings plus three batters; six runs (all earned); ten hits, two of them home runs; and one walk. His ERA for the season jumped from 4.15 to 4.51.

"It happens to every pitcher at some point but that wasn't a point where I expected it and certainly not one where it was easy to take," Glavine said. "But you don't really have a choice. I had to start thinking about how to get better for my next start."

Shortly after he arrived in the clubhouse, he received a text message from Chris, who was sitting in the stands with the boys. "Why couldn't Willie have given you another couple of batters?" she wrote.

Glavine smiled. "Because," he wrote back, "there was absolutely no evidence I was going to get anyone out between now and midnight."

It wasn't quite eight o'clock in Los Angeles. Glavine knew he probably wasn't exaggerating by much.

THE METS HELD ON THAT NIGHT to win 13–9 and took three of four in Los Angeles, including a satisfying come-from-behind 5–4 win in ten innings in the getaway game on Sunday. They flew home and had an off-day before the Pittsburgh series, meaning Glavine got to stew about his L.A. performance for an extra day since this was one of those times when Peterson had pushed him back a day in order to give him a breather.

"The one thing I wasn't after the L.A. game was tired," he said, laughing, as he got ready to face the Pirates in the middle game of three at Shea.

The Pirates were one of baseball's sadder stories, a franchise with a great history that had not had a winning season since 1992, when they had won the last of three consecutive NL East titles under Jim Leyland. Barry Bonds, who weighed less than two hundred pounds at the time, had left for San Francisco after that season, and Leyland had left a couple of years after that. Little had gone right since then. The Pirates, even with a gorgeous new ballpark, had become the classic, poorly run small-market team. They kept changing general managers and managers with no noticeable effect. They arrived in New York with a record of 41–56 on their way to firing yet another GM and manager by season's end.

The one thing the Pirates did have going for them, at least for the long-term, were some good young pitchers: Ian Snell, Paul Maholm, and Tom Gorzelanny had all flashed potential early in their big league careers. All three of them were twenty-five, and Maholm and Gorzelanny were lefties who agreed that their role model — since neither threw very hard — was Tom Glavine.

"I grew up in Massachusetts, so I was always aware of him, even when I was little," said Maholm, who had been five years old when Glavine first reached the majors. "Just watching him pitch made me want to be a pitcher. He's always so in control of things, handles himself so well. I'm not sure how you could have a better role model, especially if you're a lefty, than that."

Gorzelanny hadn't grown up in Massachusetts, but he felt pretty much the same way. It was a thrill for him to match up against Glavine on a comfortable July night. His numbers for 2007 were actually better than Glavine's: playing on a bad team, he had a record of 9–5 and an excellent 3.20 ERA.

Glavine didn't like to think about major league pitchers who had been five years old when he got to Atlanta, but he was far more concerned with bouncing back from the debacle in L.A.

Maybe it was nerves, maybe it was the presence of Tony Randazzo behind the plate (the Mets were beginning to feel as if this crew was permanently assigned to them), or maybe it was just the memories of all the shots he had given up in L.A., but Glavine started the night unable to find the plate.

After leadoff hitter Nate McLouth struck out, Glavine promptly walked the next three hitters: Freddy Sanchez, Adam LaRoche, and Jason Bay. The little voice in Glavine's head was getting louder and louder: *Here we go again.*

But an ex-teammate bailed him out. Xavier Nady, who had been traded to Pittsburgh in the deal that had brought Oliver Perez to New York, hit a perfect double-play ground ball to shortstop. Jose Reyes flipped to Damion Easley, who threw on to Carlos Delgado, and just like that Glavine was out of the inning.

As soon as the ball settled in Delgado's glove, Glavine pumped his fist, both relieved and happy.

"That might be the first time in my career I've pumped my fist after getting the side in the first inning," he said. "It was just such a relief because it looked like I was about to get off to a really bad start and then—bang!—I'm out of it. When I pumped my fist, I kind of caught myself and said, 'Whoa there, this *is* just the first inning.' But I guess it shows how tightly wound I was right then."

The Mets soon got him another early lead. After Lastings Milledge had doubled, both David Wright and Delgado walked. Gorzelanny was visibly unhappy with Randazzo's strike zone and got flustered. He gave up a two-run double down the left-field line to Lo Duca. Two more singles scored him, and the Mets were up 3–0.

This time having a lead seemed to relax Glavine. "For whatever reason, it does make a difference having an inning under your belt," he said. "You're into the rhythm of the game; you've set up the way you want to pitch. You don't walk out there thinking, 'Oh God, don't blow this lead.' You just pitch."

He pitched well, and the Mets extended the lead to 6–0 in the third, Lo Duca keying the inning with another two-run double. Before the inning was over, manager Jim Tracy had been ejected, arguing about a play in the outfield but clearly far more upset about balls and strikes than about Larry Vanover calling a ball Shawn Green had hit a trap (the Pirates still got an out on a force play) instead of a catch.

All Glavine knew was that he was up six runs and cruising. Until the fifth, when McLouth singled with one out, and Sanchez—the National League batting champion in 2006—reached out and pushed a double down the right-field line. Glavine stood on the mound cursing after that one. "I threw such a good pitch," he said. "I still don't know how he managed to turn it into a hit." LaRoche drove in a run with a ground ball out, and then Glavine got careless, leaving a fastball up to Jason Bay, who drove it into the left-field bullpen. Suddenly, 6–0 on cruise control had become 6–3, still one out short of the five innings needed by a starter to qualify for a win.

Nady promptly doubled to right—better then than in the first inning—and Glavine was wondering if he was ever going to get the third out. "It wasn't as if I panicked or I thought Willie was going to come get me," he said. "The only ball hit really hard was the home run. But still, I was standing there thinking that this had gone from easy to hard very quickly." He smiled. "I was picturing Chris in the stands staring at the dugout, ready to tackle Willie if he happened to come out of there."

It never got to that. Glavine got Ryan Doumit to tap back to the mound to end the inning. He hung in for one more inning and left, having thrown 112 pitches, pretty close to the maximum Peterson would allow him to throw. He hadn't walked anyone after the first, but he had still thrown only sixty-six strikes. Most pitchers would prefer a ball-strike ratio of at least two to one.

Glavine was comfortable with that number being lower, but when it backed toward fifty-fifty he got nervous, if only because it pushed his pitch count so high he couldn't get past the sixth inning. This had been one of those nights, meaning he had to depend on the bullpen to get the last nine outs.

Aaron Heilman and Billy Wagner made it look easy. Heilman, who thought of himself as a starting pitcher doing time as a setup man, was superb, retiring all six Pirates he faced. Wagner was almost as good, hitting McLouth with a pitch with two outs in the ninth, before ending the game by getting Sanchez to fly to Milledge. The final was 6–3.

It hadn't been pretty, but it was good enough. Glavine was 9–6 on the season, and 299–197 for his career. "Well," he said afterward. "Now it's here. At least I know I'll get a chance to walk out there and try to get this done."

No one had to ask him what it was he was trying to get done. At that moment, all of baseball was fully aware of it.

THE FIRST TRY — the only try, Glavine hoped — would come in Milwaukee. As Glavine had suspected, logistics were a bigger headache than anything else. In all, thirty people would be coming to the game as part of Team Glavine, including his parents; his sister and brother-in-law (and their three kids); his two brothers; Chris and all four of the kids; neighbors from Billerica and Atlanta; and a couple of old friends from the Braves. They would fly in from various locations around the country and be seated behind the Mets dugout on the third-base side of Miller Park.

"Had to pay for all the tickets myself," Glavine said. "God-damn IRS."

The Internal Revenue Service had changed the law several years ago on the number of comp tickets teams were allowed to give to their players, apparently because comped tickets couldn't be taxed. Glavine could afford the tickets, but he couldn't resist the half-joking swipe at the government.

Glavine tried to lie as low as he could in the days between starts, but it was close to impossible. On Friday, before the Mets began a series at home with the Washington Nationals, he had a press conference, the point being to get as many of the "three hundred" questions out of the way as possible in one fell swoop. Of course, that didn't keep reporters from stopping by his locker for "one question," and Glavine, being Glavine, wasn't about to pull the "I already talked about that in the press conference" line on them. The Mets split four games with the Nationals and flew to Milwaukee, still leading the division by three and a half games over the red-hot Phillies and by four and a half over the not-so-hot Braves. The Brewers were also in first place, clinging to a one-game lead over the Cubs, after it had looked early in the season as if they might run away with the National League Central. They were now 57–49 and not running away with anything.

Milwaukee is a town with a decidedly mixed baseball history. When the Braves first moved there from Boston in 1953, the place went baseball mad, aided by the presence of superstars Henry Aaron and Eddie Matthews. The Braves won the World Series in 1957 and lost it in seven games to the Yankees a year later. Seven years later, they were gone, spirited off to Atlanta after attendance had fallen as the team dropped in the standings. Four years later, the expansion Seattle Pilots, having spent one year in what had been a minor league ballpark, were bought by a group led by car salesman Alan (Bud) Selig and moved to Milwaukee just prior to the start of the 1970 season.

The Brewers had been bad a lot more than they had been good in their thirty-eight seasons in Milwaukee. They had won the American League pennant in 1982 but had not been in the playoffs since. They had been moved to the National League in order to accommodate the addition of the Tampa Bay Devil Rays and the Colorado Rockies as expansion teams in 1998.

But now, after years of wandering in the depths of the NL Central, the Brewers were legitimate contenders. Doug Melvin, who had scouted Mike Mussina years ago for the Baltimore Orioles, was the general manager. Ned Yost, who had first told Tom Glavine he needed another breaking pitch when he was in Double-A ball, was the manager. The star of the team was young slugger Prince Fielder, the son of former American League MVP Cecil Fielder.

The Brewers were not all that concerned about Glavine's quest for three hundred. When Ned Yost was leaving for the ballpark on Tuesday, his wife, who had known Glavine well during the days when Yost had been a coach in Atlanta, said to him, "Gee, I really hope Tom can get three hundred tonight."

"What?" Yost answered. "We're in a pennant race. We need to win every game. You can't root for him."

"Not even for one night?" she replied, sending her husband off to the park in a semihuff.

In both clubhouses there was considerably more media than would be normal for a Tuesday-night game at the end of July, even with both teams in pennant contention. It could have been far worse, but many in the national baseball media were trailing Barry Bonds, who was one home run short of Henry Aaron's record. What's more, a lot of the New York media had stayed back in the Bronx because Alex Rodriguez was one home run shy of five hundred.

"If Bridget Moynahan has her baby tonight, I might win three hundred and only make the agate," Glavine said, relaxing with his feet up in his locker.

Moynahan was the actress who was due to give birth to New England Patriots quarterback Tom Brady's child at any minute. Glavine didn't really mind the idea that he wasn't getting as much attention as he might have if not for Bonds, A-Rod, and, well, Moynahan. "It's kind of weird," he said. "I'm glad right now there aren't more people here. But if I get it, I'll probably be saying 'Where is everybody?'"

There were a number of people in the clubhouse — notably the other pitchers — who didn't think Glavine was getting the attention he deserved. Some of that stemmed from a comment Willie Randolph had made after Glavine had won number 299 the previous week.

"It's not as big a deal in the clubhouse as it is to you guys," Randolph had said to the media. "I really don't think any of our guys are talking about it very much."

Randolph has a tendency to try to low-key things. If the media thinks something is really big, he will go out of his way to tell them that it's not. This time, though, he had said something that shocked — and annoyed — some of his players.

"What is he thinking?" asked Billy Wagner. "Not talking about it? We have been talking about it all year. This is something we all want for Tom, and we all want to feel we're a part of it when he gets it. How can you say this number isn't a big deal? How many guys have done it in history — twenty-two? Plus, he might be the *last* three hundred–game winner for a very long time."

That was very possible. Roger Clemens was first in wins among active pitchers, and Greg Maddux was next, followed by Glavine. After Glavine came Randy Johnson, who was stuck on 284 and was about to undergo back surgery at the age of forty-four. Whether he would ever pitch again, much less be capable of winning sixteen more games, was a serious question mark. Next in line after Johnson? Michael Cole Mussina, who that night was going after win 245. All the other pitchers with more than two hundred wins were a long way from three hundred, and most were late in their careers: pitchers like Jamie Moyer, Kenny Rogers, and Pedro Martinez.

In fact, the argument can be made that a pitcher winning three hundred games is a far more significant achievement in this day and age than a hitter reaching five hundred home runs. Once, those were two of the numbers — along with three thousand hits — that guaranteed entry to the Hall of Fame. Now, with smaller ballparks, juiced baseballs, and juiced players, five hundred home runs isn't the iconic number it once was.

"I'm not even sure I would vote for someone with six hundred [homers]," Glavine said. "It doesn't have the same meaning."

At the same time, getting to three hundred wins has become more difficult. Pitchers aren't allowed to pitch as deep into games as they once did because they are kept on such strict pitch counts. On the day that Tom Seaver won his three hundredth game, he was forty years old and threw 146 pitches.

Because home runs have gone up—although not so much since steroid testing came to baseball—and the number of innings starters pitch has gone down, getting wins is tougher. "You're certainly far more dependent on your bullpen," Glavine said. "I would like to think whenever I get there, I'll pitch a complete game that night. But I know the chances are I won't. Billy [Wagner] will probably throw the last pitch. But that's the way it is nowadays."

The last two pitchers to reach three hundred wins were Clemens and Maddux. Clemens had pitched six innings in reaching the number; Maddux five.

The fact that A-Rod was about to reach five hundred home runs at age thirty-two was more proof of how the numbers had changed in terms of degree of difficulty. Even before he hit the home run—which, as it turned out, took him quite a while—Rodriguez was already being anointed by baseball people as the man to someday overtake Ruth and Bonds.

Clearly, no pitcher will ever challenge Cy Young's 511 wins or 749 complete games. Those numbers were achieved in a completely different era of baseball. Even so, of all the unchallengeable records in baseball, many of them dating to that period, Young's was by far the most unimaginable.

"Let's see," Glavine said. "If you win twenty games for twenty years, you're still more than one hundred wins away. I'm gonna go out on a limb and say no one quite gets there."

Later, when Randolph was asked what he meant when he said

that three hundred wasn't "that big a deal," he more or less recanted.

"I certainly wasn't trying to put Tommy down or what he was trying to do," he said. "I guess I'm still a hitter at heart. To me, five hundred home runs is a number I can identify with and understand. Three hundred wins is almost something in another sport because I never pitched. But if I think about it, I know what a big deal it is. All you have to do is look at how few guys have it and how few guys are close to it."

On a steamy night in Milwaukee, Glavine really wasn't focused on who might or might not get to three hundred after him or how many home runs Bonds or Rodriguez might ultimately hit. He was focused on the Brewers' lineup. Peterson had decided it would relax Glavine to get the pregame meeting out of the way early, so he had come into the training room with catcher Ramon Castro when Glavine first arrived, rather than waiting until an hour before game time.

That it was Castro who was catching and not Paul Lo Duca was the subject of considerable conversation in the Mets clubhouse. Lo Duca had been saying half-jokingly all season that he would catch Glavine's three hundredth win if he had to do so on a broken leg. That bit of hyperbole had ceased being a joke when Lo Duca pulled a hamstring running to first base the previous Saturday against the Nationals. Hamstrings are tricky injuries. Come back too fast, and you are likely to hurt yourself again. Lo Duca insisted he was okay to catch in Milwaukee. That wasn't what the Mets' medical people thought, and they told Randolph just that.

Lo Duca was in the clubhouse early that day to get treatment when Randolph called him into his office.

"I just can't let you go tonight," he told his catcher.

"Willie, I can do it," Lo Duca said. "I can catch tonight and then take a few days off."

Randolph shook his head. He didn't want to risk a long-term

injury, and he didn't want someone playing on one leg. Lo Duca was crushed.

Soon after, when Glavine walked into the clubhouse, he checked the lineup and saw that Castro was catching. Glavine didn't know what to say. This wasn't a "you'll get 'em next time" moment because he didn't want there to be a next time. He walked over to Lo Duca and saw that he was near tears. "They won't let me play," he told Glavine.

Catching Glavine was a thrill for Lo Duca. Like most of the Mets, he looked up to Glavine and admired everything about him. The thought that he would be spectating while Glavine went for the milestone win was heartbreaking for him.

The good news for Glavine was that having Castro catch didn't change the game much for him. Unlike some pitchers, Glavine has never been choosy about catchers. Maddux, while he was in Atlanta, didn't ever want to pitch to Javier Lopez, so the Braves always had their backup catcher assigned to Maddux. Glavine would pitch to a batting-practice cage if that was what he was asked to do.

It can be argued that there's never been a great player more low key about almost everything than Glavine. That was never more evident than in Milwaukee, as he sat at his locker and chatted with a gaggle of reporters as if he were about to throw his second bullpen session of spring training. When it was time to head out to the field, he stood up and said to the group, "I'm afraid you guys are going to have to carry on without me. I have some work to do."

If anything, everyone else in the clubhouse was tighter than Glavine. "If you've been around the guy, you just want to see it happen for him," Peterson said. "I feel a little bit like I'm caddying for a great golfer. He's doing the work, but maybe I'm helping just a little, and that's a feeling I want to hold on to."

It was a sultry midwestern summer evening, the game-time temperature eighty-six degrees, though it felt much warmer because of the humidity and because Miller Park—which has a retractable roof—is virtually enclosed, even with the roof open, meaning there is almost no breeze going in or out.

From the start, Glavine was sharp. There was no first-inning struggle at all. He retired the Brewers one-two-three, needing just twelve pitches to get two ground balls and a lazy fly ball to Shawn Green in right. He didn't give up a hit during the first three innings, the only base runner coming when he walked second baseman Tony Graffanino with one out in the third.

But the Mets weren't having any more luck at the plate than the Brewers. Jeff Suppan, who had been a key part of the Cardinals' rotation during their World Series run in 2006, was the Milwaukee starter. He had signed a big-money free-agent contract during the off-season but had done little to justify the expense. He came into the game with a record of 5–7 and an ERA of 5.21. But he picked this night to pitch the way he had a year earlier.

The Mets threatened in the first when David Wright singled and stole second with two out, but Carlos Delgado grounded to short for the third out. That was it in the early innings, as Suppan kept throwing ground balls.

What made the performance of the two pitchers even more remarkable was home-plate umpire Chad Fairchild's strike zone. "About the size of a postage stamp" was the way Ned Yost described it. "There were times I wanted to scream at him about squeezing Jeff, but he was doing the same thing to Tommy, so I really couldn't complain."

Glavine spent most of the night pitching from behind. He ended up walking five batters and threw more balls (forty-eight) than strikes (forty-seven). But the Brewers couldn't hit him. "Every time we had a man on base, he would throw an eighty-five-mile-an-hour fastball, and we'd roll one to second base or shortstop," Yost said. "If I hadn't wanted to win the game so much, I'd have just sat back and watched in awe because it was vintage Tom Glavine. We just couldn't touch him."

The Brewers finally dinged Glavine in the fourth when he walked shortstop J.J. Hardy leading off, and third baseman Ryan Braun doubled down the line in left. With the infield playing back, Glavine got Fielder to ground to newly acquired second baseman Luis Castillo. Hardy scored to make it 1–0, and Braun went to third. But Glavine got Bill Hall to pop to Delgado, and then, after a very careful walk to Kevin Mench, he induced catcher Damian Miller into a fly ball to Shawn Green in right field.

"I wasn't happy to be behind," Glavine said. "But I really figured we had to score sooner or later."

The Mets finally did score in the sixth. Jose Reyes, often the catalyst, led off with a double. Randolph, wanting to at least get the game tied, had Castillo sacrifice him to third. Wright singled to left to tie the game at 1–1, and Delgado moved him to third with another single. Sitting on the bench, Glavine sensed a chance to break the game open.

"I was thinking this inning was going to decide what kind of night it was going to be," he said. "If we could score four or five, I thought we'd be in good shape, because I felt good and we had a rested bullpen. But if we didn't score a bunch, then it was going to be a struggle."

Glavine's baseball instincts proved correct. With runners on first and third and one out, Moises Alou hit a fly ball deep enough to right field to score Wright. The Mets led 2–1. At that moment, Glavine was twelve outs from three hundred. Still, some cushion would be nice.

Shawn Green tried to get it for him. The veteran right fielder, who had struggled most of the season with men on base, smashed a ball into the gap in left-center field. With two men out, Delgado was running all the way, and he was waved in by third-base coach Sandy Alomar Sr. The Brewers executed the relay throw perfectly: center fielder Hall to second baseman Graffanino to catcher Miller, who slapped the tag on Delgado as he slid across the plate.

"Out!" was Fairchild's correct call. The middle of the Mets' lineup—Delgado, Alou, Green, and Castro (or Lo Duca)—is painfully slow of foot, and this was one of those moments when their lack of speed hurt them.

Instead of having a chance to break the game open, the Mets had a 2–1 lead. In the bottom of the inning, starting to feel the heat both literally and figuratively, Glavine walked Braun—his fifth walk of the night. He then wild-pitched Fielder, allowing Braun—the tying run—to advance to second base. With Fielder at the plate, Peterson trotted to the mound.

He put his arm on Glavine's shoulder and said quietly, "You're fine. Just take a breather here for a minute until Fairchild gets here."

Glavine understood. A minute later, Fairchild came to the mound to break up the conference. As soon as he sensed Fairchild over his shoulder, Peterson began talking. "Just keep throwing the same pitches you've been throwing," he said. "This guy is a good balls-and-strikes umpire, he's not going to keep missing these pitches all night."

Glavine smiled. He'd heard this routine before. As long as Peterson had his back to the umpire and his voice wasn't raised, he probably wasn't going to get tossed. As Peterson turned to leave, Fairchild was clearly giving him a look.

"Chad, you gotta get a better look at these pitches," Peterson said.

"Rick, we aren't going to discuss balls and strikes," Fairchild answered.

"I'm not talking about balls and strikes," Peterson said. "I'm talking about *vision*."

Fairchild said nothing, which surprised Peterson. "I've been tossed for less," he said. "If he had run me, it wouldn't have shocked me. I was trying to make a point, and I was willing to take the risk of getting tossed right there to make it."

Given both a breather and a light moment, Glavine gathered

himself and got Fielder to fly to Alou, and Mench to fly to Green to end the inning.

Green, who had been the last batter of the sixth, took the ball he caught off of Mench's bat straight into the clubhouse to put in his locker. He wanted it for Glavine to sign if he won his three hundredth that night. Billy Wagner was getting ready to leave the clubhouse to head for the bullpen, wanting to be available as early as the eighth inning if needed. He saw Green come in with the ball and laughed.

"Yeah, sure; no one on the team is thinking about three hundred," he said.

Glavine was due up third in the seventh. On another night, Randolph might have pinch-hit for him, but this night wasn't like any other night. Even with Ramon Castro on second base, Randolph let Glavine hit, hoping to at least get him through the seventh inning and to then turn the last six outs over to Heilman and Wagner.

Glavine reached on an error by Braun, with Castro holding at second. Another chance for the Mets. Reyes singled up the middle, but again the Mets' lack of speed came into play when Alomar held Castro up at third. Still, the bases were loaded. That was it for Suppan. Yost, who was also managing the game as if it might decide a pennant, brought Carlos Villanueva in to pitch to Castillo.

Although Castillo is a renowned bunter, Randolph didn't want to risk a squeeze with Castro the runner at third. Under different circumstances, he might have pinch-run for Castro, but with his other catcher hurt, he couldn't take him out of the game. So, Castillo swung away and hit a fly to left — too shallow for Castro to try to score. Wright, undoubtedly trying too hard, grounded into a force to end the inning.

Glavine went to the mound in the seventh knowing he was being watched closely by Randolph and Peterson. He had thrown ninety-two pitches, so there was no doubt this would be his final inning. It didn't last long. Damian Miller led off with a ringing single to center. It was only the Brewers' second hit, but it was enough for Randolph, who came to get his pitcher.

Glavine wasn't surprised to see someone coming to get him, but he was a little surprised to see Randolph. The manager had undergone rotator cuff surgery during the All-Star break and had been in considerable pain. He had been wearing a sling in the dugout to make sure the shoulder didn't get banged around accidentally and, by his own admission, had struggled to sleep. To make life easier, he had been sending Peterson out, not just to talk to pitchers but to make the pitching changes.

Now, he popped out of the dugout. "If someone was taking Tommy Glavine out going for his three hundredth, it was going to be me," he said. "I did it out of respect for him."

Glavine appreciated that. He was momentarily surprised to see Randolph, but when he thought about it he knew it made sense. What did surprise him was what happened when he handed Randolph the ball and started for the dugout. With the exception of Team Glavine and a handful of others—Stan Kasten had flown in for the game—everyone in the sellout crowd of 41,790 had rooted ardently for the Brewers all night. Now, as soon as Glavine left the mound, the entire stadium was on its feet, cheering.

"It took me by surprise," Glavine said. "I hadn't really thought about it much, but I guess I thought I might get a little more response than usual from a road crowd, but nothing like that. I'd never gotten a standing ovation on the road before. I wasn't sure what I should do."

As he crossed the foul line, Glavine decided one response was the right one: he took off his cap and waved it to the crowd. "When you're cheered, you should acknowledge the cheers," he said. "It really was a nice feeling getting a response like that from a road crowd."

Heilman, by his own admission as nervous as a cat, took the

ball in Glavine's stead. He quickly calmed his own nerves by getting Graffanino to ground to Delgado, who turned a nifty three-six-three double play. Bases empty. Seven outs away. Craig Counsell pinch-hit and pushed a bunt single, but Heilman got Corey Hart to ground to shortstop to end the inning.

Six outs.

Glavine went to the clubhouse to go through his postouting routine. He headed for the training room and began icing while the Mets failed to score in the eighth. He was sitting on a training table when the Brewers came up in the bottom of the inning.

J.J. Hardy, the young shortstop, led off with a bloop between Reyes and Alou. Reyes knew it was trouble right away and turned his back to the plate and ran full speed after the ball. For an instant, Glavine thought he had caught it.

"I saw him lunge for the ball and it disappeared," he said. "I thought he had it, and I went, 'Wow, what a play!' Then I saw Hosey reaching for the ball, and I realized he hadn't gotten it."

The ball had just eluded Reyes's glove. Hardy stopped at first. Then Heilman got Braun to fly to left.

Five outs to go. "At that point, I was counting outs," Glavine said. "I really thought if we could get it to Billy, there was no way we wouldn't win the game."

Wagner was in the bullpen, ready to warm up and come into the game in the eighth. He wasn't up, though, because Randolph had Pedro Feliciano and Guillermo Mota up. Feliciano was a lefty, and Randolph wanted him to pitch to Prince Fielder.

Feliciano had been one of the team's most reliable relievers against both lefties and righties, ranking just below Wagner and Heilman in the bullpen pecking order. Now, though, he plunked Fielder with his fourth pitch, putting men on first and second. Randolph came right back out and waved Mota in, which didn't thrill Glavine or anyone from Team Glavine or Team Mets.

A year earlier, Mota had been a key midseason pickup and had pitched extremely well down the stretch. Unfortunately, it turned out he'd had some extra help — from steroids. He had tested positive during the off-season and, unlike most players who test positive, had admitted his guilt. Perhaps that was why the Mets had given him a two-year contract, even though he had to sit out the first fifty games of the season under baseball's drug-testing rules.

When he had come back, Mota wasn't anywhere near the pitcher he had been a year earlier. He almost never pitched out of trouble and often pitched into it. His ERA was 5.29 and even that was deceiving because it didn't take into account inherited runners allowed to score.

Now, Mota inherited two runners. Bill Hall, who had popped out in the fourth against Glavine with runners on second and third, did considerably better against Mota. He slammed a 1–1 pitch down the line for a clean double. Both runners probably would have scored, but the ball hopped over the fence for a ground rule double, meaning only Hardy could score. Fielder stopped at third. The game was tied 2–2.

In the training room, Glavine's heart sank. Regardless of the final outcome of the game, he would not get his three hundredth win. On TV, fans could see a close-up of Chris Glavine, tears of frustration in her eyes. Later, she saw that Andruw Jones, an old friend from the Braves, had sent her a text message at that moment: "Chris, don't you know there's no crying in baseball?" Knowing that he wasn't going to be able to congratulate Glavine on number three hundred at the end of the game, Stan Kasten stood to leave. He was going to walk over to the Glavines to offer a word of consolation, but when he saw the looks on their faces, he decided to take a pass.

It took five innings and another ninety minutes before Geoff Jenkins finally ended the game with a two-run home run for the Brewers in the thirteenth inning. Surrounded by reporters, Glavine was his usual calm self. He was pleased he had pitched well, disappointed not to get the win, unhappy the team hadn't won the game. But there would be other chances; he knew that. He was disappointed but okay.

The crowd thinned. It was almost midnight. Glavine looked very tired. "The worst part of this," he said, forcing a smile, "is now I've got to figure out how to get thirty people to Chicago on Sunday night."

He would also have to dig up thirty tickets and pay for them.

"Goddamn IRS," he said, shaking his head as he walked to the door.

24

The Number Gets Named

MIKE MUSSINA BROKE his no-radio rule that night on his way home from the ballpark. He had just breezed to his easiest win of the season, the Yankees scoring eleven runs for him in the first four innings on their way to a 16–3 rout of the Chicago White Sox. Mussina had faltered briefly, giving up three runs in the second inning, but had cruised after that, coming out after six innings, not because he was tired, but because there was no reason not to give the back end of the bullpen some work with such a big lead.

It was Mussina's second straight win since the meltdown against Tampa Bay and the revamping of his stretch motion in the bullpen two days later. The Yankees had gone to Kansas City after taking three of four from the Rays, and Mussina had started the third game of four against the Royals. He had pitched extremely well, leaving in the sixth inning with a 2–1 lead, a margin the Yankees stretched to 7–1 before game's end.

"Whether I was better because I thought the changes we made were good or because they actually were good, I'm not sure," he said. "The bottom line was that I was better. I didn't feel every time I put someone on base that the next guy was going to hit a line drive. There's no doubt the difference was as much mental as it was physical."

Or to quote one of Yogi Berra's famous lines: "Ninety percent of this game is mental, and the other half is physical."

The Royals lineup hadn't reminded anyone of the Red Sox or of the Angels—or for that matter the Devil Rays—but it didn't matter. Mussina started strong and stayed strong until the sixth when he gave up a two-out double to Ross Gload and an RBI single to Reggie Sanders—who may play with all thirty major league teams before he retires—to cut the Yankee margin to 2–1.

Joe Torre didn't hesitate to take Mussina out after the back-to-back hits. To begin with, he had already thrown ninety-five pitches on a hot night. Beyond that, Torre wanted to do everything he could to give him a chance to get a win, and he didn't want to leave him in one batter too long and regret it. Mussina would have liked to have gotten through the sixth, but with left-handed hitter Alex Gordon coming up he could understand why Torre wanted to get lefty specialist Ron Villone into the game.

Villone did what he was paid to do, getting Gordon to fly to Bobby Abreu in right for the final out. On the bench, the normally stoic Mussina stood and clapped for Villone as he came to the dugout.

The bullpen did the job the rest of the way, and the Yankees scored an insurance run in the seventh and broke the game open in the eighth. Mussina had his first win since June 29. Just as important, he had some of his confidence back.

Six days later, his teammates made it relatively easy for him by bombarding White Sox starter Jose Contreras, the Cuban exile who had been the cause of one of the more famous lines in recent Yankees–Red Sox history. When Contreras had fled Cuba, the two teams had engaged in a bidding war for his services, both believing he might be the next Orlando Hernandez. The Yankees ended up signing Contreras, causing Larry Lucchino, the Red Sox team president, to call the Yankees "the evil empire."

Contreras had been a dud in New York, most notably when pitching against the Red Sox, and had been traded to Chicago, where he blossomed away from the New York crucible and had been the top pitcher for the White Sox during their World Series run in 2005. Now, though, he was struggling, with an ERA way over 6.00, and the Yankees jumped all over him. Bobby Abreu hit a three-run home run in the first, and Hideki Matsui hit a solo shot to make it 4–0. After Mussina gave up a three-run homer of his own to Juan Uribe in the second to close the gap to 4–3, the Yankees got five more runs in the third on a three-run Robinson Cano home run and a two-run shot by Cabrera. About the only Yankee who didn't homer was Alex Rodriguez, who had been sitting on 499 since Saturday.

The home-run barrage drove Contreras from the mound and made the score 7–3. Mussina had no further trouble from there and was in his car on his way home when he remembered that Glavine was going for number three hundred that night. Since Milwaukee was in the central time zone and the Yankee game had lasted less than three hours, Mussina was pretty certain they would still be playing. He flipped on the radio, and, sure enough, the Brewers were coming up in the bottom of the seventh.

"It was just as Tom was coming out of the game," he said. "I remember thinking he had to have pitched well, but now he was going to have to sweat out his bullpen trying to finish it."

Mussina was almost home when the Brewers tied the game in the eighth, and he felt for Glavine. "He obviously pitched well, and now he had to go back and do it all over again," he said. "I just didn't want to see him have to try four or five times to get there the way Roger [Clemens] did. That was tough to watch from up close."

Glavine woke up the morning after the game in Milwaukee with a hangover, even though he hadn't been drinking the night before. "I guess it's just a combination of everything," he said. "Building up to the game, the game itself, being so close, not getting it, and, most of all, knowing we have to go through the whole thing again this weekend."

Team Glavine had flown back to their various homes on

Wednesday, the plan being for Chris and the kids to come back to Chicago on Friday and for everyone else to come back Saturday or Sunday. Glavine wasn't the least bit surprised when the Met bats exploded for twenty runs during the last two games in Milwaukee—both wins. "I guess it's just not meant to be easy," he said. "This way, when I get it, I'll feel as if I've earned it, that's for sure."

The Mets made the short trip down I-94 after their 12–4 victory on Thursday and opened their series against the Cubs in Wrigley Field on Friday afternoon. The North Side of Chicago had pennant fever. The Cubs had spent a lot of money in the off-season and had hired Lou Piniella as their manager, amid high hopes that they could win the weak National League Central Division. After an awful start, the Cubs were playing much better baseball and had moved percentage points ahead of the Brewers and into first place when the Mets got to town. The Mets, after winning the last two games in Milwaukee, led the Phillies by four and the Braves by four and a half.

The teams split the first two games of the series in front of boisterous, standing-room-only crowds. The finale was ESPN's Sunday-night game. Players are accustomed to playing in the afternoon on Sunday. Playing at night, especially when the next stop was home, wasn't something anyone was looking forward to doing.

That was especially true of Glavine. It meant killing time all day rather than getting up, going to the ballpark, and pitching. As it turned out, the late start might have been a break. All four of the Glavines' children were in town for the game: Jonathan, Chris's son from her first marriage; Amber, Tom's daughter from his first marriage; and Peyton and Mason, their two sons.

On Saturday night, Jonathan was sick. He had a fever, chills, the whole twelve-year-old works. Tom stayed up with him until he finally was comfortable enough to sleep, in the early hours of the morning. Not surprisingly, Tom woke up feeling lousy—tired, maybe a little bit sick himself.

"If I'd had to pitch at one o'clock," he said, "I'm not sure I could have done it. Being able to go back to bed and get some extra sleep helped."

The day was comfortable, but late in the afternoon a warm front swept into Chicago, leaving heavy, humid air hanging over the city. By the time everyone got to the ballpark for batting practice, it was sweltering, a far more uncomfortable night than it had been in Milwaukee—and that hadn't been comfortable by any means.

"I really didn't feel great warming up," Glavine said. "I still felt as if I was a little bit sick, and I felt tired. Plus, the heat was really bothering me. It isn't as if I didn't pitch in a lot of hot weather in Atlanta. Normally, it wasn't a big deal. But I really didn't feel good at all."

While Glavine was struggling to get ready for the game, Paul Lo Duca was fighting to get into the game. He had not played on the road trip, and there was some talk that he might have to go on the disabled list. He insisted that he felt much better and was ready to play. Randolph still didn't want to take a risk and lose him for a month by bringing him back too soon.

Because the clubhouse in Chicago is so small, the two men walked out to the dugout to discuss Lo Duca's status for that night.

"Willie, you were a player, you should understand how I feel about this," Lo Duca said. "You know how much this game means to me and to all of us. I wouldn't tell you I could go if I didn't really believe I could. If you think I'm hurt that bad, you should put me on the DL. But if you aren't going to do that, let me play."

Randolph thought about it. He appreciated Lo Duca's desire and his competitiveness. He knew how close he was to Glavine and how much it had hurt him to sit out the game in Milwaukee. He decided to take a chance. "Okay," he said. "We'll give it a shot."

Thus, it was Lo Duca behind the plate when Glavine walked

out to pitch the bottom of the first, after Jason Marquis had set the Mets down in the top of the inning. Glavine very much wanted an easy first inning to get some positive adrenaline pumping so he might start to feel a little bit better.

Fortunately he got just what he needed. The always-difficult Alfonso Soriano hit a fly ball to Lastings Milledge, who was playing center field because Carlos Beltran was hurt. Ryan Theriot did the exact same thing, and Derrek Lee hit another fly ball, this one to Moises Alou. One-two-three—eleven pitches—just what the doctor ordered.

The Mets got Glavine the lead in the second. Actually, Glavine got Glavine the lead in the second. Milledge singled with two out and promptly stole second. Glavine, given a chance to drive in a run, did so, hitting a ground ball right up the middle for a base hit. Running on the pitch, Milledge scored easily, and the Mets led 1–0.

"It was nice to get the hit and the run home," Glavine said. "By then I'd almost forgotten how lousy I felt. Getting the lead early was nice, even if I had to do it myself."

He was joking, bragging—as all pitchers do—about his offense. His defense continued to be outstanding as the game wore on. The Cubs didn't get a hit until Soriano singled with two out in the third. Theriot followed with a single to center, and Soriano tried to go to third—probably not a terribly bright move with two down, and Milledge, with a solid arm, fielding the ball quickly. Whether Soriano would have been out is tough to tell because halfway to third, he pulled up, grabbing at his hamstring. He practically fell into David Wright's tag, the ball arriving long before he did.

It stayed 1–0 until the fifth, and it was beginning to look like another suspenseful night. Finally, the Mets got their pitcher a little cushion in the fifth when Luis Castillo singled, moved to second on a deep fly to center by Wright, and scored on a ringing double to right by Carlos Delgado, who was still struggling to get his batting average over .250 but seemed to be slowly finding his stroke. That made it 2–0.

A moment later, after Delgado had moved up to third on a Marquis wild pitch, Green doubled to score him. This time, there was no doubt about Delgado scoring. He was almost across the plate before the ball landed, and the Mets led 3–0.

Glavine retired the side one-two-three, and in the Mets dugout and bullpen the countdown began. "It felt like a World Series game," Billy Wagner said. "It was that kind of tension. No one said anything, but we all wanted to make sure we didn't have a repeat of Milwaukee. Tom had pitched his butt off there, and he was pitching his butt off again. It was hot, and his pitch count was starting to get up there, so we all knew we were going to have to finish it for him."

Glavine had kept his pitch count down early, but the Cubs began to do a better job waiting him out. He had only walked one—ex-teammate Cliff Floyd in the second—but, as usual, was running deep counts. He knew he wasn't going to finish, but he wanted to give the bullpen as little work to do as possible. In an ideal world, he would get through seven and let Aaron Heilman pitch the eighth and Wagner the ninth.

Because the game was on national television and it was a Sunday night, most of the baseball world was watching. Rodriguez had finally hit his five hundredth home run on Saturday—after going twenty-eight at bats without it—and Bonds had at last hit number 755 to tie Aaron on Saturday night, a moment so dramatic that Bud Selig was seen in the stands with his hands shoved deep into his pockets. Bonds hadn't played on Sunday because the Giants wanted to be sure he got his 756th at home, thus avoiding the specter of Bonds being booed after breaking baseball's most cherished record.

Bridget Moynahan had not yet given birth.

The stage was wide open for Glavine. For most, there was a feeling of inevitability about it all after the Mets scored two more in the sixth to make it 5–0, Reyes and Delgado driving in runs. The only disappointment was Green grounding out with two outs and the bases loaded, when the Mets had a chance to turn the game into a laugher.

A laugher is just what you might think it is: a game in which the margin is so great that the team in the lead can actually laugh in the dugout during the game. In his classic 1965 book *Now Wait a Minute, Casey!*, a chronicle of the Mets' pathetic first three seasons under Casey Stengel, author Maury Allen described the Mets' first true laugher, a 19–1 victory at Wrigley Field in 1964. Several writers were sitting near the Mets bullpen because it was a beautiful afternoon, and, as the lead built, they kept asking utility man Rod Kanehl if the game was a laugher yet.

At 9–0 in the fifth, they asked Kanehl if it was a laugher.

"Not yet," he answered.

At 13–1 in the seventh, they asked again.

"Not quite."

At 19–1 in the ninth, they inquired once more.

"No, not for sure yet."

Finally, with two outs in the bottom of the ninth, Kanehl turned to the writers and said, "*Now*, it's a laugher."

That same day, according to legend, a fan called the *New York Times* sports desk to see how the Mets had done.

"They scored nineteen runs," the man on the desk said.

There was a pause and then, "Did they win?"

Forty-three years later, the Mets were a lot better team, with a Hall of Fame pitcher on the mound. Any hit by Green probably would have made the game a laugher. Instead, the lead was 5–0.

"Most nights you're up five-nothing with Tommy Glavine on the mound, you figure the game is over," Rick Peterson said. "But knowing what was at stake, I don't think any of us weren't nervous."

The least nervous person in the park appeared to be Glavine. He quickly retired the first two hitters in the sixth, before Derrek

Lee hit a fly-ball double just fair down the right-field line. Aramis Ramirez followed with a double deep to center, and it was 5–1.

"It was almost inevitable they score after Lee's ball," Glavine said. "Ramirez kills me all the time, and I'd already gotten him twice. I was just happy I kept him in the ballpark."

He struck Floyd out to end the inning, and it was 5–1 with nine outs to go.

Mark DeRosa, another old teammate from Glavine's Atlanta days, started the seventh with a ground ball to Wright. Eight outs to go. Glavine was tiring in the heat, and he knew it. Realistically, he knew if he could finish this inning, that would be it for the night.

Angel Pagan followed with a shot down the left-field line that brought up chalk, bouncing directly on the foul line. "Lee hits it an inch fair to right; Pagan hits it an inch fair to left," Glavine said. "With a little luck on either ball, I think I get through the seventh."

Randolph and Peterson consulted. Pagan had doubled on Glavine's 102nd pitch of the night. Basically, they needed Guillermo Mota and Pedro Feliciano, both warming in the bullpen, to get two outs and get the ball to Heilman for the eighth. If it had been a one-run lead, Peterson might have gone out to get a read on how Glavine felt — "tired as hell" would have been the answer — but with a four-run lead they decided to trust the bullpen.

Randolph went out to get him, waving Mota in as he crossed the foul line. Glavine wasn't surprised or upset, although, if truth be told, no one on Team Glavine was jumping for joy at the sight of Mota trotting in. Peyton Glavine had been caught on camera in Milwaukee mouthing a derogatory word about Mota, not a profanity, but he had clearly been frustrated. In the SportsNet New York truck, director Bill Webb saw the shot and decided there was no need to put an eight-year-old boy on screen reacting understandably to a very disappointing moment. What's more, Peyton

Glavine probably spoke for all Met fans. At the end of the inning, he showed the shot to his announcers, Gary Cohen and Ron Darling, to see how they felt about it. Both agreed with Webb, so the shot wasn't seen in New York. It was seen in Milwaukee.

Even without the shot appearing in New York, Glavine heard about it the next day from friends. When the family returned to Chicago, he sat his boy down for a little talk about being the son of a public figure.

"I just told him he had to be aware when he was watching Dad pitch that he might be on camera," he said. "You'd rather not have to lay that on an eight-year-old, but I figured I should remind him. I also tried to explain to him that, even though he gave up the hit, Guillermo was trying just as hard as I was and just as hard as he did in his ball games."

That was almost the same message Glavine had delivered to Mota when he had come into the clubhouse in Milwaukee. "Don't worry about it; I know you tried."

"Really, that's all you can ask of anyone," Glavine said.

Now, as Mota trotted in, Glavine handed the ball to Randolph, who gave him an emphatic pat on the back as the fans began to stand en masse to cheer Glavine. He was a little less surprised than in Milwaukee—since it had already happened once—but just as moved by the gesture. "The Cubs and the Mets have had a pretty intense rivalry for a long time," he said. "For those fans to stand and do that, to me, was really something memorable."

Glavine was actually pumped as he left the game. He gave Randolph a return pat on the back with his glove—something he never did leaving the mound—and tipped his cap to the crowd.

"I had an incredible feeling of satisfaction right at that moment," he said. "I'd felt so lousy all day, and I'd gone out and really performed—pitched really well. Even if we'd somehow blown it, I would have still walked out of there feeling good about myself. I didn't want that to happen, and, to be honest, I didn't think it would. But it was a very nice feeling I had right there."

He got to the dugout, accepted all the congratulations, and watched Mota instantly give up a single to Jason Kendall, moving Pagan to third. Randolph wasn't taking any chances this time around. Mota tended to be either very good or very bad, and he didn't think he could afford to wait and find out if the Kendall hit was a fluke or a harbinger. Once Piniella had sent up left-handed-hitting Jacque Jones as a pinch hitter for pitcher Kerry Wood, Randolph waved in Feliciano.

Wanting to make up for his performance in Milwaukee, Feliciano got Jones to ground to Castillo for the second out. Pagan scored, and Kendall moved to second. Seven outs left. But Mike Fontenot, who had taken Soriano's place in the lineup when he pulled up lame, cracked a double to left, scoring Kendall and cutting the gap to 5–3.

Glavine, sitting in the dugout, couldn't help but flash back to Milwaukee. "I'd be lying if I told you that at that moment I wasn't nervous," he said. "I was. There were still seven outs left, it's Wrigley Field, and they have a good lineup. I sat there and thought, 'Oh my God, if I have to go through this again . . .'"

Randolph was thinking along those same lines. Heilman had been warming up, and Randolph decided not to wait any longer to get him in. Theriot was now coming up as the tying run. Heilman trotted in, trying to keep himself calm.

"We all felt let down when Tom didn't get the win in Milwaukee," Heilman said. "He had done his job that night; he deserved to win. This was the same situation: he had done his job. In fact, the lineup had done its job scoring five runs. It was up to us to close it out."

Heilman is a rare major leaguer in that he not only went to college — Notre Dame — but graduated. He's quiet but extremely thoughtful, one of those guys the writers who regularly cover the team go to often because he almost always has something smart to say on any given topic.

He is a fastball/slider pitcher who, at twenty-eight, wanted very much to be a starter again. Glavine had often encouraged him not to worry about that and to simply try to control that which he could control. Now, he had control of the ball and the game.

Theriot was clearly thinking about tying the game with one swing. He reached for a Heilman slider and popped it up to medium-center field. Milledge settled under it, and everyone in the dugout — most notably Glavine — breathed a sigh of relief.

Six outs to go.

With the lead down to two runs, the Mets wanted to get some insurance in the eighth against the Cubs bullpen. Will Ohman was now on the mound. Castillo and Wright started the inning with singles. Delgado doubled Castillo home, Wright stopping at third. Alou was walked intentionally, and Green struck out. But Lo Duca, in pain but happy to be playing, singled to left to score Wright, and the lead was 7–3. Milledge flied out, and then Randolph decided to go for the jugular with runners on second and third and two out. He sent up Marlon Anderson, his best pinch hitter, for Heilman, hoping to break open the game. A base hit would make the lead six. But Anderson flied to center, and it was still 7–3.

Now, with Heilman out of the game, someone had to pitch the eighth to get the ball to Wagner. Randolph chose Jorge Sosa, who had been a starter at the beginning of the season but had been moved into the bullpen in recent weeks. Sosa had live stuff and when on could be almost unhittable for an inning or two.

With everyone on the Mets bench wondering if Randolph would bring in Wagner if Sosa found trouble (he would have), Sosa got Lee and Ramirez on ground balls, walked Floyd, but then got DeRosa to fly to Milledge for the third out.

Three outs to go. And now Wagner would have the ball. The Mets added one more run in the ninth. In the clubhouse, Glavine wondered if he should go back to the dugout or stay put. His normal routine was to stay in the clubhouse, but this wasn't a normal night.

"Everyone said I should go back to the dugout," he said. "I figured they were right, especially because no one was in the clubhouse." (Almost always during a game there are players in the clubhouse for various reasons; now everyone was in the dugout.)

He walked back to the packed dugout. ESPN's camera was on Glavine more than on the field as Wagner came in to pitch. "I was glad to have a five-run lead," Wagner said. "When I had fantasized about it, I thought it would be a one-run lead, and I'd come in and blow them away. But the reality of it was I was glad to have some cushion."

Pagan lined out to right. But then Kendall doubled. Matt Murton came up to pinch-hit and foul-tipped a pitch right off of plate umpire Marty Foster's mask. Foster was knocked a little bit dizzy by the impact. He took off the mask while the Cubs' training staff ran out to check on him.

Tim McLelland, the crew chief, came in from third base to talk to Foster. As luck would have it, ESPN had miked McLelland, so people watching on TV got to hear him pleading with Foster to go back inside and let someone else finish the game in his place.

"I can't let you go on," McLelland said. "There's only two outs left. We'll finish for you."

Foster wanted to finish the game. He and McLelland and the trainers continued to talk while everyone waited.

In the stands, Glavine's sister Debbie, not knowing Tom was in the dugout and not near his BlackBerry, couldn't resist sending him a text message: "This could only happen to *you*."

Glavine was thinking roughly the same thing. "The game had been going on forever already," he said. "I was thinking we were heading for midnight."

On the East Coast, it was well past eleven o'clock when the trainers finally decided Foster could try to finish the game. Wagner, annoyed at himself for giving up the double to Kendall, struck out Murton looking.

One out to go.

Sitting in his house in Atlanta, Bobby Cox broke an old baseball rule — counting the last out before the last out. "I was just so
excited, I couldn't wait any longer," he said. He dialed Glavine's
cell phone and left a message: "I couldn't be happier for you. No
one has ever deserved it more." He paused a second before adding
the last sentence. "I just wish you could have done it in a Braves
uniform."

Everyone was standing now, knowing they were about to wit-
ness baseball history. In spite of the length of the game, the late-
ness of the hour, and the home team trailing by five, almost no
one had left the ballpark. Mike Fontenot was the Cubs' last hope.

Wagner went to 1–1 on Fontenot. He threw one more 97-mile-
an-hour fastball, and Fontenot rolled it to Castillo. Wagner was
running in the direction of first base thinking, *Throw it, throw it,
please throw it,* as Castillo, a Gold Glove second baseman in his
American League days, smoothly fielded the ball and tossed it to
Delgado, who squeezed it in his glove just to be absolutely sure.

First-base umpire Fieldin Culbreth gave the out signal, and it
was official: the Number Could Finally Be Named — three
hundred.

In the radio booth, play-by-play man Howie Rose adjusted his
usual final-out call from "Put it in the books!" to "Put it in the *history* books!"

Wagner demanded the ball from Delgado as the Mets poured
onto the field. The crowd was up again, applauding Glavine's feat.
A feeling of complete and utter satisfaction swept over Glavine as
he headed out from the dugout.

Wagner was waiting for him with the ball: he held it up,
handed it to Glavine, and the car-pool buddies hugged.

The Cubs' security people had made sure to get the Glavine
family onto the field. They were standing next to the dugout when
Glavine, ball in hand, came back from the celebration with his
teammates. He hugged Chris, and he hugged his mother. He

started to shake hands with his father because that's what he and his dad always did—they shook hands.

"I think I'll take a hug for this one," Fred Glavine said.

He turned to the kids, going youngest to oldest. He didn't lose it until he got to Amber, who was crying. Like her dad, Amber Glavine doesn't show emotion all that often, even at twelve. Now, she was crying tears of joy and pride, and it got to her father.

"She's been through a lot for a kid who is only twelve," he said. "She saw her parents go through a divorce and get remarried. Then her stepdad got killed in an accident, and, through it all, she's never been anything but a great kid. When I saw the tears in her eyes, it got to me. I had to get the lump out of my throat before I talked to the guys in the clubhouse."

When he had finished the family hugs, Glavine told them all, "I'll see you in a few minutes."

There was still work to do: postgame with ESPN, postgame radio, postgame in the interview room with everyone else. The visitors' clubhouse in Wrigley was much too small for all the media that would want to talk to him. Before all that, though, he had a moment alone with his teammates. Charlie Samuels, who had worked for the Mets since 1976 and been the clubhouse manager almost as long, had made arrangements for a celebration.

As the players walked into the clubhouse, they were each handed a T-shirt that said simply "Glavine 300" over a silhouetted photo of Glavine in his pitching motion. The number was out in the open now for all to see. Samuels had also set up champagne for everyone in the middle of the clubhouse.

The man of the hour picked up a glass as everyone else did and offered a toast: "I just want to thank all of you guys for putting up with all the stuff that's gone on surrounding this," he said. "It's been a long time coming. Now let's take care of winning the pennant."

They all drank, toasted, cheered, and hugged. Heilman felt himself tingling. "I figured this was the closest I'd ever get to three hundred wins," he said later.

It was a rare pro sports moment of pure joy. The Mets were 63–48, with a four-and-a-half-game lead and eight weeks left in the season. There was a lot of work still to do. But for this one night, they could all share in Glavine's special moment.

All of baseball felt the same way. There were many who wished Bonds hadn't reached Aaron and quite a few who felt very little emotion about A-Rod reaching five hundred. Most didn't have much of an opinion on Bridget Moynahan.

But *everyone* liked and respected Tom Glavine. He had always been a great teammate. He had stood up for his fellow players for years in his union role. He had always done things the right way.

And now, he had won three hundred games.

"It meant I didn't have to ever speculate again," he said. "It didn't have to be '*If* I can get there.' I was actually there."

Now, about that pennant race . . .

25

Autopilot

LIKE A LOT OF BASEBALL PEOPLE, Mike Mussina was watching as Glavine went for number three hundred in Chicago. He was sitting in a hotel room in Toronto, having flown there earlier in the evening with the rest of the Yankees after he had won his third straight start, beating the Kansas City Royals 8–5 in New York.

Once again, the Yankees had produced a lot of early offense, and Mussina had made it stand up—then watched the bullpen wobble before Mariano Rivera came in to wrap up the victory.

The win raised Mussina's record for the season to 7–7 and put him at 246 for his career. "Doesn't exactly roll off the tongue like three hundred, does it?" he joked.

Someone pointed out that while 246 wasn't 300, it *did* make Mussina the winningest pitcher in major league history without a twenty-win season, surpassing Dennis Martinez, who had 245. "I'm not exactly sure what that means," Mussina said. "I guess it means people have kept running me out there for a lot of years; I'm grateful for that."

The Yankees were now officially a hot team: they were 19–7 since the All-Star break and had wiped out almost their entire wild-card deficit. They were a half game behind the Tigers (who were a half game behind the Indians in the Central Division) and percentage points behind the surprising Seattle Mariners. They had even sliced the Red Sox lead to seven games.

Mussina's resurgence had coincided with the team getting hot. He had been terrible against Tampa Bay, better in Kansas City, solid in a laugher against the White Sox, and even better in his return engagement against the Royals.

"Worth noting who we're playing," he said. "Things will start to get tougher here very soon — for all of us."

After the Yankees wrapped their series against the Royals, their road trip would take them to Toronto (where the Blue Jays were playing respectably) and Cleveland. After that would come a homestand that would start with the Orioles — against whom they were 3–6 on the season — and then the toughest two weeks of the season to date: four games at home against the Tigers, three in Anaheim against the Angels, four more against the Tigers in Detroit, and then, finally, three back at Yankee Stadium against the Red Sox.

The consensus was that everyone would know a lot more about where this Yankees season was headed once the Red Sox pulled out of New York following an afternoon game on August 30.

Like everyone else in the clubhouse, Mussina was aware of the schedule but wasn't yet ready to worry about it. He had been matched against Gil Meche in the finale of the Royals series, and even though Meche had become a kind of punch line when the subject of overpaid pitchers came up — "Hey, if Gil Meche can get $55 million for five years, *anyone* can get rich in this game" — he had been a good pitcher all season. His record was only 7–8 coming into the game, but his ERA was a very respectable 3.70 on a team that was 48–61 and trying to avoid yet another last-place finish.

Meche had always pitched well against the Yankees, especially during his time in Seattle. Fortunately, this was one day when the Yankees got to him early. They scored four runs in the second inning after two were out, Bobby Abreu driving in the final pair with a single up the middle. The cushion grew to 6–0 over the next two innings, while Mussina sailed along.

"You start to feel like you're really in a groove after a while, which is one of the amazing things about the game," Mussina said. "Two weeks earlier I wondered if I would ever get anyone out again. Now, I felt comfortable on the mound, the ball felt good coming out of my hand, and I just felt like I was going to get outs."

He faltered only in the sixth inning when he hit Emil Brown with a pitch and Ross Gload hit a two-run homer on the next pitch. "Sometimes trying to get that first-pitch strike with a fastball is a mistake," he said.

The Yankees answered quickly with two more runs in the sixth. Torre let Mussina start the seventh, even though he'd thrown ninety-seven pitches and there wasn't much reason to stretch him a lot further than that. When Joey Gathright led off with a single, Torre quickly went to the bullpen, which almost turned into a disaster. Brian Bruney and Mike Myers managed to turn the 8–2 lead into an 8–5 lead with two on and two out in the eighth. Taking no chances, Torre brought in Rivera for a four-out save, and Rivera blew the Royals away—four batters, eleven pitches—to wrap up the game.

That made three straight wins in three starts for Mussina. The wins had all been over weak teams—the Royals twice and the White Sox once—but that didn't really matter. He knew he felt better on the mound, and he knew those teams probably would have pounded him a few weeks earlier.

"The next few weeks will be interesting, given the schedule," he said, as someone picked up his equipment to put it on the bus for the trip to Toronto. "We're playing well now, but there's no doubt who we have been playing has helped."

He was looking forward to getting to Toronto and relaxing in front of the television that night. "I really hope Tom gets it this time," he said. "My guess is, he'll do fine."

His guess turned out to be right. The Mets returned home for a three game series against the Braves, meaning that Glavine's wish to reach three hundred before the Mets and Braves met again had just barely been granted. It might have been a bit more dramatic if Glavine had gotten the milestone win against his old team, but he was just as glad to have it over with and to accept congratulations from old friends like Bobby Cox and Andruw and Chipper Jones.

Celebrations were being planned. On Wednesday, Glavine and family would make a trip to downtown Manhattan to accept the key to the city from Mayor Michael Bloomberg. The following Sunday, the Mets planned a ceremony to honor him. The timing had turned out perfectly: Peyton and Mason started school on August 14, and Chris was flying home with them Sunday night to get them ready.

"I can't tell you what a relief it is to have this done before they start school," he said. "I didn't want them flying all over the place and missing school so they could see me go after it. This way, they can go home and get the school year going and feel happy that they got to see me do it and got to be part of the ceremony."

Glavine was excited about going to City Hall to get the key. "It's an actual key," he said. "Apparently there was a big key that opened the back door to the building, and this is a replica. "It's kind of cool."

Alex Rodriguez would receive a similar key during the Yankees' next homestand. He didn't go to City Hall, though — Bloomberg and the key came to Yankee Stadium, and the key was presented to him behind home plate. There was, no doubt, some kind of symbolism in that. Or it just might have been that Glavine has always been able to enjoy getting to do things most people don't get to do — like being given the key to New York City.

Glavine left City Hall after the key ceremony and headed straight to the ballpark for the second game of the Braves series. He had been awash in congratulatory calls and e-mails and letters. The one that had really hit home was from another left-hander: Sandy Koufax. "That was cool," he said. "I mean, growing up, when you thought about great pitchers, you thought about Koufax. He was just terrific about it."

Koufax had only won 165 games in his career but was in the Hall of Fame largely on the strength of what were probably the four most dominant years (1963–66) any modern-day pitcher has ever had. Unlike most retired players, he didn't spend a lot of time in the public eye. He didn't do card shows, and he had given up his job as a Dodgers spring-training instructor several years ago. He might occasionally be spotted in a golf gallery, following his friend Billy Andrade, from the PGA Tour, around, and he almost always went to the Final Four since he was a basketball nut. But that was about it.

With all the calls and notes and interviews and the key to the city, Glavine hadn't given much thought to baseball. "As I was driving to the park, it suddenly occurred to me, 'Hey, I have to pitch again in a few days,'" he said. "The last time I'd been through anything that was as big a deal was when we won the World Series [in 1995]. That was different because the season was over. Our season was very much still going on. I had to pause and think for a moment about who we were playing on the weekend."

That would be the Marlins. The Mets (again) lost two of three to the Braves, leaving their record for the season against them at a dreadful 4–8. The Braves and Phillies were playing leapfrog for second place, with the Braves jumping back up after winning the final game of the series. The Braves trailed by three and a half, the Phillies by four.

The Yankees, in the meantime, were in a three-way wild-card chase coming out of Toronto. After winning two of three against the Blue Jays—with Chien-Ming Wang getting bombed in the last game of the set—they were a half game behind the Mariners and in a flat-footed tie with the Tigers.

From Toronto, they headed to Cleveland to begin a three-game series with the Indians, who had moved into first place in the Central Division, a game and a half ahead of the Tigers. Philip Hughes, finally off the disabled list, made his return in the opener and pitched well in a 6–1 win. That sent Mussina to the mound on Saturday night against soft-tossing Paul Byrd, who was kind of a poor man's Glavine. His fastball almost never touched more than 86 miles per hour but he had ninety-seven career wins and was 10–4 for the season going into the game.

For the first time in four starts, Mussina gave up a first-inning run, the kind of soft run a pitcher hates to give up: a Grady Sizemore single, a sacrifice by Kenny Lofton, a wild pitch, and a sacrifice fly by Victor Martinez. The 1–0 lead didn't last long—the Yankees bombed Byrd in the second inning for seven runs. Mussina went back to the mound in the second inning feeling very comfortable. For the next six innings, he was virtually untouchable.

"Every once in a while you pitch a game where you feel like you can't do anything wrong," Mussina said. "It's as if you're on autopilot. Everything you do turns out right: You hang a pitch, the guy fouls it off. You throw one down the middle, he takes it. They swing at your best pitches. You feel like you can throw the ball through the eye of a needle if someone asks you to. It's almost like an out-of-body experience. Once we put up the touchdown in the second, I was out there thinking, 'Now look at me go.'

"You have a game like that once, maybe twice a year. I call it pitching mindlessly. You don't have to think about anything. You look up and it's the sixth or seventh inning. You feel as if you could go out there and pitch an inning left-handed, and they'd hit three ground balls right at people."

He smiled and folded his arms. "Problem is, it's a double-edged sword. Like I said, once, maybe twice a year you can go out there in a mindless state and everything will go right. But that's not the way you normally pitch. The way you normally pitch, you need to be focused and aware of what you're doing on every pitch. Often, after you have a mindless game, the next one isn't very good.

"It's a little bit like pitching on autopilot, and then someone turns off the autopilot and there's no one in the cockpit. You do that, you're going down."

Mussina wasn't really thinking in those terms in Cleveland. He pitched into the eighth inning, coming out with two men out after a pair of doubles by the Indians narrowed the gap to 10–2. Torre, thinking long-term, figured eighty-nine pitches was enough.

"I guess the difference between now and when I was younger is when I had a mindless game in those years, I would flirt with a no-hitter or pitch a shutout. Now it means I might get to the eighth or ninth inning."

He certainly wasn't complaining. He was 8–7 on the year, the first time he had been over .500. He had started the season feeling confident he would win at least eleven games and get to 250 for his career. In mid-July that had seemed like a pipe dream. Now, sitting on 247 with, he figured, nine starts left, 250 appeared to be close to a lock.

"Two fifty isn't three hundred by any stretch," he said. "But it isn't a bad number."

Glavine no longer needed to worry about numbers. He no longer needed to talk about what he was trying to do or where he was trying to get to or the goal he was trying to reach. He could just say, "It feels great to be one of twenty-three pitchers in history with three hundred or more wins."

He was still floating when he took the mound to face the Marlins in the second game of the weekend series. As he trotted from the dugout to throw his eight warm-up pitches, many in the crowd of 50,773 began to stand and clap. By the time PA announcer Alex Anthony had finished introducing the Mets defense, concluding with "and on the mound, Tom Glavine," everyone in the place was on their feet.

"I had expected something," Glavine said. "It was my first time back home since Chicago, and I thought that I'd get a nice hand when they introduced me. But I never imagined it would be like that."

As the cheers grew louder, Glavine tried to go about the business of throwing his warm-up pitches. Finally, he knew that just wouldn't work. He stopped, backed off the rubber, took off his cap, and acknowledged the cheers, which only grew louder.

"It really was neat," he said. "Because it was spontaneous. It wasn't planned, and it wasn't part of a ceremony or anything like that. Given the rocky start I'd gotten off to in New York, it really meant a lot to me."

Glavine had to settle his emotions before Hanley Ramirez stepped in to lead off the game. He immediately gave up a leadoff single to Ramirez but then retired the Marlins without any further damage in the first. "That was kind of nice," he said. "I wouldn't have felt too good if I'd gotten an ovation like that and then given up a four-spot or something."

For five innings, he didn't give up anything. David Wright hit a two-run home run in the fourth for a 2–0 lead, and it looked like Glavine would roll to win number 301 without much resistance.

"It's hard to describe how good I felt that night," he said. "From the minute I got to the mound, even putting the ovation aside, I felt completely different than any game I had pitched in years. It was as if there was no pressure. Obviously, it was still important because we were in a pennant race, but I wasn't pitching not to screw up. When I got the lead, I didn't start thinking, 'Okay, this is an opportunity to get another win closer; don't blow it.' I think I'd been doing stuff like that without even knowing it. Now, I was just out there pitching, enjoying it, having fun. It felt almost the way I used to feel in high school. I was completely relaxed. It was actually fun again."

He gave up a run in the sixth, but Wright answered with another home run in the bottom of the inning, and Glavine took a

3–1 lead into the seventh. Cody Ross led off with a single, and Glavine got pinch hitter Todd Linden to fly to left. That was the moment when Randolph, aware of the fact that Glavine had thrown 104 pitches on a hot night, decided to go to the bullpen. And in came Guillermo Mota as everyone shuddered.

Unfortunately, the result was almost exactly the same as in Milwaukee and Chicago. Ramirez singled to put runners on first and third. Mota then struck out Alejandro De Aza, but Ramirez stole second on strike three. That left Randolph with a decision: pitch to the dangerous Miguel Cabrera or walk Cabrera intentionally to load the bases and pitch to Josh Willingham.

The sensible move was to avoid pitching to Cabrera at all costs. But loading the bases, especially for a pitcher who isn't pitching with much confidence, can be tricky.

"You always pitch a little differently with the bases loaded," Glavine said. "You're a little more concerned about falling behind because unless you have a big lead you don't want to walk in a run. It's just a different feeling psychologically when you have a base open. You're less likely to give in to a hitter if you fall behind. Most of the time, if I'm given the option, I would rather not intentionally walk someone to load the bases. But I could certainly understand Willie not wanting to pitch to Cabrera."

Mota quickly got behind Willingham 2–0, as the crowd, which had gotten in the habit of booing him whenever anything went wrong (much the way the Yankee crowd did whenever Kyle Farnsworth got into trouble), began to boo. Down 2–0, not wanting to walk in a run with a two-run lead, Mota made sure his next pitch was over the plate.

It was—a fastball right down Broadway—and Willingham crushed it over the left-field fence for a grand slam. Glavine would not get win number 301 in spite of another good performance. The Marlins now led 5–3, and Randolph had to go get Mota as the boos reached a crescendo.

"I guess I was thankful that I was at three hundred and not

trying to get there anymore because that would have really hurt," Glavine said. "As it was, it was disappointing that we ended up losing the game, but I came away feeling good because I pitched well after all the distractions of the week. I felt as if I was starting to get on the roll I really hadn't been on all season."

The team was most definitely not on a roll. The loss was their fourth in five games since Glavine's three hundredth and cut their lead over the Braves to two and a half games. It did not, however, dampen the celebration the next day when the Mets honored Glavine.

Team Glavine was back—the logistics made easier by the fact that the Billerica group could drive and a lot of the family could stay at the house. The Mets brought Tom Seaver in to be master of ceremonies. Almost always when the Mets honor someone, Seaver comes to town. He had been their first great player, the heart and soul of the Miracle Mets of 1969, and had been the first player whose bust in the Hall of Fame wore a Mets cap.

There was no escaping the irony that Seaver had won his three hundredth game in a White Sox uniform and Glavine had won his three hundredth in a Mets uniform. Glavine would go into the Hall of Fame as a Brave when his time came, but he was now the first pitcher to win his three hundredth game as a Met.

Glavine had talked to the media so much in the previous week that there really wasn't much left for anyone to ask him. It didn't matter: Seaver was going to do most of the talking anyway. "To win three hundred games, like Tom has done, you have to be an artist, not just a pitcher," Seaver said, clearly talking about himself at least as much as Glavine. "I think what's important, though, is the way Tom has conducted himself throughout his career, not just on the mound but off it."

That was the theme for the day. Glavine wasn't thrilled about all the hoopla, even though he understood it. "I like to be the center of attention when I'm on the mound and have the ball in my hands," he said. "Stuff like this is a little embarrassing."

He sat and listened while one speaker after another went on about him, and he was presented with various awards by friends and teammates and, for some reason, former New York Rangers hockey player Rod Gilbert, and he watched a videotape the Mets had put together of other great athletes congratulating him. He got a chuckle when Wayne Gretzky appeared, wondering if he might have made something of himself had he pursued hockey. The only glitch came when Seaver forgot it was time to introduce Glavine and went to sit down. Someone nudged him, and he ran back to the podium and said, "I almost forgot. Ladies and gentlemen, Tom Glavine."

Not the most dramatic introduction, but Glavine didn't mind. The only surprising moment in his thank-you speech came when Glavine went out of his way to talk about how important it was to him that he had conducted himself the way he had during his career. It was very un-Glavine-like for Glavine to pat himself on the back publicly in any way.

"I just thought it was the right forum to make the point that you can be successful as a professional athlete and not be a jerk," he said. "There's so much focus on the guys that screw up and a tendency to forget that there are guys who perform well and conduct themselves well too. I wanted to make the point that you *can* do both."

Glavine also noticed that all the Marlins were in their dugout, watching from the top step, as he spoke. He was touched by that. He knew his teammates would be out there; he wasn't so sure about the opponents. "I thought that was cool," he said. "It was a sign of respect."

As the ceremony broke up, Glavine made a point of walking in the direction of the Florida dugout to say thanks. He had no idea how the Marlins would repay him for his courtesy.

26

Crash

THERE WERE NOW just seven weeks left in a season that had started six months earlier, when pitchers and catchers reported to spring training. The weather was hot, and everyone was a little bit tired. Teams no longer in contention had to push themselves to come to the ballpark every day and give their best. For everyone, stamina was a factor. Which is why the latter days of August are known as "the dog days." You are dog tired, but there is still a long way to go to get to the finish line.

Mussina's victory in Cleveland was the middle game of an impressive three-game sweep. It boosted the Yankees' record to 66–51, putting them in a tie with Seattle for the wild-card lead and, remarkably, only four games behind the Red Sox, who were suddenly hearing people in New England whisper the dreaded words "Nineteen seventy-eight." That had been the year the Yankees had come from fourteen and a half games back in July to catch and pass the Red Sox, before beating them in the famous/infamous playoff game (depending on your point of view) in which Bucky Dent hit the famous/infamous three-run homer off of Mike Torrez.

Sweeney Murdy, the sharp young reporter who covers the Yankees for WFAN, was standing in the middle of the Yankees clubhouse in New York on the afternoon of August 13, a few hours before the team began a three-game series with the Orioles, when

Mike Mussina sidled over to him. Mussina likes Murdy because Murdy's sense of humor is similar to his (sarcastic) and because he almost never asks questions like "Are you where you want to be?" In fact, he makes fun of those who do.

"Hey, Sweeney," Mussina said. "What's our record right now?"

Murdy always knows the Yankees' record. "You're sixty-six and fifty-one, Moose," he said, wondering if Mussina had somehow lost track.

"Really?" Mussina said. "What are the Mets?"

As it happened, Murdy knew that too, and when the question came out of Mussina's mouth Murdy knew he was being set up. "They're sixty-five and fifty-two," he answered.

"Really?" Mussina said, wide-eyed. "How's that possible?"

With that, he walked back to his locker, a satisfied smile on his face.

It was nothing personal, but Mussina, like a lot of those who had been around the Yankees for a while, was more than pleased that the Yankees' record was now better than that of the Mets.

"It seemed like in May and June, whenever I turned on the radio all I heard was how New York was now a Mets town," Mussina said. "We were yesterday's news; we were done. We needed to fire our manager, our general manager, and most of our players. The Mets were *the* team. They had been in the playoffs, what, one year in a row? We'd been in twelve, right? They last won a World Series when — 1986?

"I just couldn't believe that early in the season people were just writing us off. I know some people get sick of us being in the playoffs every year, but when you're in the middle of it you take pride in it. So, when we did go past them, even though in the grand scheme of things it meant nothing, I just wanted to make sure people noticed."

The Yankees had not made any major trades at the July 31 trade deadline, resisting the urge to trade prospects for a relief pitcher like Eric Gagne or an added bat for the lineup. Instead, they were now inserting some of those prospects into the lineup and the pitching rotation and the bullpen.

Philip Hughes had finally come off the disabled list on August 3, mercifully allowing the team to take Kei Igawa out of the rotation. Jeff Karstens, who had been on the DL all season, was recalled from minor league rehab early in August, and Mike Myers was designated for assignment. But the key addition was Joba Chamberlain, a twenty-one-year-old right-hander who had started the season playing Class-A ball in Tampa but had been so good that he had been moved up to Triple-A by July. He had been a starter, but the Yankees needed someone to pitch the eighth inning since everyone who had been tried in that slot had failed. So they began using him in relief in early July, noting his 98-mile-per-hour fastball and his control.

On August 7, Chamberlain was called up, pitched two shutout innings in a 9–2 victory over the Blue Jays, and quickly began acquiring folk hero status in New York. Every time he walked to the mound in Yankee Stadium, the crowd started screaming.

As luck would have it, Chamberlain's arrival coincided with Mariano Rivera's annual slump. Every year, sometime in July or August, Rivera would go through a stretch where he struggled. Usually it was from overwork, but that wasn't the case this year. He was just having a hard time getting people out.

Rivera had been hit hard in the finale in Cleveland, even though he had held on to save the game for Andy Pettitte. The next night, he blew a save against the Orioles and was bailed out only because the Yankees scored a run in the bottom of the ninth to win the game 7–6. Two days later, he came into a tie game in the tenth inning and was shelled for three runs and the loss, as the Yankees again lost two of three to the Orioles.

Watching Rivera pitch, Mussina thought he saw something different in the way he was setting up to deliver. Mussina watches pitchers carefully, especially those on the Yankees, on the four days in between starts that he isn't pitching. Sometimes he learns something by watching; other times he may see something that he thinks needs to be brought to the pitcher's attention.

"Pitching is what I do, so it's only natural for me to study other pitchers," he said. "But I also think at this point in my career, I might be able to help out at times. Usually it's with younger guys: maybe they're tipping a pitch; maybe they're off balance for some reason or opening up. Maybe they don't know what to do when they get a scuffed ball."

Older pitchers like Glavine and Mussina are constantly amazed when they see young pitchers get a ball back after a grounder to an infielder and throw it in to the umpire asking for a new ball because it has been scuffed by the infield dirt.

"Boggles my mind when I see that," Mussina said. "You treat a scuffed ball like gold and hang on to it for as long as you can."

If a pitcher scuffs a ball himself, he is subject to ejection, fine, and suspension. But if the ball gets scuffed in the course of play and no one asks for it to be taken out of play, it can become a weapon. "You have to put it up against your third and fourth fingers instead of your second and third," Mussina said. "You throw it and twist your hand outward. The scuff makes the ball dive an extra three or four inches to the outside. A hitter should notice the difference right away, but you might get a quick out with it or, if you're lucky and no one notices, a couple."

Early in the season, Glavine had picked up a ball with a scuff on it outside the Mets dugout just before batting practice one morning. He noticed rookies Mike Pelfrey and Joe Smith standing on the top step of the dugout and walked over to them, ball in hand.

"What do you do with this ball?" he demanded, handing the ball to Pelfrey.

"Get rid of it?" Pelfrey answered.

Glavine shook his head. "*No*. Absolutely not. You hold on to it for dear life." He then spent several minutes showing Pelfrey the proper grip and motion. "Work on it," he said. "It'll make you a better pitcher."

"What about me?" Smith said.

"Nah, you can't do it throwing underhanded," Glavine said. (Smith is a side-armer who releases the ball from below the waist.)

"But *you*," he said, pointing at Pelfrey, "need to learn this. It's part of being a pitcher."

Rivera didn't need anyone to teach him about what to do with a scuffed ball. But watching him in the game in Cleveland and then the two games against the Orioles, Mussina was convinced he saw something different in his delivery. "When you've watched Mo as many times as I have, for as many years as I have, you're bound to notice any change at all. At first I wasn't sure what was different, just that something was different. I asked [Mike] Borzello if he thought he saw anything different when he was warming him up, and he said he didn't. I told him to watch that day if Mo went in.

"He saw it from the center-field window, and I saw it from the dugout. Mo always stands up very straight in the stretch [like most relievers, Rivera always pitches out of the stretch] and keeps his front [left] shoulder very high. It looked to me like he wasn't standing up as straight and his shoulder was dropping just a little. That doesn't sound like much, but it can change your balance."

Once Mussina and Borzello had agreed that they had seen the same thing, Mussina let Joe Torre and Ron Guidry know what he had observed. They both said the same thing: tell him.

"I have no problem when someone like Mike thinks he sees something," Torre said. "For one thing, he's smart and he knows pitching. For another, with his experience it's almost like having another pitching coach on the staff."

Mussina mentioned to Rivera before the Yankees began their series with the Tigers on August 16 that he and Borzello had noticed something in his stance. When he got to the bullpen that day, Rivera discussed it with Borzello.

"We need to get back to our routine from April," Rivera told

Borzello. Early in the season when Rivera had struggled, he had thrown to the Yankees' other bullpen catcher, Ramon Rodriguez (no relation to Alex), while Borzello stood in the left-hand batter's box to give him a target. When Rivera made the suggested adjustments, he instantly felt a difference, and his cutter, the pitch that has made him a surefire Hall of Famer, had noticeably more bite, diving away from Borzello as he stood on the left side of the bullpen plate.

So Rivera was fixed. He came in the next night against Detroit and pitched a one-two-three ninth. If nothing else, that quieted all the people screaming on sports radio that Chamberlain should replace Rivera as the closer.

"I heard some of that," Mussina said, shaking his head. "Are people completely out of their minds?"

Having fixed Rivera, Mussina made the start that same night in the opener against the Tigers. He had every reason to feel good about himself as he took the mound against Detroit's young ace Justin Verlander. In his four starts since the "no ball" session in the bullpen, Mussina had gone 4–0 with an ERA of 2.84. And yet, as he warmed up before the game, Mussina had a small sense of dread. Nothing felt quite as comfortable or as easy as it had in Cleveland.

"This is something that happens to everyone during a season; in fact, I'd bet it's something that happens to every athlete," he said. "You reach a point where you've worked hard and everything is clicking. That's when you have that mindless game like the one I had in Cleveland. But pitching isn't a mindless exercise. For one game, maybe even two, it can be. But most of the time you need a certain focus on your mechanics, on your release, on how you're locating the ball.

"The problem is, when you go from mindless to needing to focus, it isn't something you can just snap your fingers and make happen. I know it's hard to believe, but it's almost as if you have to learn how to pitch all over again. You go from feeling like you can't do anything wrong in one start to wondering if you have any idea how to pitch in the next start."

Mussina's sense that this happens to athletes in all sports is accurate. Consider how often golfers, after a brilliant round in which they appear capable of hitting any shot, come back the next day and shoot ten or twelve strokes higher. Or the tennis player who can't miss a serve one day and starts firing double-faults all over the place the next. Or basketball players who hit every shot they take one night and are ice cold the next. It happens in every sport.

Mussina calls it "mindlessness." A lot of people call it "being unconscious." As in "He was so hot, he was unconscious." The term is apt because an athlete in that kind of zone isn't thinking about what he's doing. That's why when someone—even someone as articulate as Glavine or Mussina—is asked about a brilliant performance, he often can't explain it because he isn't thinking about what he's doing, he's just doing it.

As Mussina says, you go from autopilot to being on a plane with the autopilot turned off and no one in the cockpit. The result is predictable: crash.

Mussina didn't exactly nosedive against the Tigers. In fact, with a little help from his defense, he might have gotten through the game in reasonable shape. In the first inning, he gave up a one-out single to ex-Yankee Marcus Thames. That brought up a far more notorious ex-Yankee, Gary Sheffield. Earlier in the season, Sheffield, who was known for an extremely quick bat and an often wayward mouth, had said in a magazine story that he believed Joe Torre treated African American players differently than he treated white and Hispanic players. The comments were so upsetting to Torre, who had gone out of his way to keep Sheffield happy while he'd been in New York, that for one of the few times in his life, he simply refused to comment. Every time Sheffield came to the plate during the weekend series, he was greeted by very loud boos.

Mussina made everyone happy when he got Sheffield to hit a ground ball to Alex Rodriguez for what should have been a five-four-three double play, especially given Sheffield's lack of speed. But Rodriguez booted the ball, and all hands were safe. Instead of being in the dugout with a relatively easy first inning behind him, Mussina was on the mound with men on first and second and cleanup hitter Magglio Ordonez, who was having a monster year, at the plate. Pitching carefully, Mussina walked Ordonez. That loaded the bases for Carlos Guillen, who was no bargain either, especially hitting lefty in Yankee Stadium.

"In that situation, you obviously don't want to walk the guy," Mussina said. "But you also don't want to make a mistake because the guy hits mistakes."

Working carefully, Mussina got to 2–2. Not wanting to go to 3–2, he tried to make the 2–2 the decisive pitch of the at bat, a fastball on the outer half of the plate. But Guillen, looking for it, extended his arms across the plate and drove the ball high into the right-field seats for a grand slam. Instead of putting a zero on the board in the first inning, the Tigers had hung a four on Mussina.

"Yeah, it's true; if Alex makes that play, maybe I get out of the inning untouched," Mussina said. "But if I'm being honest, I think that only would have meant my numbers for the night would have been better. I still wouldn't have been good. Nothing was easy."

He gave up two more runs in the second, managed to work through the third and fourth untouched, and gave up another run in the fifth, before leaving, trailing 7–3. Obviously three earned runs in five innings would have been considerably better than six earned runs in five innings, but Mussina knew if he'd gone out for a sixth inning, it probably would not have gone well.

"The home-run pitch to Guillen was kind of typical," he said. "I knew what I wanted to throw and where I wanted to throw it, and I just let it drift in a little too much. The whole night was like that."

The Tigers went on to win 8–5, giving Justin Verlander his

thirteenth win of the season. The Yankees bounced back on the strength of three good pitching performances—Pettitte, Clemens, and Wang—to win the last three games of the series. Heading to the West Coast, that gave them a three-game cushion on the Tigers in the wild-card race.

They lost the opener in Anaheim 7–6 in ten innings thanks to some sloppy outfield play and some poor relief pitching. It was Mussina's turn the next night. He had worked diligently in the bullpen on his mechanics between starts, knowing he wasn't likely to capture the mindless feeling of Cleveland any time soon but that the semi-helpless feeling of the Detroit game wasn't what he wanted to feel.

He warmed up well on a beautiful night and felt good when he came to the mound for the bottom of the first inning. The feeling didn't last very long. He walked Chone Figgins and Orlando Cabrera to start the game. In 497 major league starts, Mussina had never walked the first two batters he had faced in a game. Months later, discussing that night, he shook his head and said, "I honestly don't remember walking those guys. The only thing I remember about that first inning is getting a bad call on Garret Anderson's ground ball down the first-base line."

That came after Vladimir Guerrero had hit a long fly ball to center field for the first out. Anderson, one of many Yankee killers in the Angels lineup, hit a hard ground ball down the first-base line that was either just fair or just foul. Mussina thought it was foul and so did first baseman Andy Phillips. Paul Emmel, the first-base umpire, thought it was fair. The ball went down the right-field line while both Figgins and Cabrera scored. Anderson ended up on second.

Mussina, Phillips, and catcher Jose Molina argued the call vehemently, but Emmel wouldn't budge, and he wouldn't ask home-plate umpire Ron Kulpa for help. "He's actually a good umpire," Mussina said. "I'd never had a problem with him in the past. I just thought he missed that call."

Perhaps Mussina argued as much as he did because he knew he was skating on thin ice already. He managed to get out of the inning without further damage, and Alex Rodriguez homered in the second to make it 2–1. Then came the bottom of the second inning.

Crash.

The inning began with a Maicer Izturis single followed by ringing no-doubt doubles by Howie Kendrick and Jeff Mathis, the second making the score 4–1. Mussina managed to get two outs, but then the bottom dropped out completely: a Guerrero double in the gap made it 5–1; another double by Anderson made it 6–1; and then Gary Matthews Jr. singled up the middle to make it 7–1.

The only reason Mussina faced Matthews was that Torre couldn't get Ron Villone warmed up in time to prevent it. Ready or not, Villone was in after the Matthews hit. Mussina's line read like this: one and two-thirds innings pitched; seven runs, all earned; seven hits; two walks; one strikeout. He had thrown forty-eight pitches in less than two innings, and nine of the four-teen batters he faced reached base. Every one of the seven hits was hit hard. The only surprise was that no one had homered. By the time he walked off the mound, his ERA for the season had soared to 5.22.

"I simply couldn't keep the ball off the barrel of the bat," he said. "It was embarrassing. They hit everything hard."

The bullpen wasn't any better than Mussina, and the game turned into a nightmare, the Angels finally winning 18–9. Mussina was so bad that several Angels asked Mike Borzello if he was hurt.

The answer, as it turned out, was yes.

Mussina had been nursing a number of minor injuries for most of the season. When he had come back from the hamstring injury, he had been healthy enough to pitch but not 100 percent. "If you want to be a hundred percent after an injury like that, you probably have to do nothing for two or three months," he said. "You can't do that. You're paid to pitch. When it felt good enough to pitch, I pitched."

In mid-May, he had hurt his right foot when he misstepped going down into the dugout after batting practice one afternoon. "The dugout steps at Yankee Stadium are rounded off a little, and my foot just caught a little," he said. "I didn't think that much of it at the time, but it kept hurting to the point where I'd get out of bed in the morning and I could barely walk."

Several doctors examined him but none could find anything broken or torn. The feeling was that he had stretched one of his arches. He could have shut down for a while but — as with the hamstring — didn't want to stop pitching. "I could still pitch, and at times I pitched well," he said. "But there were times I felt like I couldn't drive down off the mound the way that I wanted to."

Other aches followed: His right knee hurt, probably connected to adjusting his delivery because of the foot. Then his left hip began to bother him, probably the result of old age.

"You know you're going to have aches and pains during the season," he said. "Especially when you're older, you have to learn to put up with them. You don't want to spend your life in the training room or on the DL or sitting out because of something minor. The funny thing is my arm never felt better. And, even with all this stuff going on, I had that four-game stretch where I pitched really well. But in August, particularly in that Anaheim game, I just seemed to feel everything. Was that the reason I pitched so poorly? I don't know. But after that game, I felt like I needed to let Joe know what was going on."

Torre already knew about the foot and the hamstring but didn't know that Mussina's knee and hip were also bothering him. When Mussina walked into his office in Anaheim the day after the debacle there and told him what was going on, Torre's first notion was to have him skip a start.

"Moose has never been a whiner or an excuse maker," Torre

said. "If he comes to me and says he's hurt, I know he's hurt. I asked him if skipping a start might help him heal up a little."

Mussina rejected that idea. Because of an off-day between the series in Anaheim and the four-game series in Detroit, he would have an extra day before he pitched next. He thought that would help. He and Torre agreed he would start the final game in Detroit and see how he felt after that game.

"Looking back, maybe I was being a little stubborn about it," Mussina said. "I didn't want to go on the DL or miss a start when we were right in the middle of this wild-card race and not completely out of the division race. Whatever it was, I just knew I wanted to pitch."

In July, when he had struggled, the Yankees really didn't have an alternative for Mussina in the starting rotation. Hughes was still on the DL then, and the feeling was that Ian Kennedy, the organization's other touted young starter, was better off staying in the minor leagues at least until September call-ups. But now Hughes was healthy and Kennedy was pitching well enough that the team might consider moving him up sooner if necessary. Mussina wasn't thinking in those terms. He was thinking only that he'd had two bad starts — one bad, one horrific — and he wanted to turn that around.

He was better in Detroit than he had been in Anaheim but not by much. The Tigers scored one in the first, two in the second, and three in the third. Mussina was consistently finding bat barrels again, and line drives were going in all directions around Comerica Park. His fastball was too close to the plate, and his breaking pitches lacked any bite at all.

"In those two games, there were times when it looked like he was throwing batting practice," Borzello said. "It seemed as if everything he was throwing, regardless of the pitch, was just flat. You can't get guys out that way."

This time, Mussina got nine guys out, getting through three innings. But the numbers were ugly again: nine hits, six runs, seventy-two pitches thrown to get through three innings. The bullpen was even worse than it had been in Anaheim, and the final was 16–0.

Mussina wasn't at wit's end, but he was close. He'd had bad streaks before in his career, but his ERA had never been 5.53 at the end of August. "What you have to do in those situations, what I've always done, is take a day to be pissed off about it and pout and then start thinking about your next start," he said. "You have to do that or you lose your mind. You have to think, 'How do I get better before my next start?' We'd been able to do it after the Tampa game. There had to be a way to do it this time too. I had to get in the bullpen with Borzy and Gator [Guidry] and figure something out."

The Yankees flew home from Detroit late on Monday night to start a three-game series with the Red Sox the next night. Their 2–5 road trip had allowed Boston to widen its lead in the division race to eight games. Clearly, the wild card was what the Yankees had to shoot for now, with less than five weeks left in the season. They had dropped two games behind the Mariners and were tied with the Tigers in that race.

Mussina wasn't scheduled to pitch in the Boston series. His next start was to come on Saturday against his old friends the Devil Rays. He arrived at the ballpark on Tuesday a little bit tired—he had gotten home at about three in the morning after the flight—and a good deal frustrated. He went through his normal day-after-pitching routine and was sitting in the office of equipment manager Rob Cucuzza about twenty minutes before the game started, looking through a sporting goods catalog for things his boys might want in the spring.

Mussina often hangs out in Cucuzza's office. It is almost directly across from Torre's office in the narrow hallway many of the players use to enter and exit the clubhouse. As he was paging through the catalog, Mussina saw Torre come out of his office and head in the direction of the field. When Torre saw Mussina, he stopped short and walked back into Cucuzza's office, sitting in a chair opposite Mussina.

"I just wanted you to know, so you don't hear it from someone else later, that we've decided we're going to let the Kennedy kid take your start on Saturday," he said.

Mussina wasn't completely shocked—he'd heard talk that Kennedy might be called up—but he was stunned, partly by the news, but also by the way Torre had more or less dropped it in his lap, as if he were letting him know that batting practice might start early the next day.

"So that's it then?" he asked Torre. "No discussion? It's just done?"

Torre nodded his head. "It's done," he said. "We talked about it a good deal, and we're going to see how he does and then decide what to do going forward after that."

"So you're saying this may not just be a one-start deal."

Torre sighed. "Yeah, I guess that is what I'm saying. I don't really know what we're going to do beyond Saturday. I can't promise you anything."

He stood up to go. He had been in Cucuzza's office for, by Mussina's estimate, ninety seconds.

"I felt bad then, I feel bad now, about the way it all came down," Torre said later. "Obviously, a lot of discussion and thought went into deciding what to do. You don't pull Mike Mussina from the rotation without giving it serious thought. But once we made the decision that afternoon, I didn't want someone — anyone — walking up to him and saying, 'So I hear you aren't starting on Saturday.' Nothing stays secret around here for very long. The tough thing was I didn't have the time to sit and talk to him about it then because it was so close to game time."

Mussina and Torre had always had an excellent relationship, dating to the phone call in November 2000 when Torre had, for all intents and purposes, recruited Mussina to play for the Yankees. Now, Mussina felt betrayed, not only by the decision but by the way it was relayed to him.

"I just couldn't believe it," Mussina said. "I'd made four hundred ninety-eight straight starts in the big leagues without ever being skipped, and I'm told in ninety seconds, 'You're out, and I can't tell you when or if you'll ever be back in.' Had I been bad for three straight starts? Yes. Awful in the last two. But the four starts before that I had been very good. All of a sudden, it felt as if my entire career had boiled down to a three-game tryout and I'd flunked.

"I was angry and I was confused. I really didn't know what to do or who to turn to."

By the time Torre told the media about the change that night, Mussina had left the clubhouse. For one of the few times in his life, he called Jana on the way home to tell her what had happened. Short of an injury, there was really no baseball news that Jana Mussina needed to hear before Mike got home. This was different.

"I really didn't sleep much that night," he said. "I had never been benched in my life in any sport at any level, and that was what had happened. If Joe had said, 'We're going to skip a start to try to get you healed up,' it would have been different. That wasn't what he had said. He said, 'You're out.' End of conversation. That hurt."

Mussina was still stewing over the whole thing the next day when he walked into the clubhouse. He walked past Torre's office en route to his locker and saw the manager sitting by himself. He poked his head into the room.

"I think we need to talk," he said.

Torre nodded. "Anytime. I'm available right now if you want."

Mussina walked to his locker to drop off his things, went back to Torre's office, and shut the door. "Joe hadn't even shut the door when he came in the day before," Mussina said. "For some reason, that burned me too. I mean, when kids get sent down to the minors, they go in the manager's office, even if it's for five minutes, and the door gets shut."

For several minutes, Mussina vented. "It wasn't so much about the decision," he said. "I might agree with it or disagree with it, but I understood where it came from. We're in a playoff race, I'm pitching badly, they want to try the kid. Tampa's a good team to do it against because even though their lineup is good, their pitching is so bad the kid will probably have a touchdown to work with.

"What I said, ultimately, was that I knew—*knew*—there was no way if Joe had to bench Jeter or Pettitte or Posada or Mo for any reason that he would have treated them that way. He just wouldn't have. And they were the only guys who had been on the team longer than me. I thought I deserved better."

Torre didn't disagree. He explained the circumstances and told Mussina he was sorry and knew he was hurt. Torre soothed—as he always did. It wasn't working. "I was just raw at that moment," Mussina said. "To be fair to Joe, there probably wasn't anything he could have said in there, short of 'We've changed our minds; you're starting on Saturday,' that was going to make me feel better."

The meeting lasted about ten minutes. Mussina walked back into the clubhouse and found a slew of reporters lingering by his locker. That was to be expected. "Not today, guys," he said.

"I just couldn't talk about it then," he said. "I was too upset, and I was afraid I might say something I'd regret."

Two days later, Mussina talked to everyone and apologized for not being willing or able to talk on the day after he had been removed from the rotation. He talked bluntly about being upset about the decision and how it had come down, without going into great detail. He said he would do whatever he could do to help the team and be ready when he was called on. What's more, he meant it.

"It took me a couple of days to wrestle the whole thing to the ground emotionally," he said. "I had always thought of myself as a guy who did what it took to help the team in any way. But this was really a test of all that. If I was the long man in the bullpen, well then, I better be ready when they called on me. What mattered, in the end, was the team. Guys pay lip service to that all the time, but in a sense this was an opportunity—granted, not one I wanted—for me to kind of put my money where my mouth was. The question was 'Is this about *me* or about *us?*' The answer had to be *us.*"

On his regular throw day, he went to the bullpen with Guidry and Borzello and a slew of others. One day it was bullpen coach Joe Kerrigan; on another it was Triple-A pitching coach Dave Eiland, who had joined the team at the end of the minor league season. Rich Monteleone, another ex-pitcher, who was listed among the Yankees' endless list of coaches as a "special pitching instructor," was out there too.

Mussina decided to alter his normal routine. He tried different pitches, mixing a few split-fingered fastballs into his session. That was the pitch that had extended Roger Clemens's career. Maybe a strikeout pitch that didn't look like anything else he threw could help him.

"I'd always been able to throw it but never really threw it in games," he said. "Maybe two, three times in my life. I figured it was worth at least thinking about."

He threw harder and longer than he normally did in his session between starts because his body wasn't as beaten up as it normally was after throwing a hundred or so pitches at maximum effort every fifth day.

"Basically, I was trying to find a way to feel comfortable throwing the ball again," he said. "Each time out, I felt a little better, a little more confident. Of course, there was no way to know if I was fooling myself or if it really was getting better until I got to pitch in a game."

He talked often to Borzello about what was going on. Guidry

had not said a word to him since his benching. "Of all the things that happened during that time, that may have been the most upsetting," he said. "I like Gator, I really do, but he just didn't seem able to handle what was going on. I'd go by him in the club-house, and he'd look right through me. It was as if I'd become a ghost. He never said a word, not even 'Hang in there'—I mean nothing. I guess he just figured he had nothing to gain by engaging me in conversation. But it bothered me a lot."

As usual, Borzello was honest with him. When Mussina talked about his whole career coming down to a three-game tryout, Borzello nodded in assent. "And you were awful," he said. "We're in a playoff race here. If this was May, it might be different. It's not. Your next start was going to be in September."

Mussina listened. He respected Borzello's opinions. Finally, one day when they were eating, Borzello asked Mussina the $11.5 million question: "If you had been Joe, would you have done what he did or not?"

Mussina thought about that one for a while. "I guess," he finally said, "I might have done the same thing. I just would have handled it differently."

Ian Kennedy started on Saturday, September 1, against the Devil Rays. He pitched extremely well: seven innings, three runs (only one earned), five hits, one walk. Although the bullpen had another semi-implosion, Mussina's touchdown prediction proved conservative and the Yankees won the game 9–6. Not surprisingly, Torre said afterward that Kennedy would start the following weekend in Kansas City. Earlier that day, Mussina had been told that he might start on Monday against the Seattle Mariners. Clemens's groin was bothering him again and if he couldn't start, Mussina was told to be ready.

Mussina had not been called on out of the bullpen since he had been sent there. Now, he was told he might be starting in two days. Or he might not. "It was very weird," he said. "I came to the park that day and went through all my usual game-day routines as if I was starting. Roger went through all of his. Then I went and sat in the dugout while he warmed up in the bullpen and waited for a call saying 'You're starting,' or 'Relax, you're not starting.' That's what my life had come down to: I was the backup. Be ready, but if we're lucky we won't need you."

The call came shortly before the 1:05 start time. Clemens said he was okay to start. Mussina headed for his new home—the bullpen—soon after the game began.

The phone rang in the fourth inning. "Roger's hurting," Kerrigan told him. "Get ready."

And so, the highest-paid long man in Major League Baseball history, one who was three wins shy of 250, got up to warm up. In the top of the fifth, with the Yankees trailing 5–1, he jogged to the mound for the first regular-season relief appearance of his life.

"I was just glad," he said later, "that I was able to get from the pen to the mound without getting lost."

27

On a Roll

WHILE MIKE MUSSINA WAS CRASHING, Tom Glavine was soaring.

He had pitched well in three straight starts after Los Angeles leading to three hundred: the win against Pittsburgh, the no-decision in Milwaukee, and the climactic win in Chicago.

Now, with the three hundred pressure removed, Glavine was enjoying pitching more than at any time since he arrived in New York, perhaps even longer than that. He pitched the opening game of a series in Washington on August 17, a night when the Mets badly needed a strong pitching performance. They had been embarrassed the night before in Pittsburgh, rallying from an early deficit to lead 7–5, only to see the bullpen completely blow up in a 10–7 loss.

The Mets still had a three-game lead, but there was evidence of some tension in the tiny visitors' clubhouse in RFK Stadium. Willie Randolph had said to the media after the game in Pitts-burgh that "you have to tip your cap to the Pirates."

In most places that would have been seen as a gracious nod to a bad team that had managed to piece together a good night. In New York it was seen as Randolph—again—not being fiery enough to go after his team when it gave away a game it should have won. Randolph had plenty of fire. He had been an extremely competitive player, and he had a temper. But, much like Torre, whom he had worked for as a coach for eleven years, he didn't often show it.

"Just because I don't jump up and down in front of the cameras and act like an asshole doesn't mean I can't be one," he said, perhaps not meaning it quite that way. His point was that he got angry behind closed doors when he felt the need. To most in New York, the need to get angry had arrived.

The players didn't feel quite that way. Glavine had said repeatedly during the season that a real pennant race was the norm; 2006 had been an aberration. And yet, there was a feeling that the chance to run away with the race had been there and hadn't been taken.

The latest issue was the catching situation. Lo Duca had strained his hamstring again during the Florida series and had been placed — angrily — on the disabled list on August 12. Within minutes, or so it seemed, of Lo Duca being deactivated for fifteen days, Ramon Castro, his backup, began complaining of back pains. Almost as if not wanting to admit they had acted hastily with Lo Duca, the club kept him active for almost a week while thirty-eight-year-old Mike Difelice, a classic journeyman major leaguer — he had played twelve seasons with seven different teams, playing in a total of 543 games — did all the catching. Finally, after the team got to Washington, Castro was DL'd and forty-one-year-old Sandy Alomar Jr. was called up. If nothing else, the Mets now had the oldest catching duo in baseball.

None of that seemed to bother Glavine. He was superb once more against the Nationals. On a typically sultry August night in Washington — it was ninety degrees at game time but felt considerably warmer with the humidity — he threw seven innings that looked effortless.

The Nats had one quick rally against him when Ryan Zimmerman singled with two outs in the third and Dmitri Young doubled him home. But that was it. The rest of the night was a breeze for the Mets and for their many fans in the small crowd (23,636 announced) that rumbled around in the old ballpark. Damion Easley got the Mets started with a home run in the second and then Jose Reyes scored a "Reyes run" in the third: walk, stolen base, advance to third on an error by the catcher, and then score easily on a David Wright single. Moises Alou homered in the fourth, and it was 4–1 by the time Glavine went out to pitch the seventh.

The beginning of that inning was his only real moment of trepidation. He had walked in the top of the inning, and after running the bases he thought Randolph and Peterson might take him out since he had thrown 104 pitches. Peterson asked him how he felt, and he told him, honestly, okay. They let him go out, in part because of that, in part because they really didn't want to go to the bullpen before they absolutely had to. Glavine proceeded to pitch a one-two-three seventh, and even though Jorge Sosa wobbled in the eighth, the final was 6–2.

"Vintage Tommy Glavine," Randolph called it. "We needed a well-pitched game from our starter tonight, and he gave us just that."

Glavine had thrown 116 pitches on a hot night and felt like he could pitch the next day if necessary. "When your pitches are going almost exactly where you want them to, it doesn't feel like work," he said. "You feel it physically, of course, but mentally you're flying. My changeup is going almost exactly where I want it to go on almost every pitch right now. When I've got that going, I'm probably going to pitch well."

Glavine's performance was the start of a roll for the Mets. They swept the Nats and won the opener of a series at Shea against the San Diego Padres, who were in a battle for the NL West title and the wild-card spot.

Glavine was in the weight room on Monday afternoon when he saw Greg Maddux coming toward him. Maddux and Glavine were the same age, and Maddux was still pitching well for the

Padres—the third team he had been with since leaving the Braves. He and Glavine were still friends but not the way Glavine and Smoltz were friends. Maddux lived in Las Vegas during the off-season, and he and Glavine weren't in touch all that often. Glavine hadn't heard from Maddux since his three hundredth win.

"Looking back, I probably should have called him or sent a message or something," Maddux said. "But I knew we were playing them in a couple weeks, so I figured I'd wait and talk to him in person."

As soon as Maddux saw Glavine, he walked right over to him with a big smile on his face.

"So," he said, "what took you so long?"

Glavine cracked up. It was exactly the kind of comment he would have hoped for from Maddux. The two then had a lengthy conversation about families, about their teams, and about next season.

"He said if I keep feeling good, I might as well pitch next year," Glavine said. "To be honest, by that point I was pretty much thinking the same thing."

There had been very little talk during the march to three hundred about 2008, even in the Glavine household. "Honestly, I have no idea what he's going to do," Chris Glavine said in mid-August. "I'm not going to be surprised if he wants to pitch. And if he does, it's fine. We'll deal with it."

There had been a little bit of a stir late in July when the *New York Daily News* had reported that the Glavines were about to put their Greenwich house on the market. The story was accurate, but Glavine didn't feel as if it committed him one way or the other: "If we get an offer, we can always turn it down," he said. "If we do sell and I come back here next year, we might want to get an apartment in Manhattan. The boys are old enough to enjoy the city now, and Chris and I have always thought it might be fun to do that for a year."

In short, he was keeping his options open. The way he was pitching, it was likely he would have a number of them. "If I do pitch, it's Atlanta or New York—period," he said. "Gregg [Clifton] told me last winter that if I went on the open market I could probably get several offers. I don't want that. Both places feel like home to me now. The difference, obviously, is in Atlanta, Chris and the kids don't have to fly back and forth all season long."

The win in the opener over the Padres had ballooned the Mets' lead to five games. Jake Peavy, who would go on to win the National League Cy Young Award, stopped the winning streak the next night.

Glavine then pitched the final game of the series. His analysis of the start was succinct: "I sucked," he said. "I guess I was due for a game like that, but it caught me by surprise because I'd been pitching so well. I kept throwing pitches in places I hadn't been throwing them since Los Angeles. It was frustrating."

The night began innocently enough, Glavine pitching out of a two-out, two-on jam in the first, and the Mets giving him a 1–0 lead when Carlos Beltran drove Wright in with a two-out double in the bottom of the inning. It unraveled for Glavine after that. The Padres scored one in the second and one in the third, which would have been more if Milton Bradley hadn't been thrown out at the plate on a call in which the Mets appeared to catch a break from plate umpire Derryl Cousins. They scored two more in the fourth and the fifth, the last two coming after two were down. Khalil Greene had doubled, Josh Bard singled with one out, and Marcus Giles tripled in a ten-pitch span. Glavine finally got the last out, but he knew he wouldn't be back for the sixth.

"I just couldn't get the third out," he said. "I think they scored five of the runs with two out. I was completely frustrated. But I really thought it was just one of those nights, not the beginning of a trend or anything. It wasn't one of those deals where Rick and I had to sit down and go over it in chapter and verse. It was just a night where I went home pissed off."

The Mets actually rallied to lead, scoring six runs in the sixth but — sound familiar? — lost in ten after another bullpen melt-down. Even so, the loss hardly appeared to be a big deal. The Mets took two of three from the Dodgers over the weekend and headed to Philadelphia for a four-game series, with a six-game lead on the Phillies and a seven-game lead on the Braves, who were fading badly, even after pulling a major trade to get slugger Mark Teixeira from Texas at the trade deadline.

"They just don't have what they always used to have," Glavine said. "Enough starting pitching."

The Mets pulled into Philadelphia thinking they had a chance to just about finish off the pennant race. After struggling to create some space all summer, they now had some. They had doubled their lead, from three games to six, since the embarrassing loss in Pittsburgh, winning six of nine while their pursuers continued to slide backward.

But the opener in Philadelphia was a disaster. Brian Lawrence had been filling the fifth starter spot while the Mets continued to wait for Pedro Martinez to have enough rehab starts to be ready to pitch. The Mets, and the media, were so obsessed with Marti-nez's return that if there wasn't a daily update on his status, every-one wondered if something had gone wrong.

Lawrence's results had been mixed at best, and he got bombed by the Phillies, the Mets losing 9–2. Glavine pitched the second game and could not have pitched better. Citizens Bank Park is as good a hitter's venue as there is in baseball, and keeping hitters in the park for an entire game is a major challenge for any pitcher. Glavine made it look easy. The Phillies appeared to be out front of everything they swung at as Glavine kept them off-balance.

Joe Kerrigan, the Yankees bullpen coach who had watched Glavine for years, laughed later when he remembered watching Glavine pitch that night. "He's made a living for twenty years out of the fact that his baseball IQ is so much higher than that of the batters he faces," he said. "He always makes them hit his pitch, and when they do, they roll over it [hitting the ball with the bottom of the bat] and hit easy ground balls. Maybe in another twenty years, they'll figure him out."

They didn't that night in Philadelphia. Glavine pitched seven shutout innnings, walking no one and scattering eight hits. Unfortunately for the Mets, Adam Eaton, who had been having a terrible year, was almost as good as Glavine, giving up just two runs in five and two-thirds innings. Even so, Glavine left with a 2–0 lead after Peterson told him 102 pitches was enough for the night.

What happened next was, as Yogi Berra liked to say, déjà vu all over again. Glavine was icing his arm when Pedro Feliciano came in to start the eighth. Jimmy Rollins hit Feliciano's fourth pitch over the left-field fence to make it 2–1. Pat Burrell walked with one out, and Shane Victorino ran for him. Feliciano managed to get Ryan Howard out, and Aaron Heilman came in needing one out to get the ball to Wagner.

He didn't get it. Victorino stole second and went to third when Paul Lo Duca, just off the DL, threw the ball into center field. Victorino scored a moment later when Aaron Rowand hit a dribbler down the third-base line and beat Heilman's throw. It was 2–2 — another chance for a Glavine win by the boards. Worse than that, the Philllies won the game 4–2 when Howard hit a mammoth two-run homer off Guillermo Mota in the tenth.

The loss was a damaging one. The Mets had wasted an excellent performance by Glavine and had allowed the Phillies to pull within four games instead of knocking them back to a six-game deficit. The next two days were even more frustrating. The Phillies won 3–2 on Wednesday, the game ending when Marlon Anderson was called for interference trying to break up a double play, while what would have been the tying run was scoring. Umpire C.B. Bucknor said that Anderson had thrown his arms into the air in an attempt to interfere with the relay throw to first base. Instead of a tie game, the Mets were in the clubhouse, literally screaming with frustration.

"That was the first time all season everyone was really mad," Glavine said. "Willie came in screaming, and a lot of guys were genuinely pissed off. I wasn't happy we lost, but I thought the anger was a good thing."

Anger is all well and good, but there's a reason for the old baseball saying that momentum is the next day's starting pitcher. For the Mets the next day, it was Orlando Hernandez, and he got shelled early, putting the Mets in a 5–0 hole. Still, they came back to lead 10–8 in the eighth, and Randolph, not trusting anyone in the bullpen but Billy Wagner, sent him out to get a two-inning save for the first time all season. It seemed like a good idea at the time, given that Wagner was rested and the rest of the bullpen had been shaky. But the Phillies got one back on a home run in the eighth by Pat Burrell and then scored two in the ninth to win 11–10.

Suddenly, the Mets' comfortable six-game lead was a two-game lead, and the Phillies were flying, the town gripped by pennant fever, not having hosted a playoff game since 1993. Jimmy Rollins, who had so angered the Mets with his "We are the team to beat" declaration in spring training, was backing up his words with his play. After going three for five in the finale, Rollins was hitting .293 with twenty-four home runs, seventy-five RBIs, and twenty-seven stolen bases. If nothing else, he was certainly the *player* to beat.

The Mets limped into Atlanta for their final road series with the Braves, knowing they needed to find something to turn them back around.

They found it: John Maine, who had appeared to be hitting the wall since the All-Star break, won the first game 7–1, out-pitching Tim Hudson. The Mets then got a huge boost when Mike Pelfrey, who had pitched so poorly the first half of the season that he had been sent to the minors, pitched his best game of the season and got his first win, 5–1, in the middle game of the set. The Phillies had split their first two games in Miami, which meant the Mets had a three-game lead again (six and a half over the Braves) going into the final game of the series. With a win, they would finish the season 5–4 in Atlanta.

The pitching matchup: Tom Glavine versus John Smoltz, naturally.

In the back of his mind, Glavine couldn't help but consider the fact that this might be his last start in Atlanta. "If it *was* going to be my last start there, I wanted it to be a good one," he said. "I wanted to beat the Braves, and I wanted to beat Smoltzie."

He was 0–2 on the year in three starts against Smoltz, even though he had pitched pretty well all three times.

It took two batters for Glavine to find trouble in the first inning. Rookie shortstop Yunel Escobar singled, and Glavine nemesis Matt Diaz singled up the middle, bringing up Chipper Jones. Glavine managed to get him to fly to deep center field, with Escobar moving to third.

Pitching carefully, Glavine walked Teixeira, loading the bases. Great. His last game, maybe, in Atlanta, and the bases were loaded with one out in the first. Glavine gave himself his usual talking to: "Don't try to do too much. Get a ground ball. Get out of this down no worse than one-nothing."

Jeff Francoeur, another headache for Glavine in '07, hit a ground ball to David Wright that wasn't hit hard enough to go for a double play. Wright threw Francoeur out as Escobar scored to make it 1–0. Still pitching carefully, Glavine walked his old pal Andruw Jones to again load the bases. That brought up catcher Brian McCann. One bad pitch—or one good pitch turned into a bad one—and the Mets might be in a hole they couldn't climb out of for the rest of the afternoon.

"You have to figure when you're facing Smoltzie that if you get down three-nothing or anything beyond that, you're in serious trouble," Glavine said. "I really wanted to hold them right there at one-nothing."

He did, reverting to his old ways—staying away from McCann

the entire at bat. On 2–2, he threw a changeup down and away, and McCann reached for it and hit a harmless ground ball to Delgado at first. Disaster averted.

Even so, Glavine was angry when he came into the dugout. "Why does this *always* happen with these guys?" he said, ostensibly to Peterson but really talking to himself out loud. "Sometimes I just feel as if they've got some kind of hex on me."

He felt less frustrated after the top of the second when he produced a run with a fly ball to center field that scored Moises Alou from third. The Mets could have scored more, but Jose Reyes struck out looking with two on and two out. Coincidence or not, Reyes hadn't been the same player since the All-Star break when Rickey Henderson and Lastings Milledge had arrived. His batting average was now under .300—.295—and at times he and Milledge had upset opponents with their post-home-run celebration dances and some of their showboating. The Mets desperately needed him to be their catalyst for the stretch drive.

In the fifth inning, with the game still locked at 1–1, Reyes did just that, leading off with a single. Two batters later, Smoltz grooved a first-pitch fastball to David Wright, and Wright hit it into orbit, giving the Mets a 3–1 lead.

Glavine kept the score right there into the seventh. When Kelly Johnson led off the inning with a single, Randolph decided one hundred pitches on a hot day was enough and went to get him. As Glavine handed the ball to Randolph and started toward the dugout, a remarkable thing happened.

For the first time since he had left Atlanta five years earlier, he heard cheers. Section after section, the fans in the sold-out stadium began standing. By the time Glavine crossed the third-base line, they were all on their feet. Of all the ovations Glavine had received before and after three hundred, this one might have meant the most. This was the place he had started as a player, the place where he had become a star, won two Cy Young Awards and a World Series. It was also the park where he had been booed more than any other place.

And now, realizing this might be the last time they saw him in a baseball uniform, Atlanta's fans were cheering him. "It meant a lot," he said. "After all that had gone on, if that was the last time I walked off a field in Atlanta, I really couldn't think of a much better ending."

Of course there was the little matter of winning the game. This time the bullpen hung on. Barely. Billy Wagner, who had been so good the first four months of the season before having a tough August, gave up a run in the ninth and allowed the tying run to reach second. But he got Diaz to ground out to second for the final out. The Mets had won 3–2. Glavine had beaten Smoltz. The Braves were seven and a half back, and the Phillies, having lost in Miami that day, were four back.

Glavine was 12–6, and his ERA was barely over 4.00 after being 4.63 following the disaster in Los Angeles. All was well. There were twenty-six games left.

THE DAY AFTER GLAVINE'S VICTORY in Atlanta, Mike Mussina got to pitch again. Called from the bullpen to replace Roger Clemens—who was officially removed from the game because he was injured but just as clearly taken out because he had given up five runs in four innings—in the top of the fifth inning against the Seattle Mariners.

Relief or not, Mussina was happy to be in a game. He had decided that whenever he was allowed to pitch again, he wasn't going to worry so much about giving up home runs, something that both Mike Borzello and Mark Mussina had counseled him on.

"I had gotten to be like Darrell Royal [the old University of Texas football coach]," he said. "I figured if I let guys hit the ball, three things could happen and two of them were bad."

Royal, who was famous for not wanting to throw the football, had once said: "If you throw the ball, three things can happen, and two of them [interception, incompletion] are bad." For Mussina the two bad things were home runs and base hits. Royal had been retired from coaching for almost thirty years, and it was time for Mussina to retire his approach from baseball.

Mussina wasn't great against the Mariners, but he was considerably better than he had been against the Angels and Tigers. The Mariners got to him for seven hits in three and two-thirds innings (Torre took him out with two down in the eighth inning so a lefty could pitch to Ichiro Suzuki), but there were far fewer ringing line drives, and there were quite a few more outs. Mussina retired eleven batters while giving up two runs. In the two starts before his benching, he had gotten fourteen batters out while giving up thirteen runs.

"It was hardly the kind of performance you write home about, but it was better," he said. "I felt like I had figured some things out about how to pitch. I was getting outs. I didn't feel like every time I threw a pitch it was going in a gap someplace."

Once Mussina had stopped brooding—"about three days, I'd say"—he had gone to strength coach Dana Cavalea and asked him to come up with a new regimen. "I needed to be doing stuff that involved more energy," he said. "I tend to get on cruise control in the weight room once the season starts. I needed to be working harder to strengthen myself so I wouldn't hurt so much anymore."

Even while he was working on some parts of his body he was resting others. All the nagging injuries were nagging a little bit less. Following a bullpen session two days after pitching against the Mariners, in which he felt as good as he had felt since July, he told Borzello, "I think I'm really close to being a good pitcher again."

Borzello agreed. "This is the best I've seen you throw in three months," he said. Mussina knew Borzello wouldn't say that if he didn't believe it.

The question was when he would get a chance to prove it. He

was still the long man in the bullpen. The Yankees won the last two games of the Mariner series to move into first place in the wild-card race. Then they went to Kansas City and swept the Royals to push their record to 81–62 — 39–19 since the All-Star break. At that stage, Mussina was just along for the ride.

"When guys go on the disabled list, they talk about feeling invisible in the clubhouse because there is no way they can help the team," Mussina said. "They're there, but they're not there. I was in that kind of place, except I wasn't on the DL. I was there but not there. It was pretty much a certainty every day that I wasn't going to help the team because I wasn't going to pitch. Having my pitching coach look right through me whenever he saw me just made it that much worse."

After a while, Mussina was able to adapt a gallows sense of humor about the whole thing. "Why should I complain about anything?" he said one day, standing at his locker. "I told my wife, 'Think about it, I get to travel the country and do absolutely nothing—for free. I get to go to Kansas City and Toronto this week—for free. I get to eat—for free. I get to stay in a nice hotel—for free.' I mean, what more could you ask?"

One of the clubhouse kids arrived at that moment with a fax Mussina had been trying to send. "You see," Mussina said, gesturing to the fax. "I get fax service—for free."

"Mike, there's something wrong with the number you gave me," the clubhouse kid said. "It didn't go through."

Mussina shrugged. "So maybe not so much the free fax service."

He was smiling. A week earlier that would have been impossible.

The first hint that he might escape from purgatory had come not long after Clemens had come out of the Seattle game. Clemens had claimed the injury was minor, and he didn't see any reason to miss a start. But as often happens with older players — especially *really* old players — the injury proved more nagging than he had expected or hoped.

Clemens's next turn was scheduled for Sunday, September 9,

in Kansas City. But the team had an off-day after the Seattle series, which gave Torre some flexibility. Rather than push Chien-Ming Wang back to start the first game in Toronto, as they would have done if Clemens had been healthy, Torre and Guidry decided to pitch him on his regular fifth day in what would have been Clemens's spot. Wang had pitched arguably his worst game of the season in the Yankees' last trip to Toronto, and the thinking was he would do better in Kansas City.

On the day before the Yankees left on the road trip, Torre told Mussina that Wang was going to pitch on Sunday in Kansas City and that Mussina might pitch the middle game in Toronto. Kennedy, who had continued to pitch well, was also experiencing some soreness, and the last thing the Yankees wanted to do was push him too hard.

"You might pitch on Wednesday in Toronto," Torre told Mussina.

"Might?"

"Can't be sure. I'll let you know as soon as I possibly can."

There wasn't much Mussina could say. "Might, maybe, could be, might not be," he said. He smiled. "Hey, just remember, I'm getting to go to Canada—for free."

"Might, maybe, could be" became "definitely" the following Monday. Clemens wasn't ready to pitch, and the Yankees had decided to let Kennedy skip at least one start. Torre told Mussina he would pitch on Wednesday against the Blue Jays "and then we'll see."

Mussina was fine with that. He had pitched once in sixteen days, throwing sixty-two pitches on Labor Day. If nothing else, he figured he was rested.

"Actually I *did* feel a lot better physically," he said. "Sometimes when Joe does things, you wonder what he's thinking. More often than not, though, he's proven right. There's no doubt after pitching once in sixteen days I felt better and stronger. The aches and pains were more or less gone, and I felt fresh, or maybe more accurately, I felt refreshed."

He didn't feel especially nervous warming up in Toronto. He knew he could pitch a shutout and might not get another start, or he could give up five runs in four and two-thirds and perhaps start again in five days. His future depended more on the health of Clemens and Kennedy than it did on him. Maybe that relaxed him just a little bit. So did the Yankees' scoring two quick runs in the top of the first.

Mussina had decided to make one tactical change, one that both his brother and Borzello had been pushing him to try all season: pitch inside more often. It wasn't all that different than what Glavine had gone through two years earlier. Mussina had become predictable and batters were diving across the plate, anticipating pitches on the outside corner.

In the first inning, working to all corners of the plate, Mussina got three ground-ball outs, the third coming after Alex Rios had singled with two out. The always-frightening Frank Thomas rolled over a slider and hit into a six-four force play.

"It wasn't as if I let out a big sigh of relief or anything," Mussina said. "It was one inning. I might have gone out there in the second and gotten bombed. But I felt good, the ball felt good coming out of my hand. My foot didn't hurt. I could really drive down the hill. It felt completely different than it had in the three starts before I got taken out."

He kept getting batters out. It was almost as if the Blue Jays were seeing a pitcher they weren't familiar with, because they were: Mussina stayed ahead of most hitters, pitched carefully when behind—he walked three—and kept getting outs. The Yankees added two runs in the fourth to make it 4–0.

Mussina rolled through the fifth, meaning he was eligible to get the win. In the sixth, he began to falter a little. After Russ Adams singled to lead off, Mussina threw another good slider and got Rios to bounce into a five-four-three double play. But Thomas walked and Matt Stairs singled. Mussina had thrown eighty-seven pitches, ordinarily a comfortable pitch count. But he hadn't pushed himself this way for sixteen days — "It was almost like a first start coming off the DL," he said later — and Torre wanted to be sure he came out of the game feeling good. A bad pitch now would leave a sour taste in his mouth.

"The funny thing about Moose is that as good as he's been for so many years, he's really kind of fragile," Torre said. "Not fragile in the way he pitches or competes but in terms of self-belief. Part of his problem was when he lost some velocity, he didn't think he was good enough to pitch to contact — when in fact he was. He had pitched really well; he was a little tired. I wanted him smiling, feeling good about what he'd done the next few days, not moping around doubting himself again."

Torre waved in Edwar Ramirez, who promptly walked Aaron Hill to load the bases and bring the tying run to the plate. But he got Lyle Overbay to fly to Abreu in right, and Mussina's line for the night was complete: five and two-thirds innings pitched, five hits, no runs, one strikeout, three walks. Obviously the stat that mattered most was the runs — or lack of them.

When he came into the dugout, the entire team greeted him with handshakes and pats on the back. "After so many years, the handshakes run together a little bit," Mussina said. "But that felt pretty good."

The Yankees went on to win the game 4–1, even though Joba Chamberlain had his first shaky outing since joining the team and had to be rescued by Mariano Rivera in the eighth.

The victory put the Yankees at 83–62 and, remarkably, in complete control of the wild-card race. Both the Mariners and the Tigers had faded badly since Labor Day, and the Yankees now led Detroit by four games and Seattle by five and a half.

"It was amazing how that happened," Mussina said. "Obviously we played very well. [Brian] Cashman and Torre deserve a lot of credit for not panicking at the trade deadline and sticking with the young guys—who came through. But I don't think people really appreciate Joe. If you look at some of the rotations we've run out there the last few years and still made the playoffs every year, I think it's amazing.

"This year we didn't have Clemens until June, and then he was up and down and hurt most of September. Andy was good; Wang was good. I had the worst year of my career. We ran a bunch of untested kids out there the first half, and then in August and September we had Hughes and the Kennedy kid in the rotation and we still played really well.

"It helped that Detroit and Seattle faded. That was a surprise. Usually teams going after the wild card play really well in September because they're good teams that have gotten hot. We were the only ones that stayed hot. I don't think any of us expected that."

The Yankees went from Toronto to Boston for what should have been a crucial series. Only it didn't feel crucial. They won two of three to cut their deficit to four and a half games, but the real suspense was gone. Barring an unlikely collapse, the Yankees were going to make the playoffs for a thirteenth straight season. They left Boston with a three-and-a-half-game lead on the Tigers with thirteen games left to play.

They went home to play the Orioles, who had won eight of twelve from them. With Kennedy and Clemens still hurting—Kennedy would not pitch again as it turned out—Mussina was told he was back in the rotation. He had never pitched all that well against his old team—he was 9–6 with a 4.45 ERA—but pitching the middle game of the series, he completely shut them down.

The case can be made that the Orioles, heading for another ninety-plus-loss season, were playing out the string, but they had played well against the Yankees all year and always came to play when Mussina was pitching. Mussina walked Brian Roberts leading off the game but got Tike Redman to hit the ball right back to him, starting a one-six-three double play. The Orioles got a single from Ramon Hernandez in the third and another single from Hernandez in the sixth. In the seventh, Miguel Tejada hit a dribbler down the third-base line and beat it out for an infield hit.

That was it. Three scratch singles, one walk. The Yankees exploded for six runs in the fourth, added a single run in the fifth, and then scored five more in the seventh against the pathetic Orioles bullpen. That made it 12–0, and Torre saw no reason to leave Mussina or any of his other starters in the game, allowing a group of September call-ups to finish it. (Major league rosters can expand to forty players on September 1. Contending teams don't often play their call-ups, but teams like the Orioles do to take a look at some of their younger players.)

Mussina had only thrown ninety-eight pitches — sixty-four of them strikes, he had been so precise — and might have been able to finish the game. Neither he nor Torre were worried about that. The time to start looking ahead to the playoffs had come, and Torre, now figuring Mussina as his number four starter in the postseason, saw no reason to leave him in a 12–0 game.

For Mussina, the win had more significance than might meet the eye. It was his tenth victory of the season, meaning he had won at least ten games in sixteen straight seasons. He had never failed to win ten games in a complete big league season. No American League pitcher had a streak as long. The only pitchers in major league history who had won at least ten games in sixteen or more seasons were Greg Maddux (twenty years), Cy Young (nineteen), Steve Carlton (eighteen), Don Sutton (seventeen), Warren Spahn (seventeen), and Nolan Ryan (sixteen). The only one of those six pitchers not in the Hall of Fame was Maddux, and the only reason he wasn't there was that he hadn't gotten around to retiring yet.

It was also the 249th win of Mussina's career.

Five days later, on a Sunday afternoon in Yankee Stadium, Mussina went for number 250 against the Blue Jays. His wife and kids were in the stands, but the game wasn't on national TV, and there was absolutely no fanfare surrounding the attempt.

"Two fifty isn't three hundred," he said. "I understand that."

Two fifty isn't three hundred, but it is still an impressive number. Among the nearly eight thousand men lucky enough to have pitched in the major leagues, Mussina was trying to become the forty-fifth to win 250 games. That would put him in pretty elite company.

Mussina hadn't allowed a run in his two starts since returning to the rotation. But he allowed three runs in the second inning, and the Yankees trailed 3–0. They answered with three in the bottom of the inning and scored three more in the fifth to give Mussina a 6–3 lead. He had settled down after the second. In fact, the Blue Jays only got three hits over the next five innings.

Mussina was now pitching with the confidence of the Mussina of old. He wasn't afraid to come inside, and he wasn't afraid to throw strikes, especially since he now felt he could hit or just miss corners whenever he wanted to. He had found the black again.

"Once I got out of Darrell Royal mode, I was a pitcher again," he said. "Unless you throw ninety-eight [miles an hour], you have to worry about how you locate your pitches. But you can't be afraid to let batters hit the ball, and you can't be predictable. I'd become predictable, and I was afraid to throw anything near the plate. Once I stopped doing that I could pitch again."

The Blue Jays made it interesting for Mussina, who waited in the clubhouse after Torre took him out following the seventh inning. Luis Vizcaino, who had pitched well for a long stretch during the summer, took over in the top of the eighth, allowed two quick runs, and Torre had to bring in Joba Chamberlain with two on and two out. Mussina was icing his arm by then. The rest of him was sweating.

"It wasn't as if not getting two fifty that day meant I wasn't going to get it," he said later. "I had another start, and I knew I was coming back next year. But I was close enough to it that I figured it would be nice to get it done then."

Chamberlain got it done for him. He struck out Adam Lind to get out of the eighth-inning jam, then pitched a one-two-three ninth, striking out Reed Johnson for the final out. The Yankees had won the game 7–5. Mussina stayed in the clubhouse in the ninth.

One of the clubhouse kids brought Mussina a ball that he had pitched with in the game. Most teams keep a bucket of game-used balls in the dugout so that players who want a game ball can have one and others can be signed by players as souvenirs. Balls are marked so that a player knows if it was in play when he was in the game. Mussina wanted Chamberlain to keep the ball Chamberlain had ended the game with because it was the kid's first major league save.

A number of players stopped by Mussina's locker to congratulate him, as did Torre and Guidry—"He was talking to me again, now that I was back in the rotation," Mussina said. He answered questions about the milestone win and talked about how good it felt to be pitching well again.

Then he got in the car and drove back to Westchester. Jana and the kids had gone directly from the game to the airport because the kids had school the next morning. He made dinner and relaxed by himself in front of the TV before going to bed.

"That was my celebration," he said. "A night at home by myself. I was happy I was pitching well again. Actually, I was happy I was *pitching* again. I didn't need a party. I was perfectly satisfied."

28

We Suck

Six days after his emotional victory in Atlanta, Tom Glavine pitched at home against the Houston Astros. Pedro Martinez had made his long-awaited season debut in Cincinnati on Labor Day, pitching five solid innings. The Mets' lead was up to six games, and the big question at Shea Stadium seemed to be who would pitch the playoff opener, Glavine or Martinez.

"I'm just glad to know we've got that option," Glavine said. "Having Petey back in the rotation should make us a lot deeper and a lot more dangerous, not to mention all his experience."

Saturday, September 8, was an uncomfortably hot, humid day in New York, and Glavine didn't feel all that good riding into the ballpark that morning with Billy Wagner. "I didn't know if it was something I ate or what it was," he said. "I just didn't feel right."

Warming up in the bullpen didn't make him feel any better. "I'm not sure I threw one pitch exactly where I wanted to throw it," he said. "I was all over the place."

Glavine knew from his years of experience that a bad warm-up doesn't necessarily lead to a bad performance, just as a good one doesn't always lead to a good day once the game begins. Nevertheless, as he left the bullpen, he turned to Aaron Sele, who was the long man in the bullpen, and said, "You might want to be ready early today; you could get a call."

Sele laughed, but Glavine wasn't joking.

446

As it turned out, Sele could have walked across the boardwalk from Shea Stadium to the National Tennis Center to watch the U.S. Open men's semifinals that afternoon, and he wouldn't have been missed.

Glavine was — at least for five innings — unhittable. He retired the first fifteen Astros he faced. Once he had gotten through a one-two-three first inning, he began to feel comfortable. His changeup was darting away from batters; his fastball was as precise as it had been all year. By the end of the fifth, there were "no hit" murmurs going around the stadium.

Glavine wasn't really thinking about that. He had once gotten within four outs of a no-hitter but didn't think of himself as a no-hit pitcher, especially at this stage of his career. "I just don't strike that many guys out," he said. "The more balls that are put into play, the more likely it is that someone is going to hit one in a hole or drop one in somewhere. I knew no one had gotten on base. I could hear the crowd getting into it a little in the fifth inning, but that is so early."

No-hitters inspire more baseball superstition than anything else in the game. For years, announcers wouldn't mention that a pitcher had a no-hitter going for fear of being a jinx. If you listen to old tapes of no-hitters, you will hear announcers saying things like "He has a chance to finish a very special game if he can get one more out." But no mention of what's so special.

Players on the bench still adhere to no-hit superstitions. No one dares mention it or says anything to a pitcher when he begins to get close to one. By the seventh or eighth inning if you look into a dugout, you are likely to see a pitcher who has a no-hitter going sitting all by himself because no one will sit close to him.

Glavine never got to that point. Cody Ransom led off the sixth inning for the Astros with a soft single to left field. The game stopped briefly while the crowd stood to give Glavine an ovation for the effort. He appreciated it. He was far more appreciative, though, when Eric Munson hit into a six-four-three double play, wiping Ransom out. He then got the side one-two-three in the seventh, meaning he had pitched to the minimum twenty-one batters.

The Mets had a 3–0 lead, having pieced together single runs in the third, fourth, and fifth. Because of the heat and because the game was close, Glavine came out after the Astros began the eighth, with Carlos Lee and Mark Loretta producing back-to-back singles.

"If I'd had the no-hitter, I would have stayed in, obviously," he said. "I hadn't thrown that many pitches [eighty-six], but the heat and the humidity were really wearing on me. It seemed to get hotter as the afternoon went on."

Aaron Heilman came on and gave up an RBI single to Ty Wigginton but then struck out the side. Billy Wagner finished it in the ninth without incident. Glavine was 13–6, the Mets were 80–61, and the lead was still a comfortable six games, with twenty-one to play.

Glavine was clearly now on the roll he had talked about throughout the first half of the season. Since the two-inning horror show in Los Angeles, he had started nine games. In eight of them he had given up three runs or less, two runs or less in seven of those eight. He'd had one bad game, against San Diego, in two months. His ERA in the other eight games during that stretch was 2.18. Even with the San Diego game included it was 3.00.

That was big-time pitching in any league. It would be hard, very hard, for someone who could still pitch that effectively to just walk away at season's end. Glavine knew that. So did his wife.

"The first thing Chris is going to say to me is 'I know you're pitching next year,'" Glavine told Wagner, as they walked out of the clubhouse.

"She'll be right, won't she?" Wagner answered.

Glavine smiled. He knew she would be right. Wagner was

right too. "You're pitching next year, aren't you?" was Chris's greeting.

"The fact is, unless my arm falls off, it doesn't make sense for me not to pitch after a year like this," he said. "With some luck, I could actually have had a shot at winning twenty games. I had two bad starts in June, one in July, and one in August. All the others [26 starts at that moment] have been either pretty good, good, or very good. I'm really happy about that."

The next question was the obvious one: if he was going to pitch, where would he pitch? He smiled. "I don't need to worry about that right now. I'm really in a good position. If the Braves made me an offer and gave me the chance to stay home and pitch, I would have to seriously consider it. But if they don't, assuming the Mets want me back, I'm very comfortable with that too. We've done this for five years now. We can certainly do it for one more."

At that moment, the Mets very much wanted Glavine back. What had started as a rocky marriage had become a very solid one. Even a happy one.

FOUR DAYS AFTER GLAVINE'S GEM against the Astros, the Mets' lead over the Phillies stood at seven games with seventeen to play. They had won two of three in their final series of the season with the Braves and had ended up splitting the season series 9–9 after the Braves had won eight of the first twelve. The Braves crawled out of town, their once promising season just about finished, and were followed into Shea by the Phillies.

The Mets were in countdown mode and with good reason. Since the Phillies had closed to within two games with their four-game sweep at the end of August, the Mets had gone 10–2. The Phillies had gone 6–7 during that stretch. With seventeen games left, the Mets' magic number to clinch the division was eleven: any combination of Met victories and Phillie losses totaling eleven and the Mets would win their second straight title. To put those numbers in perspective, if the Mets played mediocre baseball and went 8–9, the Phillies would have to go 15–2 to tie them.

Throw in the fact that thirteen of the Mets' final fourteen games of the season were against the Washington Nationals and the Florida Marlins, the two bottom-dwelling teams in the East, and it seemed almost impossible for the Mets not to win the title. "Of course, we can really take the suspense out of it if we take care of business this weekend," Glavine said on the eve of the Philadelphia series.

The Mets wanted nothing more than to blow up the Phillies' season once and for all at Shea Stadium. All the Jimmy Rollins talk and all the celebrating the Phillies had done after their late-August sweep had not been forgotten.

Glavine pitched the opener against—who else?—Jamie Moyer. Both pitchers were superb. The Mets got off to a 1–0 lead on a first-inning home run by David Wright—who was having a monster second half of the season—and scored again in the fourth on an RBI single by Moises Alou. Glavine sailed along with that lead until the sixth, when he walked Abraham Nunez to start the inning. Moyer sacrificed, but Glavine got Rollins to fly out to Alou in left. That brought up Chase Utley, one of the more dangerous left-handed hitters in the league.

Glavine worked Utley to 3–2. He had first base open and another good hitter, Aaron Rowand, on deck. A walk wouldn't be disastrous, except that Utley was a left-handed hitter and Rowand hit righty. Glavine decided to throw a changeup, figuring if Utley took it for ball four he would focus on Rowand.

"I wanted to throw it inside and I didn't," he said. "I got too much of the plate with it, and he made me pay. Good hitters do that."

Utley, knowing that Glavine was one of the few pitchers in baseball who would even think of throwing a changeup on 3–2, was looking for the breaking pitch, and he got it. He hit it into the Mets bullpen, and the score was tied at 2–2.

Neither Glavine nor Moyer gave up anything more after that, and the game fell into the hands of the two bullpens. That rarely worked out well for the Mets in 2007. The Phillies won the game in the tenth when they scratched together a run aided by an error by Mike Difelice, who dropped a Jayson Werth foul pop leading off the inning. Werth ended up singling and scoring the winning run. What made the whole thing even more galling was that the only reason Difelice was in the game was that Paul Lo Duca had been ejected by plate umpire Paul Emmel (Mussina's old friend from the Anaheim game in August) for arguing a called strike three.

The loss was disappointing. Still, the lead was five and a half, and a split of the last two games of the series would leave the Mets comfortably in front, especially given their opposition the final two weeks of the season.

Only they didn't split. The Phillies won both games for a sweep, meaning they had won the last eight games the teams had played and eleven of the last fourteen dating back to June. The manner of the losses was almost as disturbing as the losses themselves. In the Saturday game, Martinez pitched six superb innings and left with a 3–1 lead, which the bullpen blew in a 5–3 loss. The next day, the Mets rallied from a 5–2 deficit to tie the game 5–5 after five. But Mota and Sosa combined to give up five runs in the sixth, and the Phillies won 10–6.

The Mets could have won any of the three games. They won none. Their lead was down to three and a half games, and the Phillies felt as if they had life. The Mets headed to Washington to begin their final road trip of the season. The Nationals were starting the final homestand in the history of RFK Stadium since they would move into their new stadium for the start of the 2008 season.

The Mets jumped to a 4–0 lead in the opener but couldn't hold it. Brian Lawrence came out with the score tied at 4–4, and the bullpen was again miserable. The Nats—one of the weakest hitting teams in the league—won the game 12–4. In the meantime, the Phillies won in St. Louis, and the seven-game lead on September 12 was now a two-and-a-half-game lead six days later.

The Yankees were still comfortably in control of the wild-card race in the American League. That made the Mets the story in New York. "I had a seat on the columnists' charter," Mike Vaccaro, a columnist for the *New York Post*, joked in the clubhouse in Washington the next day. He was referring to the fact that most of the newspaper columnists in New York were now following the Mets in case a monumental collapse was about to happen.

The players noticed, as did Willie Randolph, whose pregame sessions with the media were becoming a bit more tense with each passing day. It was Marlon Anderson, the veteran utility player who had been brought back to the team in mid-July, who went to Randolph prior to the second game of the series in Washington and suggested that a team meeting was in order. Randolph agreed, and the clubhouse was cleared at 4:30 in the afternoon.

"It's a 'we suck' meeting," Glavine said. "The point of it really is to remind each other that we're a lot better than we've played the last few days. A lot of us have been talking about it, but calling a meeting when you play in New York isn't like calling a meeting someplace else. People are going to make a big deal out of it; they're going to wonder if we're panicking. We're not panicking, but we need to remind one another that we're still a good team. We all know it, but sometimes it can't hurt to hear it."

Randolph spoke first. He reminded the players they were still in first place and that he knew they were still the best team. All they had to do was play the way they were capable of playing, and everything would be fine. Nothing special was needed, just bearing down and playing hard.

Randolph and his coaches left the players alone after that. They spent a solid thirty minutes together, one veteran after another talking. "Everyone basically said the same thing," said Glavine, who spoke right after Anderson had opened the meeting. "If we went back to Opening Day and said, 'Okay, you're going to have a two-and-a-half-game lead with thirteen to play, would you take it?' The answer was of course, we would. We'd been in first place almost the entire season, and every time someone got close to us we'd turned it up a little and pulled away. We just had to do it one more time.

"It wasn't as if we weren't trying. If anything we were trying too hard. Our defense had gone south the past few games. We were a good defensive team. Errors on easy plays are a sure sign of nerves. We just needed to relax. That was what I said: 'Everyone, relax. We're the team in first place. We're the team that controls our own fate.'"

Most of the veterans on the team got up and delivered the same message. There was no need to worry about what anyone was saying or writing; all that mattered was that the guys in this room believed in one another.

Okay? Okay.

Thus inspired, the Mets promptly scored four runs in the first inning. They led 7–3 after four and a half, with John Maine on the mound. At least half of those in the tiny crowd of 19,966 appeared to be Mets fans. The tide, it seemed, had been stemmed.

But Maine couldn't get out of the fifth inning, allowing five runs. The Mets trailed 8–7 and never caught up. Another loss — this one 9–8 — and another Phillies win. The Mets' lead was down to one and a half.

"So much for team meetings," Glavine said. "If we had won, everyone would have said it was the meeting. Now we just have to go out and play. I mean *now,* not soon. Now."

The unlikely streak stopper the next night was Mike Pelfrey, the talented rookie who had been sent back to Triple-A after an 0–7 start. Pelfrey won his third straight start since returning to the rotation to end the five-game losing streak, and the Cardinals beat the Phillies in St. Louis. For the first time in eight days, the

Mets gained ground. The lead was two and a half with eleven to play. The magic number was nine.

Best of all, from the Mets' point of view, Glavine and Martinez would be pitching the first two games in Florida.

Glavine has never liked pitching in what is now known as — after going through several corporate names — Dolphin Stadium. To begin with, it is, as you might guess from the name, a football-first ballpark that doesn't quite feel like a place to play baseball. The weather is almost always hot and humid and frequently rainy.

Even though the Marlins have won two World Series titles in the past ten years, they have also twice broken up championship teams so that team owner Wayne Huizenga could invest more money in his football team and other businesses. As a result, the Marlins — much like the other ill-conceived Florida expansion team in Tampa — simply don't draw. In a stadium that can seat up to sixty-five thousand when seats are opened up during the postseason, crowds of under ten thousand are not uncommon.

The opener with the Marlins was no different than the norm for September baseball in Fort Lauderdale. The announced crowd of 15,132 looked like considerably less, and, as always in Florida, quite a few were transplanted New Yorkers who came out to root for the visiting team.

Right from the start, Glavine sensed trouble. "I always have a problem there because of the bullpen mounds," he said. "I know that sounds weird, but of all the parks we play in, the difference between the bullpen mound and the actual mound is the greatest there. When you stand on the bullpen mounds, at least to my eye, the plate is off-center; it's a little bit closer to the left-hand batter's box. They've checked it in the past, and they say it isn't so and maybe it's not, but it absolutely feels that way to me.

"Plus, the mounds are virtually flat. You almost feel as if you're playing catch rather than throwing off a mound. You get to the mound on the field, and you feel as if you're standing on a mountain. I remember that night saying to Rick [Peterson] after the first inning that I feel as if I'm falling straight down when I drive forward. He suggested trying to stay back a little longer, which is fine, but when you do that you're thinking way too much. I'm not trying to make excuses; it's just the way it is."

Even feeling awkward, Glavine was able to work in and out of trouble through the first four innings. He got Miguel Cabrera to pop out with two down and Dan Uggla on second in the first. He gave up a leadoff single to Josh Willingham in the second but induced Mike Jacobs into hitting into a double play before giving a single to Cody Ross that proved harmless, thanks to the double play. He struck Willingham out with men on second and third and two outs in the third.

In the meantime the Mets were putting together a 3–0 lead against the wildly inconsistent, and often wild, Dontrelle Willis. In 2005, Willis had won twenty-two games at the age of twenty-three and appeared on the verge of superstardom. He was left-handed, he had a hard-to-follow motion, he could throw hard, and he was probably the best-hitting pitcher in the game.

But he had been up and down in every possible way for two seasons, and 2007 had been more of the same, with his ERA hovering around 5.00 all year. This night was no different. In the first he hit Lastings Milledge and David Wright back to back, leading to a two-run double by Moises Alou. He gave up a third run in the third on doubles by Reyes and Wright.

"My goal was to get through six," Glavine said. "I was throwing a lot of pitches and allowing a lot of base runners. But as long as I could pitch out of trouble, I thought we'd be okay. It was one of those nights where I didn't feel all that good but had a chance to do what I needed to do for the team anyway.

"Basically, I blew it all with one pitch."

That came in the fifth. Although Glavine remembered one pitch above all others, the Marlins took him all over the park before and after, getting six hits in the inning. Willis, who was hitting .271 for the season, led off with a double, and Hanley Ramirez doubled him home to make it 3–1. Ramirez then did Glavine a favor by trying to steal third base and was thrown out by Paul Lo Duca.

Even that break wasn't enough to get Glavine out of the inning. Uggla and Jeremy Hermida singled, bringing Cabrera up. "There are certain batters that are make or break in a game," Glavine said. "Most of the time you know it when they come up. With Cabrera, the temptation is always to pitch around him, and I wasn't trying to give him anything too good to hit. Unfortunately, I did."

It was a 3–2 changeup, just as the home-run pitch six days earlier had been a 3–2 changeup to Chase Utley. The problem, again, was location. The ball drifted too close to the plate, and Cabrera crushed it. That was the first time Glavine began to wonder if his changeup wasn't behaving the way he wanted it to behave.

"Part of it was location," he said. "You put a changeup in the wrong place, and, unless you fool a guy completely because he's looking fastball, you're going to be in trouble. The pitch to Cabrera wasn't a horrible pitch. I tried to throw it in and probably didn't get it quite far enough in, but he still did a good job keeping it fair. Most hitters on a pitch like that, even though it was up, will hit it hard but get out front and hit it foul. He kept it fair. Sometimes you just have to say a guy beat you. On that pitch, he beat me."

The Mets' three-run lead had quickly became a 4–3 deficit. Glavine was disgusted with himself. "If I have a lead and I give the game to the bullpen and we still have the lead, then I've done my job," he said. "It really doesn't matter if it's a one-nothing lead or a five-nothing lead; I expect to leave the game with a lead. Two games in a row I had a lead [two-nothing versus the Phillies], and I gave the lead up before I came out. That doesn't make me happy."

He left after the fifth inning, having thrown 107 pitches, which is barely reasonable for seven innings, a lot for six innings, and way too many for five. But the Mets rallied in the ninth, scoring four runs to take a 7–4 lead. It was the kind of rally that a team will often look back on as a season-turner: trailing in the ninth, coming up with big hits and key at bats, and pulling the game out.

There was just one problem: Jorge Sosa couldn't hold the lead. Wagner had pitched the night before, and Randolph decided with a three-run lead to gamble that Sosa, who had been both good and bad out of the bullpen (as opposed to Mota, who had only been bad), could get three outs.

Sosa blew the lead in the ninth, then gave up a game-ending double to Uggla after Ramirez led off the tenth with a single. Instead of an exhilarating victory, the Mets walked away with a disastrous loss. The Phillies had won in Washington, so the lead was down to a game and a half.

"That was one that hurt, but I really don't think we were panicked by it," Glavine said. "The way we came back in the ninth was encouraging. Plus, I think in the back of our minds, we knew we had Petey going the next day, and that was comforting."

Martinez was showing no ill effects from the season-ending surgery of the previous October. The Mets were keeping him on a pitch count, basically trying to build his arm strength so that he would be 100 percent in time for the playoffs. Now they needed him to help make sure they made the playoffs.

Martinez wasn't great the next night, but he was good enough, leaving after five innings with an 8–4 lead. This time, the bullpen got the job done — notably Mota, who pitched two shutout innings — and the Mets hung on for a 9–6 victory. Buoyed by that win, the Mets won the final two games of the series. Oliver Perez, who had looked tired for much of September, pitched well on Saturday, and on Sunday the Mets finally pulled out an extra-inning win (they had lost five extra-inning games in a row) with a 7–6 victory in eleven. The Nationals, playing their final game in RFK Stadium, managed to beat the Phillies 5–3 to give the old ballpark a rousing send-off in front of a rare sellout crowd.

The Mets didn't much care about the last game at RFK or the attendance in Washington, but they were delighted when they got word the Phillies had lost. The lead was back up to two and a half games, exactly where it had been on the night of the "we suck" meeting. Only now, there were just seven games left, and the Mets were going home for those last seven games: three with the Nationals, a makeup game with the Cardinals on Thursday, and, finally, three with the team they had just beaten three straight times, the Marlins, to close out the regular season.

The message was no different than it had been during the meeting: relax; we're the best team; we're the ones in first place.

Their fate was in their own hands.

29

The Final Days

THE LAST WEEK OF THE REGULAR SEASON began in New York with a rare doubleheader: both the Mets and the Yankees playing in town on the same day. The two teams are almost always scheduled to avoid playing at home at the same time, but the Yankees had a makeup game against the Blue Jays to close out their home schedule, while the Mets were beginning their final homestand against the Nationals.

The Yankees played at 1:05 and the Mets at 7:10, meaning that a real fan could see both games by either changing subways or enduring traffic on the Triboro Bridge.

The Yankees were loving life. They had all but wrapped up the wild card and were actually making a late charge at the Red Sox. Mussina's victory on Sunday against the Blue Jays had been the Yankees' ninetieth win of the season (they were 90–65) and left them only a game and a half behind the Red Sox. Their magic number to clinch the wild card was two, even after the Blue Jays won the Yankees' home finale 4–1.

The Mets were riding a little bit of a high themselves, having won the last three games in Florida. Their lead was bigger than that of the Red Sox—two and a half—and their magic number was down to five. If they went 5–2 in the final week against three sub-.500 teams at home, there was nothing the Phillies could do to catch them. If they went 3–4, the Phillies would have to go 5–1 just to tie them.

The problem was you can't win a pennant on paper; you have to do it on the field. With the Phillies taking the day off on Monday, the Mets had a chance to extend their lead to three games. Instead, playing in front of a crowd of just under fifty thousand, they stumbled around as if it were March and lost for the third time in four games to the Nats, 13–4.

So the lead was two the next night when Glavine took the mound to face the immortal Jason Bergmann. He was convinced that the mediocre performance in Florida meant he was destined to pitch well the final week. "I'd only had two bad performances back to back all season, back in June against the Tigers and Yankees," Glavine said. "Those teams have pretty good lineups. I was a little concerned about my changeup, but I really thought I had it in pretty good shape going into the game."

The first inning was like one of those surprise cold showers Glavine talks about. He had been pitching much better in first innings throughout most of his hot streak. In fact, he had only given up a run in the first inning once in his previous eleven starts — the single run against the Braves in Atlanta — which was one of the reasons he had been so good.

Now the bad old days kicked in quickly. Felipe Lopez led off with a single and stole second. Pitching carefully, Glavine walked Ryan Zimmerman, the one real home-run threat in the Nationals' lineup. Then he hung a 3–2 changeup to Austin Kearns, hardly a home-run hitter, and Kearns hit it over the left-center-field fence for his fifteenth home run of the season. Two batters later, Tony Batista, who had once been a home-run hitter but was now a little-used utility player, hit another changeup to almost the same spot. It was 4–0 Washington, and the boo-birds were starting to make an appearance at Shea Stadium.

Jose Reyes managed to change that sound temporarily, leading off the bottom of the inning with a long home run off of Bergmann. Lastings Milledge greeted Reyes coming into the dugout, where the two did their home-run dance, which always annoyed the opposition and baffled many of their older teammates, especially in a game when the team was down by three runs.

"It wasn't my place to talk to those guys; there were other guys who were more appropriate," Glavine said later. "I know Carlos [Delgado] tried to talk to them, and Willie did too. It just never seemed to register."

The Mets got another run in the second, but Glavine gave it back in the third on a Zimmerman double and a Wily Mo Pena single. It was still 5–2 in the fourth when Justin Maxwell came to the plate for the Nationals. Maxwell was a talented young outfielder who had spent a good portion of the year playing Single-A ball. The Nationals thought he was probably still a year away from being ready to be a full-time big leaguer but wanted to give him a September look at what might be in his future.

Maxwell had performed well. But he had looked completely hopeless against Glavine in the second inning. "A young hitter like that seeing my changeup for the first time shouldn't have a chance," he said. "If I throw the pitch right, he's going to swing over it and be back in the dugout."

Maxwell did just that on the first pitch, swinging wildly as the ball darted downward. He then took a ball. Then Glavine threw another change. Only this one didn't get down enough; it simply hung up over the plate. Maxwell jumped on it, hitting it into the left-field bullpen to make the score 6–2.

"All three home runs were changeups," Glavine said. "That was bad. Having the kid hit one out was really bad. It shook me up. I'd been telling myself that the home runs Utley and Cabrera hit were mistakes that really good hitters took deep, which they were. But the three that night were bad pitches that almost anyone, even a kid a few weeks out of Class-A, could take out. That one was just a bad pitch. Not only did it hang, but it was actually going in the wrong direction. That was a major concern."

Glavine stayed away from his changeup for the remaining two innings he pitched. He threw fastballs — most of them away — and a few cutters and curveballs. He didn't want to throw the changeup anywhere near the plate until he had a chance to get to the bullpen with Peterson to figure out what was wrong. He knew something was wrong; he just wasn't sure exactly what it was.

He lasted through five innings, having thrown ninety-seven pitches. The Nationals built their lead to 10–3 before the Mets staged a furious ninth-inning rally, actually cutting the gap to 10–9 on Nats closer Chad Cordero with the tying run on second base and only one out. But Jon Rauch came in to relieve Cordero and struck out Delgado and got Lo Duca to fly to right to end the game.

So close . . . again.

"It seems like every night we either build a lead we can't hold or fall behind and come almost all the way back," Glavine said after the game. "Tonight is on me. I was bad. I put us in a hole, and we couldn't quite climb out of it."

Some pointed out that if the bullpen hadn't given up three more runs after Glavine left, the ninth-inning rally would have won the game. Others noted that in the midst of a lousy season, Delgado had again failed in the clutch. Glavine didn't want to hear that. "I had the ball in my hands," he said. "And I didn't come through."

His ERA, which he had gradually brought down to 3.88 from a season high of 4.67, had jumped back to 4.14.

The only good news of the evening had come from Philadelphia, where the Braves had come from behind to beat the Phillies, keeping the margin at two. The magic number had actually been reduced to four. With the Mets losing, the Braves' rally had created one of the stranger scenes in recent history: Mets fans, on their feet, doing the Braves' tomahawk chop, the same chop that for years had nauseated the Mets and their fans when practiced in Atlanta. Now, with the Braves out of the race and the Phillies chasing the Mets, the fans at Shea were chopping for their lives.

Prior to that night's game, someone had asked Glavine if he had talked to Randolph and Peterson about whether he would pitch on Sunday, the last day of the season, if the pennant had been clinched, or if he might just pitch a couple of innings that day to get ready for his first playoff start.

But as soon as Lo Duca's fly ball had died into Austin Kearns's glove to end the game, Glavine was beginning to prepare mentally for a start on Sunday that he was certain would be critical.

"Sometimes you just have a feel for things as a ballplayer," he said. "I was hoping we'd have it wrapped up by Sunday, but in my gut I just knew I was going to be pitching, and the season was going to be on the line.

"I don't know why I knew or how I knew; I just knew."

THERE WAS NO SUCH SUSPENSE in the Yankees clubhouse. They had flown to Tampa after the loss to Toronto, trailing the Red Sox by two but, more important, leading the Tigers by five and a half, with six games to play. That meant the magic number to clinch the wild card was one—a Yankee victory or a Detroit loss.

"I think we were all shocked that we'd pulled away as easily and as quickly as we did," Mussina said. "But we certainly weren't complaining."

The trip to Tampa meant that Mussina could sleep in one of his own beds for three nights, even though his family couldn't come because school was in session. He felt good about himself: about getting his 250th win, about keeping his ten-wins-in-a-season streak alive, but most of all he felt good about pitching well again.

"I still think if those three bad starts had come in May or June, we would have just worked it out in the pen and I would have gone out and pitched five days later," he said. "On the other hand, being out did give me a chance to heal from all those nagging injuries. My ego was hurt by it, but it may very well have worked out for the best."

Mussina was scheduled to make his last start of the regular season on Friday in Baltimore, a game the Yankees were hoping wouldn't mean much. While Torre would have been happy to run the Red Sox down and win the Division title, the goal was to get into the playoffs, and the wild card would suit that purpose. Home-field advantage means less in baseball than in any other sport as had been proven often in recent years: wild-card teams had won three straight World Series between 2002 and 2004, without the benefit of home-field advantage in either the Division Series or the Championship Series. There hadn't been a seven-game World Series since 2002, so the new All-Star-game gimmick of giving the winning league home field for the deciding game hadn't yet come into play.

"We wanted to get the wild card wrapped up in Tampa," Mussina said. "If we somehow caught the Red Sox, all the better, but it wasn't really on our minds that much."

The Yankees played the opener in Tampa as if very little was on their minds. They built a 5–0 lead, and Kei Igawa, called back up to start because both Clemens and Kennedy were still hurt, managed to hang on through five innings, even though he walked five. But Edwar Ramirez and Brian Bruney gave up six runs in the sixth, the last four scoring when second baseman Jorge Velandia, who had not homered all year, hit a grand slam off of Bruney. The Yankees tied it, but the Rays won it in the tenth, when Dioner Navarro homered off of Jeff Karstens leading off the inning.

So, the magic number was still one because the Tigers won that night. The next night, with Chien-Ming Wang pitching, the Yankees built a 9–1 lead after five innings. They weren't going to blow that. Just to be sure, Torre sent Rivera in to get the last three outs, even with a 12–4 lead. At 10:40 p.m. on the night of September 26, with all of 21,621 (announced) watching, at always overcast (indoors) Tropicana Field, the Rays' Greg Norton hit a pop-up to short right field. When the ball dropped into Robinson

Cano's glove, the Yankees were in the playoffs for a thirteenth straight year, twelve of them under Torre.

"Think about this for a minute," Mussina said later. "We were the only team that made the playoffs in '07 that also made it in '06. No one else made it two years in a row. We've made it thirteen. That's an accomplishment. The problem is, around here, anything short of winning the World Series is considered failure. It's as if they've all forgotten the Yankees didn't make postseason once between 1981 and 1995. They were a bad team when I first came up. If you're going to say that only winning the World Series is a successful season, most of your seasons are going to end as failures.

"I know that night in the clubhouse, we felt like we'd really accomplished something, given the way we started, given the injuries, given everything that had happened. It was a nice feeling."

That same night, the Mets started rookie Philip Humber against the Nationals—because they didn't want Pedro Martinez to have to start on four days' rest—and blew a 5–0 lead en route to a 9–6 loss. They had dropped five of six to the Nationals in the past two weeks. The Phillies beat the Braves, so the lead was down to one, with four games to play for both teams. There was no need, really, to discuss magic numbers.

"The magic number is one," Glavine said. "As in we need to win one game. Then we can worry about winning another one."

The day after the Nationals left town, the St. Louis Cardinals came in to play one game. It was a makeup game dating back to the four-game series in June that had been plagued by rain.

Prior to the game, Glavine went to the bullpen with Peterson and bullpen catcher Dave Racaniello for his normal second-day side session. Glavine and Peterson had talked about the changeup the previous day and decided to try some different drills to see if Glavine could get his feel back for the pitch.

Normally, Glavine will begin a bullpen session by throwing

fifteen to twenty pitches from behind the mound. "It's a way to get loose, but it also makes me feel as if I have more power once I get up on the mound," he said. "Usually I throw all my pitches — two or three of each — and then I get up on the mound."

On this particular day, every pitch he threw from behind the mound was a changeup, the hope being that if he could feel the pitch from flat ground, he would feel it even better from the mound. Then, when he got on the mound, instead of throwing from the windup, he threw about fifteen more pitches that weren't so much pitches as throws. "I kind of threw with the kind of motion an infielder throws with," he said. "You take sort of a little jump-step into the throw instead of winding up and going through your motion. It was all about trying to find the right feel for one pitch."

When he finally began to throw from his normal windup, the changeup felt a little better but not much. "To be honest, it was more of the same," he said. "Some were good; others weren't. But I did think that I had a better feel for what I needed to do to throw the good one when the session was over."

Glavine was looking for consistency. He wanted to throw the pitch the same way each time and get the same result — a pitch that fooled the hitters because of its lack of speed, and if it didn't was still hard to hit because it broke down.

"When I'm throwing it well, I just keep aiming at the catcher's feet," Glavine said. "If it starts to drift up, well, I just aim in the dirt. But if I don't know where it's going or how hard I need to throw it to get it where I want it to go, then I'm in trouble. That's where I was. Some went right where I was aiming. Others didn't.

"It's a lot like in golf when you have to start thinking about your swing. If you're playing well, you stand up to the ball, pick your target, and just take the club back and hit the ball. In pitching, it's the same thing: you stand there, pick your target, and throw at the spot, knowing the ball will go there. When it's not and you have to start thinking — 'Do I throw harder or softer? Do

I throw it lower or higher? Do I try to change my motion to make sure it goes down?'—that's when you get into trouble."

Glavine felt a little better after the side session, but not great. He felt a little bit worse when the Mets lost again that night, shut out 3–0 by Joel Pineiro, who had spent most of the season in the Red Sox bullpen, before the Cardinals, desperate for starters because of injuries, had picked him up and put him in their rotation. For one night, Pineiro was Bob Gibson, allowing three hits. Pedro Martinez pitched well but not well enough. The Phillies beat the Braves again. So much for the tomahawk chop at Shea Stadium.

The Mets were now 87–72, with three games to play. The Phillies were also 87–72. The seven-game lead was completely gone. The Marlins were coming to New York for the final three games of the season, and the Nationals headed for Philadelphia.

The Yankees flew from Tampa Bay to Baltimore, still with an outside chance to catch the Red Sox. Even if they didn't, they knew they would be playing the next week when postseason play began.

The Mets could only hope that they would be playing too.

GLAVINE AND PETERSON returned to the bullpen on Friday for Glavine's "stretch" throwing session. Most pitchers only throw in the bullpen once between starts, so they will mix that session up, throwing from the windup and from the stretch. Since Glavine throws twice between starts, the first time he will throw strictly from the windup, the second time only from the stretch.

They went through the same drills—throwing changeups from behind the mound to warm up, then working on the infield-type throws, before going through the regular throwing session. This time, Glavine felt a real difference.

"Throwing the changeup felt noticeably better from the stretch," he said. "My hope was that it was just better, period, and that it had nothing to do with whether I was throwing from the windup or from the stretch. I felt more comfortable, more like I could make the pitch do what I wanted it to do."

Some people might wonder why one pitch would be so important since Glavine could throw a fastball, a curve, a cutter, a slider. But every starting pitcher in baseball needs at least one effective breaking pitch to go with his fastball. Even someone who can throw a fastball 98 miles an hour needs a breaking pitch because batters will eventually figure out the fastball and hit it. A relief pitcher might get away with having only one pitch — Mariano Rivera throws his cutter about 90 percent of the time — because he is only going to face hitters once in a game. A starter needs different pitches for the second, third, and fourth at bats.

Glavine had become a good pitcher in 1989 when he discovered the grip that allowed him to throw his changeup at least 10 miles an hour slower than his fastball, with the exact same arm motion. The fact that the pitch went down most of the time made it that much more effective. It was what separated him from most pitchers, especially with a fastball that rarely reached 90 miles per hour. He had to count on his ability to keep hitters off-balance with change of speed. The changeup allowed him to do that.

Now, facing one of the biggest games of his career, he wasn't sure about his big pitch. Glavine without an effective changeup is the same as Tiger Woods when he can't make putts or Michael Jordan when he couldn't make a jump shot. Woods is the best player in the world because he makes more pressure putts than anyone; Jordan was Jordan because he never seemed to miss a jumper in the clutch.

"I've gone into a lot of games in my career when I knew it wasn't as good as I wanted it to be," he said. "That's kind of the frustration and the beauty of baseball. No one, and I mean *no one,* goes through a season without having stretches where they just can't do what they want to do. I've never had a season where I didn't hit stretches where I couldn't locate the ball like I wanted to or throw my changeup the way I wanted to or keep my fastball off the plate. Every pitcher goes through it, just like every hitter goes through slumps."

Mussina agrees. "I've never had a year where I didn't feel for a while like I'd never get another out," he said. "This year was worse than usual, but in my best years those periods happened. My guess is when Ron Guidry went twenty-five and three in 1978 and had one of the great years in baseball history, he had a couple times where he felt terrible." (Guidry confirms this, saying the Yankees got him off the hook on several occasions that season when he didn't feel right.)

"That's just the game. Look at the year A-Rod has had. But in May he did almost nothing. He had a twenty-five-game stretch where he hit about .220 and drove in four or five runs. Twenty-five games is most of my season. If I have twenty-five games where I'm that bad, I'm released.

"No one ever has a perfect season. No one."

Glavine had pitched remarkably well for most of 2007. Until the start in Florida, he had started thirty-one games and had produced a "quality start"—three runs or less in at least six innings—on twenty-three occasions. His record on the eight occasions when he hadn't produced a quality start was 0–4, meaning the Mets had not stolen a game or two on off-nights as would normally be expected from a good team. He had been 13–2 on the nights he had pitched well, with eight no-decisions in games he had pitched well enough to win, several of them games where he had left with a lead only to have the bullpen blow the game.

In short, he easily could have won eighteen games, perhaps more if he'd been lucky. He'd had one real slump—the games in Detroit and in New York in June when he'd been bombed by the Tigers and Yankees. He hadn't had poor back-to-back outings again until the game in Florida and the game in New York against the Nationals.

"I think, to some degree, there was a little bit of a hangover after the start in Florida," he said. "I don't want to say I lost confidence, but I got concerned about my changeup, and I didn't throw it with any consistency at all in the Washington game.

"You go through these periods during a season and you understand them. But this was the worst possible timing. I was going to pitch a game on Sunday that might mean our whole season, and I really didn't know what I was going to have going out there. I'd pitched a lot of big games in my career; I knew how to handle preparing for them mentally and physically, but wondering which breaking pitch would show up — the good one or the bad one — was a little bit unnerving.

"It wasn't as if I had any choice. They were going to give me the ball Sunday and ask me to go out and win a game. I certainly wasn't going to give it back."

After his bullpen on Friday, Glavine sat in the dugout and watched helplessly as the Mets lost again. Oliver Perez was wild from the start, giving up two runs in the first and two more in the third. The two in the third summed up the Mets' collapse: He hit Dan Uggla to load the bases with no one out, then got Jeremy Hermida to hit into a 5–2 force, keeping the bases loaded with the score still 2–1. Then he struck out Miguel Cabrera, a huge out, giving him a chance to get out of the inning unscathed. Then he hit Cody Ross to force in a run. And hit Mike Jacobs to force in another run. Three hit batsmen in one inning, two forcing in runs. The Mets lost 7–4, beaten by Byung-Hyun Kim, who lowered his ERA to 6.08. The news from Philadelphia was the same as it had been almost every night for two weeks — they won: Phillies 6, Nationals 0.

The Phillies were in first place, one game ahead of the Mets with two games to play.

"The good news was we could stop worrying about blowing the lead," Glavine said. "We'd blown it. Wasn't exactly our strategy, as in 'Way to go, guys; we're in second place now.' But in a way it almost relieved the pressure. All we could do now was try to win two games and see what happened. There was no need to worry about collapsing and getting caught. We'd already collapsed and gotten caught."

30

Götterdämmerung

Wʜɪʟᴇ Gʟᴀᴠɪɴᴇ ᴡᴀꜱ ꜱᴇᴀʀᴄʜɪɴɢ for his changeup in New York, Mussina was making his final start of the regular season in Baltimore.

The Yankees clubhouse was as loose as it ever is going into the final weekend. Mussina, even though he was pitching that night, paused for a while to help one of the coaches with a crossword. Joe Torre pushed his cap back on his head as he talked to the media before the game and wondered who he would let manage on Sunday. Traditionally, Torre has let his players run the team on the last day of the regular season with a playoff spot clinched, and he had just remembered that, once again, that would be the case.

On the day after the Yankees secured their postseason spot in Tampa, Mussina went to see Torre. He had been reading in the papers about Torre's postseason pitching plans: Chien-Ming Wang, Andy Pettitte, Roger Clemens, and Mussina were the scheduled starters, unless Clemens's elbow was still too tender for him to pitch. Clemens was insisting—as he had been for a month—that he was fine and ready to go, even though he hadn't been in a game since he'd had to come out on Labor Day.

Mussina also knew that if the Yankees played Cleveland—as was likely unless they somehow caught the Red Sox—the series would be drawn out under the crazy new postseason schedule baseball had agreed to in order to accommodate television. Game

One would be on Thursday, October 4, in Cleveland, Game Two on Friday, Game Three on Sunday in New York, Game Four on Monday, and Game Five back in Cleveland on Wednesday. The idea of two off-days in a five-game series was ludicrous, but that's the way it was.

"I just want you to know I'm ready to go wherever, whenever you need me," Mussina told Torre. "If you want me in the bullpen, I have no problem with that. If you want me to start, obviously, I'm ready to do that too. Whatever you need."

Torre was both impressed and touched by Mussina's gesture. Mussina was making a point: you don't have to worry about my ego or my feelings being hurt; I will not make it tough for you no matter what you decide.

"That meant a lot," Torre said, relaxing in the dugout in Baltimore. "I know he was hurt when I had to pull him from the rotation and by the way it came down. It was hard for me—hell, a guy gives you what he's given us, and then you have to sit him down? That's tough. For him to walk in and say, 'If me being in the bullpen is the best thing for the team, put me in the bullpen'—that says a lot about him. He just wants us to win. There aren't a lot of guys with two hundred fifty wins who would walk into your office and say that."

Mussina meant what he said. But he also wondered aloud while talking to Mike Borzello if Wang-Pettitte-Clemens-Mussina was the way to go.

"I was thinking that Wang hadn't pitched that well on the road," Mussina said. "So, what if Joe started Andy in Game One and either Roger, if he was healthy, or me in Game Two. That did several things: one, it set things up so that Andy would pitch a Game Five. Two, it meant Wang could pitch at home where he was more comfortable. Three, if it was me in Game Two, I'd always pitched pretty well against the Indians, and one of my best games all year had been in Cleveland. I thought it might set up better for everyone. Either way, I think we knew the guy Joe really wanted to throw twice if it came to that was Andy because he'd been so clutch in big games in the past."

Torre had considered that scenario. But he liked the idea of Pettitte pitching in Game Two because the argument could be made that no other pitcher in history had won more Game Twos in postseason with his team down 1–0 than Pettitte. Wang had been his best pitcher all year, and pitching him in Game One gave Torre more options—Wang, Mussina, Pettitte—in Games Four and Five if it came to that.

Mussina was hoping to end the season that night with 251 wins for his career and twelve for 2007. He was less than spectacular, but Alex Rodriguez, who was capping off a monster season—fifty-four home runs and 156 RBI—homered and doubled early in the game, and Mussina had a 7–2 lead, with two outs in the fifth inning and Tike Redman on third base. Miguel Tejada hit a one-hop shot wide of third. Rodriguez tried to make a play on the ball and couldn't, Tejada beating the throw as Redman scored.

"They scored it a hit, and it was a hit, no doubt," Mussina said later. "But A-Rod almost made the play. If he does make it, the game's a lot different."

After that, Mussina just couldn't get the third out. Aubrey Huff doubled to the gap in left-center to score Tejada; Melvin Mora singled Huff in; and Ramon Hernandez doubled to left to score Huff, making the score 7–6. Fortunately for Mussina, Hernandez foolishly tried to get to third on the throw to the plate and was thrown out to finally end the inning.

He left the game still leading, and the Yankees tacked on runs in the sixth and eighth. Then Mariano Rivera came in to wrap it up in the ninth, with the lead 9–6. Only this time he didn't wrap it up. The Orioles loaded the bases with two outs, and Jay Payton cleared them with a game-tying triple. The Orioles won the game, with a run in the tenth, 10–9.

"I guess it would have been more frustrating if I'd been going for two fifty that night," Mussina said. "But it was still a little bit upsetting. I mean, on the one hand, I didn't pitch great. On the other, how often do you see Mo blow a three-run lead in the ninth? Close to never.

"But it happens. Mo has saved enough games for me through the years that I couldn't really get on him for blowing one." He smiled. "Even though I still can't quite figure out how it happened."

The loss finally allowed the Red Sox—who beat the Minnesota Twins that night—to wrap up the Eastern Division title. The American League playoff matchups were now set: the Yankees would open their Division Series in Cleveland; the Angels would go to Boston to play the Red Sox.

The National League wasn't nearly as clear-cut. Only the Chicago Cubs had clinched a playoff spot as of Friday night. The Phillies and Mets were fighting it out in the East; the Arizona Diamondbacks had a one-game lead on the San Diego Padres in the West; and the Colorado Rockies were still alive for a wild-card berth, along with all four of the other teams.

Five teams playing for three spots. It promised to be a fascinating weekend.

THE NEW METS—the ones in second place with nothing to lose—snapped out of their lethargy very quickly on Saturday afternoon. Facing a pitcher who really didn't belong in the major leagues—twenty-three-year-old rookie Chris Seddon, who was making his fourth big league start as a September call-up—the Mets finally got their offense on track, shelling Seddon from the mound in less than two innings and continuing to pile up runs against the Marlins bullpen.

It was 8–0 after three innings, and John Maine was cruising. He would end up pitching a one-hitter, and the Mets won their first laugher in a long time, 13–0.

Unfortunately, though, the game wasn't all laughs.

It began in the third inning when Lastings Milledge hit a home run. Milledge had played pretty well since his call-up (.275 average, seven home runs, twenty-nine RBI in a part-time role), and his demeanor in the clubhouse had been markedly improved. But he and Jose Reyes were still in the habit of doing their dance outside the dugout whenever one of them got a big hit or hit a home run.

"To be honest, if they did that sort of thing when I first came up, they would go down at least once a game, every game," Glavine said. "It's one of the ways baseball has changed that isn't good. In the 'old days,' that sort of behavior was policed by the fact that guys didn't want to spend every game diving out of the way of pitches. Now, though, because the inside pitch is policed so tightly, you can behave like that and know you aren't going to go down that often.

"If you want to know why hitters pose after home runs, it's because baseball lets them. Once upon a time, you did that to a Bob Gibson, a Nolan Ryan, you better be diving for the dirt the second you stepped back in the box.

"It isn't just our team by any means. But we're from New York, which makes a lot of people resent us. We're the defending Division champions so people want to show us they can play. We spent the entire season in first place — same thing, people want to bring their best against you. The last thing we need to be doing is giving people another reason, especially an emotional reason, to want to beat our butts."

If Reyes and Milledge thought about that at all, it certainly hadn't curtailed their act. They'd been spoken to by older players and by Randolph, and their response was, essentially, we're just being ourselves. "That's fine," Glavine said. "You don't want to stop people from having fun or being enthusiastic about playing the game. But maybe they could have done it *inside* the dugout."

In the fifth, Milledge led off with another home run to make it 9–0. Reyes met him in the on-deck circle and they danced again. A moment later, Reyes doubled and moved to third on a wild pitch. Luis Castillo walked. That was it for Harvey Garcia, another September call-up who had come in to pitch.

As catcher Miguel Olivo walked to join manager Fredi Gonzales on the mound, he began jawing with Reyes, still upset about the Mets' showboating. Reyes and Olivo are friends. Reyes thought Olivo was joking and said something along the lines of "Want to fight about it?"

The answer was yes. Olivo charged Reyes, and the benches emptied. When order was restored, Olivo was ejected.

Glavine was in the clubhouse when the fight broke out. With the game in hand, he had walked back there to look at some tape of the Marlins' lineup to prepare for Sunday. He was sitting in the middle of the room in front of a tape machine when he heard a commotion coming from a nearby TV set that was tuned to the game.

"I looked up just in time to see Olivo running at Hosey throwing haymakers," Glavine said. "I was like, 'What is this about?' Maybe there was a misunderstanding between the two of them, but there's no doubt what had happened earlier had led to it."

The scene didn't thrill Glavine. "What is it about letting sleeping dogs lie?" he said. "You've got a team that's playing out the string. The last thing we want them to do is come into Sunday with the idea that it's a big game for them. There's no doubt we riled them up, and the fight just added to it."

If there was any doubt about how the Marlins felt, it was dispelled in their clubhouse after the game. "Fuck the Mets," Hanley Ramirez said. "I'd play tomorrow if I had a broken hand."

Glavine didn't know what Ramirez had said as he drove home, but he had a feeling the next day would be difficult. There was good news later on though: the Phillies, perhaps feeling the pressure of now being the hunted team, had lost to the Nationals.

That meant the Mets and Nationals were tied for first place with one game to play.

If they both won or lost on Sunday, there would be a one-game playoff in Philadelphia on Monday. If one won and the other lost on Sunday, the winner would be the Eastern Division champion.

"We have to win," Glavine said. "The rest we can't control. We control our own fate again. If we win on Sunday, the worst thing that can happen to us is that we play on Monday."

He didn't even want to think about the alternative.

Sunday dawned clear and cool, as gorgeous a day to play baseball as you could ask for. Glavine had slept well after his sister Debbie had made Chicken Parmesan and pasta for dinner. Chris, Amber, Peyton, and Mason had flown in later in the evening to be there for the game Sunday — a change from their original plans to stay home for the weekend.

"Once the game became what it became, there was no way they were going to stay home," Glavine said. "I knew that."

Normally Glavine would have driven to the park on a Sunday morning with Billy Wagner. But the team was going to leave for Philadelphia after the game if there was a playoff, and Chris and the kids were going to leave for Atlanta. Glavine's car was chock-full of stuff he was going to send to Atlanta with them, so he had to drive in alone.

"The plan if we lost was for me to go back and pack up the rest of the house on Monday," he said. "I wasn't really thinking in those terms. I was thinking we were either going to Philly or to the playoffs."

Glavine pulled into the parking lot and took a deep breath. He could feel his nerves jangling, nothing unusual, especially before a game like this one. "You've done this a million times," he told himself. "You can do it again."

He had, in fact, pitched in a game exactly like this one for the

Braves fourteen years earlier. They had gone into the last day of the season tied for first place in the NL West with the San Francisco Giants.

"We won; they lost," Glavine said, as he pulled on the white uniform top with the blue "47" on the back over his head one more time. "I feel as if I know how to handle a game like this."

The Mets clubhouse was understandably quiet before the game. None of the usual card or chess games that often took place. Players talked quietly, read newspapers, or watched TV. Glavine, who hadn't bothered to shave in the morning—"too lazy," he said—sat on the couch in the middle of the clubhouse watching the replay of a boxing match on TV. His body language was a little more tense than usual: instead of sitting back with his legs crossed, as he normally would, he was leaning forward, as if something was at stake for him in the boxing match.

"No question I was feeling nerves," he said later. "But that isn't necessarily a bad thing."

He went through his usual pregame routine and then headed to the bullpen with Rick Peterson and Dave Racaniello to warm up. Everything felt fine.

"Physically I felt good," he said. "My pitches felt good coming out of my hand. The only seed of doubt was still about the changeup. I just wasn't sure about it. I'd pitched a lot of games before where I hadn't been sure about it. The thing was, this was a game where I would rather have been sure."

All the Mets were now aware of Hanley Ramirez's postgame comments on Saturday. In fact, someone had taken a newspaper clipping, complete with a photo of the brawl, and hung it on a wall in the runway leading from the clubhouse to the dugout. Underneath the Ramirez quote was a response: "Bad Mistake to Wake Up the Sleeping Mutt . . . Someone Pays Today."

A similar message had been posted in the same spot the day before. It had said, "We've Come Too Far to Quit Now."

The atmosphere was electric as the teams went through the

last of their pregame rituals. "I'm so nervous I don't know if I can even watch the game," Scott Schoeneweis said. "I can handle the one-third of an inning that I'm in the game because I stop thinking. It's the watching that kills me."

Glavine wouldn't have to watch. As always, he was the last player out of the dugout and the last player introduced when Alex Anthony introduced the Mets defense: "And on the mound for the Mets...Number forty-seven...Tom Glavine!"

He held the last syllable of "Glavine" for a couple of extra beats, and the crowd reacted. The ovation for Glavine was longer and louder than for anyone else. He had come a long way from the boos of the first two years.

"You're trying not to pay attention to anything but getting ready to pitch at that point," he said. "But you wouldn't be human if you didn't hear the crowd. I noticed it, but I had to really make sure I was focused on the task at hand."

Ramon Castro was catching because Paul Lo Duca's knee had flared up on him again. The day was perfect: seventy-one degrees, breezy, with 54,457 in the old park ready to push the Mets across the finish line. Glavine looked around for an instant, taking in the scene. He was about to start the 669th game of his big league career.

Ramirez stepped in to lead off. The noise was almost deafening as Glavine threw a fastball that Ramirez fouled off for strike one. The noise got louder. Glavine came back with a cutter, and Ramirez fouled it off again. Now it was 0–2, and the crowd was already on its feet, two pitches into the game.

Glavine wasted a changeup outside and then threw a curve that Ramirez checked his swing on. Glavine asked home-plate umpire Joe West to check with Ed Rapuano at first base to see if Ramirez had gone around.

"I was hoping," he said later. "I didn't really think he had swung." Neither did Rapuano. It was 2–2.

The next two pitches may very well have defined the day for

Glavine and the Mets. Glavine threw two changeups, both good ones—"nasty pitches," he said—and Ramirez laid off both of them. Either could have been a strike. Neither, in West's mind, was. Ramirez walked.

A little bell went off in Glavine's head, not so much because he had walked Ramirez after being up 0–2 but because of the way he had walked him.

"He doesn't take a lot of walks," Glavine said. "He goes up swinging. It's the last day of the season, and you're facing a team in last place. What you expect is that they come up hacking at everything because they've all got planes to catch and they want to get out of Dodge. His approach to that at bat was the kind you see in a big game—he really worked at it. That told me that these guys weren't here just to get it over with and go home. They had come to play."

A sleeping mutt had been awakened on Saturday. But it wasn't the Mets.

As Dan Uggla came up, Glavine happened to glance in the direction of the Marlins dugout. What he saw gave him a little more reason to be worried: every Marlin was on the top step. He had expected to see all of his teammates on the top step—their season was at stake—but not the Marlins. Not on September 30 with a record of 70–91. *Okay then,* he thought, *this won't be easy. Back to work.*

Uggla hit a slow ground ball to Castillo on a 1–1 fastball. He forced Ramirez at second, but the ball wasn't hit hard enough to turn a double play. One on, one out, and Jeremy Hermida up. The crowd was still loud.

Glavine had thrown four changeups to the first two hitters—none for a strike, even though the last two to Ramirez had been, in his view, good pitches. He didn't want to fall behind Hermida with Miguel Cabrera on deck. He threw three fastballs to get to 2–1, then decided to try a changeup. "The pitch was down," he said. "He hit a ground ball, which was what I wanted. But he hit it in the hole."

Specifically, he hit it into right field. Uggla raced to third. First crisis of the day: runners on first and third with Cabrera, a hitter who had already driven in 118 runs, at the plate.

"Best-case scenario at that point, I'm thinking, 'Get a ground ball, and get two and get out of this right now,'" Glavine said. "Worst-case, I'm thinking, 'If it's one-nothing, we're in good shape.'"

It became 1–0 on his second pitch to Cabrera, who singled hard up the middle, a line drive that scored Uggla and moved Hermida to second.

That brought up Cody Ross, a young outfielder who'd had a solid second half of the season. "Decent hitter," Glavine said. "But I'm thinking as long as I don't give him anything middle in [of the plate], he can't really hurt me."

He started with a changeup, which bounced. Back to the fast-ball. On 2–1, Ross sliced a ball down the right-field line. The ball looked like it might go foul, but it didn't, bouncing just inside the right-field line. Milledge, positioned more toward right-center against a right-handed hitter, chased it. Hermida scored, with Cabrera following him. Milledge got to the ball and threw home. The ball arrived in plenty of time to beat the slow-footed Cabrera, but it was well wide of the plate. Castro, trying to grab it and swipe-tag Cabrera, bobbled it, and the ball dribbled to the left of home plate. Seeing the throw go home, Ross had rounded second and was heading to third. Glavine, who had been backing up the plate, spotted him and scrambled to pick the ball up after it squirted away from Castro.

"I had him by fifteen feet—at least," Glavine said. "But I was a little off-balance when I picked up the ball, and I made a bad throw."

He threw it past David Wright into left field. Instead of being an easy out, Ross scrambled to his feet and scored, while Moises Alou retrieved the errant throw. Suddenly, shockingly, the Mar-lins led 4–0. The silence was deafening.

"I can't say I was in shock at that point," Glavine said. "Stunned, yeah, probably, but not shocked because it wasn't as if they were hitting line drives all over the place. I couldn't believe we were down four-nothing just like that. But we hadn't even been up yet. Dontrelle [Willis] wasn't having a good year, so there was no reason we couldn't score runs on him. I had the bases clean. I needed to stop the bleeding right there."

He couldn't. He worked the count to 2–2 on Mike Jacobs, a left-handed batter the Marlins had gotten from the Mets in the Carlos Delgado trade two years earlier. On 2–2, Glavine threw a slider off the outside corner, and Jacobs reached out and blooped it over Reyes's head into left for another base hit.

"Now I'm starting to wonder if they are ever going to hit a ball at someone," Glavine said. "I was frustrated and shaken up."

It showed when he walked catcher Matt Treanor on five pitches. Peterson trotted to the mound. Arm on Glavine's shoulder, he told him he just needed to take a little break and get out of the inning. "It was nothing mechanical," Glavine said. "It was just, 'You're okay; just throw a good pitch now, and we've got nine at bats,'" he said. "I knew I had run out of time to get my act together."

In fact, Jorge Sosa was warming in the Mets bullpen. This wasn't one of those days when Randolph could afford to let Glavine work through early trouble or when he was going to worry about saving the bullpen. This was all hands on deck. Sosa was first up.

Glavine wasn't feeling great about his changeup so he started Alejandro De Aza with fastballs. De Aza hit the second one into left field for another hit. The bases were loaded with Willis, a good hitter, coming to the plate. Carlos Delgado trotted to the back of the mound and picked up the resin bag.

"Come on, Tommy, one good pitch and we're out of this," he said.

Glavine knew Delgado wasn't there to give him a pep talk. He was stalling to give Sosa time to get ready. "I knew if I didn't get

Dontrelle, I was done," Glavine said. "Willie couldn't wait any longer for me to find some momentum."

Glavine got ahead of Willis 1–2 — the first hitter he had gotten two strikes on since Hernandez. He had thrown three fastballs. Against most pitchers, Glavine would have thrown another fastball. But Willis was a legitimate big league hitter, and Glavine treated him as such. "The right pitch was a changeup," he said. "He'd seen three fastballs. If I put the change in the right place, he should swing early and swing over it, and that should be it."

Even though he knew the changeup was the correct pitch, there was doubt in his mind about whether he could throw it right. He had already bounced a couple. "I tried to put a little extra into it," he said. "Instead of following through and down off the hill, I actually pushed it, trying to make sure I had enough on it. I just pushed the ball out of my hand, and the result was a terrible pitch."

The ball never broke down or, for that matter, broke at all. It went straight at Willis, who tried to back out of the way. For a second it appeared Glavine might have gotten lucky, and the ball had hit the bat. Joe West — correctly as it turned out — didn't see it that way. He ruled that Willis had been hit by the pitch and sent him to first base, as Jacobs jogged in with the fifth run.

Glavine saw Randolph leaving the dugout, even while Castro was still arguing with West that the ball had hit Willis's bat. He felt sick to his stomach. As soon as Randolph crossed the first-base line, his day was over. There would be no chance to regroup, no chance to make up for what had happened. He was done.

As soon as he handed the ball to Randolph, the boos started. They followed him all the way to the dugout. Nineteen minutes after he had been cheered to the skies, boos rained down from all sides.

"I understood it," he said later. "I wasn't expecting a standing ovation."

That didn't mean it didn't hurt. He sat in the dugout for the rest of the inning while Sosa allowed two of his inherited runners to score. When Sosa finally got the third out, the entire team heard boos as the players came to the dugout trailing 7–0.

Glavine walked up the runway to the clubhouse past the sign about waking the sleeping mutt. He walked in and collapsed on the couch, where a couple of hours earlier he had watched the boxing match, and stared at the TV.

Wagner, still inside, said something to him. Glavine didn't really hear it. He stared at the television. He really didn't see it. Everything had gone blank.

THE METS AND MARLINS had started playing at 1:11. The Yankees and Orioles were starting their finale in Baltimore that day at 1:35. Joe Torre had made Jorge Posada manager for the day, and he had made Mike Mussina the pitching coach.

Shortly before 1:30, Mussina walked into the dugout and glanced out toward right field where the out-of-town scores were flashed.

He looked at the Marlins-Mets score and saw a "7" next to "FLA" on the board.

"What?" he said out loud. "They scored seven in the first? Is that a mistake?"

Someone told him it was no mistake. "Glavine was pitching," Mussina said, still speaking to no one and everyone. "Glavine gave up seven in the first? I can't believe that."

All around Major League Baseball, that was the response as the score was posted. As the Phillies took the field for their 1:35 start with the Nationals, a huge roar went up in Citizens Bank Park's sellout crowd of 44,865. The Phillies glanced around to see what the commotion was about, and there it was on the scoreboard: Florida 7, New York 0.

"How much do you think it helped those guys to see we'd given up seven in the first," Glavine said later. "They were playing with house money before a pitch was thrown."

That first pitch was thrown by Jamie Moyer, who was going for his fourteenth win of the season and the 230th of his career. For Moyer, who had grown up a Phillies fan, this day was a dream come true: a chance to pitch the Phillies into the playoffs before a wild, sellout crowd. Glavine's nightmare made Moyer's dream even better than he had dared imagine.

Back in New York, the Mets tried gamely to get something going against Willis, whose 5.20 ERA for the season had to give them some hope.

Willis was hardly dominant. After Jose Reyes—whose batting average had dropped to .280—had flied to right to start the first inning, Luis Castillo doubled. David Wright also flied out, but Carlos Beltran dribbled a ball in front of the plate and beat the throw for an infield single. Willis then threw a wild pitch with Moises Alou at the plate, and it was 7–1. The crowd stirred. Alou blooped a single to right, and Delgado was hit on the hand by a pitch. The bases were loaded. Willis was all over the place. An extra base hit by Castro, and the Mets could be right back in the game.

Willis fell behind 2–0, and Castro looked for a fastball. He got it, and the ball flew off his bat, headed toward the left-field fence. The crowd screeched. In the clubhouse, Glavine, who had come out of his trance as the inning developed, almost jumped off the couch.

"I thought he'd gotten it," he said. "I thought we were right back in the game."

But Castro hadn't quite gotten it. As the ball got closer to the fence, it began to die. It settled, finally, in Cody Ross's glove on the warning track. Glavine sat down with a thud. In the press box, public relations director Jay Horwitz, who had been following the ball through his binoculars, slammed them on the desk in front of him in frustration. In a sense, he spoke for all Mets fans at that moment.

That turned out to be the Mets' best chance. In the third,

Willis walked the bases loaded with two outs, and manager Fredi Gonzales, again showing that he was taking the game very seriously, yanked him. Logan Kensing came in and got Lo Duca—pinch-hitting for Orlando Hernandez, who had come in to pitch in the top of the inning—to tap back to the mound to end the inning.

The only hope left really was the Nationals. The Phillies had taken a 1–0 lead in the first when Jimmy Rollins, of course, singled, stole second, stole third, and scored on a Chase Utley sacrifice fly. They extended the lead to 3–0 in the third before the Nationals got one back in the fourth. In the sixth, Moyer tired. Ronnie Belliard singled and, with one out, Dmitri Young also singled.

Phillies manager Charlie Manuel—whose job was no longer in jeopardy—was taking no chances. He brought in Tom Gordon, normally his eighth-inning pitcher. In the press box at Shea, a feed of the Phillies game was on a TV in the back row. The two games were now both in the sixth inning, the Phillies and Nats having caught up, since the first inning in New York had taken forty-three minutes. The Marlins were leading 8–1, and people crowded around the TV to see if the Nats could rally.

They couldn't. Gordon got Austin Kearns to hit a ground ball up the middle, which was scooped by Utley, who stepped on second and threw to first for a double play. The Phillies got two more in the sixth and another in the seventh on Ryan Howard's forty-seventh home run of the year and took a 6–1 lead in the eighth.

The Mets could do nothing with the Marlins bullpen. The outs dwindled. In the clubhouse, Glavine had gone through several different emotions: He had been angry. "I blew it. I cost my team the season. I had the ball in my hands, and I dropped it." Then he became analytical. "I sat there and went through every batter. If I get a call on Hernandez, if Uggla's ball is hit a little harder, if Hermida's grounder goes at someone.... The only really hard-hit ball was Cabrera. The one truly awful pitch had been the changeup to Dontrelle. The results were terrible, but I hadn't been *that* bad. Put it this way: I've pitched worse, but I've never had a worse result at a worse time."

He began preparing himself for what he knew was coming after the game. Billy Wagner would point out that twenty-five guys had blown the pennant, that it had taken a team effort to lose a seven-game lead in seventeen games. But it was Glavine who would now be the poster boy for the collapse. "I knew," he said, "that I was going to have to wear it. I was going to have to answer the questions. The only thing comparable in my career had been in '92 in Atlanta, when I got knocked out of Game Six of the playoffs in the second inning. That night I *really* got hit hard. But even that was different. We were still tied three-three. We had another game to play. After a while, watching what was going on in Philly, it was apparent we weren't going to have another game to play."

He thought about the day, about his family sitting in the stands, and, remarkably, began to feel a little better. "I knew how disappointing it was for them and for everyone," he said. "But at moments like that, you almost find yourself rationalizing. It's *still* just a baseball game. It was the most disappointing baseball game of my life. But I still had a wonderful life and a wonderful family. The world wasn't ending. The day sucked, but my life didn't."

In the eighth inning, Horwitz came into the clubhouse to begin to prepare for the postgame. He asked Glavine how he wanted to meet the media. "I just thought I'd stand by my locker like I usually do and talk," Glavine said.

Horwitz suggested he come into the interview room next door after Randolph had finished. The place was swarming with media, and this way he could get everything done at once.

"Whatever you say, Jay," Glavine said.

He wasn't going to argue. "Either way, it wasn't going to be fun," he said.

The Mets came up in the ninth needing seven runs to tie. The

Nationals were coming up in the ninth in Philadelphia. Marlon Anderson, who had sparked so many rallies with pinch hits late in the season, led off, pinch-hitting for Aaron Heilman. He popped to Ramirez. Reyes, now hearing boos whenever he came to the plate, grounded meekly to second base.

The Mets were down to one last out. Luis Castillo came up to face Kevin Gregg, the Marlins' sixth pitcher. Those who were left in the stadium tried bravely to conjure one last "Let's Go, Mets" chant. It faded quickly. Castillo swung at a 1–2 fastball for strike three.

At 4:31 p.m. the Mets' season was over: Marlins 8, Mets 1. Four minutes later, while the players were still shuffling silently into the clubhouse, Phillies closer Brett Myers froze Wily Mo Pena with a rising fastball for strike three in south Philadelphia.

Phillies 6, Nationals 1.

Phillies 89–73, Mets 88–74.

It was over. The 2007 Mets, like the once-mighty gods of *Götterdämmerung*, the final opera of Wagner's Ring Cycle, had been destroyed.

31

Into the Twilight

TOM GLAVINE WAS DRESSED in a green shirt and blue jeans when he followed Willie Randolph into the interview room at a few minutes before five. He'd had three hours to think about dealing with this moment, had thought about all the questions he would face and the answers he would give in response.

It was the very first question that set the tone.

"Tom," someone asked, "how devastating is this?"

Glavine visibly flinched. He was not, under any circumstances, going to sit in front of the media and get weepy eyed. That wasn't him. He was the stoic New Englander. Never let them see you sweat. Beyond that, he simply couldn't bring himself to attach the word *devastating* to baseball.

And so, he said that.

"*Devastation* is for much more important things in life than baseball," he said. "I wouldn't use that word."

Glavine's press conference, like Randolph's, was being broadcast live on WFAN, the Mets' flagship station. Thousands of fans—most of them pretty close to devastated—were sitting in their cars trying to get out of the parking lot when they heard Glavine, sounding cool, calm, and collected, say that he wasn't devastated.

The screaming and yelling that "he doesn't even *care*" began before Glavine had left the interview room.

Weeks later, Glavine understood the fans' reaction but also believed his answer had been misunderstood.

"I think once you become a parent, your entire outlook on life changes," he said. "To me, *devastating* is finding out that a neighbor's eight-year-old is going to lose a leg to cancer. Hurricane Katrina was devastating. *Devastating* to me involves life and death or the health of a child.

"If the question had been 'Tom, how disappointing is this?' I think my answer would have been something like 'I've never had a more disappointing day on a baseball field.' So maybe I should have said that right then and there. Because it was. I mean, I was beyond pissed; I was upset, I was angry, I was frustrated. But I just wasn't going to let someone put the word *devastated* in my mouth."

Glavine talked about the season getting away, the day getting away, the balls that had found holes, the changeup to Willis that got away. He said he couldn't really think of anything in terms of his pitch sequences that he would change. "It's a bitter pill," he said. "You start in February and work to get to this point. I thought we could win a World Series this year. I've had twenty years in the big leagues and nineteen of them have ended this way in one form or another."

Maybe, he said later, he would have rephrased that. "Obviously losing is losing, but some losses are worse than others. This one, the way we collapsed down the stretch, was as bad as it can possibly get."

He answered all the questions. He talked about not knowing what next year would hold for him. He left quickly when it was over, not even going back into the clubhouse. Standing next to Glavine's empty locker, Billy Wagner talked about the boos. "Those people weren't booing Tom Glavine," he said. "They were booing the result.

"Tom didn't lose the pennant, all twenty-five of us did. We're going to have to live with this a long time. When teams collapse in the future, they'll be compared to the '07 Mets—the way we were compared to the '64 Phillies. That's tough to take. Next year, if we're leading in September, everyone's going to bring this up. We're going to have to take that because we didn't hold up our end of the bargain. We embarrassed ourselves."

He glanced over at his friend's now empty locker. "It wasn't like he got rocked," he said softly. "Ground ball here, bloop there. All part of baseball. I just hate to see it happen to him. Tom Glavine is the most stand-up, accountable teammate any of us will ever have.

"Of all the guys in here, he's the one you would want with the ball today. It just wasn't meant to be—for any of us."

AS IT TURNED OUT, the Yankees' season lasted eight days longer than the Mets'. They went to Cleveland for the Division Series against the Indians—a team they had gone 6–0 against during the regular season—and promptly dropped the first two games. Chien-Ming Wang was rocked in Game One, and, after Andy Pettitte pitched superbly in Game Two, the Indians tied the game at 1–1 in the eighth and won it 2–1 in eleven innings.

There was controversy in that game because Jacobs Field was invaded by giant gnats in the eighth inning, and crew chief Bruce Froemming refused to delay the game because of them. The Indians tied the game in that inning en route to their win.

Two days later, Ian O'Connor of the *Bergen Record* took a shot at reaching George Steinbrenner. Amid all the rumors about his health, Steinbrenner rarely spoke to the media anymore. Almost all of his comments were carefully crafted statements written by a publicist.

But he took O'Connor's call. He ranted about the gnats, saying among other things that Bruce Froemming "will never work any of our games again." Froemming, naturally, worked the next night. What he said that mattered, though, had nothing to do with Froemming or gnats. He said that if the Yankees lost to the Indians, Joe Torre "would not be back" in 2008.

Torre's job status thus became the story for the rest of the series. Many of his players, including Mike Mussina, leaped to his defense, pointing out that his calm hand at the tiller was a major reason they were even in postseason.

This was before Game Three of the series in Yankee Stadium. While he was defending Torre, Mussina was wondering who would start Game Four—if the Yankees survived Game Three. Torre had said he might start Wang, who had only thrown ninety-four pitches in the opening game. And because Wang is a sinker-ball pitcher, Torre thought it might not hurt him to pitch when he was a little tired.

"I was almost certain after we lost the first two games that Joe was going to start Wang in Game Four," Mussina said. "He'd been a different pitcher at home all year. What worried me though was that Wanger was really beat up by then. He was hurting, and he was tired. I wasn't sure if pitching him on three days' rest, even after a short start, was a great idea."

Standing in the outfield during batting practice before Game Three, Mussina asked Wang—speaking slowly as he always did—"Can you start tomorrow?" Wang understands English well, even though his speech is limited. Now, though, he looked confused.

"No, Mike," he said, pointing his finger at Mussina. "*You* pitch tomorrow."

Mussina shook his head. "No, that's not what I am asking you. I'm asking you *can* you pitch tomorrow?"

Wang again looked confused. In his mind, Mussina was pitching the next day, and he or Pettitte, more likely Pettitte, would pitch a Game Five if there was one.

The Yankees rallied from a 3–0 deficit that night to force a Game Four. Mussina was standing in front of his locker before the media was let into the clubhouse when Torre stopped on his way to his office. "Wang's going to start tomorrow," he said.

"I understand," Mussina answered.

"I did understand," he said later. "He'd been our best pitcher all year. I might have made the argument that the Indians have more trouble with soft stuff than hard stuff, but it wasn't my place to make it right then. It was Joe's decision, and he thought this was the best thing for the team."

That did not turn out to be the case. After Wang had warmed up the next night, Mike Borzello told Mussina he had better be in the bullpen at the start of the game rather than in the second or third inning. "I don't think he's got much," Borzello said.

Mussina knew from his own experience that a pitcher can look terrible in the bullpen and pitch well once the game starts. He also knew that Borzello had a pretty keen eye. Mussina was in the bullpen in the first inning. The Indians scored twice to jump to a 2–0 lead.

In the top of the second, Mussina was sitting in the bullpen watching the game through the center-field window, with Borzello on one side of him and Ramon Rodriguez, the other bullpen catcher, on the other. He knew Wang was on a short leash and that Philip Hughes, the other candidate for long relief, had pitched three and two-thirds innings the night before because Clemens had come out of the game hurt in the third inning.

Franklin Gutierrez led off the second for the Indians with a line-drive single to right-center. Peering into the dugout, Mussina saw Ron Guidry reach for the phone. He jumped off the bench and began taking off his jacket. He was standing on one of the bullpen mounds with a ball in his hands when bullpen coach Joe Kerrigan hung up the phone. Kerrigan didn't say anything because Mussina was already doing what the dugout had called to tell him to do.

"It went fast after that," Mussina said. "Casey Blake got a hit, and I started throwing breaking pitches because I was thinking, 'Even if he gets out of this, he's not going to last long.' I knew I was going into the game soon."

It was even sooner than he thought. Wang hit Kelly Shoppach with a pitch to load the bases. Jorge Posada walked slowly to the mound. Mussina knew a stall when he saw one. Sure enough, a few seconds later, Torre popped out of the dugout.

"I threw four more pitches as fast as I could," Mussina said. "I think I threw fifteen, sixteen or so altogether, which is about twenty to twenty-five less than I'd normally throw. But they were waving me in. I couldn't call time-out."

He walked in with the bases loaded, no one out, and the Yankees' season about to go down the drain. The situation was not all that different than Game Seven in 2003, when Mussina had come in with no one out in the fourth inning, Red Sox on first and third, and Boston already leading 4–0.

In 2003, he had gotten a strikeout and a double play to escape with no further damage. This time, he got a double-play ball from Grady Sizemore on a ground ball to second base. Gutierrez scored, and Blake moved to third, but Mussina now had a chance to get out of the inning with the score just 3–0. Paul Byrd, the Indians' starter, didn't really strike fear into Yankee hearts, and they had come from 3–0 down the previous night.

But Asdrubal Cabrera singled up the middle to score Blake, and it was 4–0 before Mussina got Victor Martinez to ground out to end the inning.

"I was mad at myself for not holding it to three-nothing," Mussina said. "Still, we had a chance until I gave up the two in the fourth."

The Yankees had scored a run to make it 4–1, when Shoppach led off the fourth with a double, Sizemore walked, and Cabrera moved them up with a sacrifice bunt. Mussina walked Travis Hafner to set up a double play, but Martinez blew up the plan with a two-run single that made it 6–1. Mussina settled down after that and ended up pitching four and two-thirds innings, giving up just those two runs.

The Yankees managed three solo home runs in the late

innings — Cano in the sixth, Rodriguez in the seventh, and Bobby Abreu in the ninth. Seeing his team score four runs made the two runs surrendered in the fourth inning that much more irksome to Mussina.

"It's an 'if, if, if' game," he said. "Who knows what would have happened? I just would have felt better about it all if I'd held them at four or even three. Who knows what would have happened. The bottom line is we lost again in the first round."

Mussina sat in the clubhouse watching the final three innings of the season tick away. The feeling wasn't all that different than it had been the previous two years when the Yankees had failed to get out of the first round of postseason. The difference was that he knew this would be Joe Torre's last game as Yankees manager.

"It had to be," Mussina said. "After everything that had been said, after everything he had been put through, I knew he wasn't going to be back. He didn't deserve anything — *anything* — that they did to him. The front office just never understood what an amazing job he did handling everything and everyone for twelve years."

In an unfair twist, the last two outs were made by Rodriguez and Posada, both of whom had had sensational seasons. Rodriguez flied to right for the second out of the ninth and then Posada struck out. Final: Indians 6, Yankees 4. Mussina's longest season was over — too soon.

When the team assembled in the clubhouse before the media was allowed in, Torre thanked his players and told them how proud he was of everything they had accomplished and overcome. His voice was steady but filled with emotion. Mussina, not normally an emotional guy, felt distinct sadness realizing Torre was no longer going to be his manager.

"Even when you thought Joe had gotten something wrong, like when he took me out of the rotation, he always seemed to be proven right," he said. "I just felt the whole thing was wrong."

Most of the veterans lingered, unusual for a team that has just been eliminated. "I think everyone wanted to be sure they had a minute alone with Joe," Mussina said.

Mussina and Roger Clemens sat in Rob Cucuzza's office, away from the eyes of the prying media, waiting for a chance to talk to Torre in private. Finally, Torre walked down the off-limits hallway toward his office. Mussina spotted him and walked out to talk to him.

"There wasn't much to say," he said. "I just thanked him."

The two men started to shake hands, then hugged.

Other than celebratory moments with champagne being splashed on people, it was one of very few hugs Mussina could remember being involved in during his baseball career. But he was glad it happened.

THINGS HAPPENED SWIFTLY for the Yankees in the postseason: the Yankees "offered" Joe Torre an incentive-laden, one-year contract to return, which, to no one's surprise, he turned down. The Los Angeles Dodgers hired him to manage soon after, a move that made Mike Mussina very happy.

"I'm glad someone out there understood how good he is, and I'm glad he still wants to manage," he said. "I think it's great."

Joe Girardi was hired over Don Mattingly as Torre's replacement. Mussina would have been happy with either one. "You never know how someone will be as a manager," he said. "It will be different, no doubt about that, but I've always liked Joe. I like Don too. Either one would have been fine with me."

Dave Eiland, whom Mussina had worked with a little bit in September, was hired to replace Ron Guidry as pitching coach. Mussina was pleased with that move too. "I liked working with Dave in September," he said. "I think he'll be good. He's only been retired a few years, so I think he'll be able to relate to today's players better than Gator did. I liked Gator — in spite of what happened when I was out of the rotation, I liked him. But it always felt a little awkward working with him. He hadn't been around baseball at all after he retired, and I think that made coming back harder for him. I think this will be good."

The Yankees re-signed all their key free agents: Alex Rodriguez signed a ten-year contract worth $275 million, after a melodramatic negotiation that would have made the writers of a soap opera blush. Mariano Rivera and Jorge Posada also re-signed, meaning the Yankees would have the guts of their team back in 2008.

The key, though, would be pitching. Even before the Mitchell Report, it was a given that Roger Clemens would not be back. Wang, Pettitte, Mussina, Hughes, and Ian Kennedy would be. The Yankees were talking about restoring Joba Chamberlain to the starting rotation. Mussina thought that was a mistake.

"The key to being successful in postseason and when you play good teams are the middle innings," he said. "All good teams have good starters and a good closer. Postseason games are different than the regular season. Starters have to work harder because they're facing good hitters who are going to have good at bats. You have to have guys who can get outs in the sixth, seventh, and eighth innings.

"When the Yankees won World Series, they had guys like Mo in '96, who always pitched the seventh and eighth, and then people like Mike Stanton, Jeff Nelson, and Ramiro Mendoza, who got outs in those innings and got to Mo. Chamberlain can be that guy next year. Andy and I will probably be gone in another year and then you're going to need him to start."

He smiled. "Clearly, they aren't going to consult me on this." Perhaps not, but Chamberlain did start the season in the bullpen.

AS IT TURNED OUT, Tom Glavine flew back to Atlanta with his family right after the Mets' season had ended.

"Chris just said to me, 'No way you're staying here tonight,'" he said. "I don't think she wanted me to see, read, or hear what was going to be said. She was probably right."

She was completely right. Glavine's comments about not being devastated and having had other seasons end the way this one had generated a firestorm in New York. In fact, his postgame comments were the subject of more discussion than his performance during the game.

Glavine first heard about what was going on when Jeff Wilpon called him at home on Tuesday. Wilpon knew that Glavine was scheduled to make his final appearance with Christopher Russo and Mike Francesa the next day, and he wanted Glavine to know that they and many others had been attacking him for his comments.

"To be honest, I was surprised," Glavine said. "I really couldn't believe people would think I didn't care. I mean, I've never been one to show a lot of emotion, but anyone who knows anything about me knows how much I care. I really felt as if it came down to the one word — *devastated*."

He said that to Francesa and Russo, who told him up front that they had been, to use Russo's word, "killing" him for his comments. "They were honest about it," Glavine said. "I appreciated that. Some guys will kill you and then act as if you're their best friend on the air. They didn't do that."

There was a lot of sentiment in New York that Glavine should not return there under any circumstances. Cooler heads looked at the two hundred innings, the fact that he was fifth in the league in quality starts, and had seventeen starts in which he allowed two runs or less.

Glavine had four potential options for 2008. The least likely option was retiring. "There are days when I think I don't want to go through all the work to get ready again," he said. "And if playing again makes it tough for my family, I won't play. But most of the time, I think I want to play again. I pitched well last year until the very end. There's no doubt in my mind I can do that again next year."

Option number three was Washington: Stan Kasten had called Glavine as soon as he had officially filed for free agency and, in "typical Stan" fashion, had said: "Look, I'd really like to see you sign with the Braves or the Mets so we can spend next year kicking your ass, but if that doesn't work out give me a call." Translation: The Nationals, with a very young pitching staff, would be interested in bringing Glavine in as an anchor and a mentor when they opened their new park in 2008.

"If that was my only option, I would think about it," Glavine said. "But realistically, that has the same logistical problems as New York, and it's a new team for me and a team that probably won't contend next year. I would have to ask myself, 'Am I doing this for the money or because it might be fun?' If I thought it was for the money, I wouldn't do it."

Option number two was New York. The biggest issue, once again, was the travel. On a rainy night late in September, Chris, Peyton, and Mason had been on the runway getting ready to fly to New York, when a plane in front of them skid off the runway. No one was hurt, but the incident shook Glavine. Since his first day in New York, he had worried about the amount of time his family spent flying.

"It isn't as if I lie awake at night and worry about it all the time," he said. "If I did that, I wouldn't have stayed in New York for five years. But you do think about it. I don't think I'd be human if I didn't."

Glavine had talked with Jeff Wilpon before the end of the season about the possibility of a Roger Clemens–type schedule if he returned in 2008, meaning he might occasionally fly home to Atlanta between starts rather than having his family fly to him. "I would say Jeff was lukewarm about it at best," he said. "I understood. I don't blame him. I'm just thinking about ways I could do this and make it easier on my family."

There was also the issue of the fallout after the Marlins game. That could have been handled. All Glavine would have had to do was say at the press conference announcing his signing that September 30 had been the most disappointing day of his baseball career, and he was coming back in 2008 to finish the job that hadn't been finished in 2006 or 2007. He might have heard some boos the first time he took the mound at Shea Stadium, but they would have turned to cheers as soon as he started getting people out.

Choice number one — again — was Atlanta. The Braves had shaken up their front office after the 2007 season. John Schuerholz, after seventeen years as general manager, was named team president. His longtime assistant and GM-in-waiting, Frank Wren, was promoted to take his place. That meant Wren, with Schuerholz's approval, would be making personnel decisions.

"John is going to be involved," Glavine said. "He has to be. You don't give someone the keys to the car for the first time and not supervise the way he drives."

Glavine and Schuerholz had never had the rapprochement after the 2002 negotiations that he and Kasten had been able to reach. But they had talked after Schuerholz's autobiography, and Glavine hoped that any hard feelings were in the past. His first hint that his hopes might be realized came the day after the filing deadline for free agency, when Wren asked Gregg Clifton to let Glavine know the Braves were very interested in signing him.

"We'll see what happens," Glavine said that week. "I don't think Frank would have called Gregg if they weren't serious, but there's no reason to get excited until there's an actual offer."

A week later there was an offer: one year, $8 million. If Glavine wanted to negotiate with the Mets or the Nationals, he might have been able to get more, but he wasn't going to do that. He happily accepted the Braves' offer, and on November 16 he was officially welcomed back to Atlanta.

He would finish his career in a Braves uniform. He had proved, once and for all, that you can go home again.

EPILOGUE

ON DECEMBER 13, 2007, former U.S. senator George Mitchell finally made public his long-awaited report on steroid use in baseball, twenty-one months after MLB commissioner Bud Selig had asked him to undertake the project.

Neither Mussina nor Glavine was among the eighty-nine names that appeared in Mitchell's report. Glavine had used the supplement creatine for a couple of years but had stopped using it when baseball began drug testing in 2003.

"It was cleared by everyone, but I didn't want to take any chances at all," Glavine said. "Every time someone tests positive, their excuse is that they were using a legal supplement and got a bad batch. I didn't want to be the one guy who *was* taking a legal supplement, *did* get a bad batch, and had his name sullied forever. It just wasn't worth the risk, no matter how small."

Glavine said the creatine, which he took after starts in season and occasionally during his preseason training, definitely helped him. "I felt a noticeable difference," he said. "I recovered much more quickly from physical stress when I was on it. I would drink it in the car on the way home after I had pitched, and I was far more able to do my off-day exercises than when I wasn't taking it."

In the end, though, he didn't think even a 1 percent risk of blowing up his chances for the Hall of Fame was worth it.

Mussina still took creatine. "I was told categorically that it was

503

legal and taking it would never lead to a positive test," he said. "So far, that's proven to be true. I still take it, and I've never tested positive."

Like Glavine, Mussina could feel the difference when he took creatine, which he only did during the season.

Neither man was surprised by what was in the Mitchell Report or who was in the Mitchell Report. "The only real surprise to me were some of the names *not* in the report," Glavine said. "I think we all know there are guys out there who took steroids who weren't named. There wasn't anyone in there who I went, 'Oh my God, no way.'"

The most prominent Met named in the report was Paul Lo Duca, who signed a free-agent contract with the Washington Nationals when the Mets had no interest in re-signing him. Glavine considered Lo Duca a friend, but, like most baseball people, knew there were far more users than the public suspected.

Mussina felt the same way. The two most prominent Yankee names in the report were Roger Clemens and Andy Pettitte, both teammates of his in 2007. Clemens's miraculous pitching in his midforties—considerably better than he had pitched in his late thirties—was viewed by many with skepticism, in spite of all the stories about his extraordinary workout regimen.

Earlier in the season, long before the Mitchell Report became public, Ron Darling, who had been on the Oakland Athletics "Bash Brothers" teams led by Jose Canseco and Mark McGwire in the early 1990s, explained the fallacy of the "he works out like crazy; therefore, he doesn't use steroids" theory.

"When I was with the Mets in the '80s, we would come in at the end of a game, eat the postgame meal, and talk about where we were going that night," he said. "When I got to the A's in '92, guys would come in after the game, change into a T-shirt and shorts, and go down to the weight room for an hour. Then they would come back the next day and do it again—sometimes twice—before the game.

"What people don't understand is that steroids don't just make you big, they allow you to work much harder in order to get big. It's about recovery. There is no way you can work weights that hard two or three times a day *and* play baseball without help, without something inside you that allows your body to recover so you can keep up that workout regimen."

Like many others, Mussina wasn't that surprised to see Clemens named in the report. He was surprised to see Pettitte named but not stunned.

One thing the report made clear, in addition to the names, is that more and more players (in all sports, not just baseball) are using human growth hormone (HGH) as their drug of choice, in large part because it cannot be detected by urinalysis, the current method used to test players in both Major League Baseball and the National Football League. Only through a blood test is it possible to detect HGH, and even that is not infallible.

"I think there are too many questions about blood testing to start doing it," Glavine said. "How long do you keep the blood? Who gets to see the test? How reliable is it? I just think they have to come up with some kind of reliable urinalysis test for it as soon as possible."

Mussina disagreed. "If you really are serious about stopping guys, I don't think there's any choice," he said. "I know there would be issues and questions, but you have to thrash that all out between the union and the owners. If they wait, then this thing is far from over."

Clearly, it is far from over.

PLAYING BASEBALL will be over for Glavine and Mussina soon. Both went into 2008 thinking it would be their last season — Glavine in his twenty-second year in the majors, Mussina in his eighteenth.

It is worth noting that Glavine honestly believed that 2007 would be his final year as a pitcher. He never completely closed the door on coming back in 2008, but he said repeatedly, "Once I do what I'm trying to do [this was in the days of the Number That Could Not Be Named], I think I'll probably want to hang it up."

He did what he was trying to do — and more — but could not resist the urge to return to Atlanta for one more season. "Let's face it," he said. "I have the rest of my life to not pitch."

Mussina's future was perhaps a little more complicated, though he insisted it wasn't. He had one year left on his contract for $11.5 million.

"I'm not going to be one of these players who announces his retirement five different times. But right now, I don't see myself pitching after this year. I'm not going to be close enough to three hundred, even if I have a good year, that I'm going to want to come back for at least two more years and, realistically, three more years.

"In 2006, I pitched about as well as I could have hoped to pitch, and I won fifteen games. If I win fifteen games a year — stay healthy, pitch well, all of that — for the next three years, I would *still* be five wins short of three hundred, and I'd be forty-two years old. What's more, my older son will be a teenager by then, and my younger one is only a few years behind. I don't want to come home just when they're saying, 'See ya, Dad.'

"I've had a good career. I'm lucky to be in a position that whenever I retire, I don't *have* to do anything. I can pick and choose what I want to do or what I don't want to do. If I have a great year, that might make it harder to walk away. But my plan right now is to walk away, and when the calls come the next spring from teams desperate for pitching, my answer — even if I'm tempted — will be no."

Whenever Glavine finishes, he will no doubt remain in baseball. He can have a job in TV the day he retires, and with TBS located in Atlanta he could work for them and never leave home. Or he might do one game a week on the road for ESPN or Fox. "Just nothing that means I travel all the time," he said. "I don't see myself back in uniform because of the travel."

But a front-office job would not be out of the question some-where down the line. In any event, Glavine will remain around baseball.

Not Mussina. "The hardest part will be that there's no gradual pulling away," he said. "You just cut the cord, and it's over. You aren't a player anymore. That will be hard; I know that. But I don't think I'll have any problem just hanging out at home, at least for a while. Could I be a pretty good pitching coach or a manager? I'd like to think so. But it isn't what I want to do."

He smiled. "The Little League World Series is right here in town [Williamsport] every August. I'll go do TV for that for ten days and sleep in my own bed every night. That will be enough."

Time will tell for both men. If 2008 is their last season as pitch-ers, each can walk away from the game—as difficult as that will be—knowing that he got everything he could possibly get from the talent he was given. Neither ever came up short on effort.

"I think all of us are the same in one sense," Mussina said. "When we're kids and we're playing the game strictly for fun, we never seriously think we'll pitch in the major leagues. We dream it, but we don't really think it will happen. I grew up in a small town; I know Tom did too. We both loved the game and wanted to play it for as long as we could, as well as we could.

"Neither one of us ever imagined we would pitch as long as we have, get paid anywhere close to what we've been paid, or pitch as well as we've both pitched."

In fact, when Glavine wrote his autobiography in 1995 at the age of twenty-nine after the Braves won the World Series, he wrote, "I can see myself pitching until I'm thirty-five but not beyond that."

When Mussina signed his six-year contract with the Yankees that would keep him in the majors until he was thirty-seven, a friend he had grown up with in Montoursville pointed out to him that he had said he wouldn't pitch much past thirty and certainly not past thirty-five.

"I know that," Mussina joked. "But I never thought I'd be this good."

Glavine and Mussina are still out there, grinding through another off-season, and another spring training, and another marathon season because they love what they do and they can still do it well.

They are pitchers. Even when they stop pitching, they will still be pitchers. According to the Elias Sports Bureau, just under eight thousand men had pitched in the major leagues through the end of the 2007 season.

Among them, Glavine ranks twenty-first in all-time victories. Mussina is forty-fifth.

Put simply, they are two of the best pitchers of all time. And they aren't quite done yet.

ACKNOWLEDGMENTS

As MIKE MUSSINA AND I wrapped up our final interview for this book last December, I thanked him for all the time he had given me during 2007 and for his patience in answering all my questions, even in what was the most difficult season of his baseball career.

"I know it wasn't always fun for you," I said. "At the very least I think I learned a lot about pitching."

Mussina gave me one of his "tell me something I don't already know" smiles and said, "Two guys with five hundred fifty-three wins should know *something* about pitching, right?"

Indeed. Mussina has won 250 games in seventeen major league seasons; Tom Glavine has won 303 in twenty-one. They both know how to pitch and how to explain what goes into pitching, which is why I asked them to be the subjects of this book. They agreed, and even though each went through what may have been the most emotionally charged season of his career, neither backed away from any questions; both were remarkably patient; and, yes, I think I learned a lot about pitching, especially for someone whose career as a baseball player didn't last a second beyond high school.

There really is no way for me to adequately thank Tom and Mike for all the time they gave me. The best I can hope for is that this book is a reflection of how they feel about what they do, and, in spite of the ups and downs of the season, something they will look back on with at least some fondness.

509

Mike and Tom made this book happen. But they, and I, needed a lot of help.

In the Mets' clubhouse I have to thank Willie Randolph and Rick Peterson, first and foremost, for all of their time and patience. Thanks also to Omar Minaya, Billy Wagner, Aaron Heilman, Paul Lo Duca, Shawn Green, and Scott Schoeneweis.

I told Jay Horwitz, who has been the Mets' PR guy since the beginning of time, that I might dedicate the book to him. I lied. But Jay was helpful enough to deserve serious consideration from beginning to end, in what was a difficult season. I can't thank him enough for putting up with me, dating back to our first meeting in 1983. Additional thanks to Ethan Wilson and Shannon Forde from Jay's staff.

On the Yankees' side, I owe huge thanks to Joe Torre, whose ability to find time for everyone who asks for it and make it look easy constantly amazes me. The team will miss him in 2008; the New York media—with all due respect to Joe Girardi—will miss him more. Thanks also to Brian Cashman, Jorge Posada, Wil Nieves, Alex Rodriguez, Ron Guidry, Don Mattingly, and Joe Kerrigan. Extra special thanks to Mike Borzello, Mussina's best friend on the team, who spent a lot of time helping me understand Mike, the Yankees, and pitching.

Jason Zillo walked into one of the hardest jobs in baseball—Yankees' PR director in 2007—and had the added bonus of some guy who wasn't really covering the team hanging around most of the year. He could not have been more gracious or helpful. Thanks also to his assistant, Michael Margolis.

Obviously, I talked to a lot of baseball people from a lot of baseball teams, and I'm grateful to them for their time too. Among them are: Bobby Cox, Bill Acree, Tony LaRussa, Jim Leyland, Ned Yost, Leo Mazzone, Frank Wren, Mike Scioscia, Bud Black, Doug Melvin, and my old friend Stan Kasten, who was funny, forthright, honest, and, as Glavine likes to say, "typical Stan" throughout the project. Thanks also to players on other teams:

Jamie Moyer, Aaron Boone, Ken Griffey Jr., David Wells, Paul Maholm, Mike Cameron, and, of course, John Smoltz, who himself is more than worthy of a book on pitching. Thanks also to expitchers Don Sutton and Ron Darling, who know both the pitchers I wrote about—and pitching—as well as anyone.

I have known Phyllis Merhige and Rich Levin from MLB since 1992, when I did my first baseball book. They helped me greatly then, and they both helped me greatly again in 2007. They're very good at what they do and are terrific friends. Thanks also to Mike Port, who patiently answered all my questions about umpires and umpiring. In 1992 one of the people who helped me most was Andy Dolich, then of the Oakland Athletics. Somehow, I didn't thank him then. So, fifteen years later, I thank him now, if only for putting up with me for the past twenty-five years as a friend.

Thanks also to Bill Stetka in Baltimore and John Dever in Washington, who went out of their way to help me on a project that had little to do with their teams. I'm also grateful for the help I received from Warren Miller, Greg Casterioto, Mike Swanson, Tim Mead, Mike Herman, Kevin Behan, and my old pal Rick Vaughn.

I spent a lot of time from spring training to season's end in press rooms and press boxes. I was, as Marty Noble of MLB.com pointed out to me, an adjunct member of the New York chapter of the baseball writers for one season. The list of writers and broadcasters who welcomed me to that group is a lengthy one, and I will undoubtedly fail to mention people here who should be mentioned. But I thank all of the writers for their hospitality to an outsider, notably: Jay Cohen, Mike Vaccaro, Joel Sherman, Wally Matthews, Mark Herrmann, Kat O'Brien, Adam Rubin, Bill Madden, Roger Rubin, John Harper, Ben Shpigel, Peter Boddy, Tyler Kepner, Jack Curry, Dave Anderson, George Vecsey, Ian O'Connor, Bob Klapisch, and the aforementioned Marty Noble.

On the broadcast side, the list is equally lengthy: Gary Cohen,

Keith Hernandez, Howie Rose, Tom McCarthy, Ed Coleman, John Sterling, Suzyn Waldman, Michael Kay, Ken Singleton, Chip Caray, and the always entertaining Sweeney Murdy. Thanks again to my local guys: Joe Angel, Fred Manfra, Bob Carpenter, Dave Jaegler, and Charlie Slowes, for pregame meal entertainment and stories. Thanks also to Ted Robinson, who has been a baseball/tennis friend for many years, and to Skip Caray, who is still as good a baseball listen as anyone out there. Special thanks also to Bill Shannon, Jordan Sprechman, and Howie Karpin.

And then, of course, there are the usual suspects, starting, as always, with my agent Esther Newberg, who gritted her teeth and put up with a book that was about a hated Yankee and a not-as-hated Met. Esther believes the Red Sox should win the World Series every year from here to eternity, and the way things are going, they might. Her patience is often tried working with me, and, when it (often) fails, Kari Stuart usually picks up the pieces.

Michael Pietsch has proven himself as an editor and a friend more times than I can count. He even went along with this title although not quite sure what it meant. Thanks also to Michael's many assistants: Eve Rabinovits, Vanessa Kehren, and, gone but not forgotten, Stacey Brody. Michael and I and everyone at Little, Brown are fortunate to have Heather Fain, Heather Rizzo, Katherine Molina, and Marlena Bittner working in the publicity department. Holly Wilkinson is gone but also not forgotten. She would kill me if it were otherwise.

Friends, never more important than in the past year: Keith and Barbie Drum, Bob and Anne DeStefano, Jackson Diehl and Jean Halperin, David and Linda Maraniss, Lexie Verdon and Steve Barr, Jill and Holland Mickle, Shelley Crist, Bill and Jane Brill, Terry and Patti Hanson, Mary Carillo, Bud Collins and Anita Klaussen, Doug and Beth Doughty, David Teel, Beth (Shumway) Brown, Beth Sherry-Downes, Erin Laissen, Bob Socci, Pete Van Poppel, Omar Nelson (who owes me a *lot* of food), Frank DaVin-ney, Chet Gladchuk, Eric Ruden, Scott Strasemeier, Billy Stone, Mike Werteen, Chris Day, Chris Knocke, Andrew Thompson, Phil Hoffmann, Joe Speed, Jack Hecker, Dick Hall (my hero), Steve (Moose) Stirling, Jim and Tiffany Cantelupe, Derek and Christina Klein, Anthony and Kristen Noto, Pete Teeley, Bob Zurfluh, Vivian Thompson, Phil Hochberg (who proved he can take a hit), Al Hunt, Bob Novak, Wayne Zell, Mike and David Sanders, Bob Whitmore, Tony Kornheiser, Mike Wilbon, Mark Maske, Ken Denlinger, the ever-patient Matt Rennie, Kathy Orton, Camille Powell, Dan Steinberg (who needs a real job), Jim Brady, Jon DeNunzio, Jim Rome, Travis Rodgers, Jason Stewart, Mike Purkey, Bob Edwards, Tom and Jane Goldman, Ellen McDonnell, Bruce Auster, Jim Wildman, Jeffrey Katz, Mike Gastineau (Seattle's Best), Mary Bromley, Kenny and Christina Lewis, Dick (Hoops) Weiss and Joanie Weiss, Jim O'Connell, Bob Ryan, David Fay, Frank Hannigan, Mike Butz, Mike Davis, Mary Lopuszynski, Jerry Tarde, Mike O'Malley, Larry Dorman (to quote Paul Henreid, "Welcome back to the fight"), Marsha Edwards, Jay and Natalie Edwards, Len and Gwyn Edwards-Dieterle, Chris Edwards and John Cutcher, Aunt Joan, Tom Watson, Andy North, Neil Oxman, Bill Leahey, Dennis Satyshur, Mike Muehr, Bob Low, Joe Durant, Bob Heintz, John Cook, Peter Jacobsen, Paul Goydos, and Brian Henninger. Extra special thanks to Olga Rivera.

And more of the same to Mark Russell, Laura Russell, Alex Russell, Steve Rintoul, Jon Brendle, and Slugger White.

Norbert Doyle might well have won three hundred games if not for a bad hip, a bad knee, a bad shoulder, and a bad arm.

Basketball people: Gary Williams, Roy Williams, Mike Krzyzewski, Rick Barnes, Mike Brey, Karl Hobbs, Phil Martelli, Fran Dunphy, Jim Calhoun, Jim Boeheim, Billy Donovan, Rick Pitino, Thad Matta, Ed Brennan, Tom Brennan, Tommy Amaker, Dave Odom, Jim Larranaga, Mack McCarthy, Jim Crews, Billy Lange,

Pat Flannery, Emmette Davis, Jeff Jones, Billy Taylor and the irrepressible Ralph Willard, David Stern, and Tim Frank. Frank Sullivan should be coaching. Harvard should be ashamed of itself. Thanks again to orthopods Eddie McDevitt, Bob Arciero, Gus Mazzocca, and Dean Taylor, and my official trainer Tim Kelly. It takes a village to try to keep me in one piece.

Howard Garfinkel cannot be made up — there is only one of him. Tom Konchalski will always be the only honest man in the gym.

Swimmers, in spite of my miserable year in the water: Jeff Roddin, Jason Crist, Clay F. (Daddy) Britt, Wally Dicks, Mike Fell, Erik (Dr. Post) Osborne, John Craig, Mark Pugliese, Doug Chestnut, Peter Ward, Penny Bates, Carole Kammel, Margot Pettijohn, Tom Denes, A.J. Block, Danny Pick, Warren Friedland, Marshall Greer, Paul Doremus, Bob Hansen, and Mary Dowling.

The China Doll/Shanghai Village Gang: Aubre Jones, Rob Ades, Jack Kvancz, Joe McKeown, Stanley Copeland, Reid Collins, Arnie Heft, Bob Campbell, Pete Dowling (still in absentia), Chris (the right winger) Wallace, Herman Greenberg, Joe Greenberg, Harry Huang, George Solomon, Ric McPherson, Geoff Kaplan, and Murray Lieberman, who continues to be the group's representative to Boston. Red, Zang, and Hymie are still there. I just wish Red could have seen this Celtics season, even with cheerleaders.

The Rio Gang: Tate Armstrong, Mark Alarie, Clay (LB) Buckley, and, in the role of Alberto Gonzales, Terry Chili.

The Feinstein Advisory Board: Keith Drum, Frank Mastrandrea, Wes Seeley, Dave Kindred, and the only man I know with a press room named in his honor, Bill Brill.

This has been a long year for my family. I am more than lucky to be Danny and Brigid's dad. I am also fortunate to have Bobby and Jennifer, Margaret and David, and Marcia supporting me through the proverbial thick and thin. I have a cadre of smart, funny nephews: Ethan and Ben, Matthew and Brian.

Believe it or not, I owe a lot to every single person mentioned here. It's a long list. I must be very lucky.

John Feinstein
Potomac, Maryland, January 2008

INDEX

John Feinstein is the bestselling author of *Tales from Q School, Last Dance, Next Man Up, Let Me Tell You a Story* (with Red Auerbach), *Caddy for Life, Open, The Punch, The Last Amateurs, The Majors, A Good Walk Spoiled, A Civil War, A Season on the Brink, Play Ball, Hard Courts,* and three sports mystery novels for young readers. He writes for the *Washington Post,* Washington Post.com, and *Golf Digest,* and is a regular commentator on National Public Radio's *Morning Edition.*